RESEARCHING THEORIES OF CRIME AND DEVIANCE

Charis E. Kubrin

George Washington University

Thomas D. Stucky

Indiana University–Purdue University at Indianapolis

Marvin D. Krohn

University of Florida

New York   Oxford
Oxford University Press
2009

Oxford University Press, Inc., publishes works that further Oxford University's objective of excellence in research, scholarship, and education.

Oxford New York
Auckland Cape Town Dar es Salaam Hong Kong Karachi
Kuala Lumpur Madrid Melbourne Mexico City Nairobi
New Delhi Shanghai Taipei Toronto

With offices in
Argentina Austria Brazil Chile Czech Republic France Greece
Guatemala Hungary Italy Japan Poland Portugal Singapore
South Korea Switzerland Thailand Turkey Ukraine Vietnam

Copyright © 2009 by Oxford University Press, Inc.

Published by Oxford University Press, Inc.
198 Madison Avenue, New York, New York 10016
http://www.oup.com

Oxford is a registered trademark of Oxford University Press

ISBN: 978-0-19-534086-0

Printed in the United States of America
on acid-free paper

CONTENTS

PREFACE

C ritically important to effectively reducing crime is an understanding of why crime occurs. And what we know about the etiology of crime and deviance depends on the quality of research that is conducted. Research on deviant or criminal behavior is inherently difficult to undertake. Much of what we study is done in an uncontrolled environment, often relying on reports of behavior or attitudes rather than on direct observations. This makes both the measurement of concepts imprecise and the assessment of causal order among those concepts difficult to establish. Those of us who have taught courses on theories of crime and deviance know that students can become frustrated with the imprecision involved in researching those theories.

We believe it is important that students come to understand the lack of definitiveness in what we can say about crime and deviance not as a source of frustration and dissatisfaction but rather as a challenge—a challenge in which they can ultimately engage. To do so, however, they must be aware of how researchers have examined the major theoretical perspectives in our field. Moreover, deficiencies in the research as well as the implications of those deficiencies for what we conclude about the viability of our theories need to be emphasized to enable students to assess critically the status of theoretical research.

We have written this text with that goal in mind. Our emphasis is on the research literature on major theoretical perspectives in the field of criminology and deviance. Specifically, we assess the methods used, pointing out the advantages and disadvantages of those approaches. Most texts that explore criminological theories emphasize the substantive core of the theories and provide little detail about the research that examines that core. We shift the emphasis to a methodological critique of the research literature, providing a comparatively brief description of the theories. By doing so we hope that students will come to appreciate just how difficult it is to do research on crime and, more importantly, how interesting the pursuit of solutions to the conceptual and methodological problems can be.

ACKNOWLEDGMENTS

This book could not have been produced without the assistance of several people. Claude Teweles oversaw much of the project and offered wonderful guidance from first discussions to the production stage. Claude's tireless enthusiasm and patience with our schedules helped carry us through the demanding challenges of writing this book. Sherith Pankratz provided excellent support as we moved through the production process, ensuring that all went smoothly. We are appreciative of the careful attention that Leigh-Ann Todd-Enyame brought to her duties as editorial assistant (as well as other OUP staff members who assisted in this respect). We are also grateful to the many individuals who provided feedback and offered suggestions at various stages in the review process.

Charis Kubrin thanks Erin Dooling for her excellent research assistance. I am particularly grateful to family, friends, and colleagues not just for their ideas and suggestions regarding the book, but for their untiring support and encouragement along the way.

Tom Stucky wishes to thank Eric Bleich and Kendall McCaig, who provided tremendous research assistance in the production of this book. Most especially, I wish to thank my family for their love and support throughout this long journey. Thanks to Michelle, Sam, and Emily, who ground me, humble me, and spend all I make.

Marv Krohn extends his thanks to Pat Lambrecht, who provided both research and editorial assistance. I also thank my partner, Kathy Bice, whose love has brightened my life and facilitated my work.

RESEARCHING THEORIES OF CRIME AND DEVIANCE

CHAPTER 1

INTRODUCTION

At a dissertation defense, the Ph.D. candidate concluded his research summary by explaining the failure to find significant results in support of his theory as likely due to inadequacies in the methods he used. The first examiner, a wise old professor, reminded the student that the Ph.D. was awarded to those who demonstrated research expertise in their discipline. He then asked the candidate why the professor should agree to award a Ph.D. to the candidate if, indeed, the lack of supportive findings was not due to the theory being wrong but rather was due to the inadequate or inappropriate methods the student had employed. As the student contemplated how to respond, the professor offered him a way out. He asked whether the candidate would like to reconsider his conclusion and acknowledge that perhaps the theory was not an adequate explanation of the phenomena being studied. The candidate declined, standing firmly behind his theory.

This true story illustrates a few of the difficulties encountered in doing social science research. We generate theories to explain phenomena. We design methods to examine whether the ideas incorporated in those theories provide a sufficient explanation to warrant our continued attention. However, we often examine phenomena that are difficult to study. This is particularly true when researching crime and deviance. It is very difficult, and in some cases unethical, to design a study focusing on disapproved behavior in which such behavior can be manipulated, as might be done in studying the effect of adding a chemical to some solution to determine its effect on that solution. With human behavior, a number of factors that are difficult to screen out may be operating at any one time. Our problem is further complicated because humans store experiences, and it is difficult to access what they have stored. Add to this the fact that humans have the capacity to interpret those experiences and the task becomes even more complex. It is no wonder that the task of determining how to examine our theory is so difficult. Because of the elusive nature of our focus of study, some level of error typically is introduced in testing our theories. This error makes the examination of any theory problematic, as the results could be interpreted as being due to a problem with the research as opposed to a problem with the theoretical explanation itself. Hence, the Ph.D. candidate in the opening story illustrates the ambiguity we sometimes feel regarding our research.

Unfortunately, the research literature is replete with examples of inadequacies in the methods we use to examine our theories. These inadequacies may include a number of problems ranging from identifying the appropriate people or sources from which to collect data; designing a measurement or observational strategy; acquiring the data with minimal and unbiased loss of subjects; and determining, applying, and interpreting the appropriate analytical technique. Of course, our task can be made more difficult if our theories contain concepts that are not adequately defined or propositions that are poorly constructed or are ambiguous, or too complex, to be reasonably researched.

Most textbooks on theories of crime and deviance are concerned with communicating the basic ideas contained within theories. Many also include sections on the historical development of these ideas and a critical analysis of the logic and substance of the theories. If a section on research on theories is included, it is too often presented in a summary fashion with little or no critical assessment of the research methods used to examine the theories. Thus, students have no way of evaluating the appropriateness of the research design and the way in which it was implemented. This lends itself to an uncritical acceptance of the research results and may lead to a naïve acceptance or rejection of the theory.

In this book, we reverse the emphasis. We are concerned primarily with how theories have been researched. Although we also review the intellectual history and substance of criminological theories, including their hypotheses and concepts, our major focus is on critically assessing the research methods used to examine these theories.

It is important that you understand just what we are trying to do in this text and what we are not trying to do. We want to focus on the problems and pitfalls that researchers encounter in researching theories of crime and deviance. To do this, we must review the background and major components of those theories. But, we do not provide a comprehensive statement and substantive critique of each theory. We need to introduce you to some standard methodological issues that are essential to understand when evaluating research on theories. However, we do not provide a thorough discussion of each methodological issue. Finally, we review the research literature on each theoretical perspective, but our goal is not to incorporate every study that has been done on these perspectives. Rather, we select studies that illustrate the theoretical, conceptual, or methodological points we are making. In short, the information we provide in this text will enable you to become critical consumers of the research literature on theories of crime and deviance and, therefore, to be critical consumers of the theories themselves. Before we begin our exploration of the methods used to research theories of crime and deviance, we need to discuss just what we mean by a theory.

Theory

R. P. Cuzzort calls theory "a kind of controlled fantasy" (1989:10). Theory is fantasy in the sense that it encourages us to speculate, to explore alternative explanations. Indeed, according to Cuzzort, theory "is a place where speculation is not only allowed, but where it is essential" (p. 19). These speculations need to be grounded in both logic and experience.

Most people have ideas about why some things occur, why some people behave in the way that they do, and even how the things that occur are related to the way in which people behave. But few of us would characterize our thoughts as "theory." Why not? What differentiates the explanations that we all tend to generate from theory?

Both the ideas that we all generate concerning the why and how of phenomena and those bodies of thoughts we designate as theory have one thing in common: They both are interested in explanation. By a theoretical explanation, we mean the process of linking some observation, event, or fact to a logically related body of statements that help us understand why the phenomenon we observed occurs. This may sound complicated, but really it is not. Let us say we observe that adolescents who do poorly in school are more likely to commit delinquent behavior. We might explain this observation in a number of different ways. The relationship may exist because youth who perform poorly in school are less capable of distinguishing right from wrong and, therefore, are more likely to do something wrong. Or it may be that those who do poorly are less committed to what we consider conventional goals (e.g., getting a well-paying job) and, therefore, are less concerned with whether they get in trouble. Note how both explanations take the observation of the relationship between school performance and delinquency and link it to a statement that helps us understand why the relationship exists. Those statements, in turn, could be linked with other statements to provide a more complete understanding of the observed relationship.

To be useful, theoretical thought, unlike the explanations you and I may have, must be communicated to a wider audience. Not only is communication to a wide audience essential, but the form of communication (the format in which it is communicated) is also important to ensure a degree of precision. The way in which we communicate theoretical ideas also needs to have certain characteristics to allow for understanding. In communicating our theoretical ideas, we want to let others know what is important to consider in doing research on the theory and to provide sufficient information to guide researchers in their efforts. If the substance of a theory does not communicate to all members of its audience the same meaning, the value of that theory for scientific development will be minimal. Hence a theory, unlike an idea that a layperson may have, takes a particular form that requires precision in the definition of its concepts and a clear statement of its predictions, or hypotheses.

An essential purpose of communicating our thoughts through a theoretical statement is to instruct us as to what it is we must look at to support or refute our theory. That is, theory directs our research. Here again, the form that our theory takes is important in enabling us to identify the research questions. Precision in the definition of concepts informs us of what variables to examine. Social control theory (see Chapter 7), for example, suggests that we look at variables that represent the bond youth have with conventional society, such as attachment to parents. Clearly stated hypotheses identify the relationships between variables that we will need to observe to continue to entertain our theory. Social control theory hypothesizes that if attachment to parents is strong, the probability of delinquent behavior is lower than if attachment to parents is weak.

The building blocks of theory are **concepts**. Concepts may vary in their degree of abstractness, with some pertaining to concrete phenomena and others referring to general properties. Concepts must be defined in a way that allows the audience to identify the phenomenon to which the concept refers. Most importantly, the definition of the concept should convey the same meaning to all who read it. It is easy to see how a poorly defined concept may lead to confusion. If we define crime as bad behavior, there are myriad behaviors that some people, but not others, would identify as bad and, hence, criminal. Such a definition would render the concept useless in studying social phenomenon.

Some concepts refer to specific phenomena (concrete concepts), while others refer to general properties (abstract concepts) (Turner 1986). If we are to use abstract concepts in our research, we need to develop operational definitions of them. For example, a key concept in most versions of strain theory (see Chapter 5) is anomie. While Durkheim, who originated the term, and Merton, who applied it to American society, have slightly different definitions of anomie, both would be considered abstract definitions. Anomie refers to how well our cultural norms limit our desires. If cultural norms are not effective in limiting desires, deviant behavior is more likely. To examine some of the implications of the concept of anomie for crime and deviance, the term would have to be anchored in some concrete phenomena so the researcher would know what to consider. **Operational definitions** are procedures that tell the researcher how to discern phenomena (Turner 1986:6). How would you operationalize the concept of anomie? One way may be to construct a measure comparing the importance that citizens place on adhering to the norms of society to their emphasis on attaining material goods. Although the term is more often thought of as applying to research that attempts to quantify phenomena through measurement procedures, even when we do an observational study that relies more on an understanding of the phenomena rather than on quantifiable measures, we have to be guided by a specific notion of what phenomena the researcher is to investigate.

Theories are intended to explain the relationship between concepts. Hence, theories contain a set of assertions relating concepts to one another (Wagner 1984). The specific form that these assertions take may vary, but, regardless of style, these assertions are intended to relate the concepts to one another and to phenomena that can be observed in the real world. The propositions are what direct the research agenda.

Wagner (1984), in identifying the minimum components of what he calls unit theories—that is, those theories that are theoretically testable—includes not only concepts and assertions but also the specification of the scope of application of the assertions. For example, Cohen's status frustration theory (see Chapter 5) was intended to explain the formation of delinquent gangs; it was not intended to explain general delinquency. As we review the research on the various theories, we will see a number of examples in which the scope of the research (i.e., what was examined) exceeded or was inconsistent with the stated or implied scope of the theory.

Theory, then, is simply a systematic way of stating our ideas on the how and why of social phenomena. Theory must be stated in a systematic way to convey the same meaning to scholars who wish to use the ideas. Without this, our ideas would have little value to scientific development because one of the requirements for scientific knowledge accumulation is that we must be able to replicate the knowledge any one scholar may acquire. If, for example, one researcher reports that there is a relationship between two phenomena but other researchers are unable to find the same relationship, that first re-searcher's finding will not be accepted as scientific fact and will have little use in explaining whatever it was intended to explain. To replicate findings, the meaning of concepts, the relationship among those concepts, and the scope of the application of these relationships must be similarly defined across re-search efforts. Without such consistency, we would not know how to make sense of the many relationships we might discover among concepts that we did not define in a similar way.

Methods

Assuming our theory is stated in such a way as to both generate similar meaning and direct research questions, we still need to determine how we are going to collect information concerning concepts and propositions incorpo-rated in the theory. The methods that we use to do this are critical. If we do not choose appropriate methods, if the methods do not reflect the meaning of the concepts or are inadequate in assessing the predicted relationships among those concepts, we will be unable to evaluate the usefulness of the explanation that constitutes our theory. There are many steps to designing a study that will elicit theoretically meaningful information and, therefore, many places where problematic decisions can be made. We do not have the space, nor is it our purpose, to discuss how to do social science research. Instead, in this chapter we want to highlight some of the critical decision-making points in the research process. Problems with decisions that have been made in the research literature will be discussed within subsequent chapters that focus specifically on the literature relevant to that theory.

Qualitative or Quantitative Data

Once we have derived appropriate research questions (hypotheses) from our theory, an important decision point in doing research is to determine what methodology to use in collecting data. Several factors might be considered in making this determination. The most important are assumptions on which the theory is based. The types of assumptions that might be relevant to determining how we go about researching our theory are referred to as **ontological** and **epistemological** assumptions.

Ontological assumptions are basic beliefs we have about the nature of human beings. For example, we may assume that people are active participants in the socialization process; that is, people not only perceive the stimuli they encounter but are also an important part of the learning process. People have the ability to interpret those experiences. If a theory is based on this type of assumption, it will be important to "get into the head" of subjects to acquire a true understanding of what is causing their behavior. On the other hand, we might not think it is essential to understand how subjects interpret events but, rather, simply need to know what events they experience to understand outcomes. For example, we may assume that people who have more delinquent friends are more likely to commit delinquency than people who have fewer delinquent friends. If we do not assume that different people will react or interpret their friendship with delinquents differently, there is little reason to determine how subjects interpret such friendships.

Certain methods of obtaining knowledge may be more or less appropriate given our ontological assumptions. The philosophy that addresses how we obtain valid knowledge given our ontological assumptions is called epistemology. More formally, epistemology "is the branch of philosophy that investigates the origin, structure, methods and validity of knowledge" (Runes 1962:94). For example, we might believe that the only appropriate way to acquire an understanding about what is going on in someone's head is to observe that person over an extended period of time and that such knowledge could not be achieved by asking the subject questions.

In the study of crime and deviance, research is typically divided into two primary methodological approaches: **qualitative** and **quantitative** methods. Qualitative approaches emphasize the importance of the researcher acquiring an understanding of behavior by interpreting what is observed, what the respondents tell the researcher, or what the subjects of the research have written. The most frequent type of qualitative research is observing behavior in the natural context in which it occurs. With direct observation of behavior and an understanding of the context in which it occurred, the researcher may be in a better position to determine why, from the actor's perspective, the behavior did occur.

Often such observational studies involve the researcher becoming a participant in the subjects' social world. That is, the researcher interacts with the subjects, typically for an extended period of time, establishing a rapport with them. Once rapport is established and the researcher believes the subjects will now behave more or less normally in the presence of the researcher, systematic observations are made and field notes taken. Several observational studies of gangs (Decker and Van Winkle 1996; Hagedorn 1988; Jankowski 1991; Moore 1978; Padilla 1992; Vigil 1988) have provided insight into why youth join gangs and what they do as gang members. In one of the most extensive studies undertaken, Jankowski (1991) observed gangs in three cities over a 10-year period. In describing his research methods, he states:

In sum, I participated in nearly all the things they did. I ate where they ate, slept where they slept, I stayed with their families, I traveled where they went, and in certain situations where I could not remain neutral, I fought with them. The only things that I did not participate in were those activities that were illegal. (p. 13)

As part of his observational strategy, Jankowski took detailed field notes and, on occasion, interviewed gang members about ongoing events.

Qualitative methods can provide tremendous insight into what is going on in the lives of the subjects of the study. With this understanding, theoretical explanations and research hypotheses can be generated. Glaser and Strauss (1967) call this approach **grounded theory**, suggesting that the theory is developed while it is grounded in the real world as opposed to generating hypotheses without the benefit of experiencing the social world of the subjects. Although all theoretical development is based on some level of understanding of the world, grounded theory builds from the empirical observations as opposed to having hypotheses derived from a more abstract level.

Qualitative methods have limitations, however, in terms of testing research hypotheses. Qualitative research tends to be very time-consuming and is typically limited to one set of research subjects. For example, Vigil (1988) spent three years observing 67 gang members. His insights on the lives of these gang members provide a wealth of information. However, are these gang members characteristic of all gang members or even some definable subset of gang members? Gang members in one locale can be very different from gang members in another locale. Are the life histories of gang members that Vigil acquired significantly different from those of non-gang members? Of course, to answer this question one would need to observe non-gang members in the same way that Vigil observed gang members. Can you imagine how much time and effort it would take a researcher to address these issues? Not many researchers are willing or able to spend 10 years in the field as Jankowski did.

Even if one could invest the time and effort, qualitative methods are problematic for theory testing because of the very advantage they offer. Qualitative methods provide the researcher with good insight into the world of delinquents and criminals. That insight comes from the researcher's perception and interpretation of what is being observed. If one of the reasons for doing qualitative research rests on the assumption that each person interprets the social world differently and only by observation will the researcher understand the actor, then it follows that different researchers may interpret what they are observing differently. Hence, it would be difficult to test theories in any objective way.

Because of the challenges inherent in theory testing with qualitative methods, most research that examines theoretically derived hypotheses is quantitative in nature. That is, researchers try to measure phenomena by recording subjects' responses to questions, obtaining official counts of behavior like arrest records, or recording behaviors that take place in small group studies or even in the natural environments of subjects. What is lost is the researcher's personal involvement in the social world of the subjects and, perhaps, an insight into how the actors perceived that world. What is gained is a method that other researchers can use to study the same issues to determine if the findings are replicated. In addition, such studies can more easily be done over larger and potentially diverse samples of respondents to allow for a more systematic way of testing hypotheses.

As a contrast to Jankowski's qualitative study, we briefly describe Thornberry, Krohn, Lizotte, Smith, and Tobin's (2003) quantitative study of gangs. Thornberry and his colleagues conducted a survey study from which they obtained interview data on gang members and non-gang members. They interviewed the respondents 12 times over about a 10-year period. They then used this data to compare the characteristics of gang and non-gang members (e.g., gang members are more likely to come from dysfunctional families and have experienced more negative life experiences such as deaths in their families) to determine what the impact of the gang was on behavior and to examine the long-term impact of being a gang member on their life chances.

In this book, we primarily review quantitative research because this is the methodological style that is used most in testing theoretical hypotheses, although we will point out and comment on qualitative studies that have been used to test theories where appropriate.

Sampling Techniques

Regardless of the type of study design chosen, the researcher typically cannot gather information from or about all potential subjects, localities, archival records, and so on. The researcher studying gang behavior within an observational study or a survey design, for example, cannot acquire information from all gang members in all localities. Yet, when examining theoretical perspectives, we would like to be able to generalize to everyone or everything that falls within the province of our theory. Therefore, a selection of what the researcher will study as well as what will not be studied must be made. The goal is to draw a sample of the total population that is at least as representative as possible of the population that our theory addresses.

Often a sample is drawn for convenience purposes and not because it reflects the type of people the theory would suggest should be examined. This is particularly true in the area of juvenile delinquency, where samples are often determined by the schools or communities that are most convenient for the researcher to survey. For example, some studies have intended to examine theories of delinquency that hypothesize that youth growing up in households that are economically disadvantaged are more likely to commit delinquent behavior, using samples from a population that included households ranging from lower middle-class to upper middle-class families. So, by selecting a middle-class sample, instead of examining the hypothesis that youth who are truly economically disadvantaged commit more delinquency, those studies can at best examine the hypothesis that youth who are relatively disadvantaged (compared to other middle-class youth) are more likely to commit delinquency. By not choosing the sample correctly, some studies fail to examine the hypotheses they purport to study.

Even if one selects the appropriate population from which to sample, many difficulties can arise in acquiring data from a representative sample of that population. For example, most studies involving juveniles use the school system to acquire data since locating and gaining access to youth is easier and less costly when they are at school. Often respondents who were supposed to be sampled are not because they have either dropped out of school or are not in attendance on the day the survey was administered. There is good reason to suspect that dropouts and truants are more likely to be involved in delinquent behavior than those who attend school regularly (Thornberry, Bjerregaard, and Miles 1993). Hence the findings, and possibly what we conclude about our theory, might be misleading.

How many subjects should we include in our sample? A primary reason we select a sample rather than studying the entire target population is to make our task more manageable. We have a finite amount of time and resources, so we endeavor to study a sufficient number of subjects to be able to make scientifically reliable conclusions. Within the limitations of our resources, it is always better to obtain a larger sample. The larger the sample size the more likely it will be representative of the characteristics of the population. In addition, the larger the sample size the more likely that any observed differences will be important. To illustrate this point, consider the simple technique of flipping a coin. One would expect that if you flipped the coin thousands of times, heads would come up about 50% and tails about 50% of the time. But what if you flipped the coin 10 times and heads came up 8 times? You would probably not be very surprised, attributing the outcome to chance. But if you flipped the coin 1,000 times and it came up heads 800 times, you might be wise to check out the weight distribution in the coin. The point is that the 80% to 20% distribution in the outcome of the coin flips is a much more significant finding when there are 1,000 cases in the sample than when there are only 10. It is, therefore, preferable to obtain as large a sample size as possible within the limitations of one's resources.

Researchers are continually concerned with the ability to falsify a theory or, as in the previous example, a hypothesis. If a theory or hypothesis does not have the potential of being falsified, it is not very useful. The **power** of a test of a hypothesis is defined as the probability of rejecting a hypothesis when it is false. The power or probability of rejecting a false hypothesis is increased when the sample size is larger because it enables a rejection of the hypothesis when there are smaller differences.

A number of other pitfalls can be encountered in choosing whom to study. Our purpose is neither to identify sampling strategies nor to identify all the potential problems in drawing a sample. Rather, we will raise these issues in our review of the research for each theory when we feel that the sampling process threatened the usefulness of the research, and thus the proper testing of the theory.

Measurement

Perhaps the most important step in the process of researching theoretically derived hypotheses is determining how the theoretical constructs are going to be measured. Our theoretical concepts vary in terms of the degree to which they have direct empirical referents. For example, if our theory includes the concept of poverty, there is a direct empirical referent that we can measure. At the individual level, we could determine how much money is earned by household members and compare that sum to the government's defined poverty level. On the other hand, for some concepts, determining just what to measure or how to measure it is more difficult. This is particularly true when the concept refers to a feeling, state, or attitude rather than to a behavior (crime) or economic state (poverty). For example, attachment is one of the elements of the social bond identified by Hirschi (1969) in his social control theory (see Chapter 7). The most important source of attachment for adolescents is their parents. To be attached to parents refers to the quality of the relationship between child and parent. The better the relationship between child and parent, the more influence the parent will have over the behavior of the child and the less likely the child will be to engage in behavior that would jeopardize the relationship with the parent. But how does one measure how the child feels about the parent or how bonded he or she is with the parent?

To examine hypotheses including a construct such as attachment, we must **operationalize** the concept; that is, we must identify dimensions that we can measure. How would you measure how a child feels about his or her parents? The researcher attempting to measure the concept of attachment might first identify dimensions that would be consistent with what Hirschi (1969) meant by attachment. For example, adolescents who have good relationships with parents might be likely to confide in them, spend time with them, want to be like them, respect them, and so on. To increase the likelihood that the operationalization of the concept taps the meaning of that concept, researchers typically provide several statements that are intended to reflect what is meant by the construct. Table 1.1 contains items from one measure of attachment, the Hudson scale (1982), which has been used to operationalize the attachment construct (see, e.g., Krohn, Stern, Thornberry, and Jang 1992).

In examining the Hudson scale, the first thing you might consider is: Do these items tap into what I think Hirschi (1969) meant by attachment? In addressing this question, we would be discussing the **validity** of the measure. Different types of validity are associated with the way in which you determine if the questions are measuring what they are supposed to be measuring. If you looked at the items in Table 1.1 and you thought about whether they measured attachment, you would have used a form of establishing validity known as face or content validity. You would have used your understanding of the logic of Hirschi's theory to determine if the items are consistent with his concept of attachment.

Table 1.1 Hudson Scale: Parental Attachment to Child*

Questions
How often would you say that... (4 = Often, 3 = Sometimes, 2 = Seldom, 1 = Never)
You get along well with your child.
You feel that you can really trust your child.
You just do not understand your child.
Your child is too demanding.
You really enjoy your child.
Your child interferes with your activities.
You think your child is terrific.
You feel very angry toward your child.
You feel violent toward your child.
You feel proud of your child.
You wish your child was more like others that you know.
Reliability coefficient N of cases = 782.0 N of items = 11 Cronbach's alpha = .84

*Data come from the Wave 7 Parent Interview of the Rochester Youth Development Study.

A number of other ways can determine the validity of a measure (see Champion 1993), which we will not discuss here. We will, however, consider the issue of whether respondents provide honest answers to the questions. If they do not, our data are not valid regardless of how appropriate the measure may be. We discuss how to establish the validity of responses in the next section, on measuring crime and delinquency.

Having developed a measure of a concept from the theory that we think captures the meaning of the concept, we need to determine if the measure provides consistent or reliable results. If we obtained quite different results when asking the same person the same questions, then we would have to question whether the measure really is a valid indicator of the construct. For example, if we gave the Hudson scale to respondents on two different occasions within the same month and the cumulated results were very different, we would question the validity of those results because it is unlikely that the respondents would have changed their assessment of relationships with their parents dramatically over the course of a month.

This example of reliability is known as an **external check on reliability**. We can also examine the **internal reliability** of a measure. Again, we refer to Table 1.1. The Hudson scale has a number of items, all intended to measure the overall construct of attachment to parents. If they all do measure attachment, there should be some consistency in how a respondent answers the items. One way to examine whether there is consistency across the items is to do an item analysis to determine how consistent any one item is to the accumulated score of all items. If a measure is not internally reliable, we cannot confidently assume that it measures the construct it was intended to measure. The Cronbach's alpha statistic included in Table 1.1 is a measure of internal reliability (the coefficient normally ranges between 0 and 1; usually scores above .70 are considered acceptable in social science research). An alpha of .84 indicates that the Hudson scale has high internal reliability.

Creating a reliable measure of concepts that tap the meaning of those concepts is difficult for the researcher who designs the study. It is even more difficult for the researcher who uses data that were collected by someone else, possibly for some other purpose. We refer to this practice—using data that were collected by someone else—as **secondary data analysis**. Why would someone do secondary data analysis? Doing research is a costly enterprise demanding much time and resources. If the data are collected in more than one locale (e.g., a nationally representative sample) or at more than one time (e.g., longitudinal research), it is particularly costly. The difficulty in using secondary data is that the study may not have been designed with the particular theory in mind that the secondary data analyst would like to examine. Often this requires the researcher to use measures that are the best approximations of the meaning of the concept or that are expected to be related to the concept. A compromise is made between the desire to use a particularly high-quality data set and the ability to measure precisely the concepts that are included in the theoretical perspective. We will review several examples of secondary data analysis in the chapters to follow and will pay particular attention to how well the concepts are represented by the measures used.

Measuring Crime and Delinquency

In examining theories of crime and delinquency, it is essential we determine which behaviors we are going to include in our operational definition of crime and delinquency, as well as how we are going to measure those behaviors. Unfortunately, the measurement of crime is one of the more controversial issues in the discipline.

Early work on theories of crime and delinquency almost exclusively relied on official crime data. By **official crime data,** we are referring to those data that are collected by the police, courts, or correctional agencies. The most frequently used of these sources are the data on crimes recorded by the police. Police data include those crimes that are known to the police, those crimes that result in an arrest, and some limited demographic information on the people arrested. The Federal Bureau of Investigation gathers crime data from around the country and incorporates it into the Uniform Crime Reports, an annual publication.

Using official data, early studies found that crime and delinquency were disproportionately located in areas that were poor. They also found that people who were arrested were more likely to be from lower socioeconomic classes. Based in part on these findings, the theoretical perspectives developed from the turn of the twentieth century through the 1960s were predicated on the assumption that crime was primarily a lower-class phenomenon.

This assumption was questioned with the introduction of a different method of measuring criminal behavior, the **self-report survey.** Self-report surveys ask respondents whether they have committed any of a checklist of criminal and delinquent behaviors either in their lifetime or over some specified time period (most often, the past year). Porterfield (1943) conducted one of the first such surveys, asking college students if they had committed delinquent behaviors. He found that every one of the 337 college students surveyed had indeed committed at least one delinquent act, and many had done so repeatedly. Yet few of these college students had come before the juvenile court for their offenses. Why? Because most college students, particularly at that time, came from middle- to upper-class backgrounds, it is possible that juvenile justice authorities treated adolescents from lower-class backgrounds differently than they treated those from the middle class. If so, the findings questioned the assumption on which most theories were based—that crime was disproportionately a lower-class phenomenon. A series of subsequent self-report studies indicated that, at the very least, official data overestimate the relationship between social class and crime (see Thornberry and Krohn 2000 for a review of this literature).

As early as 1931, Thorsten Sellin observed, "the value of a crime rate for index purposes decreases as the distance from the crime itself in terms of procedure increases" (p. 337). Essentially, Sellin was suggesting that crime data are better if they are measured as close to the actual behavior as possible. For example, it would be best if the researcher could actually observe all criminal events. Of course, this is not possible, so the next best source would be finding out about the crime from the person who committed the behavior or the person who was victimized. The problem with official data as an estimate of the prevalence or incidence of crime is that the data involve not only the behaviors of the perpetrators of crime, but also potentially the behaviors of the victims, police, and other law enforcement agents. Not all crimes are reported to the police, and the police do not catch all offenders. When they do apprehend an offender, the police exercise discretion in deciding whether to handle the case in an official manner. Prosecutors and court officials also make discretionary decisions on cases. Thus, the crimes known to the police and the people who are arrested and convicted are but a rather small percentage of all crimes and people who commit crime.

When designing a self-report study of crime or delinquency, the researcher must be sensitive to a number of issues. First, researchers need to determine what behaviors are to be included in the survey. Some self-report surveys have been criticized for including only minor delinquent behavior (e.g., truancy, running away, teenage drinking). It is possible that minor delinquent behavior will be related to other variables of theoretical interest differently than more serious forms of delinquent behavior such as assault and robbery will be. When comparing both self-reported delinquent behavior with official delinquency to a third data source, for example, victimization studies (surveys asking respondents if they have been a victim of a crime), Hindelang, Hirschi, and Weis (1979) found that differences in the relationship between these measures and demographic variables such as race were due to the fact that self-reports and official data tap different "domains of delinquency." Self-report measures tap less serious offenses that are not likely to result in many arrests, while official data (and victimization studies) measure the types of offenses that are likely to result in an arrest. Therefore, it is not surprising that one does not always obtain comparable results when using these two measures.

When self-report studies do include measures of more serious delinquent and criminal behavior, there is the problem of having a sufficient prevalence of those behaviors to obtain reliable results. Serious delinquent behavior is less prevalent, particularly among certain samples. For example, if you draw a sample of 100 juveniles and 5% have committed a burglary, you would have only five burglars to use in your analysis. Think about comparing across a variable like sex. Let us say that three of those burglars were male and two were female. Would we be willing to make a general statement that males are more likely than females to commit burglary based on those five cases? To obtain reliable measures of serious delinquent behavior, samples of youth who are at risk for such behavior have to be drawn (e.g., oversampling high-crime areas where youth at risk are more likely to be).

Once researchers select the behaviors to be included in the survey, they have to be concerned with the response categories that are included. Many of the early surveys included response sets similar to the following:

Over the past year, how many times did you steal something worth over $50?

1. None
2. Once or twice
3. Three to five times
4. Six to nine times
5. Ten or more times

The problem with this way of asking the question is that some juveniles commit many more crimes than 10. By including an upper limit of 10 or more, researchers are, in effect, placing an artificial cap on the number of times such events actually would be committed by some juveniles. Elliott and Ageton (1980) explored the implications of placing a cap on the upper limit of offenses. They allowed respondents to indicate just how many times they committed offenses. What they found is that some respondents reported committing 200–300 delinquent acts over the course of a year! Moreover, when they compared the relationships between variables like race and social class and delinquent behavior by first capping the total number of offenses (in a similar fashion as was just illustrated) and then by allowing the upper limit to vary to the maximum offenses reported, they found that the findings differed. When a cap was placed on the maximum number of offenses, there was no difference in the amount of delinquent acts committed by the different classes. However, when allowed to extend to the maximum number, lower-class youth were more likely to be in the highest categories of offenses than were middle-class youth. Elliott and Ageton concluded that when looking at those youth who contribute disproportionately to the crime problem, lower-class juveniles are, in fact, more likely to be represented.

Of course, a researcher can ask all the right questions with the right categories and respondents can still threaten the results by not being honest. This may be particularly true when asking questions about sensitive issues or issues that may get someone in trouble, such as having committed a crime. A number of studies have examined the reliability and validity of self-report surveys. It is generally agreed that the method produces reliable results (Hindelang, Hirschi, and Weis 1981; Thornberry and Krohn 2000). If respondents are good liars, they will respond in a similar manner when asked the same or similar questions more than once and, therefore, have reliable results. However, if they are not telling the truth, the measure would not be a valid measure of crime.

The issue of whether this method produces valid or truthful results is more difficult to assess. The type of validity that is of most interest for our discussion is **criterion validity**. Criterion validity "refers to the relationship between test scores and some known external criterion that adequately indicates the quantity being measured" (Huizinga and Elliott 1986:308), for example, comparing self-reported data on crime with arrest rates. The problem with establishing the criterion validity of self-report measures, as Thornberry and Krohn (2000:52) point out, is identifying a standard measure against which self-reports can be judged. We have already discussed some of the problems with official data. If there is a difference in the findings from self-report measures and official data, does it mean that respondents are lying, or does it reflect the biases of law enforcement in determining who gets arrested?

A number of different methods have been used to establish the criterion validity of self-report measures, including the use of official data (e.g. Farrington, Loeber, Stouthamer-Loeber, Van Kammen, and Schmidt 1996; Huizinga and Elliott 1986); reports by friends and classmates concerning the respondents' behavior (e.g., Gold 1970); and, for substance use, physiological measures (e.g., Akers, Massey, Clarke, and Lauer 1983; U.S. Department of Justice 1990). Overall, these studies have found that the validity of self-report methods is moderate to strong (Thornberry and Krohn 2000). However, some studies have found some systematic bias in results from self-report studies. For example, Hindelang et al. (1981) and Huizinga and Elliott (1986) find that African-American males self-report fewer of the offenses found in their official criminal histories. On the other hand, Farrington et al. (1996) did not find any systematic bias in results from self-report measures.

In sum, we need to be cognizant of how crime and delinquency are measured when reviewing studies that examine theoretical propositions. Sensitivity to how the selection of one or another measure may affect the observed results will allow us to be better able to critically assess those results.

Analyzing the Data

Once the data are collected, decisions must be made on how to make sense of the information. To provide a basic understanding of the statistical techniques used to analyze data would require a text dedicated to that purpose (see Bachman and Paternoster 2004 for a discussion of the application of statistical techniques to issues of crime and justice). In this chapter, we briefly introduce four statistical terms that you will need to understand the material that follows: association or correlation, multivariate analysis, statistical significance, and causal inference.

Most theoretical hypotheses are stated in terms of two or more variables that are expected to be related to one another. For example, differential association theory (Chapter 6) suggests that a relationship exists between having friends who engage in delinquent behavior and one's own delinquency. In testing this hypothesis, we would want to know if there is an association or correlation between having friends who commit delinquency and one's own delinquency. To determine this, we would compute a measure of association or **correlation** between the two variables. Which measure of association is appropriate depends on the type of information you have. For example, if you only know if someone has a friend or friends who commit delinquent behavior but do not know how many friends committed such behavior, and if you only know that the respondents have committed delinquent behavior and not how much of such behavior they committed, you would use a statistical measure that is appropriate for nominal-level data (data that are categorical, e.g., yes or no, male or female). If, on the other hand, you know how many delinquent friends or the proportion of their friends who commit delinquent behavior and know how much delinquent behavior they committed, you would use a measure appropriate for ordinal- or interval-level data. Ordinal data refer to information that has categories that have an internal order to them. For example, we might ask respondents to answer a question about how often they committed a delinquent act by indicating the category that represents about how many acts they committed (e.g., 1–2 acts, 3–5, 6–10, or 10 or more). Those categories would have an internal order to them, with category 1 representing less than categories 2 through 4. Interval-level data refers to data that have an equal and known quantity between categories. So, the difference between 1 delinquent act and 2 delinquent acts is the same as the difference between 16 delinquent acts and 17 delinquent acts. Measures of association range from 1.0 to −1.0. A perfect positive relationship would be 1.0, indicating that with every unit increase in one variable, the other variable increases one unit as well. A perfect negative association would be −1.0, indicating that with every unit increase in one variable, the other variable decreases by one unit. If the two variables are not related, the value would be 0.

We have already mentioned the concept of **statistical significance**. Recall that the concept refers to whether the finding you have observed is large enough to be beyond chance (we illustrated this with the coin-flip example). You can estimate the statistical significance of the difference between the occurrences of some phenomenon in two or more categories of another variable. For example, comparing someone who has never committed a delinquent act with someone who has, you can estimate whether the difference in their mean number of delinquent friends is beyond what you could expect from a chance finding. You can also estimate whether an association or correlation between two variables is large enough to be beyond chance. Often, statistical significance is the criterion by which we determine whether our hypothesis has been supported.

In discussing association and significance, we have used **bivariate** examples; that is, we have illustrated the concepts by referring to what happens between two variables. However, much of the work that will be reviewed in this book examines what is happening among several variables in the same analysis. We refer to this as **multivariate analysis**. For example, differential association theory not only states that there should be a relationship between having delinquent friends and one's own delinquency but also hypothesizes that definitions favorable to delinquent behavior (e.g., it is okay to fight back if you are wronged) should be related to one's own delinquency. To determine if both delinquent friends and delinquent definitions are related to one's own delinquency, you would need to see if, after controlling for (or taking out) the effects of one these variables, the other variable remains related to delinquency.

Multivariate analysis is used not only to examine the relative effects of two or more variables but also to examine the impact of variables that are not included in our hypotheses but may impact the hypothesized relationships. For example, we might expect that gender is related both to one's own delinquent behavior and to the type of people with whom one associates. Therefore, we would include gender in our statistical analysis as a control variable. Multivariate analysis is important for making causal inferences, a topic to which we now turn.

Causal Inference

Most theoretical hypotheses imply, if not actually state, that one or more variables cause or result in a higher probability of delinquent or criminal behavior. Yet, establishing the causal order between any two variables can be a very difficult task. Let us take the example of the relationship between having friends who commit delinquent behavior and one's own delinquency. The causal order between these two variables in differential association theory is that association with friends who commit delinquency will increase the probability of coming into contact with definitions favorable to the violation of delinquency, which, in turn, will increase the probability of one's own delinquent behavior. However, an equally plausible hypothesis is that people who like to engage in delinquent behavior are more likely to seek out friends who behave in a similar (delinquent) way. How do we determine the appropriate causal order?

The first criterion to establish causality is that the two variables have to be associated or correlated with one another. If a change in one variable is not related to a change in the other variable, then there cannot be a causal relationship between the two. Correlation, however, does not suggest a direction for the causal relationship. In the example involving delinquent friends and one's own delinquency, the same correlation could be found regardless of which variable causes the other. A correlation simply means that two variables vary together.

To establish a direction to the relationship between these variables, we need to determine their order in time. If we could establish that people associate with delinquent friends before they begin to commit delinquent behavior and that the two variables are related to one another, then we can more confidently conclude that associating with delinquent friends causes delinquent behavior. In this example, delinquent behavior could not be the cause of the initial association with delinquent friends if delinquent behavior occurs only after such association. Establishing time order presents a challenge for researchers. In most cases, it requires data collected over time (longitudinal data), which is difficult and costly to do.

Even if you have established a correlation and the right time order, one more step must be done before you can infer causality. It is possible that the relationship between association with delinquent friends and delinquent behavior is really the result of a third variable that precedes the other two in time and is correlated with both. For example, let us say that a lack of parental supervision precedes in time both the association with delinquent friends and one's own delinquent behavior. If the relationship between association with delinquent friends and delinquent behavior is eliminated or significantly reduced when we take into consideration parental supervision, then we would say that the relationship between association and delinquent behavior is **spurious**; it is simply an artifact of the fact that parental supervision predicts both of the other two variables. Thus, the third criterion in establishing causality is to determine that there is no spuriousness in the relationship between the two variables you are examining.

Most theories contain hypotheses involving more than two variables, often placing them in a causal sequence. For example, using the same variables we employed in our example of spuriousness, we can illustrate an alternative causal sequence involving those three variables. If the relationship between associating with delinquent friends and one's own delinquency was not substantially reduced when we introduced the antecedent variable of parental supervision, our causal sequence would look like the Figure 1.1.

In this example, both parental supervision and delinquent friends are directly related to delinquent behavior (the solid arrows). In addition, parental supervision is indirectly related through its effects on delinquent friends (the broken arrow). It is, of course, possible that when both parental supervision and delinquent friends exercise their respective effects on delinquent behavior, the direct effect of parental supervision may be eliminated by the stronger, more proximate impact of delinquent friends. If so, the solid arrow from parental supervision would be eliminated, indicating that the only causal impact parental supervision has on delinquent behavior is indirect through delinquent friends. Delinquent friends would be considered an **intervening** or **mediating variable**.

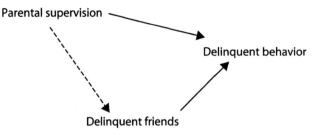

Figure 1.1 Relationships among Parental Supervision, Delinquent Friends, and Delinquent Behavior.

The increased availability of longitudinal data and the development of more sophisticated statistical techniques have allowed our causal models to become more and more complex, reflecting the complexity of the dynamics of human interaction. One result has been the recognition that variables may be reciprocally related over time. To illustrate, recall the discussion of the possibility that delinquent friends may cause delinquent behavior or that delinquent behavior may cause an increase in associating with delinquent friends. Is it not likely that both statements are correct? For example, one could begin to associate with delinquent friends, increasing the probability of delinquent behavior. Increased involvement in delinquent behavior could lead people to further involve themselves in delinquent peer networks, increasing their association with delinquent friends. The relationship between delinquent friends and one's own delinquency would thus be described as a **reciprocal relationship**.

Summary

The purpose of this book is to examine the way in which theories of crime and deviance have been researched. Several excellent reviews of the intellectual background and content of these theories can be found. Some texts include a section reviewing relevant findings regarding those theories. However, they do not devote much, if any, space to a critical assessment of the methods that were used in generating those findings, a necessary task for determining how useful our theories are for understanding criminal behavior. The emphasis in this book is on the latter issue.

In this chapter, a number of issues essential to the research enterprise have been introduced: what methodological approach should we take, whom we should study, how we should measure our concepts, what is the meaning of basic terms we frequently use in describing the statistical analysis of our data, and how we infer causal order from our results. We have provided only a brief introduction to these procedures and terms to enable you to follow the critical review of research, but they are necessary for any critical evaluation of research that purports to test theory.

Each chapter to follow examines a theoretical perspective that has been developed to explain criminal, delinquent, or some other form of deviant behavior. Within each perspective, there may be more than one actual theory. For example, in the chapter on strain theory (Chapter 5), we discuss a number of different theories that share a common assumption. For each theory, we discuss its intellectual history, the content of the theory including its hypotheses and definitions of concepts, the measurement of concepts, analytical issues, and the directions that future research on theory should take. In some cases, this format may vary slightly to more effectively and efficiently present the relevant information. At the end of the chapters, we assess the current state of research support for the theories in light of our critical assessment of relevant methodological issues.

Discussion Questions

1. Why is theory testing particularly challenging for researchers studying crime?
2. What differentiates the explanations that individuals tend to generate about some phenomenon from theory?
3. How do researchers decide whether to use qualitative or quantitative research methods in their tests of criminological theory?
4. What are some of the major challenges researchers face in drawing representative samples? Discuss those challenges in the context of studying, say, sex offenders.
5. What is the difference between correlation and causation? Can you think of an example in which two variables are correlated but do not necessarily have a causal relationship?

CHAPTER 2

RATIONAL CHOICE AND DETERRENCE THEORIES

Introduction

Even young children learn to avoid touching hot stoves because the consequences can be quite unpleasant. It is common sense that people's behavior is guided by the expected consequences of their actions. The idea that people's behavior, including criminal behavior, is influenced by the potential consequences of their actions forms the basis of the one of the earliest theories of crime—deterrence theory (and its modern counterpart, rational choice theory). From this perspective, the likelihood of an individual committing a crime will depend on the relative balance of risks and rewards. Crime can be *deterred* if the negative consequences for criminal behavior outweigh the expected rewards that follow from the crime. The likelihood of shoplifting an MP3 player, therefore, will depend on whether a person believes he or she is likely to get caught and fears the punishment that would follow more than he or she desires an MP3 player that could not otherwise be afforded. Of course, the notions that an individual's behavior is rational and that punishments can deter crime, although straightforward in principle, are not so simple in practice. In the next section we discuss the roots of this explanation of crime.

Intellectual History of Deterrence and Rational Choice Theories

To understand the roots of deterrence and rational choice theories (and criminology as a discipline), we must turn the clock back several centuries. For hundreds of years until the seventeenth and eighteenth centuries, religious views dominated thinking about crime (see Vold, Bernard, and Snipes 1998, for a discussion). From this perspective, crime was viewed as a sin against God. This meant that the state was not just punishing crime but punishing sin. Beginning in the 1600s, some philosophers began to adopt more naturalistic views of behavior. In particular, Thomas Hobbes argued that people are rational and will pursue their own interests, regardless of how their behavior affects other people. If all individuals do this, then chaos follows as each person tries to look out for himself. In this situation, a person's belongings are only his until a bigger, stronger person comes along and takes them. The solution to this problem is what Hobbes called the "social contract," which is an agreement to sacrifice some of an individual's freedom to do as one pleases in exchange for living in a safe and orderly society.

Cesare Beccaria (1996 [1764]) applied some of these ideas to crime. His writings, along with those of Jeremy Bentham, formed the foundation for what later came to be known as classical criminology. Both argued that people possess free will to choose their behavior and will seek to maximize their own pleasure and avoid pain. From this view, because people are rational, they will weigh the costs and benefits of courses of action, including crime. Crime occurs because some people believe that the expected benefits of crime outweigh the potential consequences, or that crime is easier than law-abiding behavior. Anyone who has worked long hours at a minimum wage job will tell you that it would be much quicker to rob a convenience store. Therefore to reduce crime, the punishment for unlawful behavior must outweigh the potential gain or reward from it. Beccaria also posited that the more swift, certain, and severe a punishment was, the more likely it would be to deter crime. These ideas form the basis of the deterrence doctrine. Beccaria also noted that punishments should be proportional to the crime to prevent criminals from committing more serious offenses. So, for example, if the punishment for both purse snatching and homicide is execution, the criminal who wishes to avoid capture might as well kill his or her victim to eliminate any witnesses. From this view, all similar crimes are equal and should be punished equally, regardless of the individual circumstances under which they were committed. The idea that individual circumstances were irrelevant was later modified in the neoclassical school to consider personal factors such as age and mental competence. Classical criminology had a major impact on thinkers of the time, and the criminal justice systems of both the United States and France were founded on classical criminological principles (Vold et al. 1998). Many of these criminal justice policies survive today, and the efficacy of these deterrence-based policies will be discussed later. The notion that people freely chose their behavior was challenged with the development of determinism, which stated that people's behavior is influenced by outside forces. As a consequence, deterrence-based theories of crime gave way to biological, psychological, and sociological explanations, which we discuss in subsequent chapters.

Modern Deterrence and Rational Choice Theories

Despite its initial decline, in the 1970s deterrence reemerged as a popular theory of crime (for early discussions, see Chiricos and Waldo 1970; Gibbs 1968, 1975; Tittle 1969, 1975, 1980; Zimring 1971; Zimring and Hawkins 1968). One reason for this was the perceived failure of rehabilitation programs, which relied on deterministic views of criminals (Clarke and Cornish 1985). The modern notion of deterrence is largely consistent with that of Beccaria and Bentham: "Deterrence refers to any instance in which an individual contemplates a criminal act but refrains entirely from or curtails the commission of such an act because he or she perceives some risk of legal punishment and fears the consequence" (Gibbs 1986:325–326). Thus, crime is a function of personal choice following the weighing of potential risks of punishment versus the relative rewards to be gained from the act. As in the classical view, the certainty and severity of punishment are key elements that affect the likelihood of crime commission. Gibbs (1986:324), however, objects to the notion that deterrence can be summarized adequately with a single statement that crime is a function of the certainty, severity, and celerity of punishment, arguing that deterrence doctrine cannot be reduced to one simple proposition and, instead, has three premises and two corollaries:

Premise I: A direct relationship obtains between the objective properties of punishment and their perceptual properties.

Premise II: A direct relationship obtains between the perceptual properties of punishment and deterrence.

Premise III: An inverse relationship obtains between deterrence and some kind of crime rate.

Corollary I: An inverse relationship obtains between the perceptual properties of punishments and some kind of crime rate.

Corollary II: An inverse relationship obtains between the objective properties of punishments and some kind of crime rate.

This statement of deterrence theory moves beyond the prior conception in important ways. First, it expands the properties of punishment that could be relevant beyond simply certainty, severity, and swiftness. In other words, other properties of punishment may be relevant for deterring crime. And second, it explicitly deals with perception. Because deterrence is a function of the thought processes of the individual, it forces one to recognize the distinction between objective properties of punishments and the way they are perceived by the offender.

Implicit within both the classical view of criminals and modern deterrence theory is the idea that criminals are rational actors. In other words, people rationally weigh the costs and benefits of their actions in deciding whether or not to commit crime. Such a view is consistent with the rational choice perspective in economics. In fact, both traditions arose from the same sources (see Akers and Sellers 2004). Rational choice theories of economics argue that people's behavior is a function of their "expected utility." "The expected utility principle simply states that people will make rational decisions based on the extent to which they expect the choice to maximize their profits or benefits and minimize the costs or losses" (Akers and Sellers 2004:26). Thus, all behavior, including crime, is a function of whether the offender perceives that the benefits outweigh the costs or risks (Clarke and Cornish 1985; Cornish and Clarke 1986). The degree to which individuals, especially criminals, are rational actors consistent with economic rational choice theories is the subject of substantial debate.

In recent years, important extensions have been made to deterrence and rational choice theories of crime. For example, several authors have suggested that deterrence can be expanded beyond the formal sanctions applied through the law (Paternoster 1985; Zimring and Hawkins 1973). "Informal deterrence" refers to the negative reactions of others when they find out about the arrest and conviction of the offender. Such negative consequences can include the loss of jobs or friendships, divorce, and social stigma. Yet, some question whether such an expansion reshapes deterrence into another theory that resembles other traditional theories of crime (Akers and Sellers 2004).

Another recent development is Stafford and Warr's (1993) reconceptualization of deterrence theory. In most discussions of deterrence theory, general and specific deterrence are considered to be separate. General deterrence refers to the idea that others are deterred from committing crime when they see an offender being punished. Specific deterrence refers to the idea that the punished offender will be deterred from committing another crime because he or she fears suffering punishment again. Stafford and Warr argue that separating general and specific deterrence is inappropriate because they operate together: "[P]eople are likely to have a mixture of indirect and direct experience with punishment and [what they call] punishment avoidance" (p. 126). Stafford and Warr argue that general deterrence refers to indirect experience with punishment and punishment avoidance, whereas specific deterrence refers to direct experience with punishment and punishment avoidance. One advantage of their approach is that both general and specific deterrence can operate on the same person or population. Their reconceptualization also suggests more active involvement in the deterrence process by the potential offender. In the previous conceptions of deterrence theory, the potential offender simply weighed the rewards versus the consequences as they were presented (whether accurately or not). Punishment avoidance suggests that potential offenders actively manipulate the risks of punishments by trying to avoid getting caught (Jacobs 1996; Paternoster and Piquero 1995; Piquero and Paternoster 1998; Piquero and Pogarsky 2002). Other theoretical developments are consistent with the rational view of the offender. In the next section, we discuss one of the most prominent—routine activities theory.

Routine Activities Theory

The routine activities perspective arose from Hawley's (1950) theory of human ecology. Hawley identified three important temporal components of community structure—rhythm (the regular periodicity with which events occur), tempo (the number of events per unit of time), and timing (the coordination among different activities that are more or less interdependent, such as the coordination of an offender's movements with that of a victim). These ideas formed the basis of the theory, which states that crime can be understood in terms of the "routine activities" of everyday life—that is, in terms of what we do, where we go, and with whom we interact on a daily basis (Cohen and Felson 1979). Routine activities theory does not examine why individuals are inclined to commit crimes, but takes that inclination as given and examines how the organization of activities in space helps people translate criminal inclinations into action.

According to Cohen and Felson (1979), three things must be present for victimization to occur: (1) a motivated offender (one who plans to commit a crime), (2) a suitable target (potential victim), and (3) an absence of capable guardians (those who might thwart the victimization). A crime is more likely to happen when a potential offender is able to find a suitable target for victimization in an area with few or no bystanders to intervene, such as in a dark alley or secluded area. Routine activities theory focuses on how everyday life assembles these elements in time and space and predicts that potential victims are likely to become actual victims when all three converge. Cohen and Felson use these concepts to explain macro-level changes in crime rates in recent decades. They note several changes in daily activities that have led to higher crime: First, more people work outside the home, which increases the likelihood of exposure to would-be criminals in public places such as parking garages or bus stops and reduces the guardianship of one's home and personal goods, and second, the number of portable goods that are easier to steal has increased.

In addition to explaining variation in crime rates, routine activities theory explains individual differences in the likelihood of crime or victimization. Osgood et al. (1996) use routine activities theory to explain individual differences in delinquent behavior. They note that much delinquency occurs during unstructured, unsupervised periods—times when capable guardians are absent. They found that routine activities are associated with a wide range of delinquent and deviant behaviors and explain a substantial portion of the age, sex, and social class correlations with delinquency.

Cohen, Kluegel, and Land (1981) use routine activities concepts to develop a more formal opportunity theory of victimization (for recent discussions, see Bernburg and Thorlindson 2001; Felson 1998; Miethe and Meier 1994; Wilcox, Land, and Hunt 2003). They argue that predatory criminal victimization is a function of guardianship, exposure, proximity, and target attractiveness. Exposure and residential proximity to populations of motivated offenders are expected to increase victimization risk, as will higher target attractiveness and lower guardianship of potential victims or targets. We discuss research on opportunities and crime in further detail later.

Concepts and Measurement Issues

An important first step in testing a theory is to identify hypotheses. Table 2.1 lists some hypotheses that have been or could be examined for deterrence, rational choice, and routine activities theories. Several hypotheses can be derived from these perspectives. For instance, one would expect that increasing the certainty of punishment should reduce crime. In addition, more severe punishments are expected to be associated with lower crime. From the standpoint of the theory, it also makes sense that the most severe punishments are likely to be the most effective deterrents. The death penalty is widely considered to be the most severe punishment. Therefore, one hypothesis that has been tested is that the use of the death penalty should reduce the likelihood of homicide.

Table 2.1 Hypotheses Based on Rational Choice and Routine Activities Theories

Deterrence/Rational Choice Theory

1. Increasing the certainty of punishment should reduce crime rates (general deterrence).
2. Increasing the severity of punishments should reduce crime rates (general deterrence).
3. The use of the death penalty should deter homicide (general deterrence).
4. Punishment should prevent future crime by convicted criminals (specific deterrence).

Routine Activities Theory

5. Crime rates will be higher when routine activities take more people away from home.
6. Crime is more likely when motivated offenders and suitable targets meet in the absence of capable guardians.
7. Crime is a function of opportunity.
8. Crime can be prevented by reducing opportunities.

The celerity or swiftness of punishment has rarely been tested but appears to be unrelated to the likelihood of punishment (Nagin and Pogarsky 2001). This is probably due to the nature of our criminal justice system. It might be that immediate consequences, such as having one's hand cut off in the marketplace for getting caught stealing an apple, would make punishments more effective deterrents. In the United States, constitutional safeguards on due process prevent such quick action because of the potential for error and vigilante justice. Therefore, punishments typically follow weeks, months, or years after a criminal act rather than minutes. Changing the celerity of punishments in the absence of substantial (and improbable) changes in the constitution is unlikely to make punishments swift enough to impact the decision to commit a crime. Therefore, we do not discuss celerity of deterrence.

As noted earlier, there are two kinds of deterrence, general and specific. From the standpoint of general deterrence, one would expect that the more certain and severe the punishments are, the more likely they are to lead to lower crime rates in society. Specific deterrence refers to the effect of having been punished on the convicted offender. One would expect that increases in the severity of punishment would reduce the likelihood of future crime by the offender due to greater fear of punishment.

Routine activities theory also provides a number of hypotheses that can be tested. The theory suggests that opportunities for offenders and victims to meet will be structured by the daily activities that people engage in, particularly those that take them away from home. Therefore, one could hypothesize that crime rates will vary with the amount of time people spend away from home. Similarly, at the individual level, victimization is more likely when motivated offenders and potential victims meet in the absence of capable guardians. This suggests that crime is a function of opportunity. The corollary to this view is that crime can be prevented by reducing opportunities. A substantial research literature has assessed the ways in which crime can be prevented in individual situations.

These hypotheses provide a starting point for discussing the measurement issues in research on deterrence, rational choice, and routine activities theories. The next step in theory testing is to specify clearly the concepts to be measured. Here, we discuss some key concepts, how they have been measured, and whether the measurement strategies adequately capture the underlying constructs in these perspectives. Specifically, we consider deterrence, certainty, severity, risk perception, rational choice, routine activities, and crime.

Deterrence

One key issue in deterrence and rational choice research is how deterrence is defined. It is important to make a distinction between absolute and marginal deterrence. Absolute deterrence refers to the existence of legal punishments for crimes generally. Few would argue that crime rates would be unaffected if there were no legal mechanism for punishment of offenders. Indeed, Gibbs (1986) claims that in the absence of a government-run criminal justice system, a private system of protection and punishment would rapidly develop. To say that legal punishments have some absolute deterrent effect is not very helpful, however. Since very few advocate the abolition of legal punishments, the real question is to what extent *changes* in legal punishments improve upon having any legal sanctions. The incremental reductions in crime that result from incremental changes in laws and punishment refer to marginal deterrence. As we will see in the context of our discussion of research on the certainty and severity of punishment, the evidence in support of marginal deterrence is considerably less encouraging than many lawmakers and citizens imagine.

Certainty

Studies that have considered certainty of punishment generally focus on the number of police or on changes in police activities such as crackdowns on drunk driving or drug sales (Cohen, Gorr, and Singh 2003; Sherman 1990), changes in patrol patterns (Kelling, Pate, Diekman, and Brown 1974), or pro-arrest policies for domestic violence (Berk, Campbell, Klap, and Western 1992; Sherman and Berk 1984). Each of these interventions is based on the idea that the increased presence of police or changes in police activities will increase the certainty of arrest, thereby deterring crime. As we will see, the evidence for this assertion is mixed at best.

The idea that more police equals less crime is a popular one. A number of studies have examined whether greater police presence is associated with less crime. For example, Greenberg, Kessler, and Logan (1979) estimate a multi-wave panel model of the relationship between crime rates and arrest rates for a sample of 98 U.S. cities with 25,000 or more residents from 1964 to 1970. They find no meaningful relationship between crime rates and arrest rates, concluding there is no support for the existence of a deterrent effect (they note that criminals may simply be unaware of marginal changes in the likelihood of detection or punishment). Similarly, Greenberg and Kessler (1982) analyze the relationship between crime rates and arrest rates, finding little effect of arrests on crime, controlling for other factors. Using a different approach, Loftin and McDowall (1982) conduct a longitudinal study of Detroit from 1926 to 1977, comparing the number of police and index crimes per 100,000. They find no relationship between crime and number of police. It could be that larger variations in police strength may be necessary before they have an impact on crime rates. Finally, in their study of 252 Northern areas in 1970, Huff and Stahura (1980) do find that police employment and crime are related but *positively* (opposite of the direction predicted by rational choice theory).

A few studies have documented more support for what Nagin (1998) refers to as "deterrent-like" effects of the police on crime. Levitt (1997) examines the relationship between crime and police employment for 59 cities with 250,000 or more residents from 1970 to 1992, finding that increases in police employment significantly reduce violent crime, and to a lesser degree property crime, in these cities. Nagin notes that Marvell and Moody (1996), using essentially the same data (but different statistical techniques), also conclude there is a deterrent-like effect of the number of police per capita on crime.

In a review of this literature, Nagin (1998) concludes the evidence suggests that the *activities* of the police (e.g., community policing, proactive policing), rather than their sheer numbers, are far more likely to influence crime rates (see also Sampson and Cohen 1988; Sherman 1990). One possible explanation for this is that greater police presence makes the reporting of crime easier, which would lead to a positive relationship between the number of police and reported crime. Or police forces may increase in response to changes in the crime rate rather than the reverse. Therefore, it is not uncommon for high crime cities also to have the highest numbers of police per capita. As we discuss in the analytical section, this presents a challenge when designing studies to capture the effects of police presence on crime that can only be resolved using certain statistical techniques.

One of the earliest studies of police activities considered variation in routine police patrol. Conventional wisdom suggested that having police officers drive around on routine patrol deterred crime. The Kansas City Preventative Patrol experiment (Kelling et al. 1974) set out to test this notion by dividing the city into three kinds of patrol beats. One group had standard amounts of routine patrol, the second group had double the amount of routine patrol, and the third had no routine patrol. Presumably the double patrol beats would have higher certainty of arrest, and therefore lower crime, than the standard or no-patrol beats. After nearly a year, they found no appreciable differences in crime or fear of crime across the three types of beats, suggesting that random patrol was not a deterrent.

Another police intervention to increase the certainty of punishment is the use of roadblocks or random stops to reduce drunk driving. Studies suggest these enforcement efforts produce a short-term reduction in drunk driving (see Briscoe 2004; Ross 1984 for overviews). Unfortunately, the reductions do not last. This phenomenon is known as extinction, where a policy intervention has an initial impact on crime that declines over time (see also Sherman et al. 1995 for an example of extinction effects in law enforcement crackdowns on crack houses). Some suggest the reason for extinction effects is that people initially overestimate the increased certainty of punishment due to the publicity of the intervention but over time adjust their perception of certainty as the reality of the low odds of detection become clear (Nagin 1998). Extinction effects are common in criminal justice policy interventions.

Another potential limitation of police-based policies on deterrence is the possibility of displacement, where crime is shifted from one place to another by enforcement efforts. An example of displacement would be when drug dealers move away from areas where police crackdowns are focused. Such displacement could be problematic because it means that crime is not deterred, just moved from one place to another. Some research has considered this issue and has found that crime displacement is less common than one might expect (see Barr and Pease 1990; Cornish and Clarke 1987; Green 1995; Sherman 1990 for discussions). Moreover, it appears there can be a diffusion of beneficial crime-control effects in some cases. Recent research finds that focusing police resources on high crime areas (so-called hot spots) does not displace crime to immediate areas, but rather leads to a diffusion of crime control benefits in areas immediately surrounding targeted sites (Weisburd et al. 2006).

Another example of targeted police activities to deter crime through increased certainty is pro-arrest policies for domestic violence. The idea is that domestic violence can be deterred if potential offenders believe there is an increased certainty of arrest. Sherman and Berk (1984) set out to test this idea in Minneapolis using an innovative experiment. During the study, police officers were randomly assigned one of three options in responding to a domestic violence call: Provide counseling to the parties to diffuse the conflict; make an arrest; or force the aggressor to leave for six hours (presumably to become sober in many cases). Sherman and Berk found that subsequent calls for domestic violence were significantly lower for arrestees compared to the other two groups. As a consequence, many police departments instituted pro-arrest policies for domestic violence. Subsequent studies, however, failed to replicate these findings and suggested that arrest only deterred offenders who were employed and might actually *increase* the likelihood of offending for others (see Berk et al. 1992 for a discussion). This may result because those without jobs have little to lose by being arrested and would likely become angry about being arrested and potentially take it out on the very person the arrest is supposed to protect. This illustrates an important issue in deterrence research. The same penalties may not deter equally in all cases. We discuss this issue further later. In sum, the evidence in support of certainty effects is mixed. Increasing the certainty of punishment seems to work in some cases, but often reductions are short-term or limited to certain kinds of offenders.

Severity

From the time of Beccaria, it has been argued that more severe punishments should constitute more effective deterrents. Such arguments commonly have been used to support demands for increasingly harsh punishments since

1970, such as the so-called three strikes laws enacted in many states in recent years. Three strikes laws enhance penalties as the number of prior offenses increase. Analogous to baseball, an offender would strike out (be sentenced to life in prison) upon conviction for a third serious offense. Yet research on the effects of three strikes laws has generally found no deterrent effects (Kovandzic, Sloan, and Vieraitis 2002, 2004; Worrall 2004; Zimring, Hawkins, and Kamin 2001). Other policies aimed at increasing the severity of punishments have been instituted, including increases in specific penalties for drunk driving and drug use/sale. As we discuss later, the results do not suggest strong support for deterrent effects of increasing severity.

In response to widespread concern over the harm caused by drunk drivers, many states have implemented increases in the penalties for these offenses, including license suspension for first offenses, revocation for repeat offenders, and stiffer fines and jail terms. Although a few studies indicate these changes deterred drunk driving and reduced accidents (see Briscoe 2004:980 for a discussion), the majority fail to show reductions following changes in the laws (Briscoe 2004; Ross 1984, 1986). For example, Ross, McCleary, and La-Free (1990) examined the effect of mandatory jail time for offenders in Arizona. The law apparently had no deterrent effect on drunk driving. The authors suggest two reasons for this failure. The first is that the law allowed alternative sentences for offenders with a reasonably low blood-alcohol content, where no injury occurred. The second is that drivers likely perceived the certainty of arrest as being very low. Therefore, increases in the severity of punishment had no impact because drivers did not think they would get caught. More recently, Briscoe analyzed the impact of stiffer penalties for drunk driving on the rate of road accidents in New South Wales, Australia, from 1994 to 2001. She found that the rate of accidents actually *increased* following changes in the law. Thus, the evidence does not suggest that stiffer penalties reduce drunk driving. Ironically, drunk driving fatalities have declined in recent years, but this is likely due to increased social stigma (Grasmick, Bursik, and Arneklev 1993).

A variety of reasons can explain why increasing the severity of prescribed punishments may not have a deterrent effect. One is that lawmakers cannot control actual changes in the severity of punishment. Police officers, judges, juries, and correctional officials all have discretion over the imposition of actual punishments (Nagin 1998). They can therefore use this discretion to limit the impact of punishments they perceive to be excessive. Increases in the severity of punishment may also have perverse effects on crime. Increasing punishment severity for one kind of crime may simply result in the substitution of another kind of crime. So, harsher sentences for robbery may reduce robbery but increase burglaries and theft. Another potentially perverse effect is that increases in punishment severity may increase the incentive to kill witnesses or police. A suspect facing life in prison would have much more incentive to violently resist police or kill witnesses.

As we have noted, if deterrence theory is correct that increasing the severity of punishments should deter crime, then threat of the ultimate punishment—the death penalty—should have a strong deterrent effect on homicide. Three types of studies have examined the deterrent effect of the death penalty. The first compares homicide rates in states with the death penalty (currently 38) to those without it. Generally, this type of study shows no support for deterrence theory (see Cook 1980; Donohue and Wolfers 2006; Gibbs 1986; Nagin 1998 for discussions). In fact, states with the death penalty often have *higher* homicide rates, perhaps because these states institute the death penalty in response to greater levels of violence. The second type of death penalty study is time series analysis, which compares homicide rates over time in comparison to the number of executions. A famous early study is Ehrlich's (1975) national time series analysis of executions and homicide from 1932 to 1970. Ehrlich showed that each execution prevented about eight homicides. The study was highly controversial and has been criticized on methodological grounds (Blumstein, Cohen, and Nagin 1978; Cook 1980). Some research suggests that the finding of deterrent effects depends on the years included in the study (Levitt 2001). Although a few studies do find a deterrent effect of the death penalty on homicide (e.g., Lott and Landes 1999), the evidence does not suggest that the death penalty is an effective deterrent to homicide. Levitt (2001) concludes that even if there is a deterrent effect, it is likely to have little impact on homicide overall because there are so few executions compared to the number of homicides in any given year (see also Donohue and Wolfers 2006).

Some have suggested that executions may have a short-term impact on homicide that is not captured in the annual homicide figures used in time series studies. Some studies, therefore, have considered the immediate impact of executions on homicides in the weeks and months following a publicized execution. Most studies do not show that homicides go down in the periods shortly after an execution (Cochran and Chamlin, 2000; Cochran, Chamlin, and Seth 1994; Stolzenberg and D'Alessio 2004), although one study does (Stack 1998). In fact, some studies find that homicides actually increase in the periods immediately following executions, producing a "brutalization" effect (Cochran et al. 1994). In short, the literature on the deterrent effects of increasing punishment severity indicates that overall it is not an effective strategy for general deterrence.

Specific Deterrence

Policies such as police crackdowns or changes in the law are usually aimed at general deterrence—reducing crime by increasing the likelihood or severity of punishment, causing would-be offenders to avoid crime. Theorists also focus on specific deterrence, where the punished offender refrains from future crime for fear of again suffering the punishment they endured for the first offense. Although this idea seems reasonable, the evidence for specific deterrence is decidedly mixed. Some studies find that experience with the criminal justice system reduces future offending (Shapiro and Votey 1984; Smith and Gartin 1989). Others find that the experience of being punished has no influence on future criminality (Weisburd, Waring, and Chayet 1995), that being punished can actually lead to increased offending (Spohn and Holleran 2002), or that specific deterrence varies based on individual characteristics (Dejong 1997). One study is particularly discouraging for specific deterrence. Weisburd et al. examined the effect of imprisonment on 742 white-collar offenders sentenced in federal court from 1976 to 1978. In the 126-month (10.5-year) follow-up period, there were no significant differences in the likelihood of recidivism for those receiving prison sentences compared to those receiving probation. Presumably white-collar criminals would be most likely to consider their previous experience with punishment in deciding whether to engage in further criminality. This study suggests little support for such a view and casts doubt on the validity of specific deterrent effects.

Risk Perception

Recall that our definition of deterrence refers to an individual who considers criminal activity but refrains from it because "he or she perceives some risk of legal punishment and fears the consequence" (Gibbs 1986:325–326). This definition does not refer to the objective properties of punishment (i.e., how long the real possible jail time would be) but how the offender subjectively perceives them. In measuring the effects of deterrence on crime, therefore, it is necessary to consider how offenders perceive the risk of punishment (also called perceptual deterrence).

A number of studies have considered whether the perceived risk of sanctions deters criminal behavior (Erickson and Gibbs 1978; Jensen, Erickson, and Gibbs 1978; Klepper and Nagin 1989; Minor and Harry 1982; Paternoster, Saltzman, Waldo, and Chiricos 1983a, 1983b; Williams and Hawkins 1986). Cross-sectional and scenario-based studies find that increasing the perceived risk of punishment reduces the likelihood of crime (Nagin 1998). Longitudinal studies have been less likely to find deterrent effects of risk perception. Research also suggests that perceived certainty of punishment is a more effective deterrent than perceived severity (Nagin 1998).

One important issue is the extent to which the perception of risk is accurately tied to the objective risk of punishment. Research finds that people do not accurately perceive their objective risk of punishment (Cook 1980). In fact, some argue that noncriminals dramatically overestimate their punishment risk, whereas offenders may have accurately low perceptions of risk. One recent study challenges this claim. In a telephone survey of 1,500 residents of large urban counties, Kleck, Sever, Li, and Gertz (2005) found that criminals are not more aware of actual punishment risks than noncriminals. Cook argues that deterrence may still operate effectively even if subjective perceptions of risk of punishment are not accurate but are systematically related to criminal justice activities.

Related to the accuracy of information is what kind of information the potential offender uses to evaluate punishment risk. Cook (1980) notes there are several potential sources of information about the threat of punishment— the media, visibility of law enforcement, personal experience or observation, word of mouth, rumor, and observation of other criminal activity in an area. He also notes deterrence and rational choice theories generally assume that apprehension of criminals will influence other criminals, but it is more likely that each individual apprehension has a large impact on the perceptions of a few offenders and none on everyone else. Our earlier discussion of Stafford and Warr's (1993) reconceptualization of deterrence theory has implications for this issue. If both personal and vicarious experiences with punishment and avoidance are relevant for risk perceptions, then tests of deterrence theory need to be more nuanced. Stafford and Warr argue:

> [F]or example, tests based on survey data would need to include, at a mini- mum, measures of (a) person's perceptions of their own certainty and severity of legal punishment for crimes, (b) persons' perceptions of the certainty and severity of legal punishment for others (presumably those within their imme- diate social network), (c) self-reported criminal behavior, including self-reports of direct experience with punishment and punishment avoidance, and (d) es- timates of peers' criminal behavior, including their experiences with punish- ment and punishment avoidance. (p. 133)

Several studies have used Stafford and Warr's (1993) expanded model of deterrence (Jacobs 1996; Paternoster and Piquero 1995; Piquero and Pa- ternoster 1998; Piquero and Pogarsky 2002). Piquero and Paternoster exam- ined people's intentions to drink and drive using a 1989 phone survey of 1,686 respondents. They note that drinking and driving is a good offense to ex- amine because people are likely to have both personal and vicarious expe- riences. Piquero and Paternoster's results support Stafford and Warr's model. They found that respondents' expressed intentions to drink and drive were influenced by their own and other people's experiences with punishment and avoiding punishment. These deterrent effects of risk perception also re- mained after controlling for moral beliefs and peer drinking and driving.

Another important issue is whether individuals differ in their risk per- ceptions. Deterrence and rational choice theories generally assume that ev- eryone will perceive risk in the same way, but this is likely an unrealistic assumption. Cook (1980) argues that individuals differ in their subjective view of risk and reward because they will differ in their willingness to accept risks, their preferences for law-abiding behavior, and how they evaluate profit (e.g., $50 may be a lot of money to one person but not much to another). As an example, some people are more risk averse, or less willing to take risks, than are others. Risk averse people may be more influenced by the threat of sanctions than are others. Research suggests that offenders are particularly likely to be impulsive or risk-seeking (see, for example, low self-control the- ory in Chapter 7). Therefore, offenders may be the least likely to see risks as serious impediments to action. Similarly, some individuals are more present- oriented whereas others are more future-oriented (Nagin and Pogarsky 2001, 2003). It appears that those who are more present-oriented are less likely to be deterred by sanctions. One reason for this may be that those with a present orientation invest less in social bonds and therefore have less to lose from crime (Nagin and Paternoster 1994). Similarly, Gibbs (1986) argues that perceptions of risk likely vary by age, race, socioeconomic status, and gender, and evidence suggests this may be the case (Grasmick, Sims-Blackwell, and Bursik 1993; Sims-Blackwell 2000). In sum, research suggests that the perception of risk is related to the likelihood of offending but that all offenders do not perceive risk similarly.

Rational Choice

Recall that the deterrence and rational choice perspective assumes the potential offender weighs the potential costs and benefits of crime and decides on a course of action in light of these costs and benefits. This view of the offender is controversial. In this section, we discuss what it means to act rationally and the degree to which offenders (or people more generally) act rationally.

Whether individuals are rational depends very much on the way that rationality is defined. Most people act in predictable ways. Imagine how difficult driving in traffic would be if people did not engage in reasonably predictable behavior. Similarly, few people act in ways that most others would consider irrational; those that talk to themselves or hear voices are often referred to mental health professionals. In this sense, people are "rational." Yet the term **rational** means something more in the context of rational choice theories of economics or crime. From this perspective, individuals will make decisions based on the expected utility of their actions. This conception of rationality is considerably more controversial because it implies that potential offenders have realistic perceptions of sanction severity and probability and they rationally calculate behavior rather than acting on impulse (Jacob 1979).

One component of this economically rational view is that individuals must possess accurate information to make informed choices about the relative costs and benefits of actions. As we have seen, such an assumption is likely unjustified. Cook (1980) notes that it is not necessary for individuals to possess full and accurate information as long as people rationally weigh the costs and benefits of behavioral options with the information available to them. This is often called "limited rationality." Yet, even this view of the offender suggests that costs and benefits of behavioral choices are consciously weighed and a "correct" choice is made based on available information. This view may be inaccurate for several reasons. First, not everyone is equally able to weigh costs and benefits of actions (Clarke and Cornish 1985). Some will be better able to make "smart" choices with respect to crime, just as some people get better deals when shopping for cars. The economic rational choice view also assumes that criminals and noncriminals will think similarly, yet research suggests they may not (Clarke and Cornish 1985:161). And second, people make predictable errors in decision making (see Cook 1980 for a discussion). Individuals often ignore events they believe have a low probability of occurrence. This is especially relevant for deterrent effects of punishment if arrest is perceived to be relatively rare. Sometimes rare events will be overly weighted because they are vivid. For example, flying in an airplane is statistically safer than riding in a car, but many fear plane travel because plane crashes are highly publicized. Other complexities in people's decision making are not well accounted for by a rational choice view. Piquero and Pogarsky (2002) find that being punished seems to encourage offending for some rather than discouraging it, which the authors refer to as an "emboldening effect." Such an effect may be the result of the gambler's fallacy (I would have to be really unlucky to get caught again). To add even greater complexity, Pogarsky and Piquero (2003) suggest such effects operate only for some types of offenders.

Another question is the extent to which people *consciously* weigh their options. Simon (1957) claims people have rules of thumb so that not every decision must be reevaluated each time. For example, some people have developed rules of thumb that prohibit robbery under any circumstances. Or people may act on impulse according to their rules of thumb. So the choice to drink alcohol may be based on a rational calculation of the costs and benefits, even if the behavior of the intoxicated individual is not rational per se.

The rational choice model also implies that decisions to commit crimes are offense-specific. A potential offender may conclude that committing a burglary is a good idea but that robbery is not. Along these lines, Clarke and Cornish (1985) claim we need separate models of decision making for each crime. This claim suggests the need to develop and presumably test relatively narrow models of criminal behavior. As such, a model of decisions on whether to commit a burglary may be too broad. We may need different decision models for commercial and residential burglaries. Such model specificity could become cumbersome when considering the sheer number of different kinds of crime in which offenders could engage. This approach also suggests a degree of offender specialization, which may not reflect reality. Gottfredson and Hirschi (1990) and others suggest that criminals do not specialize. They maintain that today's burglar is tomorrow's convenience store robber.

There also may be multiple decision points in the commission of a crime (Clarke and Cornish 1985). The first is willingness to engage in any crime. The second is the decision to commit a particular offense. It is quite possible that rational choice may be more applicable to the decision to engage in a particular offense than the willingness to engage in crime at all. Individual experiences or circumstances may drive only some to be in a position where commission of a crime is a realistic course of action. Yet current views of rational choice imply that we all are potential offenders and weigh the consequences and rewards of criminal behavior.

Finally, most research focuses on punishment risk. The rational choice model suggests that the potential criminal weighs both the risks of punishment and the expected rewards. Piliavin, Thornton, Gartner, and Matsueda (1986), however, argue that most previous deterrence research does not take reward aspects into account. Using a relatively unique sample of previously incarcerated and drug-using adults and teenage high school dropouts, Piliavin et al. found support for reward but not risk aspects of rational choice. Similarly, Piquero and Rengert (1999) found that active burglars responded to risks but their perceptions of the potential rewards were stronger influences on their behavior. More research is needed to determine whether this is true for all potential offenders.

Routine Activities and Opportunity

Routine activities and opportunity theories focus on the factors that converge to produce predatory criminal victimization, including motivated offenders, a lack of capable guardians (reduced guardianship), suitable or attractive targets, exposure, and proximity. Many studies have used routine activities and opportunity concepts, taking one of two approaches. The first is to consider variation in crime or victimization rates. As described earlier, Cohen and Felson (1979) used the theory to determine whether the dramatic increase in U.S. crime rates since 1960 was linked to changes in the routine activity structure of American society, such as increases in labor force participation among married females, an increase in the number of single person households, and a sizable rise in the proportion of households unattended at 8:00 a.m. They hypothesized that these changes affected the daily routine activities of millions of residents, increasing target suitability and decreasing guardian presence, two necessary elements for victimization. Using victimization evidence to support their contentions, they calculated a household activity ratio and compared it to five index offenses. In a national-level analysis from 1947 to 1974, they found that nonhousehold activities vary directly with homicide, burglary, rape, aggravated assault, and robbery. Similarly, Cohen, Felson, and Land (1980) find that national crime rates for robbery, burglary, and auto theft from 1947 to 1972 are related to routine activities.

Other research has used smaller units of aggregation such as standard metropolitan statistical areas (SMSAs). Messner and Blau (1987), focusing on leisure activities and using index offenses for 1980 and 1981 (murder, rape, robbery, aggravated assault, burglary, larceny, and motor vehicle theft) as the dependent variable, generally find support for routine activities theory in a sample of 124 SMSAs. Other research has considered variation in crime across smaller areas within cities. Roncek and Maier (1991) examine whether areas with bars and taverns have more crime. They examine 4,937 residential blocks in Cleveland, using three-year crime averages in city blocks from 1979 to 1981. They find that crime is substantially higher in blocks with bars, even controlling for socioeconomic variables that might also affect crime. In contrast, in a pooled analysis of 584 cities in 1960, 1970, and 1980, Miethe, Hughes, and McDowall (1991) find greater support for social disorganization (see Chapter 4) than routine activities but note that neither is a strong predictor of crime. Models including variables derived from both perspectives only explained about 20% of the variation in homicide, robbery, and burglary rates across cities.

Although macro-level studies generally find results consistent with routine activities theory, some researchers argue that individual-level data are necessary to test the theory since differences in routine activities, and therefore opportunities for victimization, occur across individuals (Birkbeck and La-Free 1993). Several individual-level tests have used information from the National Crime Victimization Survey (NCVS), a nationally representative annual survey. Cohen and Cantor (1980) used 1975–1976 NCVS data to examine whether the risk of larceny victimization varied by age, race, gender, and economic activities. And, as we mentioned earlier, Cohen et al. (1981) used 1974 and 1977 NCVS data to consider how victimization patterns vary by dimensions of social stratification such as race, income, and age. Results of these early studies are generally consistent with the theoretical predictions of routine activities theory.

Other individual-level studies document mixed support. Miethe, Stafford, and Long (1987) examined individual-level data on routine activities for 107,678 residents in 13 cities in 1975. They find that routine activities explain property crime victimization reasonably well but not violent crime victimization. Massey, Krohn, and Bonati (1989) used data from six neighborhoods in Atlanta in 1979 to compute three types of property victimization measures at the individual level. Their results provide some support for the theory. In contrast, Sampson and Wooldredge (1987) document minimal support for routine activities using the British Crime Survey (BCS), finding instead that neighborhood social structure is a better determinant of victimization.

Noting the mixed results of prior individual-level studies, Kennedy and Forde (1990) use the Canadian Urban Victimization Survey (CUVS) to examine whether routine activities holds for violent as well as property victimization and whether structural differences in people's living environments account for victimization patterns rather than routine activities. The CUVS contains data unavailable in the NCVS or BCS. The data were collected from seven large cities via a telephone survey. The final sample included 74,463 respondents. The study includes demographic variables such as measures of sex, age, income, and marital status as well as both daytime and evening activities and information from the areas where the respondent lived such as percentage of one-person households, unemployment, divorce, low-income families, and population density. Kennedy and Forde (1990) use logistic regression to estimate the dichotomous (yes/no) outcome of victimization. They find that routine activities predict breaking and entering but not vehicle theft. They find some support for the routine activity perspective across property and violent victimization, even when the demographic nature of the areas was taken into account. They argue that these results contradict Miethe et al. and suggest that even violent victimization depends on patterned exposure.

A major limitation of most studies of routine activities and opportunity theories is the failure to measure variation in motivation. Early research assumed the supply of motivated offenders was relatively constant. Recent studies have begun to consider variation in motivation. For example, Osgood et al. (1996) highlight the importance of unsupervised time for teens (absence of guardians) as a factor in delinquency. They argue that the very periods or activities that decrease guardianship also increase motivation for crime as well. Osgood et al. find support for these ideas using five waves of the Monitoring the Future (MTF) study, a nationally representative sample of 18- to 26-year-olds who were high school seniors from 1977 to 1981. Similarly, Osgood and Anderson (2004) argue that the time kids spend unsupervised and socializing with each other is conducive to delinquency. They claim that neighborhood rates of monitoring provide a contextual effect on delinquency above and beyond the individual parent effect. They test this in a hierarchical linear model of 4,359 students in 36 schools across 10 cities. They find that unstructured socializing has a strong impact on delinquency at the individual and school levels and that there was a contextual effect of parental monitoring. This study highlights the importance of social context in determining routine activities (see also Bernburg and Thorlindson 2001; Miethe and Meier 1994).

One advantage of the routine activities and opportunity approach is that it leads fairly straightforwardly to potential strategies for crime reduction by reducing the *opportunities* for crime. If predatory crimes occur in given situations with predictable characteristics, then it may be possible to reduce crime using this knowledge. Many studies have examined the possibility of situational crime prevention. Although space precludes a thorough discussion of this research, it appears that crime prevention measures can be effective at preventing some kinds of crimes (without displacement). For more on situational crime prevention, see Brantingham, Brantingham, and Taylor (2005); Clarke (1983, 1992, 1995, 1997); Felson (1998); Lab (1997); and Newman, Clarke, and Shoham (1997).

Measuring Crime

Many studies testing deterrence and rational choice theories have employed the number of crimes known to the police and arrest rates. However, Gibbs (1986) is sharply critical of employing "official" crime rates to test these theories for two reasons: (1) Not all crimes are reported to the police, and (2) official statistics may not accurately reflect the relative numbers of different kinds of crimes being committed because certain kinds of crimes are more likely to be reported than others.

Some also claim the relationship between crime and punishment found in studies of deterrence is a statistical artifact because the variables being correlated have a common term—crime. The crime rate is typically expressed as C/P (where P = population and C = crime). The certainty of punishment is usually expressed as S/C (S = number of sanctions and C = crime). Since crime is a common term in both formulas, the correlation between crime and punishment rates could be a statistical artifact. Gibbs and Firebaugh (1990) disprove the artifact argument but suggest that measurement error could still underlie this correlation. Recent research has shown, however, that even when measurement error is large, as in the case of official crime measures, the practical impact of this error is small and unlikely to influence substantive conclusions regarding deterrent effects (Levitt 1998; Pudney, Deadman, and Pyle 2000).

A second limitation of using official crime rates is the aggregated nature of crime categories reported (Cook 1980; Gibbs 1986). All types of burglaries are lumped together, for example. As noted earlier, the same factors may not explain residential and business burglaries (Cook 1980). Official data are therefore limited because they do not allow distinctions to be made within broad offense categories. Another example of this limitation is the use of general homicide estimates in death penalty research when not all homicides are death penalty eligible (Gibbs 1986). Because of such limitations, Gibbs claims only self-reported data offer valid measures for evaluating deterrence. Indeed, perceptual studies of deterrence are much more likely to employ self-report data, yet many studies still use official crime data to test deterrence arguments.

Another important question is whether all kinds of crime are equally driven by rational considerations. The economically rational components of burglary or theft certainly seem more apparent than taking revenge on the man with whom one's wife is cheating. Yet, Clarke and Cornish (1985) argue that both expressive and economic goals can be considered in rational terms. Thus, all types of crimes appear to be eligible. One could still question whether drug use is rational. Likewise, it would seem that white-collar crimes are most likely to be guided by rational considerations, although some studies suggest that white-collar offenders are not effectively deterred by sanctions (Weisburd et al. 1995).

Finally, some deterrence studies use intended crime rather than actual crime measures. Pogarsky and Piquero (2003) ask subjects to estimate the likelihood they would drive while intoxicated on a scale from 0 to 100 based on scenarios with varying sanction risks. But the stated intention to engage in a behavior is not the same as actually engaging in it. Similarly, some studies consider minor kinds of deviance such as cheating. Nagin and Pogarsky (2003) conducted a randomized experiment that measured the likelihood of cheating on a task to earn a nominal reward in a university research setting. It could be, however, that rational calculations are more likely to influence relatively minor acts of deviance such as cheating on a test than more serious criminal behaviors such as homicide, which may be driven by strong emotions. Using intentions to engage in a behavior or minor deviant acts can artificially inflate perceived support for deterrence theory.

With respect to routine activities and opportunity theories, it is not clear whether they are expected to apply to all crime types or only predatory crimes (those involving the meeting of an offender and a victim). If an offender and victim are required to meet, then this would limit the scope of the theory to crimes of interpersonal victimization. This may appear more limiting than it is in reality because even minor crimes such as pick-pocketing are interpersonal, although not necessarily violent. But the theory also seems to apply to instances where the property of the victim is left untended, creating an opportunity for crime (e.g., thefts of personal belongings left unattended while a student goes to find a book in the library stacks). Similarly, a question arises as to whether all crimes are equally influenced by opportunity. It would seem that some crimes arise from chance circumstances whereas others arise from careful creation of opportunity. Certainly, evidence suggests that sex offenders actively try to create situations where they are alone with potential victims to increase their opportunities to offend. Alternatively, homicides that occur as the result of an argument fit less clearly within an opportunity model.

Summary Critique of Measurement Strategy

The evidence that deterrence-based policy interventions reduce crime is mixed at best. Some studies find "deterrent-like effects" (Nagin 1998), whereas many others do not. For example, increased punishments for DUI seem to have limited effects (Ross 1984, 1986), whereas DUI interlock ignition devices, which physically prevent drunk driving by forcing the driver to blow into a machine, seem to be more effective (Fulkerson 2003; Morse and Elliot 1992). In contrast, studies of the death penalty do not show consistent deterrent effects (Donohue and Wolfers 2006). Other ecological studies of deterrence produce mixed results. Studies of police interventions, for example, sometimes find deterrent effects (Braga et al. 1999; Kovandzic and Sloan 2002; Sherman and Rogan 1995; Smith 2001), sometimes find no effects (Novak et al. 1999), and sometimes find that the deterrent effects are contingent on specific aspects of police activity, vary by location (Fritsch, Caeti, and Taylor 1999; Kennedy 1998), or have short-term effects that extinguish over time (Sherman et al. 1995).

Research also concludes that certainty is generally a more effective deterrent than severity when considered separately. Yet certainty and severity are likely related to one another (Gibbs 1986). The effect of a particular sanction level likely depends on the certainty of its application. Research does not suggest strong support for specific deterrence. Offenders do not seem to be deterred by being punished. In fact, some offenders are more likely to engage in crime after being punished.

Of course, the strength or weakness of policy interventions does not exclusively determine the value of deterrence and rational choice theories of crime. The approach could still be valid, even if it does not lead to policies to reduce crime. As we noted, the theory suggests that individuals rationally consider risks when determining whether to commit crime. Research has also considered whether risk perceptions influence the likelihood of criminal activities. The evidence suggests that risk perceptions vary across individuals in ways that are not accounted for in rational choice models. Likewise, people do not appear to be economically rational actors, although they appear to act predictably. Given this limited rationality, Akers and Sellers (2004) argue that there is minimal value added by a rational choice perspective because many other theories of crime (such as social learning theory, discussed in Chapter 6) also assume that offenders will act in reasonably predictable ways.

It is also possible that decisions made in an artificial research setting do not occur in the same way as in the real world. For one, the presence of alcohol or drugs may lead to less than optimal decisions being reached (Clarke and Cornish 1985). Clarke and Cornish also note that decisions made as part of a group will be different than those for individuals acting alone. This point is crucial because many crimes are committed in groups. Decisions must be made rapidly in many cases, under considerable and varying levels of uncertainty, with varying levels of information, by actors who differ in the way they process information as well as the kinds of information they rely on to make decisions. Certainly, more research is needed on decisions to commit crime in "real-world" settings (e.g., Tunnell 1992).

Research on routine activities and opportunity theories is generally supportive, although the measures employed to tap concepts are often too general and measures of the motivated offender concept are rarely included in studies. More recent individual-level studies tend to support the opportunity approach, yet some find that when measures from alternative theories—such as social learning—are included in models, the influence of routine activities variables is weaker (Bernburg and Thorlindson 2001). Similarly, Jensen and Brownfield (1986) note that criminal victimizations often occur during criminal activity. It may also be that criminal activities structure future routine activities. If a youth gets suspended from school for fighting, for example, he or she is much more likely to have spare time on his or her hands to engage in delinquent acts.

Analytical Issues

In this section we consider how studies have been designed to test rational choice theories. We also consider issues related to causal modeling and causal ordering of variables suggested by rational choice theories. Finally, we consider potential alternative explanations that must be ruled out. (Note: Space limitations preclude the discussion of routine activity and opportunity theories in this section. This is not meant to imply that such issues do not arise in research on those theories).

Sample Selection

Decisions on how to design a study to test a theory are just as important as the concepts to be measured. Several key questions must be addressed. First, who should be studied? At first glance, it might appear that deterrence and rational choice theories could be tested on all kinds of research subjects. After all, the theories claim to apply to everyone. Again, the assumption is that all potential offenders consider the relative risks and rewards of criminal action. If this were true, then it would not matter who was included in the study. Yet, this assumption may not be realistic. First, one must consider whether everyone is a potential offender in a meaningful sense. Some people may not actively consider the possibility of committing a crime, even if the opportunity presents itself. We sometimes hear news stories of people who turn in lost money. So, the first question to address is whether all people can be considered potential offenders. If not, samples from the general population, who might not actively consider crime under any circumstances, could be misleading. Unfortunately, most research has been conducted on subjects who might not really be potential offenders because they have so much to lose (jobs, family, friends) from committing crime, irrespective of the potential for formal punishment (Foglia 1997).

Perhaps to properly test deterrence theory, studies must identify "potential" criminals. Piliavin et al. (1986) address this issue by drawing a relatively unique sample from three different sources: subjects with prior prison records, drug users, and teenage high school dropouts. Crime is likely to be a viable option these individuals might consider. Similarly, Foglia (1997) employs a sample of 298 teenagers from low-income, high-crime inner-city high schools in a Northeastern city. Her study finds no deterrent effect of the perceived risk of arrest, which she attributes to the fact that these youth likely had little to lose by being arrested. Rather, they were influenced by their peers' behavior, their own norms, and their parents. It thus appears that for this population, informal sanctions constitute a more viable threat than formal sanctions through arrest.

Another issue related to sampling is whether to choose adults or juveniles. Many (if not most) studies discussed in this book rely on juvenile samples because teenagers are congregated in schools and because a disproportionate amount of crime is committed by juveniles. Yet, if teenagers have not fully developed their ability to make rational choices, then such samples could be problematic. These samples also might not generalize to adults because the juvenile justice system has different punishments than the adult system does. Therefore, risk calculations among teenagers might be different than adults.

Another question is whether risk perceptions vary across individuals (Gibbs 1986). If such variation is random, this is not particularly problematic. A much more serious problem arises, however, if groups systematically vary along these dimensions. It could be that women are inherently more risk averse than men. Or risk perceptions might systematically vary by racial and ethnic groups. If true, the best solution is to test deterrence arguments using samples with varying characteristics to determine how consistent such processes are across different populations.

Model Specification and Causal Ordering

In testing a theory, it is also important to consider the nature of the relationship between the concepts. This refers to issues of model specification and causal ordering. Most theoretical treatments of deterrence theory suggest there is an unconditional linear negative relationship between certainty and severity of punishment and the likelihood of crime (i.e., as one variable goes up, the other goes down). Although it is tempting to think of deterrence in terms of linear relationships, the reality is likely more complex. For example, there may be threshold effects for certainty of punishment. A threshold effect refers to a situation in which a variable only has an effect on an outcome once it reaches a certain threshold. In other words, the certainty of punishment may need to reach a certain level before it is effective in deterring crime. If the actual risk of apprehension is below this threshold, then the threat of punishment would have no effect. Deterrence may also have ceiling effects, such that above a certain severity level, additional increases in severity may produce minimal impact. An example of a ceiling effect is in the toxicity of certain drugs—once the lethal dose of arsenic is reached, additional amounts won't make the person any more dead. It could be that the punishments for many crimes are already so severe that any additional increases in severity will have no additional marginal deterrent effect (Cook 1980:231–233). This may be the case with the death penalty. The death penalty, in reality, is only an incremental increase in punishment beyond spending the rest of one's life in prison. So, capital punishment only affects potential offenders willing to commit a homicide in the face of a sentence of life in prison but unwilling to risk execution.

The distinct possibility also exists that deterrent effects are conditional, meaning that the effect of one variable on the likelihood of crime depends on others. The effect of punishment severity on rational choices to commit crime likely depends on the corresponding level of certainty of apprehension. An extremely severe punishment in a situation in which the potential offender thinks getting caught is highly unlikely will be less of an effective deterrent than an equally severe punishment when risk of punishment is more certain. Thus, certainty and severity effects are likely conditional upon one another, although most deterrence research considers them separately.

Causal ordering (i.e., which is the cause and which is the effect when two variables are correlated) is another important issue in deterrence research. Recall that one area of research has examined the relationship between various policies and crime. Such research raises difficult causal order issues. For example, conventional wisdom suggests that more police means less crime. Thus, one could simply measure the number of police and the amount of crime and should find that in places where there are more police there is less crime. But such research often finds the opposite—places with more police often have more crime. The difficulty is that jurisdictions will often hire more police officers in *response* to rising crime rates. As a result, more police is the effect of higher crime. Another real possibility is that more police will mean higher reported crime because there are more people to report crime to, and the police may also observe more crime. Such a relationship is known as a reciprocal one (i.e., crime and increased police presence are both causes and effects), and it presents thorny methodological issues for a variety of areas of research on deterrence (Nagin 1978, 1998). We discuss the issue of reciprocal relationships further in Chapters 3, 5, and 6.

Related to reciprocal effects is the issue of reverse causation. Reverse causation is when the suspected cause is actually the outcome. Cook (1980) notes that one must be concerned about reverse causation when studying policy effects such as those often used to test the implications of deterrence research. If the policy being examined was implemented in response to a problem, it could be that what the researcher is saying is the outcome is actually the cause. For example, we noted earlier that states with the death penalty often have higher homicide rates than states without it. This would suggest that the death penalty leads to increases in homicide. The more likely scenario is that states that have instituted (or retained) the death penalty are those that have high homicide rates to begin with. This would mean that homicide causes the death penalty to be instituted rather than the death penalty leading to changes in homicide rates. Both reciprocal effects and reverse causation raise questions of research design, which we discuss next.

Research Design

As discussed in Chapter 1, to test theories of crime, it is necessary to choose a method for collecting the data. The first consideration is usually whether individual- or group-level data will be used. Studies of deterrence have used both individual and aggregate data. Aggregate data are often used to study the deterrent effects of policies. Recall that studies have compared the crime rates of cities with more police officers per capita to those with fewer. If deterrence works, cities with more police officers per capita should have lower crime rates, all else being equal (it rarely is).

A number of researchers have suggested that individual-level data are necessary to test deterrence arguments (see, e.g., Gibbs 1986) because deterrence is something that happens in the potential offender's head. Recent studies of deterrence such as the studies of risk perception discussed earlier have been much more likely to employ individual-level data.

Another important consideration is whether to use cross-sectional data (collected at one point in time) or longitudinal data (collected over time). Both individual-level and aggregate studies have relied mainly on cross-sectional data. For example, the cross-state comparisons of the homicide rates in states with or without the death penalty are cross-sectional. Yet, such studies are limited because they cannot tell which factor is the cause and which is the effect. Studies of the deterrent effect of the death penalty have also employed longitudinal designs. One type of longitudinal study of the death penalty is an interrupted time series design. Here, one examines homicide rates in a particular jurisdiction before and after the death penalty is instituted or repealed. If the death penalty has a deterrent effect, one would expect homicide rates to decline in that jurisdiction during the time that capital punishment is a legal sentencing option. The accumulated evidence does not support this. One reason for this finding may be that the time lag used in longitudinal research may be too long to detect any effects of the death penalty. Longitudinal studies typically use periods of one year between observations. Some have suggested that the deterrent effects of an execution may be much shorter and would be missed in such a design (Chamlin, Grasmick, Bursik, and Cochran 1992). A few studies have used shorter time lags, but the results of these "immediate impact" studies are not encouraging. In fact, some show that homicide actually increases in the immediate aftermath of a publicized execution (Cochran and Chamlin 2000; Cochran et al. 1994).

Studies of risk perception have employed three types of research designs—cross-sectional surveys, scenario-based studies, and panel studies (Nagin 1998). In cross-sectional surveys, respondents are questioned about their perceptions of the certainty and severity of sanctions and about either their prior offending behavior or their future intentions to offend. In scenario-based studies individuals are questioned about their perceptions of the risks of committing a crime based on a detailed description of a scenario, including the risks of punishment, which the researchers systematically vary across individuals (Nagin 1998). The likelihood of a particular crime being committed should vary with the perceived certainty and/or severity of sanctions, and studies find that it typically does. Yet, both types of studies are potentially problematic. The scenario-based studies are limited because they do not measure actual offending and scenarios often refer to relatively minor kinds of crime such as intentions to drink and drive (e.g., Pogarsky and Piquero 2003). Cross-sectional risk perception surveys are also limited because they cannot assess cause and effect. This is especially problematic in research on risk perceptions. If risk perceptions work in the way that deterrence theory suggests, then one would expect a person would perceive the risk of punishment and respond accordingly, either by committing the crime or not. Yet, it could be that people's perceptions of risk respond to whether they were apprehended or not. So if they commit a crime and don't get caught, it may reduce their perceived level of punishment risk, raising the potential for reciprocal effects. Such situations require longitudinal designs to determine causality (see also Minor and Harry 1982).

Some risk perception studies have employed panel survey designs, in which a sample is repeatedly surveyed on both risk perceptions and criminal behavior. This allows the researcher to disentangle which came first—the choice of whether to commit a crime or the risk perception. Paternoster (1988) uses a three-wave panel model of 265 high school students to test deterrence. Survey questions regarding theft and marijuana use were administered in the fall of the students' tenth-, eleventh-, and twelfth-grade years. Paternoster did find some effects of perceived certainty of punishment on marijuana use and theft but noted that other effects such as peer and parental influences were often stronger. Nagin (1998) claims that panel studies of risk perception are least likely to show "deterrent-like" effects of certainty or severity of punishment. Minor and Harry (1982) conducted a two-wave panel study of 488 undergraduate students in 1978 employing a three-month lag between surveys, rather than the standard one-year gap. They find that risk perceptions are unstable over time. Therefore, one explanation for the lack of support for deterrence in longitudinal risk perception studies may be that too long of a lag was used.

Potential Alternative Explanations

In testing a theory, it is also necessary to rule out alternative explanations before researchers can claim that one variable is the cause of another.

Alternative explanations are an issue in both aggregate- and individual-level deterrence studies. In aggregate-level studies, one important alternative explanation is incapacitation. Incapacitation refers to when an offender is incapable of committing a crime regardless of his or her intentions. Prison sentences certainly incapacitate offenders (at least with respect to committing crimes against nonprisoners). Therefore, aggregate studies such as those examining the deterrent effect of adding police must consider the possibility that more offenders are incapacitated by arrest and imprisonment rather than deterred (for research on incapacitation, see Greenberg 1975, 1982; Greenberg and Larkin 1998). Yet including estimates of incapacitation effects in macrolevel deterrence studies is problematic because it requires assumptions about the number of offenses that would be prevented through the incapacitation of each offender (Gibbs 1986). Without accurate estimates of incapacitation effects, the deterrent effects of punishment will be misleading.

For individual-level deterrence studies, a number of alternative explanations must be considered, especially *informal* sanctions. Deterrence theories suggest that the fear of formal sanctions through punishment by the state is the primary consideration of the potential criminal. Numerous studies find, however, that the fear of shame, embarrassment, job loss, damage to family relationships, and loss of friendships may be a stronger determinant of criminal behavior than fear of arrest (Anderson, Chiricos, and Waldo 1977; Layton, MacKenzie, and De Li 2002; Peete, Milner, and Welch 1994; Thomas and Bishop 1984). Related to this is the effect of laws on the moral condemnation of crime. People could perceive that society considers an act wrong when actions are made illegal and respond to that rather than to the fear of arrest itself. Because of this, one must consider the degree of moral commitment individuals have to the law. In other words, most people obey the law because they believe it is the right thing to do. In this case, it is the moral authority of the law, rather than the threat of punishment, that operates to "deter" a person from committing crime. Such potential effects must be ruled out before one can conclude that fear of punishment (or lack of fear) is the driving force behind criminal behavior (see Burkett and Ward 1993; Erickson and Gibbs 1978; Grasmick and Bursik 1990).

Summary Critique of Analytical Strategy

As discussed, studies of deterrence have often employed cross-sectional research designs to test deterrence arguments, but such designs are inherently limited because they cannot reliably determine cause and effect. Cross-sectional designs are also unable to disentangle reciprocal effects, sometimes leading to seemingly incongruous findings such as the conclusion that more police equals more crime. Longitudinal designs are needed to assess the effects of most policy interventions, and recent research has begun to employ more sophisticated pooled cross-sectional time series models (Levitt 1998; Marvell and Moody 1995). More research using such sophisticated research methods is desirable in studies of policy effects.

At the individual level, research has begun to move past the early cross-sectional studies of risk perception. Longitudinal studies of risk perception and crime are also desirable. Yet the typical time lag in such research—one year—may be too long to capture risk perceptions that appear to be more dynamic over time. In addition, more research on how criminal decisions come to be made as they are happening would be useful (Clarke and Cornish 1985:160). Such examinations would likely entail field research rather than the more typical survey methods employed in most individual-level deterrence research.

More studies also need to take into consideration the possibility that deterrent effects are nonlinear. It seems likely that threshold or ceiling effects could operate for certainty and severity of punishment. It also seems likely that certainty and severity of punishment depend on one another (Mendes 2004). Finally, more studies must consider alternative explanations. Until alternative explanations are ruled out, support for deterrence and rational choice arguments is suggestive, at best.

Directions for Future Research

Although there is some support for "deterrent-like" effects (Nagin 1998), the evidence is mixed, particularly with respect to deterrence-based policy interventions. It seems clear that the rational choice view of offenders is unrealistic if considered in the economic terms of utility maximization (De Haan and Vos 2003). At the same time, offenders (like people more generally) are not irrational, and they respond predictably to situations. More research is necessary on how individuals develop their perceptions of risk and when the risk of formal punishment operates to deter crime, especially net of other factors. Studies show that many factors other than the fear of punishment are important influences on the behavior of criminals. A serious gap in deterrence research is the failure to consider that the choice to commit a crime is based on both the perceived risk of punishment *and* the expected rewards. Too few studies seriously consider the reward side of the equation. Some research, however, suggests that rewards are stronger influences on behavior than expected punishments (Piquero and Rengert 1999). This also underscores a neglected potential link between deterrence theories and social learning theories of crime (see Chapter 6), which argue that crime is more likely when it is rewarded (Akers 1990). The deterrence model is also limited because it assumes that the motivations to commit crime are constant over time. Recent research suggests, however, that motivations for crime vary over time (Tittle and Botchkovar 2005; Uggen and Thompson 2003). The effects of threats of punishment may also differ according to a person's motivation or propensity to commit crime (Wright, Caspi, Moffitt, and Paternoster 2004). Future research needs to take motivation, as well as the alternative explanations discussed here, into consideration.

Perhaps the greatest strength (and weakness) of deterrence and rational choice theories is their policy relevance. The seemingly straightforward policy implications of the certainty and severity of punishment no doubt account for much of the perspective's popularity. Still, the discussion in this chapter has shown that such policy effects are anything but straightforward. They often depend on a variety of factors and are inconsistent. Perhaps most disturbing is that policies with short-term deterrent effects may lead to completely unintended long-term consequences. If part of the deterrent effect of punishment comes from fear of social stigma, then what happens when the experience of criminal punishment becomes commonplace (Nagin 1998), as it has for too many disadvantaged inner-city minority men? The increasing use of imprisonment for less and less serious offenders has potentially weakened the overall deterrent effect of punishment for a significant segment of potential criminals. This, along with the other issues discussed, raises serious questions about the desirability of deterrence-based policies.

Discussion Questions

1. Are people rational? What does this tell us about their propensity to commit crime?
2. Given the mixed or limited effects of deterrence-based policy interventions on crime rates, why do you think this perspective is so popular among the public and officials?
3. How could we improve the theory to better account for individual differences in risk perception and the importance of nonlegal factors (e.g., socioeconomic status, race, ethnicity, age)?
4. Why does crime occur according to routine activities and opportunity theories?
5. How are rational choice and routine activities theories similar, and how do they differ?

CHAPTER 3

TRAIT THEORIES

Introduction

Media images of criminals—from hockey-masked murderers to cannibalistic geniuses—can lead one to believe that criminals are somehow fundamentally different from noncriminals. Although most theories in this book assume that all individuals are basically similar and will be driven, free, or choose to commit crime under certain conditions, the biological and psychological "trait" theories discussed in this chapter assume there are basic differences that distinguish criminals from noncriminals.

Intellectual History of Trait Theories

The view of the criminal outlined in the previous chapter suggests that people choose to act in a certain way of their own "free will," based on classical views of human nature. This conception of the criminal was dominant until the beginning of the nineteenth century, when positivism began to emerge. Positivism assumes that forces beyond the individual's control influence behavior, which is referred to as determinism. Positivists also believed in the use of the scientific method, which emphasized observation in advancing science. When scientific methods began to be used to explain human behavior, it also seemed reasonable to use scientific methods to explain criminal behavior.

The earliest positivist theorists of crime focused on biological explanations. For example, phrenologists such as Franz Joseph Gall examined the shape of a person's skull to predict criminality (Siegel 2006). The most famous of the early biologists was Cesare Lombroso, an Italian physician studying the physical characteristics of prisoners. Using Darwinian concepts, Lombroso argued that criminals were physically inferior to noncriminals and were what he called "atavistic anomalies," or essentially physical throwbacks to pre–homo sapiens species. Lombroso is considered to be the "father of criminology." Ironically, though, the biological determinism of Lombroso and others led early sociologists studying crime to reject biological explanations to the point they were considered taboo for much of the twentieth century (Jeffery 1979). In the 1970s, more nuanced, less deterministic biologically based theories began to emerge. Many of these modern biosocial theories now explicitly recognize that both biology and the social environment are important for understanding criminal behavior.

Although much of the focus in early criminology was on biological explanations, the nineteenth century also saw similar developments in psychology, based on the work of Phillipe Pinel and Benjamin Rush (Siegel 2006). The most famous early psychologist was Sigmund Freud, widely considered to be the father of psychology. Freud's work paved the way for modern psychological explanations of crime. In the next section we discuss broad categories of biological trait theories in more detail, followed by a discussion of the various branches of psychological trait theories.

Modern Biosocial Theories

Because early biological theories focusing on the shape of the skull are now historical curiosities, space limitations preclude discussion of them here (for more information on early theories, see Jeffery 1994). One longstanding line of research conducted by biologically oriented theorists concerns the "nature versus nurture" debate. Although the field of criminology began with theorists who believed there was something about the biological makeup of an individual that caused him or her to commit crime (nature), by the early 1900s, the study of crime was dominated by sociologically oriented explanations. Sociologists denied the relevance of biological factors for behavior, arguing that criminal or law-abiding behavior was the result of a person's social environment (nurture). In other words, sociologists generally believe that a person's environment, rather than his or her genetic makeup, influences behavior. The nature–nurture debate led to one of the earliest and longest lines of biosocial research—heritability studies. Generally, heritability studies examine the degree to which criminological traits are biologically passed from one generation to the next. This research is described later.

Another set of studies has also attempted to show that genetics influence behavior by examining genetic anomalies (see Raine 1993:53–54; Herrnstein 1995:57–58 for reviews). Although the majority of people have 46 chromosomes, some are born with additional X or Y chromosomes, which determine gender. Researchers argued that XYY males (with an extra Y chromosome) would be more likely to exhibit criminal, especially violent, behavior. Although a number of studies exist, little evidence supports the notion of a "supercriminal" male (Raine 1993:53–54). But some research does find that people with extra chromosomes are more likely to be criminal, although *nonviolent* rather than violent offenders. The increased criminality may result because those with chromosomal abnormalities might have lower intelligence and thus more difficulties in school, which leads to crime. Even if chromosomal abnormalities are associated with crime, this would only apply to an extremely small proportion of the population. Although important, heritability and genetic anomaly studies can only establish *whether* biology plays a role in determining criminal behavior. They cannot explain *how* biology influences criminal behavior. A wide variety of biosocial theories that suggest specific ways that biology influences criminality have been developed.

Biosocial theories of crime generally focus on the influence of biochemical conditions, brain chemistry, hormone levels, arousal levels, neurological conditions, and evolutionary psychology. Because a full description of these theories is impossible in one chapter, we focus on a few of the more prominent lines of research from each category to illustrate some of the methodological issues in trait research. For more complete discussions of biosocial theories of crime, see Raine (1993, 2002a, 2002b); Reiss, Miczek, and Roth (1994); Raine, Brennan, Farrington, and Mednick (1997); and Fishbein (2001).

A number of recent biosocial explanations have examined the relationship between biochemical conditions and crime. These theories focus on the role of factors such as diet (Fishbein and Pease 1994; Kanarek 1994; Rosen et al. 1985; Werbach, 1995), vitamin deficiencies (Walsh, Isaacson, Rehman, and Hall 1997), and birth complications (Kandel and Mednick 1991; Piquero and Tibbets 1999; Raine, Brennan, and Mednick 1994; Tibbets and Piquero 1999), to name a few. For example, research has shown that lead exposure can reduce the ability to learn (Neisser et al. 1996). Other research, discussed throughout this book, finds that youth who do poorly in school are more likely to engage in delinquent behavior. One explanation for poor school achievement could be lead exposure. Thus, it could be that lead exposure reduces mental ability, causing poor school achievement, which ultimately affects crime.

Other research suggests that brain chemistry may influence criminal behavior. Information is transmitted within the brain and to the rest of the body through chemical reactions. Two of these chemical information systems have been studied in relation to aggression—neurotransmitters and hormones. Neurotransmitters are chemicals that carry information in the brain, whereas hormones are released by glands and carry information to the brain and other parts of the body regulating brain activities and other organs. "Neurotransmitters regulate emotion, mood, hunger, thirst, sleep, and a host of other behavioral and psychological processes" (Fishbein 2001:37). Although there are several kinds of neurotransmitters, scientists have studied dopamine, serotonin, and norepinephrine extensively. Some studies have found that these neurotransmitters are related to aggression, impulse control, learning, and fight-or-flight responses. For example, low levels of serotonin have been found to be related to lower impulse control and aggressive behavior (Fishbein 2001:39).

Hormones are a second set of chemicals studied in relation to antisocial behavior (Brain 1994; Brain and Susman 1997; Raine 1993). They can influence body size and strength, sensory perception, emotional regulation, and aggression. Researchers primarily have considered sex hormones, particularly testosterone, in relation to aggression, antisocial behavior, and criminality. Testosterone is known to increase aggression in animals, but the relationship between testosterone and aggression in humans is less clear. Some argue that testosterone causes aggressive behavior, whereas some suggest it is a consequence of aggression. Research on both neurotransmitters and hormones is discussed in greater detail later.

Another biosocial theory that has received significant attention in biological research but relatively little attention by criminologists is the relationship between psychological states and physiological responses. Numerous studies have found that criminals appear to have very low levels of arousal, as measured by brain activity, electroencephalograms (EEG), low skin conductance, or low resting heart rate (Fishbein 2001; Raine 1993, 2002a). Several potential explanations exist for the correlation between arousal and crime. First, it could be that low-arousal individuals have lower fear levels (Raine 1993), making them more willing to engage in risky activities such as crime or reducing their fear of punishment. A second explanation suggests that low-arousal people are more likely to seek stimulation to relieve their under-arousal. Sensation-seeking behaviors are more likely to be risky and in many cases criminal. Finally, it could be that low-arousal individuals are both bored and fearless, leading them to have a higher propensity to commit crime (Raine 2002a). We discuss the research on this issue later.

Although many other biosocial theories are worth discussing, we will mention two additional theories here. Beyond biochemical differences in the brain, research also suggests that there may be structural differences in the brains of those involved in antisocial behavior. Interest in structural differences between the brains of criminals and noncriminals dates back at least to the 1800s. Fishbein (2001:57–58) relates the story of Phineas Gage, who was injured in a construction accident in 1848. Prior to the accident, Gage was a well-liked, successful businessman. An explosion drove a spike through the front part of Gage's skull. Miraculously he survived the accident, but those who knew him said he became short-tempered, impatient, and driven by his passions. Similarly, Siegel (2006) mentions the story of Charles Whitman, who killed 16 people and wounded 24 others at the University of Texas. It was later found that he had an infiltrating brain tumor and wrote of having uncontrollable homicidal thoughts prior to the incident. These examples suggest that there may be physical differences between the brains of criminals and those of noncriminals, a claim supported by some research. Evans and Park (1997), for example, found a number of types of brain dysfunctions in a sample of 20 murderers using EEG readings. Similarly, Raine, Buchsbaum, Stanley, et al. (1994) found that 22 convicted murderers showed evidence of poor prefrontal lobe functioning using PET analyses compared to 22 non-criminals. Raine (2002a) suggests that reduced prefrontal lobe functioning can limit a person's ability to control aggressive feelings. Likewise, some studies suggest that attention-deficit hyperactivity disorder (ADHD) and minimal brain dysfunction (MBD) may be related to differences in brain functioning (see Raine 1993). Because the brain-imaging techniques used in these studies are so new and the sample sizes are typically very small, any conclusions on the relationship between brain structural differences and antisocial and criminal behavior should be considered preliminary. Still, the early results of these studies suggest that there indeed may be something physically different about criminals, as the early biological determinists suggested. One important question is whether these differences in brain structures are a cause or consequence of criminal behavior, an issue we discuss further in the chapter.

Finally, some biosocial theorists suggest that evolution has influenced criminal behavior. They argue that what we call criminal behavior is actually "adaptive" from the standpoint of evolution (see Fishbein 2001:21–22 for a discussion). The theory of evolution states that all animal and plant species change over time as a result of reproduction. Some characteristics of species make them more or less able to survive in given environments. Characteristics that help an animal to survive are more likely to be passed on through reproduction. So, for example, giraffes have very long necks because the plants they eat tend to be high off the ground. The taller giraffes were better able to compete for limited food resources and reproduce, passing on long-neck genes more frequently than short-neck ones. Evolutionary psychologists believe that evolution has had an impact on criminal behavior as well (Daly and Wilson 1988, 1997). There are several evolutionary theories of crime. One is r/K theory, which applies a more general approach regarding reproductive strategies to criminal behavior. Evolutionary theorists note that the main goal of any species is reproduction and that there are two broad strategies to accomplish this. One strategy produces many offspring but devotes minimal time to their care. The other strategy is to produce few offspring but devote many resources to their development. Species vary along a continuum, ranging from r-strategies producing many offspring at relatively low cost to K-strategies producing few offspring at high cost. As a species, humans tend toward the K end of the spectrum, with much energy and resources devoted to a few offspring. But even within the species, some variation occurs along the r/K spectrum. Ellis (1987a) argues that those at the r end of the spectrum are more likely to engage in selfish, deceptive, or victimizing behavior to reproduce, which in extreme cases can be criminal (see also Rushton 1990, 1995).

A second related evolutionary theory of crime is cheater theory, which focuses on reproductive strategies and suggests that men can increase their offspring by engaging in sexual relations with multiple partners; these men are also known as "cads" (Mealey 1995). Women, on the other hand, prefer mates who will provide resources for the children; these men are known as "dads." The cads increase their chances of reproducing their genes by tricking women into believing they are dads. The theory suggests that these deceptive, selfish strategies may be adopted in other situations, leading to crime. Of course, these theories say very little about female crime.

As this overview suggests, a variety of biosocial theories consider hereditary, biochemical, neurological, and evolutionary causes of crime. For additional reading on biosocial theories, see Fishbein (2001); Raine (1993, 2002a); Raine, Brennan, Farrington, and Mednick (1997); Reiss et al. (1994); Rowe (2002); and Walsh (2002). In the next section, we discuss several psychological trait theories of crime beginning with Freud's psychodynamic theory.

Psychological Theories

Psychological trait theories focus on factors such as unresolved developmental issues, differences in cognitive or moral development, and personality and intelligence to understand criminal behavior. One cannot, therefore, speak of a single psychological theory of crime or antisocial conduct. In this section we discuss some of the major psychological explanations for antisocial behavior beginning with Freudian psychodynamic theories.

Perhaps the most influential figure in the development of modern psychology is Sigmund Freud (1856–1939), an Austrian psychiatrist. Freud (1953) argued that much of people's behavior was the result of unconscious factors. He suggested that a person's psychological makeup was divided into three components—id, ego, and superego. The id is the source of our most basic desires, such as food, shelter, and procreation. The ego develops relatively early in life to provide ways to help satisfy the desires of the id in realistic ways. And the superego is a person's conscience, which judges the acceptability of the choices the ego offers to satisfy the desires of the id. Freud also argued that there are stages of psychosexual development that a person goes through as he or she matures and that psychological conflicts must be resolved at each stage or a person can become "fixated" and develop psychological disorders. Although Freud dealt primarily with psychological disorders, some aspects of his theory are relevant for criminal behavior (see Andrews and Bonta 1998:Chapter 3). For example, if the desires of the id are not properly balanced by the ego and the superego, then people are more likely to act inappropriately to achieve satisfaction of their desires, which can lead to crime (weak superego theory). Others may "stumble into crime" as a result of immaturity, poor social skills, or willingness to be led into crime and drug use by others (weak ego theory). Although Freud had a tremendous influence on the development of psychology, few psychologists still directly ascribe to his theories.

One branch of modern psychology is behaviorism. Behavioral theorists argue that behavior, including criminal behavior, is learned in specific ways through processes of reinforcement or punishment. Theorists such as Bandura (1973) argue that aggressive and criminal behavior is not inherent but is learned. To explain how behaviors, even criminal behaviors, are learned, behaviorists focus on imitation and conditioning. As babies and young children develop they observe the behavior of others and imitate it. People can also learn through a process of conditioning. In conditioning, the likelihood of a behavior is increased if it is rewarded. Thus, for a behavioral psychologist, criminal behavior is more likely to result to the extent that it is observed and imitated or rewarded (or not punished). Because this argument is conceptually and empirically similar to the arguments advanced in social learning theory (Chapter 6), we do not discuss this research here.

A third area of psychology is the cognitive perspective, which focuses on how people mentally construct and interpret the world around them. Within the cognitive psychological branch, moral development and information processing have been related to crime. Jean Piaget (1932) argued that people's moral and intellectual development occurred in four stages until approximately the beginning of puberty. Similarly, Lawrence Kohlberg (1981) argues that there are six stages of moral development (see Table 3.1).

Kohlberg and his colleagues (1973) found that criminals operated at lower stages of moral development than noncriminals did. Subsequent research has shown that criminals tend to operate at stages 1 and 2 compared to noncriminals, who operate in stages 3 and 4 (Andrews and Bonta 1998:199–200; Raine 1993:236–239). Some research also suggests the determinants of whether to commit a crime or not depend on one's stage of development. Veneziano and Veneziano (1992) found that those at the lowest stage of moral development were deterred by the threat of punishment, whereas those in middle stages were most concerned about the reactions of family and friends. Those at the highest levels of moral development chose not to commit crimes because of their concern for the rights of others. Krebs and Denton (2005) have argued that Kohlberg's theory may be useful in an abstract sense but that it does not adequately describe how people make concrete decisions in their lives. Andrews and Bonta (1998) conclude that general levels of moral reasoning may have a small correlation with crime. One important question is whether increasing moral reasoning levels can be used as a strategy to reduce criminal activity. Some research suggests that interventions can increase moral reasoning skills and reduce crime, but more research is necessary to determine whether long-term changes are possible (Raine 1993).

A second area of research in cognitive psychology focuses on how people process information. Cognitive psychologists argue that people must process information about the world around them to make decisions about how to respond in particular situations. So, for example, in driving a car a person must be aware of traffic, road signs, weather conditions, and a number of other factors. Quickly processing the information in one's environment while driving is a key factor in not hitting or being hit by other cars. Cognitive theorists note, however, that not everyone is able to process information efficiently or to interpret information correctly. Criminals, according to the theory, have less ability to quickly and correctly process information, which

Table 3.1 Kohlberg's Stages of Development

Stage 1 Right is obedience to power and avoidance of punishment.

Stage 2 Right is taking responsibility for oneself, meeting one's own needs, and leaving to others the responsibility for themselves.

Stage 3 Right is being good in the sense of having good motives, having concern for others, and "putting yourself in the other person's shoes."

Stage 4 Right is maintaining the rules of a society and serving the welfare of the group or society.

Stage 5 Right is based on recognized individual rights within a society with agreed-upon rules—a social contract.

Stage 6 Right is an assumed obligation to principles applying to all humankind—principles of justice, equality, and respect for human life.

---

can lead to improper behavior. Similarly, much information in the environment is ambiguous. Research has shown that those with tendencies toward violence or aggression are more likely to interpret others' intentions as hostile and to use fewer environmental cues to determine behavioral choices (see Raine 1993). For example, Lipton, McDonel, and McFall (1987) found that sexually violent males were more likely to believe that dates were playing games or wanted to be taken forcefully when they were declining sexual advances. Some evidence also suggests that the ability to process external information has a biological basis (see Brain 1994).

Finally, psychological researchers have focused on two "traits"— personality and intelligence—thought to be related to crime (Gottfredson and Hirschi's low self-control theory also has traitlike aspects; see the discussion in Chapter 7). Criminologists have long compared criminals and noncriminals on various personality traits (Glueck and Glueck 1950; Schuessler and Cressey 1950). These traits are assumed to be stable across various situations. A second set of studies focuses on the relationship between one's intelligence quotient (IQ) score and crime. This is perhaps one of the most controversial research topics in criminology. Some argue that there are innate differences in intelligence between criminals and noncriminals (Wilson and Herrnstein 1985), while others strongly dispute this notion (Cullen et al. 1997). We discuss research on personality and the IQ–crime link in detail later.

Concepts and Measurement Issues

Now that we have identified the basic tenets of trait theories, we can begin to discuss how to test them. A logical first step in testing a theory is to identify testable hypotheses. Table 3.2 lists hypotheses derived from various biological and psychological trait theories that have been tested. Although trait theories can produce numerous hypotheses, we focus on some of the more central and widely researched hypotheses.

One of the earliest biologically based hypotheses is that crime is heritable, or genetically passed from parent to offspring. There are three types of studies of the heritability of crime: family studies, twin studies, and adoption studies. It is important to keep in mind that heritability refers to a *propensity or liability*

Table 3.2 Hypotheses Based on Modern Trait Theories

Biosocial Theories

1. The tendency to commit crime is genetically passed from parent to offspring.
2. Neurotransmitter levels are related to antisocial behavior.
3. Hormone levels are related to antisocial behavior.
4. People with low levels of arousal are more likely to be criminal.

Psychological Theories

5. Those with lower levels of intelligence will be more likely to commit crime.
6. Criminals are more likely to possess certain personality traits than are noncriminals.

to commit crime, rather than actual behavior (Carey 1994:23). In other words, there is no criminal gene (contrary to early views), only a set of genetic packages, that might predispose one to behave in ways legally defined as criminal or to react to situations in ways that make crime more likely, such as taking undue offense in a social situation leading to a fight (see Akers and Sellers 2004:53 for a discussion). Family studies examine the likelihood of criminality in children based on whether parents are criminals (Rowe and Farrington 1997). Twin studies determine whether similarity in the propensity for criminal behavior is greater for identical twins (monozygotic, one egg splits) than fraternal twins (dizygotic, two different eggs in one womb). Because identical twins have identical genetic material, if genes influence criminality, there should be greater similarity in their likelihood of criminality than fraternal twins, who share no more genetic material than other siblings. Finally, adoption studies consider whether the criminality of adoptees is more similar to that of biological parents than to adoptive parents. Similarity to criminality of biological parents would suggest the importance of biological factors, whereas similarity to criminality of adoptive parents would suggest that environmental influences are more important. The research on the nature–nurture question is detailed later, but the general point is that if crime is "heritable" it implies strong support for a biological component to crime. Yet heritability studies can only suggest that there is a biological component to crime, not explain *why* biology is important. Ultimately, any adequate theory must go beyond correlation to causation.

As noted earlier, several explanations of antisocial behavior focus on the role of information systems within the body, specifically neurotransmitters and hormones. Although they account for a small proportion of all neurotransmitters, studies have focused mainly on dopamine, serotonin, and norepinephrine. Some research suggests that neurotransmitters are directly associated with aggression, specifically, that lower levels of serotonin and higher levels of dopamine and norepinephrine are associated with aggressive or antisocial behavior (see Berman, Kavoussi, and Coccaro 1997; Raine 1993, 2002a for overviews). Studies have shown that drugs that increase serotonin and reduce norepinephrine and dopamine tend to reduce violent behavior in mental patients. Other research finds an indirect relationship between neurotransmitters and antisocial behavior. For example, dopamine levels are associated with novelty-seeking, and some criminologists suggest that crime can provide a thrill-seeking opportunity. Serotonin levels may also be related to the ability to control impulses. Those with lower serotonin levels appear to be less able to regulate impulses. In certain situations, lack of impulse control could lead to criminal behaviors like shoplifting or fighting, if negative emotions are aroused in a situation such as being bumped by a stranger in a bar. Thus, it seems reasonable to hypothesize that there could be direct and indirect effects of neurotransmitters on crime.

A second line of research on biochemical information systems within the body focuses on the role of hormones. Several possible relationships between hormones and behavior could exist (Susman and Ponirakis 1997). Hormones could directly influence behavior, such that higher levels of certain hormones would cause aggression. Or it could be that aggressive behavior causes certain hormones to increase. It could also be that the two are reciprocally related such that hormones influence behavior, which, in turn, influences hormone levels. For example, athletic people with higher testosterone levels may be more likely to engage in competition, and winning these competitions might then raise testosterone levels. Finally, it could be that hormones, situations, and behavior all interact in complex ways, such that the release and effect of hormones on behavior depend on the situation.

Another biosocial explanation for antisocial behavior considers people's arousal levels. There are two mechanisms by which arousal and criminal behavior could be related (Raine 1993, 2002a). First, "fearlessness theory" posits that low-arousal people have lower levels of fear and arousal in stressful situations and that this facilitates criminal acts requiring a certain amount of fearlessness. So, for example, higher fear levels would likely prevent a person who is angry from fighting compared to someone who has relatively lower fear levels. Similarly, it could be that the only thing preventing a girl from shoplifting her favorite CD is fear of punishment. For some, this fear may be lower on average, freeing them to commit criminal acts. Second, it could also be that some people have unusually low levels of arousal, which would cause them to seek out excitement. "Stimulation-seeking theory" suggests that those with low arousal levels perceive life to be unpleasant (e.g., boredom) and engage in risky (sometimes criminal) behavior to increase their arousal levels. Arousal theory thus posits that those with low biological arousal levels are more likely to engage in criminal behavior either because they have less fear or because they seek stimulation (or both). Of course, these are only a few of the hypotheses that can be examined from a biosocial trait perspective.

Several hypotheses have also been considered from the psychological perspective. As noted earlier, some argue that what and how people learn will influence the likelihood of crime. Because this issue is considered extensively in Chapter 6 on social learning theories, we do not discuss the hypotheses and research in this chapter. But it is important to keep in mind that the strength or weakness of this line of research is important for evaluating a psychological perspective on crime. Because of limited space we focus on two psychological traits—personality and intelligence.

The search for unique personality traits that would differentiate criminals from noncriminals has a long history. Within sociology, Glueck and Glueck (1950) identified several personality traits they believed were linked to antisocial behavior, including hostility, defiance, resentment, suspiciousness, social assertiveness, and ambivalence toward authority. Researchers have also considered traits such as impulsiveness, extraversion (being outgoing), and instability (see Caspi, Roberts, and Shiner 2005; Miller and Lynam 2001 for a discussion). Thus, one could hypothesize that a person with these particular personality traits will be more likely to engage in crime. For example, impulsive people may be more likely to shoplift because they do not consider the possibility of getting caught or are unable to delay the gratification of their desires for a new sweater.

Similarly, a voluminous body of research has attempted to determine whether there is a link between innate intelligence levels and crime. Researchers hypothesize that those with lower intelligence levels are more likely to engage in crime, although the reasons one would expect for such a relationship to exist are often not explicitly stated. The search for innate differences in intelligence is itself a controversial undertaking. We discuss the research on IQ generally, whether a link between IQ and crime exists, and potential explanations for how and why intelligence and crime may be associated later. As we will see, one of the key questions has to do with the interpretation of the findings.

Now that we have specified some hypotheses that can be examined with respect to trait theories, we describe the concepts that must be measured and the research that has considered these hypotheses. Specifically, we discuss heritability, neurotransmitters, arousal, hormone levels, cognitive/moral development, personality, intelligence, and the dependent variables used in trait theory research. Because the outcomes vary so widely across studies, we begin with a discussion of this issue.

Dependent Variables: Crime and Antisocial Behavior

The dependent variable in studies of trait theories is often somewhat different than that in other theories of crime. The outcomes that researchers explain in most theories of crime (except labeling theory, which includes the broader topic of deviance) are relatively uniform, focusing on behavior that is defined as unlawful by the government. This is not the case for trait theories, which focus on explaining aggression, antisocial behavior, antisocial personality, conduct disorder, and psychopathy. These concepts often overlap with crime but are not synonymous with it.

A brief exploration of the various ways these concepts have been measured will illustrate the difficulty of comparisons to other studies of crime and possible reasons for mixed findings in past research. Many trait studies have considered aggression, partly because biosocial theorists often study animal behavior. Animals only behave aggressively or nonaggressively. They cannot, by definition, commit a crime. Brain (1994) notes some of the difficulties in defining aggression as it applies to human behavior. Aggression can be physical or verbal, active or passive, and direct or indirect. Physical aggression is clearly more likely to be seen as criminal in some cases, unless the aggressive behavior is in response to an attack (self-defense). Verbal aggression such as yelling or threatening could constitute criminal behavior in some situations but is not what we normally consider a crime. Likewise, active aggressive behaviors certainly are more likely to be considered criminal than the failure to do something (passive aggression). This creates problems for researchers trying to apply findings from animal research on aggression to humans.

Similarly, trait researchers frequently try to explain antisocial behavior. Fishbein (2001) notes that antisocial and criminal behavior often overlap. Certainly, serious crimes such as murder are generally considered antisocial. However, minor offenses such as illegal gambling or recreational drug use are often illegal but may or may not be considered antisocial depending on the degree to which they harm the individual gambler/drug user or his or her families. So, occasional illegal gambling is likely not antisocial, whereas a man gambling away his paycheck at the local bar on a Saturday could seriously harm his family and therefore could be considered antisocial. To further complicate matters, these terms are sometimes used interchangeably. For example, Rhee and Waldman (2002), in their meta-analysis of twin and adoption studies of antisocial behavior, describe three different ways that antisocial behavior has been defined. Some studies consider specific psychological diagnoses such as antisocial personality disorder (APD) or conduct disorder (CD), which are often based on violations of law; others define antisocial behavior specifically as criminal behavior; and still others treat aggressive behavior and antisocial behavior as synonymous. To illustrate the wide variety of outcomes that are often lumped together, consider Moore, Scarpa, and Raine's (2002) meta-analysis of serotonin and antisocial behavior. They considered studies of aggression (variously defined), homicide offenders, arsonists, violent offenders, self-mutilators, personality disorders, and domestic violence, but specifically excluded studies that only included nonviolent property offenses such as theft.

Psychopathy is another outcome often studied. Fishbein (2001:53) lists 14 different characteristics that are typical of psychopathy, including, among others, untruthfulness, insincerity, lack of remorse or shame, (inadequately motivated) antisocial behavior, poor judgment, and incapacity for love. None of these factors automatically refers to criminal behavior, although some, such as lack of remorse or antisocial behavior, could. Yet the same explanatory factors are often applied to both psychopathy and crime (for a review of the link between psychopathy and crime, see Hart and Hare 1997).

Even studies that specifically consider crime do so in a variety of ways. Some focus on violent crimes such as murder (Raine, Buchsbaum, and La Casse 1997), while others examine property crimes (Cornell and Wilson 1992; Mednick, Gabrielli, and Hutchings 1984). Some focus on dichotomous (yes or no) measures of criminality, whereas others use continuous measures. The heritability studies discussed later typically employ dichotomous measures of the dependent variable, so individuals are classified as criminal or not, usually based on having been convicted of a crime. This is different than considering the number of offenses that a person has committed, as is often done in studies described in other chapters of this book.

The wide variety of outcomes used in biosocial and psychological research makes it much more difficult to determine exactly what is being explained by trait theories and how the findings fit with the other crime studies discussed in this book. Although concepts such as aggression, antisocial behavior, psychopathy, and crime overlap, we must be cautious about applying the findings of studies using one concept to the findings of studies using other concepts. It may very well be that biosocial theories explain psychopathy but not minor forms of crime or that theories of crime may explain some types of antisocial behavior but not others. As we discuss the research here, it is important to keep in mind that these various outcomes are not necessarily interchangeable.

Heritability

One of the longest research efforts to demonstrate the biological basis of criminality is based on the idea that criminal characteristics can be passed down genetically. Because there has been extensive research on the heritability of crime, we examine this research in some detail. Three types of studies examine the heritability of crime: family, twin, and adoption studies.

One of the earliest observations people made about crime is that it runs in families, leading many to believe that criminality could be inherited just like hair and eye color. The problem with this line of reasoning is that parents contribute both genetic and environmental influences to their offspring. So the fact that crime runs in families could mean that parents pass on genetic predispositions to crime or it could mean that parents socialize (or fail to socialize) their children in ways that cause them to commit crime. Indeed, social learning theory (Chapter 6) maintains that crime runs in families because the parents reward (or don't punish) their children for antisocial and criminal behaviors. Because family studies cannot distinguish between genetic and environmental influences, a different method must be used that can differentiate between biological and environmental influences on children's behavior.

Studying twins can separate genetic and environmental influences. Because identical (monozygotic, or MZ) twins share 100% of their genetic material, whereas fraternal (dizygotic, or DZ) twins share no more genetic material than other siblings do, if genetic factors influence criminal behavior, MZ twins should exhibit greater similarity in behavior than DZ twins do. Studies that examine the similarity of twin behavior use the concordance or discordance of twin behavior as a measure of association. When both twins are criminals or law-abiding, they are said to be concordant. When only one twin is criminal, they are discordant. One would expect that the concordance rates for MZ twins should be higher than those for DZ twins.

Studies have compared the concordance rates for MZ and DZ twins with respect to both criminal and antisocial behavior (see Hutchings and Mednick 1977 for an early review). For example, Christiansen (1977) used a relatively unique data set called the Danish Twin Register to examine the concordance rates of 3,586 twin pairs born between 1881 and 1910. He used official police, court, and corrections records to determine criminality for each of the 7,172 twins. In all, 926 individuals from 799 twin pairs were considered criminal. The MZ twins were nearly three times more likely to be concordant than were DZ twins for both males (35% to 13%) and females (21% to 8%), which suggests support for genetic influences on criminal behavior. Yet the authors acknowledge that one major methodological limitation in their study, as well as in other twin studies, is that they assume environmental influences of MZ and DZ twins are equivalent so that any remaining differences between MZ and DZ twins are likely genetic. There are several reasons to doubt the validity of this assumption. First, MZ twins might be treated more similarly by parents than DZ twins are. MZ twins also tend to spend greater time with each other and have more similar groups of friends than DZ twins do (Carey and Goldman 1997:243). Such differences could result in overestimating the genetic influence on behavioral similarities for MZ twins.

One remedy is to consider twins reared apart (i.e., in different environments). Very few studies have used this approach, in large part because such situations are extremely rare. One study was conducted by Grove et al. (1990). The authors studied 32 sets of MZ twins raised in separate homes from 1979 to 1988. They examined alcohol use, drug use, and antisocial personality disorder. They found concordance rates of 33% for alcohol use, 36% for drug use, and 29% for antisocial personality disorder. Based on their analyses, they concluded that drug problems and antisocial personality disorder showed significant evidence of heritability but that alcohol use did not. Because few studies of this type have been conducted, it is difficult to know how representative these findings are.

A second way to eliminate concerns over differential environmental influences on twins is to compare adopted children to their biological parents or siblings. This method eliminates potential environmental influences of biological parents on their children's behavior because the adopted children are not in the same social environment as their parents. Therefore, similarities in behavior between biological parents and offspring raised by others are more likely to be genetic than environmental. Mednick, Gabrielli, and Hutchings (1984) compared the similarity of 14,427 parents, adopted children, and their siblings from 1927 to 1947 using conviction records in Denmark. They found that criminal convictions of the biological parents predicted criminality of their adopted offspring (for property crimes only) but convictions of adoptive parents did not. As the number of convictions of biological parents increased, so did the likelihood of criminal convictions of their adopted offspring. Only about 13% of adoptees with biological parents with no convictions had convictions for property offenses, whereas 25% of adoptees with biological parents convicted of three or more offenses had criminal convictions. This relationship held even after controlling for the socioeconomic status of the adoptee and biological parents.

Because many twin and adoption studies have been performed, their findings can be summarized statistically using a technique called meta-analysis. Meta-analysis treats the individual study as the unit of analysis, rather than the person or twin pair. Using studies as the unit of analysis allows one to determine the average sizes of genetic and environmental effects on criminal behavior across a large number of studies. Walters (1992) conducted a meta-analysis of 54 "effect-sizes" from 32 family, twin, and adoption studies conducted from 1930 to 1989 to determine the level of support for a gene–crime relationship. He found evidence for a genetic influence on criminality, but the strength of this relationship depended on the type of study and how methodologically rigorous it was. Older presumably less sophisticated studies showed stronger heritability estimates. Adoption studies, which he argued were the strongest methodologically, showed the lowest heritability estimates. Walters concludes that there is evidence for the heritability of propensity to crime but the relationship is weak. He also suggests a more fruitful approach is to consider genetic–environmental interactions as explanations for crime (see also Rowe and Osgood 1984). For example, he argues that heritable factors such as intelligence, temperament, and physical reactivity should be integrated with more traditional environmentally based explanations of crime.

More recently, Rhee and Waldman (2002) completed a meta-analysis of 52 twin and adoption studies of antisocial behaviors including nearly 56,000 pairs of participants from 1965 to 2000. The authors found evidence of genetic as well as shared and nonshared environmental influences on antisocial behaviors. They estimated that approximately 40% of the variation in antisocial behaviors is genetic. Similar to Walters (1992), Rhee and Waldman noted that the type of study influenced the strength of heritability estimates. Adoption studies yielded the lowest heritability estimates. They additionally found that the method of determining whether twins were MZ or DZ also influenced heritability estimates. Typically, blood grouping, questionnaire methods regarding similarity of appearance, or a combination of the two were used to determine whether twins were identical or fraternal. The only sure method of determining whether twins are MZ or DZ is DNA testing, but this has developed recently and is not often used in twin studies.

Although heritability studies suggest that there may be a biological component to criminal behavior, they cannot tell us what it is about the individual's genetics that causes him or her to be more likely to commit crime. The next step, therefore, is to determine which genetic differences lead to crime. In the following sections we consider some mechanisms relating biology and crime.

Neurotransmitters

Levels of neurotransmitters in the brain may be directly or indirectly related to aggression and antisocial behavior. Most research has focused on three neurotransmitters: serotonin, dopamine, and norepinephrine (Moore, Scarpa, and Raine 2002; Raine 1993). Because neurotransmitter levels cannot be measured directly in the brain, they must be measured indirectly in cerebrospinal fluid (CSF), blood, or urine samples. CSF measurements tend to be more reliable but are more difficult and expensive because they require a lumbar puncture (inserting a needle in the area around the spinal cord). No tests measure neurotransmitters directly—only the chemical precursors or byproducts of their action in the brain. This presents difficulties for interpreting these studies because neurotransmitters may act differently in different parts of the brain. This would be like determining the problem with an automobile engine by examining the ground underneath a car on a hill. The fact that oil is pooling on the ground at the bottom of the hill only tells you that there is an oil leak, not which part of the engine it is coming from. To complicate matters, unlike oil, which serves one function, neurotransmitters have different functions depending on where they are located in the brain. Despite these difficulties, some studies have found evidence of a link between neurotransmitters and human antisocial behavior.

There have been a sufficient number of studies on the relationship between neurotransmitters and antisocial behavior to permit meta-analysis. Raine (1993) examined the relationship between serotonin, norepenephrine, dopamine, and a number of antisocial behaviors or psychiatric conditions. He analyzed 29 studies of alcohol abuse, borderline personality disorder, suicide, and antisocial behavior finding that serotonin levels were somewhat negatively correlated with antisocial behavior and psychiatric problems. Norepinephrine was also negatively related to these conditions but only in studies using CSF measures. He did not find support for a relationship between dopamine and antisocial behavior. More recently, Moore, Scarpa, and Raine (2002) conducted a meta-analysis of 20 studies from 1978 to 2000 on the link between serotonin metabolites in CSF and antisocial behavior. Moore et al. find that antisocial individuals had significantly lower serotonin levels.

Although these results suggest that neurotransmitters, particularly serotonin, may be related to antisocial behavior, limitations of these studies preclude firm conclusions (see Raine 1993:99–102 for a discussion). First, there are several limitations in the way neurotransmitters have been measured. While neurotransmitter levels vary over time for many reasons (weather, age, and diet), most studies use only single measures. Related to this, the indirect ways that neurotransmitters have been measured in these studies severely limit researchers' ability to determine *how* neurotransmitters work to influence aggression. There is no reason to believe that neurotransmitters act uniformly in all areas of the brain, so Raine (1993) suggests the use of more direct measures of brain activity such as positron emission tomography (PET) imaging, which can highlight which brain areas are related to certain neurotransmitters and how this activity affects antisocial behavior. Second, measures of neurotransmitters are typically studied in isolation (Berman et al. 1997), but in fact neurotransmitter systems are complex and interact. Therefore, future studies need to examine combinations of neurotransmitters. In addition, Berman et al. suggest that future research should consider other neurotransmitters such as acetylcholine, gamma-aminobutyric acid (GABA), and monoamine oxidase A (MAOA). One recent study by Caspi et al. (2002) found that some children were genetically predisposed to emit high levels of MAOA, which seemed to shield them from the effects of childhood maltreatment. These children were less likely to exhibit antisocial behaviors in adulthood. The weight of the evidence suggests that neurotransmitters play some role in antisocial behavior. Future research and theory must specify exactly what that role is and how it specifically relates to *criminal* behavior.

Hormones

One well-known "fact" in criminology is that men commit more crime than women, particularly violent crime. To account for the gender–crime correlation, one might consider several biological differences between males and females. One such difference is the relative presence of "male" hormones (androgens), the most common of which is testosterone. Because men have higher levels of androgens and higher levels of aggressive behavior, it could be that male hormones cause increased aggressiveness. Consistent with this logic, some studies (e.g., Berenbaum and Resnick 1997) have found that girls exposed to abnormally high levels of testosterone before birth became "masculinized." Animal studies have also shown that testosterone and aggressiveness are related (see Brain 1994 for an overview).

Hormones have been hypothesized to have different effects on behavior depending on the stage of development. Some argue that prenatal (before birth) exposure to high levels of testosterone influences later behavior by making the child more impulsive and aggressive (Olweus 1984), although the specific behavioral influence is not always clearly identified (Brain 1994). Prenatal influences of testosterone are called "organizational" because they change the way the brain is organized by increasing the number of testosterone receptors in the brain. Others argue that hormones have influences at puberty, when large increases in hormone levels generally occur for both males and females. Still others argue that hormone levels continue to influence behavior throughout adulthood (Brain 1994).

Earlier we mentioned several possible relationships between hormones and behavior. Hormones could cause changes in behavior, could be consequences of behavior, or both. Therefore, it could be that testosterone levels increase aggression, that aggressive behavior increases testosterone levels, or that high testosterone levels cause aggressive behavior and subsequently increase as a result of aggressive behavior. Or it could be that hormones influence behavior only under certain conditions. Olweus et al. (1988) found that levels of testosterone in the blood were related to increased aggression in a study of 58 healthy Swedish 15- to 17-year-old boys. They found that testosterone levels were directly related to provoked aggressive behavior and indirectly related to unprovoked aggressive behavior by causing greater irritability and impatience. Similarly, Booth and Osgood (1993) found that higher testosterone levels were associated with lower levels of "social integration," which lead to higher offending.

The measurement of testosterone in early studies was taken from blood samples, but only 2% of blood testosterone is "free" to act in the system. More recently, a test has been developed that measures "free" testosterone in the saliva. Although saliva samples are relatively simple and inexpensive to collect, such a test cannot determine where in the body the testosterone is active because testosterone can act on many parts of the body including different parts of the brain. Zitzmann and Nieschlag (2001) also note that tobacco use can increase, and the use of certain illegal drugs such as cocaine and heroine can reduce, testosterone levels. Given the frequency of these behaviors, especially among criminal populations, failure to control for them is likely to compromise the findings of studies on testosterone and aggression.

It may also be the case that testosterone only causes aggression above a certain threshold. Testosterone may only cause aggression at abnormally high levels, but be unrelated to aggression for those with normal testosterone levels. Or it could be that testosterone is related only to certain types of offenses. Some evidence exists that testosterone levels increase offending for sex offenders (Raine 1993:207). For example, Wille and Beier (1989) found that voluntarily castrated sex offenders in Germany (who have drastically lower testosterone levels) had much lower rates of sexual recidivism (3%) than uncastrated offenders did (46%). Other studies have demonstrated that "chemical castration" (testosterone-reducing drugs) is also associated with reduced levels of violence and sexual aggression (Archer 1991).

The relationship between testosterone and aggression has been studied frequently enough to permit meta-analysis. A meta-analysis of 45 effects across 30 studies by Archer, Graham-Kevan, and Davies (2005) found a small overall correlation (.08) between testosterone and aggression, and the correlation depended on whether saliva or blood tests were used. Thus, it seems unlikely that testosterone is a direct and powerful cause of aggression or violence. It should be clear from this brief review that the hormone–aggression relationship is much more complex than to simply claim that hormones cause aggression. The effects of hormones likely depend on a number of social and biological factors, and much more research is necessary to isolate the specific role that hormones play in criminal behavior.

Arousal

Researchers argue that biological indicators of physiological arousal are related to crime and antisocial behavior in at least two ways. Some claim that low arousal levels among criminals are indicators of a lack of fear or stress. "Fearlessness theory" suggests that some individuals exhibit lower arousal levels in stressful situations, making the commission of crimes more likely since many criminal acts require a certain degree of fearlessness (Raine 1993, 2002a). It could also be that some individuals do not react to negative stimuli as quickly or as strongly as others and, therefore, do not learn to avoid these negative stimuli in the way that others do. The criminal justice system is predicated on the idea that those considering crime will refrain from it because of the potentially unpleasant consequences that follow from being caught and punished (see rational choice and deterrence theories, Chapter 2). This assumption could be unrealistic for some people because they are less likely to fear punishment or less likely to learn from prior punishments. Therefore, if criminals are more "fearless," punishments in the criminal justice system may be least likely to influence the behavior of those they are most directed at—criminals!

Others maintain that low levels of arousal are viewed as a negative state by the individual. "Stimulation-seeking theory" suggests that underaroused people engage in criminal behavior to relieve boredom. A number of sociologists have suggested that some crime is at least partly thrill-seeking behavior (e.g., Katz 1988). Stimulation-seeking theory provides a biological basis for this claim. Researchers also argue that the relationship between sensation-seeking and crime explains correlations between religiosity and crime or between school achievement and crime (Cochran, Wood, and Arneklev 1994; Cochran, Wareham, Wood, and Arneklev 2002; Ellis 1987b, 1996; Forthun, Bell, Peek, and Sun 1999).

Arousal can be measured in brain wave patterns through EEG, skin conductance of electricity, and heart rate. EEG is measured by placing electrodes on the skull to record four patterns of brain activity. Mednick, Volavka, Gabrielli, and Itil (1981) studied the relationship between EEG patterns at roughly age 10 and officially recorded thefts until age 18 for 265 Danish boys born from 1959 to 1961. They found that certain EEG patterns (consistent with lower arousal) in 1972 predicted both incidence and frequency of later thefts among the boys. Raine (1997:289–290) notes that many studies have examined the relationship between EEG patterns and violence. Research finds that EEG levels are abnormal in 25–50% of violent people, although only 5–20% of "normals" exhibit these abnormalities.

Other studies have measured arousal through skin conductance, which captures the amount of electrical activity in the skin (Fishbein 2001:51). Skin conductance levels are used in polygraph examinations to determine lying. For most people, lying causes an emotional reaction (because we have been taught that lying is bad) that is measurable in terms of increased skin conductance. Some studies have shown a link between low arousal and crime using skin conductance measures. For example, Raine, Venables, and Williams (1990) found that lower resting skin conductance levels at age 15 among 101 British boys predicted officially recorded criminality at age 24. This study is one of the few that has combined multiple measures of arousal in one study. The authors correctly identified nearly 75% of the boys as criminal or noncriminal based on the three indicators of arousal included (EEG, heart rate, and skin conductance). Skin conductance levels are somewhat less clearly linked to criminal behavior than EEG or heart rate are (see Raine 1997:290 for a discussion).

Raine (1997, 2002a) notes that the link between low resting heart rates and crime is one of the best-replicated findings in all biosocial research. Raine, Venables, and Mednick (1997) found that low resting heart rates at age 3 predicted aggressive behavior at age 11 for boys and girls regardless of race and ethnicity. Because so many studies of heart rate levels and antisocial behavior have been conducted, Ortiz and Raine (2004) performed a meta-analysis on this research, examining 40 studies from 1971 to 2002. They concluded that both resting heart rate levels and heart rate levels measured under stress were lower for antisocial children than "normals." This effect did not depend on gender, age, or method of measurement. Such a finding is important because other studies have suggested that chronic offenders are more likely to start criminal activity earlier and to exhibit conduct problems as children (Moffitt 1993). Moreover, heart rate level is much easier to measure than many of the other biological markers we have discussed. Resting heart rate levels are partly heritable (Raine 2002a).

If low arousal predicts criminal or antisocial behavior, it also appears that the reverse may be true. High arousal levels seem to be associated with reduced likelihood of criminal behavior. Raine, Venables, and Williams (1995) found that high autonomic arousal among teenagers predicted lower criminal behavior at age 29. Similarly, Brennan et al. (1997) found that high arousal levels predicted lower criminal activity, even among those considered to be "at risk" by having criminal parents.

Recent studies suggest that one of the reasons for these lower arousal levels could be damage or dysfunction in some parts of the brain. Raine, Buchsbaum, and La Casse (1997) documented evidence of brain abnormalities in murderers using PET compared to matched controls. Similarly, Raine, Lencz, Bihrle, La Casse, and Colleti (2000) found evidence of reduced prefrontal gray matter and reduced autonomic activity in subjects with APD, concluding that structural deficits in the brain may underlie this disorder. Evans and Park (1997) compared the EEG readings of 20 men under death sentence for murder with the brain wave activity one would expect in the "normal" population. They found significant indications of a number of brain abnormalities among these men. In contrast, Pillmann et al. (1999) noted no overall EEG differences but found them to be localized in the left hemisphere. Collectively, this research suggests that there may indeed be something "different" about the brains of criminals. The challenge is to clarify exactly which dysfunctions influence which behaviors and how.

One interesting implication of a link between arousal and crime is that it could be mediated by social or environmental factors (Raine 1997). So if a person has low arousal and seeks to change that arousal level, both prosocial and antisocial options are available. If true, it could be possible to channel low-arousal people into socially acceptable behaviors that provide the stimulation they are seeking. Competitive sports may provide just as much stimulation as shoplifting does. Of course, this is based on sensation-seeking or fearlessness interpretations of arousal rather than on brain damage/dysfunction interpretations. Future research needs to clarify which of the two mechanisms underlies this correlation or under what circumstances each operates. In the next section, we turn to research on two psychological constructs that have been hypothesized to be related to crime: intelligence and personality.

Intelligence

Investigations of a purported relationship between intelligence (as measured by IQ scores) and crime date back to at least the 1920s (Ellis and Walsh 2003). Then researchers believed that criminals were "feebleminded," and the earliest studies appeared to support an IQ–crime relationship. Sutherland (1931) reviewed existing research at the time and concluded that the evidence was unconvincing because of serious methodological flaws in the studies. Additional evidence against a "feeblemindedness" explanation for criminality came from widespread IQ testing of American World War II draftees, which placed significant portions of the adult male population in the feebleminded category (despite the fact that most were not criminal). Some even suggested that since low IQ was an innate biological trait that led to criminality, to reduce crime, those with low IQs should not be allowed to reproduce. This line of reasoning sounded eerily similar to the Nazi propaganda of social engineering, and, combined with early methodological problems in IQ-crime studies, it drove such research from the criminological mainstream. The topic reemerged in the 1970s partly because of the publication of Hirschi and Hindelang's (1977) review of more recent studies, which suggested that IQ was a better predictor of crime than was race or socioeconomic class. To this day debate continues on several issues that we discuss in this section: First, what is measured by intelligence tests? Second, does the evidence support a link between intelligence and crime? Third, if IQ and crime are related, what are the reasons for this link?

Nearly from the outset of IQ testing, debate has centered on what exactly is measured by IQ tests. Clearly "individuals differ from one another in their ability to understand complex ideas, to adapt effectively to the environment, to learn from experience, to engage in various forms of reasoning, to overcome obstacles by taking thought" (Neisser et al. 1996:77). Some argue that these differences are evidence of innate differences in ability that are mainly biologically determined (Herrnstein and Murray 1994) and can be characterized along a single dimension (g) that is captured by ranking on an IQ test. For example, research shows that the IQs of MZ twins are more highly correlated than those of other siblings (Walsh 2003). Others contend that IQ is largely environmentally determined (see Dickens and Flynn 2001 for a discussion). A number of studies show that environmental contaminants such as lead or early diet can strongly influence IQ (Neisser et al. 1996). In addition, there have been substantial overall gains in IQ in recent years, which some argue are too rapid to have biological origins (Neisser 1998).

Evidence is emerging that biology and the environment interact in complex ways to produce IQ. For example, one recent study found that the (biological) heritability of IQ was strong in high socioeconomic status (SES) families but weak in low SES families (Turkheimer et al. 2003). Similarly, Dickens and Flynn (2001) argue that both strong environmental and genetic effects are possible. For example, let's say that a child with low IQ is born to low IQ parents. The child is not likely to show an aptitude toward learning based on his or her genes, nor are the low IQ parents likely to push the child toward pursuing learning (environment). The opposite is likely to occur in high IQ families. High IQ children are likely to be interested in learning and rewarded for such learning by their high IQ parents. Now imagine a high IQ child is born to low IQ parents or vice versa. In such cases, a low IQ child might be pushed to achieve by their high IQ parents or high IQ children might be held back by their low IQ parents. It is easy to see how the actual outcomes of such interactions between the genes and the environment might vary considerably.

Others dispute the notion of a unidimensional intelligence factor (g), contending that there are different categories or kinds of intelligence (Neisser et al. 1996:79) and that individuals vary substantially across these various subcategories. For example, IQ tests typically break down into verbal reasoning (VIQ) and nonverbal reasoning (performance, or PIQ). Some maintain that only some kinds of intelligence are measured in typical IQ tests. Sternberg (1985) claims that there are three basic kinds of intelligence: analytical (measured by traditional IQ tests), practical (coping with basic problems), and creative intelligence. Others contend that intelligence is context specific. Lave (1988) found that women could do complex price comparisons in a grocery store but were unable to perform similar calculations on a standardized test. Thus, evidence exists that intelligence is both environmentally and genetically determined in complex ways and also that it is multifaceted.

Despite continuing disagreement over what exactly it is that IQ tests measure, a number of studies have shown a link between IQ and crime (see Ellis and Walsh 2003; Walsh 2003 for overviews). The weight of the evidence suggests that there is a weak to moderate correlation between IQ test scores (whatever it is they measure) and crime, controlling for other factors. For example, Ellis and Walsh found that IQ and crime were linked in 88% of 68 studies of juveniles and in 79% of 19 studies of adults. Generally, research documents that the correlation between IQ and crime is .2 or less.

There is also some evidence that crime may be more highly correlated with some types of intelligence than others. Some studies show that the verbal or VIQ deficits may be more strongly linked to criminality than performance or PIQ deficits. Cornell and Wilson (1992) found more than one third of 149 juveniles convicted of serious crimes had VIQs at least 12 points lower than their PIQ scores, and this relationship held for violent and property crimes and regardless of the race of the offender (cf. Raine et al. 2005).

IQ and crime may also be linked only for some criminals. Moffitt (1993) describes two types of offenders: life-course persistent (LCP) and adolescence-limited (AL). LCP offenders are hypothesized to have early conduct problems that escalate during the teenage years and continue in many cases throughout adulthood (see also Piquero 2000). AL offenders are youth that engage in criminal behavior for a variety of social reasons and essentially grow out of crime as they enter more adult roles. Raine et al. (2005) found that the IQs of LCP offenders in the sample were 10 points lower than controls, compared to only 3-point differences between AL offenders and controls. Thus, the IQ–crime relationship may be limited to some types of intelligence and some types of offenders.

Despite the concerns often raised about the meaning of IQ tests, the IQ–crime correlation appears to be real. The question is: What does this correlation mean? As we reiterate throughout the book, correlation does not equal causation. It is important, therefore, to determine how and why IQ and crime are linked. A number of scholars have suggested plausible explanations. One is the "differential detection" hypothesis (Walsh 2003), which suggests that crime and intelligence are unrelated but those with lower IQs are less able to avoid getting caught. The evidence does not appear to support this notion. Studies using official crime data as well as self-report data show similar IQ–crime correlations. Moffit and Silva (1988) specifically set out to test the differential detection hypothesis using a birth cohort from New Zealand. The authors measured both self-reported delinquency (unknown to the police) and officially recorded delinquency, as well as IQ scores. They found that self-reported and officially recorded delinquents had similar IQ scores and delinquency rates, but had overall IQs roughly 6 points lower than nondelinquents. Thus, the IQ–crime link does not appear to be explained by only "dumb criminals getting caught." In addition, recidivism rates do not appear to be related to IQ once one has begun to commit crime (Ellis and Walsh 2003).

A second explanation is that IQ and crime are related through problems in school. One version of this argument is that lower IQ leads to school failure (see Ward and Tittle 1994 for a discussion), which much evidence has linked to crime (school performance). A second explanation is that tracking because of intelligence tests leads to lower self-esteem, causing individuals to engage in delinquency as a result (school reaction). Ward and Tittle sought to test these competing explanations using data from the first three waves of the Youth in Transition project. When tested in separate models, using VIQ scores, they found some support for both models. In combined models, the school performance model provided a better explanation than the school reaction model did.

Finally, some suggest the IQ–crime relationship may be due to the fact that those with lower IQs may have slower rates of moral maturation (Ellis and Walsh 2003:352). Recall that Kohlberg et al. (1973) argue that stages of moral development and crime are related. If those with lower IQs proceed through stages of moral development more slowly, then this could explain the IQ–crime relationship.

In sum, IQ tests predict school performance well but predict later crime less accurately. Yet the best evidence suggests that there is a weak to moderate correlation between IQ (whatever the tests really measure) and crime, controlling for other factors. Debate now centers on the exact reason(s) for this correlation. Such debate is likely to provide the greatest contribution to criminological theory.

Personality

One of the first to study personality was Freud. Recall that he divided the mind into its conscious and unconscious elements—the ego, id, and superego. Although Freud didn't focus much on crime, followers using the psychoanalytic approach suggested that crime could result from either an underactive or overactive superego (Andrews and Bonta 1998:Chapter 3; Fredl and Toch 1979). Although some case studies have been conducted, larger studies have not. Part of this may be because of the practical difficulty of measuring unconscious constructs such as the id, ego, and superego. For a variety of reasons, psychoanalytic theory has not had much influence on modern criminological theories. Yet Freud's work helped further the belief that stable elements of a person's personality influence behavior in consistent ways across situations (Vold et al. 1998). Miller and Lynam (2001:765) refer to personality as "characteristic ways of thinking, feeling, and behaving." The search for personality traits that could predict crime has a long history in criminology. In their study of 500 delinquent and nondelinquent boys, Glueck and Glueck (1950:274–275) suggested that a variety of personality traits were related to delinquency. Specifically, the delinquents were more likely to be hostile, defiant, resentful, suspicious, socially assertive, less cooperative, and more ambivalent toward authority. And consistent with a number of other theorists such as Gottfredson and Hirschi (1990), the delinquent boys were found to be more impulsive and to exhibit less self-control than the nondelinquents.

Although a number of early studies documented a link between personality and crime, this research was roundly criticized (Schuessler and Cressey 1950; Tennenbaum 1977; Waldo and Dinitz 1967), especially for the measurement techniques used to measure personality. For example, the Gluecks used the Rorschach test, where the person being tested views a number of ink blots and responds to them. The exam proctor then interprets the subject's responses. This method of identifying personality traits is highly subjective and could reflect the personality of the tester as much as the subject. Personality has also been measured through the Minnesota Multiphasic Personality Inventory (MMPI) or the California Personality Inventory (CPI). These tests ask a series of questions that are then used to identify various personality dimensions. Yet the questions often refer to deviant or criminal behavior to infer personality dimensions, which are then used to predict criminal behavior (e.g., Hathaway and Monachesi 1953). This creates a tautology problem. In other words, the tests use crime to predict crime (likely to be highly accurate but not very helpful).

In recent years, the study of personality has reemerged in criminology. Miller and Lynam (2001) note four predominant models of personality, with anywhere from three to seven major personality elements. The first is McCrae and Costa's (1990) five-factor model (FFM), which focuses on neuroticism, extraversion, openness to experience, agreeableness, and conscientiousness. The second is Eysenck's (1977) model, which identifies psychoticism, extraversion, and neuroticism (PEN) as the three key elements of personality (with several subelements). The third is Tellegen's (1985) three-factor model, which focuses on positive emotionality, negative emotionality, and constraint. Finally, Cloninger et al. (1993) disaggregate personality into temperament (novelty-seeking, harm avoidance, reward dependence, persistence) and character (self-directedness, cooperativeness, self-transcendence).

Some studies support a link between personality and crime using all of the models (Miller and Lynam 2001:796–798). For example, supporting the Tellegen model, Krueger et al. (1994) found that greater negative emotionality and lower constraint were associated with delinquency among 862 18-year-olds from a birth cohort in New Zealand (see also Caspi et al. 1994). Similarly, Tremblay et al. (1994) found some support for Cloninger et al.'s (1993) model because high impulsivity, low anxiety, and low reward dependence measured in kindergarten predicted delinquency from ages 11 to 13. Miller and Lynam (2001) performed a meta-analysis of 59 studies of personality and crime that used these four personality models. They found that 8 of collective 18 dimensions are at least moderately related to antisocial behavior (which, you recall, may or may not be crime). They note that all 8 of these personality elements may be thought of as dimensions of agreeableness or conscientiousness from the FFM.

Personality concepts also overlap with concepts from mainstream criminological research. For example, several models focus on impulsivity and sensation-seeking, although describing it in different ways (see also White et al. 1994). These elements can be found in Gottfredson and Hirschi's (1990) low self-control theory discussed in Chapter 7. Similarly, the negative emotionality discussed in the Tellegen model is similar to recent discussions of "anger people" in research on Agnew's general strain theory (see Chapter 5). Therefore, one major challenge to those who wish to claim personality as a major predictor of crime is to show how these personality traits relate to constructs found in mainstream theories of crime.

Despite studies that document a link between personality traits and crime, future research should address several methodological issues. We noted before that early tests of personality were mainly subjective. Current research on personality has generally moved past this problem, but until some level of agreement exists among researchers on how to measure personality, it seems unlikely this work will add much to mainstream criminological theory. Most personality research also uses cross-sectional, correlational research designs (Andrews and Bonta 2003), but longitudinal studies are necessary to show causation in most cases. Therefore, additional longitudinal studies showing that stable personality traits exist *prior* to criminal behavior (and ruling out alternative explanations) are necessary.

In addition, most studies have suggested the relationship between personality and crime is linear, meaning the more impulsive a person is, for example, the more likely he or she is to become criminal. It may be, however, that both being *low* or *high* on some traits predict criminal behavior (Miller and Lynam 2001). This would suggest a nonlinear relationship between personality and crime. It may also be that the effect of personality on crime depends on the environment in which one is raised. For example, being a person who tends to follow others would be likely to lead to conventional behavior if raised in a law-abiding environment but could lead to crime if exposed to criminals, suggesting a *conditional* relationship between personality, environmental factors, and crime.

Another question is whether personality is stable over time and across situations. While studies find that personality does tend to be stable over time (Caspi 2000; Pulkkinen et al. 2000), researchers challenge the assumption that it is invariant across situations. Horney (2006) argues that humans are considerably more complex than the current views of personality suggest. As a result, personality is not something that manifests itself similarly across all situations. She uses the example of self-control. Some people exhibit tremendous self-control in some situations but very little in others. Thus, the manifestation of the trait (e.g., self-control) will not be uniform across situations but will depend specifically on the situation. From this view, current models of personality are too simplistic to have predictive value because they assume that personality will operate similarly across a variety of situations. In the future, research on personality and crime should find ways to account for this complexity.

Summary Critique of Measurement Strategy

The measurement strategies used in biosocial research have severely limited researchers' ability to specify the influences of specific biological or psychological factors on crime or antisocial behavior. The fact that studies include such a wide range of dependent variables makes comparisons difficult. Unlike many other studies in which crime is clearly the outcome of interest, it is not immediately obvious what the dependent variable is in these studies (see Fishbein 1990:31–32). It is crucial that researchers specify dependent variables in ways that are more similar to mainstream criminological research if biosocial research is to be of use to criminologists. Aggression and antisocial personality disorders may or may not be synonymous with criminal behavior, leading to questions of what is being explained. One way to address this issue is to consider scope conditions, such that biosocial theories could be limited to certain types of behaviors. For example, research shows that reduction of testosterone through actual or chemical castration reduces some types of sex offending. Testosterone levels might thus be helpful in explaining sex offenses but not shoplifting. Properly specifying scope conditions will likely improve the ability to distinguish when and how biosocial traits influence criminal behavior. There is also a tendency in this research not to include specific descriptions of the dependent variable that is being used so that it is often difficult to determine exactly what outcome is being measured and how results compare with other studies. It is imperative that the criminal components of outcomes be clear if trait theory research is to be accepted in mainstream criminology.

In addition to improving measurement of the dependent variable, biosocial trait theories would benefit from improving the measurement of key independent variables. For example, many twin studies have not used DNA testing, which introduces measurement error and reduces confidence in these studies. Similarly, the indirect way that neurotransmitters have been

measured in most research sharply limits researchers' ability to make informed judgments about their effects. In addition, the use of single measurements of neurotransmitters and hormone levels in many studies is
problematic because these levels vary over time. More studies should follow
the approach of Raine, Venables, and Williams (1990), who included three
different measures of arousal.

Fishbein (2001) notes that there are also links between central nervous
system (CNS) and autonomic nervous system (ANS) activity so that ANS
indicators of low arousal may be related to problems with neurotransmitter
action in the brain. Because studies generally consider these influences separately, it is impossible to describe fully the relationship between these two
systems and how they influence criminal behavior. Future research, therefore,
should consider the interrelationships among neurotransmitters, arousal, and
hormone levels. Oversimplification of the biological processes by separating
research into hormonal, neurotransmitter, and arousal effects likely accounts
for some of the confusing findings in past research.

Future research must also take advantage of scientific advances in measurement techniques. It is likely that in the near future we will be able to map
the effects of neurotransmitters, hormones, and arousal levels in ways that are
not currently possible, which will provide a much better understanding of
their specific roles in generating violent, aggressive, or criminal behavior.

With respect to studies of intelligence and crime, a number of issues remain. Debate continues on what intelligence is and what IQ tests measure
(Sternberg and Grigorenko 2002). The best evidence suggests that IQ has some
biological basis but is greatly influenced by the environment. Research also
generally supports the conclusion that IQ and crime are somewhat correlated.
Research should now focus on how this correlation fits with, or can be used to,
modify existing crime theories. Perhaps research should also consider what
Simpson and Hogg (2001) refer to as "intellectual disability," rather than the
narrower concept of IQ. Siegel (2006) also notes several problems for the IQ–
crime relationship. If IQ and crime are related, why does aging out of crime
occur? Of course, Moffit (1993) would argue that IQ and crime are only linked
for LCP offenders, who do not age out of crime. Second, why are there large
gender gaps in crime without corresponding gender gaps in IQ?

Finally, recent research suggests that some elements of personality predict
crime (Miller and Lynam 2001). Yet there is conceptual overlap among personality constructs across models of personality and between personality
constructs and concepts from mainstream criminological theories such as
impulsivity and low self-control theories (see Chapter 7). Future research
must clarify exactly how personality constructs are similar to, or distinct
from, concepts in mainstream crime theories. Research also needs to clarify
the circumstances under which one would expect personality factors to operate similarly across situations. Horney (2006) persuasively argues that behavior can vary substantially across seemingly similar situations in which
current models of personality would suggest similar behavior.

Analytical Issues

In this section, we discuss analytical issues in testing trait theories. We consider how subjects have been selected in the various studies, study design issues, and model specification issues. Because of the variety of studies that fall under the trait theory umbrella, we choose some of the more representative lines of research to serve as examples of points that apply to much of the trait theory literature.

Sample Selection

As discussed in Chapter 1, the choice of study subjects is a critical issue in criminological research. Trait theory studies generally have several limitations related to sample selection. The first is sample size. Many studies across a number of biosocial research programs employ very small sample sizes (Fishbein 2001; Raine 1993). For example, Rhee and Waldman (2002), in their meta-analysis of heritability and antisocial behavior, included studies with samples as small as 15. Similarly, Raine (1993) notes an average sample size of 30 in her meta-analysis of neurotransmitter studies. One implication of small sample sizes is that it is much more difficult to find effects due to the lack of statistical power to reject the null hypothesis that results are due to random chance. Another issue is whether the samples used are representative of the larger population. Rhee and Waldman (p. 496) note that volunteers for studies tend to be above average in SES, but this may make them unrepresentative. Similarly, criminality is very low in Danish populations, so extrapolation to other populations from Danish studies is potentially problematic (Carey and Goldman 1997; Rhee and Waldman 2002). Arousal, hormonal, and other biological studies often use samples of institutionalized criminals. Several potential problems arise when using these samples. First, the criminals that have been caught and convicted may or may not be like the ones that have not been officially processed. Second, these studies often fail to include control groups comprised of similar but noncriminal individuals for comparison (Fishbein 2001:83). And third, if control groups are used they may not be properly chosen so that they differ only with respect to the variable of interest.

The results of biosocial studies may also depend on the characteristics of the sample in other ways. Walsh (2000:1084) notes that environmental effects on behavior appear to be stronger than genetic effects for juveniles but that the opposite is true for adults. Walsh also notes that heritability is more likely to be seen in better social environments than in poorer ones. Thus, whether support is shown for heritability may depend on the sample used. Raine (1993) additionally notes that most studies of neurotransmitters and crime have been done on males and argues that we need more studies of neurotransmitters on females. This critique appears to be true of biosocial research more generally (for an exception, see Fishbein 1992). Given differences between males and females in terms of both criminality and biology, more research should explicitly compare males and females on the factors hypothesized as relevant to crime.

For some biosocial factors discussed here, the effect may only appear at extreme levels of the variable. For example, testosterone may only cause aggression above a certain threshold. If so, samples composed mainly of people with average or even relatively high or low levels of testosterone might not show a relationship, whereas samples containing individuals with extreme testosterone levels might.

Model Specification and Causal Ordering

To properly test theories of crime, one must accurately model the relationships between the variables. If not, then failure to show support for a hypothesized relationship may simply mean that the test has been poorly designed. It is important, therefore, to think about how biosocial and psychological traits are expected to be related to crime. Traits have been hypothesized to be direct causes of criminal behavior, consequences of criminal behavior, indirect causes through their effect on other variables such as impulsiveness or antisocial personality traits, and causes that are conditional, depending on other factors such as the environment (Raine 2002a:52–54; Raine, Brennan, and Farrington 1997:5–6). Because this issue applies to many biosocial theories, we consider one example (hormone studies) to illustrate the complexities of properly modeling these relationships.

As shown in Table 3.3, several possible relationships between hormones and crime may exist (Brain 1994; Susman and Ponirakis 1997; Tremblay et al. 1997). Hormones could influence behavior directly, or certain aggressive crimes such as robbery or assault may cause certain hormones to increase. Hormones and crime also may be reciprocally related such that hormones influence criminal behavior, which, in turn, influences hormone levels. For example, individuals with higher testosterone levels may be more likely to get in fights, and winning these fights might further raise testosterone levels. It could also be that hormones indirectly influence crime. Recall that Olweus et al. (1988) found that circulating levels of testosterone in the blood were indirectly related to unprovoked aggressive behavior by causing greater irritability and impatience. Or recall Booth and Osgood (1993), who found that higher testosterone levels were associated with lower levels of "social integration," leading to more offending. Finally, it could be that hormones, situations, and crime all interact in complex ways such that the release and effect of hormones on crime depend on the situation.

Table 3.3 Potential Relationships between Hormones and Crime

1. Hormones → Crime
2. Crime → Hormones
3. Hormones → Crime → Hormones
4. Hormones → Environment → Crime
5. Hormones → Interaction differences → Crime

It should be clear from this brief review that the hormone–aggression relationship is much more complex than simply to say that hormones cause aggression. Many of the relationships suggested in biosocial trait theories are similarly complex. Teasing out these effects requires nuanced research designs to model these complexities.

Research Design

To have confidence that one variable causes another, we must show that the two are correlated and that the purported cause comes prior to the supposed effect. Thus, we must first show correlation between the two variables. If hormones are thought to be a cause of crime, studies must show that higher levels of the hormone are associated with criminal behavior. As discussed earlier, such a finding is not uncommon. The more difficult task is to show that the higher hormone levels came first. Unfortunately, most research on biosocial trait theories has been cross-sectional and correlational (Fishbein 2001), but such studies cannot tell which came first—hormones or crime—and cannot tease out reciprocal relationships. Experimental designs, which are excellent vehicles for isolating cause-and-effect relationships, can be problematic in many cases when doing biosocial research. For example, it would be unethical to give testosterone to an experimental group to see if the members of the group become more antisocial or aggressive (see Susman and Ponirakis 1997:266). This is true of a variety of the biochemicals, such as neurotransmitters, hormones, environmental contaminants, and diet. Determining cause and effect in most cases can only be accomplished through longitudinal studies.

Although not as common as cross-sectional studies, some studies use longitudinal research designs. Recall Raine, Venables, and Williams' (1990) study of 101 British boys, where resting skin conductance levels at age 15 predicted officially recorded criminality at age 24. Similarly, Raine, Venables, and Mednick (1997) found that low resting heart rates at age 3 predicted aggressive behavior at age 11 for boys and girls.

Some IQ studies have also been longitudinal in nature. For example, Stattin and Klackenburg-Larsson (1993) found that language impairment at 6 months predicted criminal behavior at age 19. Consistent with this, Brownlie et al. (2004) found that language impairment among 5-year-old Canadian boys also predicted later crime. One important issue that must be considered in longitudinal trait studies is the time interval between measurements. Most crime studies use intervals of one or two years between measurements. But such a time frame may be too short or too long, depending on the biosocial process that is being tested. Testosterone levels could vary dramatically over fairly short periods of time right before or after a criminal offense. Short intervals between measurements, therefore, may be necessary to capture these effects. Conversely, some processes are expected to operate at, or shortly after, birth but not show their impact on aggression or criminal behavior for many years. In this case, researchers need much longer time frames to adequately test whether these factors influence crime.

Controlling for Alternative Explanations

To determine that one variable is the cause of another, we also need to rule out alternative explanations. One of the biggest shortcomings of biosocial research is that studies frequently fail to control for potential alternative explanations that other criminologists consider important. Sociological theories of crime discussed in other chapters of this book focus on a variety of factors that are thought to influence whether a person becomes a criminal or not. Too few biosocial studies control for environmental factors such as peer and parental influences, attitudes, and socioeconomic status.

It is also important to control for relevant alternative *biological* explanations. It is likely that the effects of some biosocial variables depend on the presence of others. Recall, for example, that the use of tobacco can increase testosterone levels, whereas cocaine and heroine can reduce levels (Zitzmann and Nieschlag 2001). Because criminals are likely to be tobacco and/or drug users, failure to control for their use is likely to compromise the findings of studies on the effects of testosterone. In short, it is crucial that alternative biological and environmental factors be included in these studies.

Summary Critique of Analytical Strategy

The analytical strategies chosen to evaluate trait theories have improved dramatically from early studies that simply noted that crime ran in families. Studies employ increasingly sophisticated ways of measuring key variables such as neurotransmitters, testosterone, and brain activity. Yet a number of unresolved issues remain. One important limitation of most trait research is that too many studies rely on very small sample sizes. This creates two potential problems. First, it may be difficult to find significant effects of biological differences because of the lack of statistical power, suggesting that there might be more support for these theories if larger samples were used. The other issue is potentially more problematic. If the small samples are not representative of the larger population with respect to the variables of concern, then study results may mislead researchers. Related to this is the question of whether to sample from the general population or groups with identified problems such as mental patients or known offenders. Studying known offenders may make traits appear to be more important than they really are because it is not known to what extent these traits exist among nonoffender populations. The solution is to use appropriate comparison groups, but determining such groups is not always obvious with respect to traits. For example, known offenders may have certain kinds of psychological problems that manifest themselves in increased aggression. Yet nonoffender populations may have similar psychological problems that may not lead to offending but to other behavioral problems.

Another critical issue is that studies must make a distinction between trait and state effects when testing a variety of trait theories such as neurotransmitters and hormones (see Kruesi and Jacobsen 1997). Individuals vary in their average hormone levels (trait effects), for example. Individuals also vary in the extent to which certain situations will be associated with increases in hormone levels (state effects). It is crucial that researchers consider both kinds of effects to really understand the effects of hormones. Capturing trait effects may require very different study designs than capturing state effects.

Directions for Future Research

It seems we can move past the question of whether biology and psychology matter for crime. Research demonstrates that they do. The important questions at this point are when and how biology and psychology matter for crime. By the same token, research discussed throughout the book consistently shows that social environment also matters for crime. The debate, therefore, should no longer be nature versus nurture but should instead focus on when and how nature and nurture combine to influence behavior. One approach is to consider environmental and biosocial factors separately in the same study. For example, Rowe (1985) (see also Rowe 1986) found support for genetic effects using a sample of 265 twin pairs in Ohio high schools from 1979 to 1981, controlling for a number of environmental variables from differential association (see Chapter 6) and social control (see Chapter 7) theories such as association with delinquent peers and social bonds. Another example is Cauffman, Steinberg, and Piquero (2005), who found that low self-control (see Chapter 7) and resting heart rate were both independent predictors of offending. Perhaps a more promising approach is to consider how biological and social factors interact to influence behavior. Recent studies suggest that biological factors can condition the effects of certain social events on antisocial behaviors. Caspi et al. (2002, 2003) found that certain variations in brain chemistry made individuals more or less susceptible to depression or antisocial behavior as a result of negative life events such as child maltreatment. Thus, the effect of a social experience on later antisocial behavior depends on certain biological variations that naturally occur (see also Moffitt 2005; Moffitt et al. 2006 for a discussion of gene–environment interactions and their effects on antisocial behavior).

Another approach is to consider ways to integrate biosocial and psychological trait theories into mainstream criminological theories. A number of recent studies provide good examples of this integrative approach. Wright and Beaver (2005) use a twin study design to consider genetic influences in their test of Gottfredson and Hirschi's assertion that parents teach self-control. Another example comes from research that shows that sensation-seeking (arousal) may help explain the correlation between religiosity and crime and between school achievement and crime (Cochran, Wood, and Arneklev 1994; Cochran et al. 2002; Ellis 1987b, 1996; Forthun et al. 1999). A final example is Walsh (2002), who integrates biosocial concepts into traditional mainstream criminological theories.

Insights from trait theories could also help explain some of the major correlates of crime, including age, gender, and SES. A number of biological changes in the teen years occur at roughly the same period in the life course as the period of highest criminal activity. Such coincidences raise the potential that (some of) the age–crime relationship has a biological basis. Likewise, gender differences in crime rates are likely to have at least some biological basis, although the degree of this influence relative to environmental influences remains unclear. Similarly, the well-established links between lead exposure and poor school performance, combined with a great deal of research showing that poor school performance and crime are related, could help explain the SES–crime relationship. If poor children are more likely to be exposed to environmental contaminants that reduce their ability to perform in school, this could partly explain why the poor are more likely to engage in crime. In sum, it seems clear that criminology as a field can no longer afford to ignore trait theories. Yet much work remains to fully integrate the insights of biological and psychological perspectives into criminology. Doing so can only strengthen our understanding of crime.

Discussion Questions

1. What are the basic assumptions of trait theories, particularly with respect to human behavior?
2. What distinguishes trait theories from other theories in the book?
3. How are biological and psychological trait theories different from one another?
4. What are the major methodological challenges in testing trait theories?
5. Let us imagine that trait theories have correctly identified a major biological (e.g., neurotransmitters) and psychological (e.g., IQ) correlate of crime and delinquency. What policy recommendations would you suggest to help lower crime rates in light of these findings?

CHAPTER 4

SOCIAL DISORGANIZATION THEORY

Introduction

Picture a map of the city where you live. Now imagine placing pins on the map to plot the crime that has occurred over the last year. How might the pins look? Would they be randomly placed throughout the city, or might they cluster in certain areas? If you imagined they would cluster, you are correct. It is a well-established fact that crime does not occur randomly in a city but instead is concentrated in certain neighborhoods. It is for this reason that most residents can tell you where the "good" and "bad" areas of a city are.

Social disorganization theory takes this fact—the nonrandom distribution of crime across areas—as a point of departure for explaining crime. Rather than being concerned with the criminality of individuals, as we have seen in the last two chapters, social disorganization theory is interested in where crime occurs. As such, the theory's emphasis is on the geographic or spatial distribution of crime. Two key questions that guide the theory are: Why is crime higher in some neighborhoods than others? Is there something about the characteristics of these neighborhoods themselves (above and beyond the residents who live there) that fosters crime?

In answering these questions, social disorganization theory roots the examination of crime and deviance in the social norms and activities of communities—basically, in what is going on within the community. Theorists pay particular attention to how residents interact and get along with one another. This is important because interaction determines, in large part, the ability of residents to "patrol" their neighborhood, or what theorists refer to as "informal social control." According to the theory, neighborhoods can be classified along a continuum: Some neighborhoods are "organized" with high levels of informal control and, therefore, little crime; others are "disorganized" with low levels of control and, therefore, much crime; and still others are somewhere in the middle. The differences between organized and disorganized communities are responsible for the differences in crime rates across areas.

This is a quick introduction to social disorganization theory, one that only scratches the surface. Before going any further, it is useful to understand the intellectual history of social disorganization theory, a history that is intimately linked to what was going on in our country when the theory took shape. Social disorganization, like several other theories discussed in this book, cannot be understood outside the historical context of the time.

Intellectual History of Social Disorganization Theory

Social disorganization theory developed in the United States during the first part of the twentieth century, a period marked by rapid political, economic, and social change that affected virtually all aspects of life. Industrialization, urbanization, and immigration were central features of the American landscape in the 1920s and 1930s. A clear link between what was happening at the time and the development of social disorganization theory emphasized the "problems" of this country's heterogeneous, rapidly changing society.

The perspective has its roots in Chicago, a characteristic city that embodies these changes. Chicago began as a small town of approximately 4,000 residents in 1833, but by 1910 there were 2 million people, primarily due to the influx of foreign-born immigrants. This increase in population created cultural, religious, and ethnic heterogeneity among residents. And, like so many other cities at the time, Chicago also experienced a boom in industrialization.

These rapid changes paved the way for the creation of social disorganization theory, which was first developed in the studies of urban crime and delinquency by sociologists at the University of Chicago and the Institute for Juvenile Research in Chicago during the 1920s and 1930s (Akers and Sellers 2004:160). Because the early research was conducted primarily by scholars in Chicago, the theory's pioneers formed what is commonly referred to as the "Chicago School of Sociology."

Two professors in particular studied how the changes of the time were affecting the city, and they did so from a somewhat unique perspective. Robert E. Park and Ernest W. Burgess had backgrounds in human ecology, which uses concepts derived from plant and animal ecology to understand social processes. Mixing human ecology with their observations of Chicago city life, they proposed a theory that viewed the metropolis as analogous to the natural ecological communities of plants and animals. From this perspective, human behavior is determined by social conditions that affect the social and physical environment of which humans are a part. Theorists likened the growth of a city to ecological competition; just as there is a natural ecology where animals and plants compete for space and existence, so there is a social ecology where humans compete for scarce and desirable space. Park and Burgess closely studied the changing composition of the city for years. Chicago was the perfect natural laboratory.

In a 1925 publication titled "The Growth of the City: An Introduction to a Research Project," Park and Burgess described the process they were witnessing. This "natural" process was one of invasion, dominance, and succession, much like the way a new species of plant takes control of an ecosystem. First, they noted the expansion of the central business district (CBD), the downtown area of the city that is the center of action. In the 1930s, cities were not as spread out as they are today; instead, everything culminated at the city center. Before automobiles, or at least their mass production, trolley cars and public transportation all had routes that converged in the city center. One thing Park and Burgess noted about the CBD was that it continually expanded over time. As Chicago grew in population, the CBD kept expanding outward in successive stages.

With the expansion of the CBD came the deterioration of residential properties in the area. As residents moved farther away from the hustle and bustle of the CBD, existing properties began to deteriorate because few inhabited these residences, and even fewer took care of them. At the same time, businesses began buying these properties and converting them into workspaces. This deterioration and change caused "social disorganization."

These observations comprised, in part, the concentric zone theory eventually proposed by Park and Burgess. As noted earlier, the researchers described how cities underwent an evolutionary process and how the structures of neighborhoods changed in relation to this process. The result was that some neighborhoods were organized with a high degree of informal social control while others were highly disorganized and exhibited little control. In their zone theory, Park and Burgess explained that cities can be divided into sections or zones that correspond to areas of social (dis)organization (see Figure 4.1).

Park and Burgess identified the city center as Zone 1, or the CBD. Few residents lived in Zone 1 because it was occupied by stores, business offices, light industry, and places of amusement. Zone 1 was marked by low levels of social control.

Moving out from the city center, Zone 2, or the Zone in Transition, was so named because it was in a continual state of transition. Zone 2 was repeatedly invaded by business and manufacturing interests from the CBD. These changes led residents who could afford to move to do so, leaving behind the

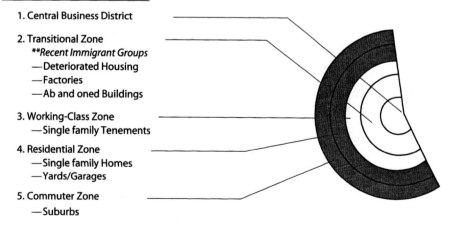

The Concentric Zone Model

1. Central Business District

2. Transitional Zone
   **Recent Immigrant Groups*
   —Deteriorated Housing
   —Factories
   —Ab and oned Buildings

3. Working-Class Zone
   —Single family Tenements

4. Residential Zone
   —Single family Homes
   —Yards/Garages

5. Commuter Zone
   —Suburbs

Figure 4.1 The Concentric Zone Model.
(*Image by Bruce Hoffman, crimetheory.com*)

most economically disadvantaged. At the same time, residents who owned properties in Zone 2 converted their units to apartments to maximize the return on their investments. The zone in transition was thus characterized by physical decay; cheap housing; broken families; and an ever-changing, heterogeneous population. Its residents, many foreign immigrants new to the United States, were at the bottom of the socioeconomic scale with little income, education, and undesirable occupations. Levels of social control were considered lowest in this zone.

Zone 3, the Working-Class Zone, was also referred to as the Zone of Workingmen's Homes. A somewhat more stable population of skilled blue-collar laborers inhabited the residences in this area. Park and Burgess viewed Zone 3 as the intermediate between the slum and the residential areas where moderate levels of social control operated.

Finally, Zones 4 (Residential Zone) and 5 (Commuter Zone) were inhabited by middle-class and upper middle-class families, mostly native-born whites. In these zones, residents owned their homes and resided in the community for long periods of time, so there was little residential turnover. Not surprisingly, social disorganization was nearly absent and there were high levels of social control.

The concentric zone theory was born from the systematic observations of Park and Burgess over many years. It was destined to become a hallmark contribution to sociological and criminological theory. Although the depiction of five zones seems rather simplistic, by emphasizing *social causation* as opposed to rational choice or illness (see Chapters 2 and 3) the Chicago school departed greatly from the individualistic focus of classical and pathological theorizing that was popular at the time.

Still, at this point crime wasn't a part of the equation. Park and Burgess were urban sociologists not specifically interested in crime. Two other Chicago school researchers, Clifford Shaw and Henry McKay, eventually brought crime to the forefront. They applied the zone theory to the study of delinquency in their 1942 influential work *Juvenile Delinquency in Urban Areas*.

Shaw and McKay's primary interest was to study the relationship between community and delinquency and to determine the extent to which differences in economic and social characteristics of local areas paralleled variation in rates of delinquency. Their detailed Chicago studies that spanned decades plotted out the residential location of male youths who had been referred to juvenile court from different areas of the city (think back to the plotting of pins example at the beginning of this chapter). Using the Census to get population counts for each area, they constructed delinquency rates to determine how many youth in each community (per 1,000) were officially labeled delinquent by the court. Shaw and McKay also examined how these rates varied across the different zones identified by Park and Burgess. In this way, they were able to directly compare community characteristics and delinquency across neighborhoods. Consistent with the concentric zone theory, Shaw and McKay's results revealed a concentration of delinquency in certain areas of the city.

Shaw and McKay supplemented their maps and findings with extensive qualitative data. Through interviews they collected information from residents of high-crime communities in the form of case studies or "life histories" from a first-person narrative. Much of this information was later used by Shaw in a series of books about delinquent youth. These books contained the accounts of the process that led to a delinquent career. One of the most famous was *The Jack-roller* (Shaw 1930) which tells the story of a delinquent youth named Stanley from a poor Chicago neighborhood. Unlike his previous research, in these life histories Shaw describes the micro- or individual-level processes that contribute to delinquency, focusing on factors such as the role of deviant peers and lack of parental control.

Collectively, the findings from Chicago school studies formed the basis of social disorganization theory. These studies shaped the development and direction of the theory for years to come. Two findings in particular proved extremely influential, with implications not only for the development of the theory but also for the study of crime more generally.

First, these studies showed that delinquency, crime, and deviance co-occurred with other social problems including poverty, unemployment, and residential turnover. These two sets of things—deviance and community characteristics—appeared together, seemingly related. For the Chicagoans, this implied a connection between social and economic conditions of places and crime. Thus, in the 1920s a social-ecological explanation of crime was effectively introduced which, in large part, offset the prevalent perspectives on biological determinism (see Chapter 3).

Second, the researchers noted that some areas in the city appeared to be high crime or deviance areas, regardless of the characteristics or nationality of the people living within them. Stated differently, no matter which group or nationality of people inhabited a certain area, the crime rate remained high, suggesting that crime and delinquency persisted in some areas despite drastic changes in the social and ethnic composition of residents. The clear conclusion for Chicago school theorists was that crime and delinquency are linked to social conditions of areas, not the ethnic composition of the residents that inhabit the areas. Faris (1967) sums up this important point:

> The Chicago research...showed that with few exceptions, each racial or national population that poured into the slum areas of the city experienced the same severe disorganization, and that as each of these populations in time prospered and migrated outward into more settled residential districts, the symptoms of disorganization declined. The human behavior pathologies thus were found to be consistently associated with the type of urban area and not with the particular ethnic group which inhabited it. (p. 57)

The implications of these findings were clear. First, crime is present in certain areas of the city where there is social, cultural, and economic deprivation. Chicago sociologists emphasized that residents in these areas were not biologically or psychologically abnormal. Rather, their crime and deviance was simply "the normal reaction of normal people to abnormal social conditions" (Plant 1937:248). And, second, that these trends occur suggests that more than "kinds of people" explanations are needed to account for the ecological concentration of deviance—we also need to develop "kinds of places" explanations (Stark 1987). This is exactly what Chicago theorists and those who continued to develop social disorganization theory did.

Social Disorganization Theory

A key question for Chicago school and subsequent researchers was: What is it about some neighborhoods that consistently breed high crime rates? The theory's fundamental concept in explaining high crime areas is "social disorganization." In general terms, social disorganization refers to the inability of a community to realize the common values of its residents and maintain effective social controls (Kornhauser 1978:63). In other words, socially disorganized communities are ineffective in combating crime. On the other hand, crime is more successfully prevented in socially organized communities.

But what constitutes a socially organized or disorganized community? A socially organized community has (1) solidarity, or an internal consensus on important norms and values (e.g., residents want and value the same things, such as a crime-free community); (2) cohesion, or a strong bond among neighbors (e.g., residents know and like one another); and (3) integration, with social interaction occurring on a regular basis (e.g., residents spend time with one another). Imagine a community where like-minded neighbors know one another, interact in public, and spend time together, where community clubs and associations flourish. This is considered a socially organized community.

Conversely, disorganized communities have little solidarity among residents and lack social cohesion or integration. Imagine a neighborhood where residents have little in common with each other, where they can't identify who their neighbors are, and where they don't speak to or spend time with each other. This is considered a socially disorganized community. As we'll see in a moment, neighborhood characteristics like poverty, racial heterogeneity, and residential mobility, among others, affect levels of social organization.

But why should community solidarity, cohesion, and integration matter for crime? According to the theory, they are fundamental because they foster informal social control, a key weapon in the fight against crime. Informal social control can be defined as the scope of collective intervention that the community directs toward local problems (Kornhauser 1978; Shaw and McKay 1969 [1942]). It is the informal, nonofficial actions taken by residents to combat crime in their communities. Consider residents who prevent or sanction disorderly and criminal conduct through informal surveillance of the streets, such as the retired neighbor who day after day sits on his porch and watches the traffic go by or the neighbor who frequently walks the streets for exercise. These individuals are the "eyes and ears" of the community, and their presence is often enough to deter people from committing crimes. Now consider residents who directly intervene by questioning persons about suspicious activity, admonishing those who are misbehaving, and informing parents about their children's misconduct. Each of these informal practices helps to reduce crime in a community. In short, informal social control implies a specific focus on reducing crime through the regulation of behavior.

Socially organized neighborhoods have high levels of informal control primarily because residents share the similar goals and values of a crime-free community and because integration among neighbors is high. Integrated communities have residents who care about one another, are invested in their communities, and feel comfortable admonishing others who are misbehaving. On the other hand, socially disorganized neighborhoods have low levels of informal control given little integration among residents. According to the theory, differences between organized and disorganized communities are responsible, in large part, for differences in crime rates across areas. As disorganization increases, rates of crime and deviance rise as well. Stated differently, disorganization creates conditions for crime and deviance.

The social disorganization approach is grounded in the systemic model (see Figure 4.2) in which the local community is viewed as a "complex system of friendship and kinship networks and formal and informal associational ties rooted in family life and ongoing socialization processes" (Kasarda and Janowitz 1974:329). In the systemic model, social organization and disorganization can be viewed as opposite ends of the same continuum with respect to networks of community social control.

You might be wondering how characteristics of communities such as poverty, racial heterogeneity, or population density factor into the equation. Are poor neighborhoods more likely to suffer from social disorganization? If so, why? A central notion of social disorganization theory is that, in fact, community characteristics matter. Ecological characteristics of neighborhoods can influence the degree of social disorganization.

Certain ecological characteristics can impede the development of social ties that promote the ability to solve common problems, the process described earlier. For example, consider residential mobility, or the frequency with which people move in and out of a neighborhood. Some communities are stable, with people living in the same homes for decades, while others are unstable and witness lots of turnover in the properties. It is not difficult to understand how residential mobility can disrupt a community's network of social relations. If people continually move in and out, it becomes more difficult for residents to

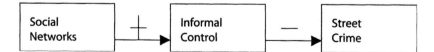

Figure 4.2 Systemic Crime Model.
(*From Bellair 2000:139*)

know, trust, and interact with one another. Without interaction, residents are less likely to engage in informal social control. In short, mobility operates as a barrier to the development of extensive friendship networks, kinship bonds, and local associational ties. Communities marked by high rates of residential turnover, therefore, should experience high crime rates, precisely because weakened social ties lead to reduced informal control. Indeed, social disorganization studies find just this (Bellair 2000; Chamlin 1989; Kubrin 2000; Sampson and Groves 1989; Warner and Rountree 1997).

Consider another example—racial/ethnic heterogeneity. According to social disorganization theory, racial composition bears directly on community solidarity, cohesion, and integration. Racial heterogeneity is hypothesized to prevent the ability of residents to achieve consensus. Since residents are of different races and come from different cultural backgrounds, the likelihood they share similar values, beliefs, and goals is reduced. Moreover, racial heterogeneity is thought to impede communication and interaction among residents because of cultural differences between racial groups, language incompatibility, and the fact that individuals prefer members of their own race to members of different races (Blau and Schwartz 1984:14; Gans 1968). As a result, residents will be less likely to look out for one another and will not as frequently take an interest in their neighbors' activities. Communities marked by racial/ethnic heterogeneity, therefore, should experience high crime rates because they have fewer social ties and less informal control, similar to residential mobility. Studies have also found support for this (Kubrin 2000; Warner and Pierce 1993; Warner and Rountree 1997).

Two important points should be noted with respect to this theory. First, social disorganization is a property of neighborhoods or communities, not individuals. It is incorrect to state that the residents of a neighborhood are disorganized. One must argue that the community in which they reside is disorganized. This point, combined with the fact that it's not a "kind of people" but "kind of place" approach, makes social disorganization a macro-level theory. By this we mean that the theory is not intended to explain the behavior of individuals but rather differences in crime rates across areas.

Second, although community characteristics such as residential mobility and racial/ethnic heterogeneity are related to crime, the theory is clear that these factors themselves don't directly cause crime. That is, residential mobility is related to crime only indirectly through the neighborhood processes of social ties and informal control. As such, community characteristics are important only because they affect the mediating processes of social disorganization. Here mediating means that community characteristics such as poverty *work through* social ties and informal control to influence crime. Bursik (1988) explains this point with respect to poverty and racial composition:

> [B]ecause only the ecological indicators appear in most models, the social disorganization framework may therefore appear... to implicitly assume that lower class neighborhoods with a large proportion of black or foreign-born residents are disorganized. Yet, it is important to emphasize that this is definitely

not an inherent assumption of the theory. Rather, the degree to which these ecological processes are associated with the ability of a community to regulate itself [e.g., informal control] is an empirical question. (p. 531)

A related point about the importance of the intervening mechanisms is made by Kornhauser (1978), who claims that many theories take similar independent variables as their point of departure. She uses poverty as an example. Its correlation with crime and delinquency is assumed by strain, social control, and cultural deviance theories. Because of this, she argues, it is the variables that intervene between poverty and crime that are of importance. For social disorganization theory, social ties and informal control take center stage.

Let's return for a moment to the historical development of social disorganization theory. At the time, the work of Shaw and McKay and others had a profound impact on the study of crime. However, interest in the relationship between community characteristics and crime began to ebb in the 1950s when the field of criminology moved toward micro-level or individual theories of crime causation, the most influential of which were social learning (Chapter 6), social control (Chapter 7), and labeling theories (Chapter 8) (Paternoster and Bachman 2001:120). In addition to this shift, a number of criticisms surfaced.

For example, many criticized the assumptions they saw as inherent in the writings of disorganization theorists, assumptions about deviant behavior that reflected the relatively homogeneous, middle-class backgrounds of the theorists. Critics questioned: Is it true that physical, economic, and population characteristics are objective indicators of disorganization, or does the term reflect a value judgment by the theorists about lower-class lifestyle and living conditions (Akers and Sellers 2004:161)? In other words, who were these theorists to decide what is "organized" or "disorganized"? What may appear as disorganization may actually be quite highly organized systems of competing norms and values. Many subcultures of deviant behavior such as youth gangs, prostitution, and white-collar crime are, in fact, highly organized. Even the norms and values of the slums are highly organized, as Whyte (1943) showed in his classic study of a slum area, *Street Corner Society*. This criticism was so compelling that by the 1940s the term "differential social organization" (Sutherland 1947) was introduced to emphasize that some urban neighborhoods may not be so much disorganized as simply organized around different values and concerns.

The most damaging criticism, however, revolved around researchers' limited ability to test social disorganization theory. Given the primitive nature of data analysis during the early 1900s, researchers were not able to conduct sophisticated analyses. Chicago school theorists "tested" the theory mainly by plotting the spatial distribution of crime in the city to determine whether it was consistent with the theory's predictions. The researchers also correlated characteristics of neighborhoods such as poverty and population instability with crime rates. Although informative, this did not constitute a formal test of the theory. Moreover, they were only able to hypothesize that social ties and informal control mediated the relationship between poverty and crime, for example, as they did not have measures of both across neighborhoods. In sum, these criticisms, in conjunction with a shift toward micro-level explanations, caused social disorganization theory to gradually fade into the background.

But after a period of decline, the theory enjoyed a revived appreciation in the 1980s that continues today. Although a number of important works jump-started this revival, we highlight just a few. Reiss and Tonry (1986) produced a volume titled *Communities and Crime*, which signified a renewed interest in ecological studies of crime. And Bursik (1988) published a statement in the field's major journal, *Criminology*, which proposed attempts to address the major criticisms lodged at the theory. Finally, Stark (1987) argued for the return of "kinds of places" theories and proposed a series of hypotheses to investigate.

Social disorganization theory really sprang back to life with the 1989 study by Robert J. Sampson and W. Byron Groves. Their study was critical because it addressed the main criticism that social disorganization theory had not been properly tested. Previous research had included the "front end" of the human ecology model—attributes of the community—and the "back end"—crime or delinquency outcomes, but left out the crucial middle—indicators reflecting how much social disorganization is actually occurring in a neighborhood (Taylor 2001:132 in Paternoster and Bachman 2001). Sampson and Groves used data from a large national survey of Great Britain to formally test the theory. They constructed community-level measures of neighborhoods (e.g., poverty, racial/ethnic heterogeneity) and the mediating dimensions of social disorganization and determined how both sets of factors influenced neighborhood crime rates. Their causal model is shown in Figure 4.3.

The findings were largely supportive of social disorganization theory: Communities characterized by strong social ties and informal control had lower rates of crime and delinquency, and, more importantly, these dimensions of social disorganization were found to explain, in large part, the effects of community structural characteristics (e.g., poverty) on crime rates. This latter finding was important because it verified for the first time that the structural factors themselves don't influence crime; rather, they are important only inasmuch as they produce social disorganization. Sampson and Groves concluded: "We have thus demonstrated that social disorganization theory has vitality and renewed relevance for explaining macro-level variations in crime rates" (p. 799).

Studies of social disorganization theory have become more common (e.g., Bellair 1997, 2000; Elliott et al. 1996; Kubrin 2000; Markowitz et al. 2001; Sampson 1997; Warner and Rountree 1997), as have reformulations of the theory. In a 1993 book, Bursik and Grasmick sought to make it easier to conceptually differentiate social disorganization from the ecological processes that make internal self-regulation problematic and from the crime and delinquency that result. One hallmark of their reformulation has been "the

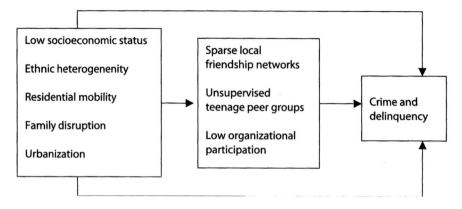

Figure 4.3 Sampson and Groves (1989) Causal Model.
(From Sampson and Groves 1989:783)

formal definition of social disorganization as the regulatory capacity of a neighborhood that is imbedded in the structure of that community's affiliational, interactional and communication ties among the residents" (Bursik 1999:86). Bursik and Grasmick identified three types of social control, with implications for preventing crime: (1) private, including intimate friendship and kinship relationships; (2) parochial, including less intimate and secondary group relationships; and (3) public, including linkages to groups and institutions located outside the neighborhood.

More recently, Sampson, Raudenbush, and Earls (1997) proposed modifications to the intervening measures of social disorganization. They argued that social ties and networks may be necessary, but not sufficient, for social control and that what was missing was the key factor of purposive action (i.e., how ties are activated and resources mobilized to enhance social control). For the latter to occur, according to the researchers, residents must be willing to take action, which depends in large part on conditions of mutual trust and solidarity among neighbors, conditions that had not been considered in previous work. Sampson et al. therefore proposed a new construct, collective efficacy, which captures this linkage of trust and intervention for the common good. They argued that neighborhoods with high levels of collective efficacy should have low levels of crime and that collective efficacy (like social ties and informal control) should largely reduce the effects of poverty, residential instability, and other community factors on crime. A study of Chicago neighborhoods finds just this (Sampson and Raudenbush 1999).

Other innovations have taken place throughout the theory's development. One has involved incorporating ideas from a perspective that began to garner attention in criminology in the late 1970s—the routine activities perspective. Although this perspective has some conceptual overlap with social disorganization theory, we discuss routine activities in the "Rational Choice and Deterrence Theories" chapter (Chapter 2), largely because routine activities and deterrence and rational choice theories share fundamental ideas that are consistent with the rational view of the offender.

Concepts and Measurement Issues

Now that you understand how social disorganization theory works, let's consider some issues in testing the theory. Remember that a good theory requires precision in the definition of concepts, and the concepts must be defined in a way that allows the audience to identify the phenomenon to which the concept refers. So, before we discuss measurement issues in the testing of the theory, it is first useful to review the key concepts that must be measured in any analysis of social disorganization theory.

Recall Sampson and Groves' (1989) causal model in which they identified three sets of measures that are central to the theory. Reading from left to right, they first listed the exogenous (external) sources of social disorganization, or the structural factors that promote disorganization such as poverty, residential mobility, and racial/ethnic heterogeneity. In the middle, they listed a second set of measures—the intervening measures of disorganization as reflected in the amount and extent of social ties, informal control, and (eventually) collective efficacy. Finally, on the right-hand side of the equation, they identified a third set of factors that represent the outcome of disorganization— crime. We'll discuss each set of measures as they relate to the theory.

Poverty, racial/ethnic heterogeneity, and residential mobility were the most common exogenous sources of disorganization studied by Chicago school theorists. This is not surprising given what was happening in Chicago at the time. But research in the last several decades has identified other important community characteristics that may influence social ties and informal control, including family disruption (reflected in the divorce rate and/or the number of one-parent households with children), population density, unemployment, young males, and dilapidation, among others.

While these exogenous characteristics are important for social disorganization theory, their importance mainly lies in how they affect the intervening measures of disorganization—social ties, informal social control, and collective efficacy. Recall that social ties reflect the prevalence and interdependence of social networks in a community. This concept measures the nature and extent of neighboring in communities and describes the types of activities and relationships that community members have. While the activities and relationships do not necessarily revolve around regulating crime, they are important as precursors to informal social control. When residents form local ties, their capacity for community social control is strengthened because they are better able to recognize strangers and more apt to engage in guardianship behavior against victimization (Skogan 1986:216).

Recall that informal social control is defined as the scope of collective intervention that the community directs toward local problems. The concept encompasses activities performed by residents that attempt to control the behavior of people in the community. As such, informal control implies a specific focus on reducing crime through regulation of behavior (e.g., stopping kids who are fighting on the street). This regulation, however, does not result from police presence, or formal control. Rather, informal control is nonofficial, nonformal actions taken by residents to solve local problems. Likewise, social control should not be equated with social repression, as it is in other theories like conflict or labeling, but with the collective pursuit of shared values that are rewarding and meaningful (Janowitz 1975). Social disorganization theory assumes general consensus among residents about what is best for the community.

A final mediating concept is collective efficacy. Collective efficacy is defined as social cohesion among neighbors combined with their willingness to intervene on behalf of the common good—a combination of ties and informal control. Of particular importance in the measurement of this concept is the linkage of mutual trust and the willingness to intervene for the common good. Both elements are needed to measure collective efficacy accurately.

Finally, any complete test of social disorganization theory must include some "outcome" measure. Common outcomes of social disorganization include, but are not limited to, crime, delinquency, victimization, and deviance. The theory predicts that neighborhood ecological characteristics influence ties, informal control, and collective efficacy to create conditions favorable to these outcomes in communities.

All theories pose a challenge to researchers when it comes to measuring the major concepts, and social disorganization theory is no exception. Measuring neighborhood characteristics such as poverty or residential mobility as well as crime are difficult enough, but what about the intervening concepts? How does one measure social ties, informal control, or collective efficacy? The question of measurement, or, more importantly, accurate measurement, is paramount. As noted in Chapter 1, if concepts are not measured properly, then the result is a faulty test of the theory. Think about measuring a person's age by eyeballing him or her; you'll come up with a number, but how accurate that number is remains up for debate. Precise measurement is key to testing any theory successfully.

What Is Social Disorganization?

Before you can measure a theoretical concept you must fully understand what that concept is, or the concept's definition, as discussed earlier. Seems logical, but this was a serious problem initially for social disorganization theorists. The problem centered on the theory's central concept of social disorganization, which according to some was confusing and ill-defined. Cohen (1959:474) noted, "Few terms in sociology are so variously and obscurely defined as social disorganization." While Chicagoans conceptualized social disorganization as a cause of deviance (social disorganization $\rightarrow$ deviance), they sometimes used deviance as an index of social disorganization. In other words, they did not clearly differentiate the presumed outcome of social disorganization (i.e., crime/delinquency) from disorganization itself. For example, Schmid (1928) used houses of prostitution and homicides as indices of social disorganization, yet social disorganization is predicted to cause these precise things. So, in a sense, theorists wound up arguing that crime predicts crime, creating a tautology, or circular reasoning. Clearly this was not informative, and researchers began to realize that social disorganization must be measured separately from what it is supposed to predict—crime. Other measurement issues have continued to plague the theory. Before we discuss them, let's first review some studies to determine just how they measured the key theoretical concepts. This review is by no means exhaustive, but it should give you an idea of how the concepts are typically measured.

Measuring Intervening Concepts

One of the greatest methodological challenges for social disorganization theory has involved empirically measuring the intervening concepts: social ties, informal social control, and, recently, collective efficacy. Given the difficulty of collecting data to measure these theoretical constructs, most early studies simply inferred their presence; they showed that poor, residentially unstable, racially/ethnically heterogeneous neighborhoods had higher crime rates and assumed this was because they also had lower levels of social ties, informal control, and/or collective efficacy. But recall that this changed with the work of Sampson and Groves (1989), who analyzed survey data collected from over 10,000 residents in 238 localities to test the theory. The survey was quite extensive. Residents were asked numerous questions about the areas in which they lived. Sampson and Groves used many of these questions to create measures of social ties and informal control. One element of social ties was what Sampson and Groves called "local friendship networks," or the extent to which your friends live in the same community as you do. Communities with residents who have most of their friends residing nearby arguably have greater social ties than communities where residents have few friends in the neighborhood. The survey question, "How many of your friends reside in the local community, defined as the area within a 15-minute walk of your home?" was used to capture local friendship networks. Residents answered this question using a 5-point scale that ranged from none to all.

But note that this measure does not include any elements of informal social control. To tap into this the researchers used two other questions. The first captured the extent of control over street-corner teenage peer groups. Using a 4-point scale respondents were asked, "How common is it for groups of teenagers to hang out in public in the neighborhood and make nuisances of themselves?" The second question reflected the prevalence of organizational participation. Respondents were asked about their social and leisure activities for each night of the week, broken down by type of activity (given that, for example, participation in the bowling club is not as critical for informal control as is participation in a neighborhood crime watch group). Sampson and Groves hypothesized that low levels of social control existed in those communities where teens commonly hung out unsupervised and where few residents participated in organizations. These communities, according to the theory, should have the highest crime/delinquency levels—a finding the authors report.

Sampson and Groves' study was the first to include the intervening measures of social disorganization. Reflecting on their measures, how successful do you think they were? Do you think the survey questions accurately captured the spirit of social ties and informal control? It is important to remember that these concepts are extremely difficult to measure given their abstractness, complexity, and "messiness." Unlike chemists in a lab who can take precise measurements of things, social scientists often have to rely on rough approximations since concepts like social ties and informal control are intangible. Still, one must continually question how "successful" researchers are at measuring key concepts. For comparison purposes, let's examine how other studies have operationalized the mediating concepts of social disorganization.

In their 1997 study, Barbara D. Warner and Pamela Wilcox Rountree set out to test the role of local social ties as a mediator between structural conditions such as poverty, ethnic heterogeneity, and residential stability and crime rates in Seattle neighborhoods. Like Sampson and Groves, the authors used survey data (on 5,302 residents) to construct their social ties concept. These questions concerned whether respondents (1) had borrowed tools or food from neighbors, (2) had lunch or dinner with neighbors, and (3) had helped neighbors with problems. Higher values on this measure are indicative of more social ties and hence a greater capacity to control crime. Because Warner and Rountree did not include a measure of informal control, theirs is only a partial test. The results, nonetheless, were interesting. While they found that social ties directly reduced crime, they did not find that they mediated the effects of community characteristics on crime, as the theory predicts. These findings had significance for the development and refinement of social disorganization theory (discussed later). But of interest methodologically is whether, and to what extent, the measures used by Warner and Rountree accurately capture the definition of social ties. How does their measure compare to that of Sampson and Groves?

Another study by Bellair (1997) using 1977 victimization survey data from cities in New York, Florida, and Missouri explored the role of social ties. Bellair's study, however, takes a slightly different approach by determining whether the type of interaction among neighbors matters. Bellair constructed a variety of alternative measures of social interaction and separately examined the effect of each on crime rates. The measures of social interaction were constructed from a survey question that asked respondents how often they, or members of their household, got together with their neighbors either in their neighbor's or their own home. Responses to this question were daily, several times a week, several times a month, once a month, once a year, and very infrequently. Bellair finds that, somewhat surprisingly, both frequent and infrequent social interaction among neighbors establishes community controls. Why are community controls strengthened even by infrequent interaction? According to Bellair, "Neighbors may be willing to engage in supervision and guardianship regardless of whether they consider themselves to be close friends with their neighbors" (p. 697). Unlike Warner and Rountree (1997), Bellair finds that the social interaction measures mediate a significant proportion of the effect of ecological characteristics on community crime, consistent with social disorganization theory.

A 1996 study by Elliott et al. has provided one of the most complete tests of social disorganization theory to date. The authors studied the relationship between neighborhood "disadvantage" (comprised of poverty, residential mobility, unemployment, single-parent families, among other things) and delinquency. They wanted to know whether social ties and informal control mediated the effect of disadvantage on delinquency. The researchers used survey data from Chicago and Denver to create their measures. Unlike the studies just mentioned, Elliott et al. had many more questions to choose from to measure the concepts.

For the informal control measure they included the following: How likely is it that one of your neighbors would do something about it if: (1) Someone was breaking into your house in plain sight? (2) Someone was trying to sell drugs to one of your children in plain sight? (3) There was a fight in front of your house and someone was being beaten up? and (4) Your kids were getting into trouble?

Their social ties measure was even more extensive, including questions about the following:

- *Social support*: Is there anyone you could talk to or go to for help if: (1) One of your children was thinking of dropping out of school? (2) One of your children wanted to go to college? (3) Your unmarried teenage daughter was pregnant? and (4) Your teenage child was looking for a summer job?
- *Neighborhood bonding*: (1) Overall, how satisfied are you with this neighborhood? (2) Do you think that you will be living in this neighborhood five years from now? (3) Would you move out of this neighborhood if you could? and (4) Are there things you like about this neighborhood?
- *Neighbor activity*: During an average month last year, how many times have you: (1) Had someone over to your home or gone to his or her home during the day for coffee or just to talk? (2) Gone out for an evening with someone to a movie, to a sports event, for a drink, or for some other activity? (3) Asked someone over to your house or gone over to his or her house for a meal, to play cards, or to watch TV? (4) Asked someone for help, like getting your car started, getting a ride with him or her, borrowing a tool, or asking him or her to watch your kids while you ran an errand? (5) Talked to someone about personal problems you were having or he or she was having? (6) Talked to

someone about stores and sales, programs for neighborhood kids, church activities, and so forth? and (7) Asked someone if you could borrow some money?

- *Neighborhood kids known by name*: How many children or teenagers living in your neighborhood do you know by name?
- *Family and friends in neighborhood*: (1) Not counting family members living with you, how many family members live in your neighborhood? (2) Not counting people you live with, how many good friends do you have who live in your neighborhood? and (3) How many good friends do you have who live outside of your neighborhood?
- *Organizations/activities in neighborhood*: Respondents select from a list which organizations/activities are present in their neighborhood, including community watch program, a library, a police station, a community family health service, community athletic teams, a family-planning clinic, and so on.

Elliott et al. combined these sets of questions into a single measure of social ties, which they labeled "local social integration." Clearly this measure is much improved over measures used in previous research. The findings from Elliott et al. offer mixed support for social disorganization theory. On the one hand, informal social control is significantly related to delinquency and mediates the effect of neighborhood disadvantage on delinquent behavior. On the other hand, social integration is not significantly related to delinquency, nor does it mediate the effect of neighborhood disadvantage on delinquency.

More recently studies have shifted their focus to the notion of collective efficacy, proposed by Sampson, Raudenbush, and Earls (1997). Recall that collective efficacy captures the linkage of trust and intervention for the common good, both of which are necessary precursors for combating crime. Sampson et al. measured collective efficacy by combining a scale of questions on informal social control with a social cohesion and trust scale from a survey of 8,872 Chicago residents. With respect to informal social control, residents were asked about the likelihood ("Would you say it is very likely, likely, neither likely nor unlikely, or very unlikely?") that their neighbors could be counted on to intervene if: (1) Children were skipping school and hanging on a street corner, (2) Children were spraypainting graffiti on a local building, (3) Children were showing disrespect to an adult, (4) A fight broke out in front of their house, and (5) The fire station closest to their home was threatened with budget cuts. The social cohesion and trust scale consisted of five conceptually related items. Respondents were asked how strongly they agreed (on a 5-point scale) that "People around here are willing to help their neighbors," "This is a close-knit neighborhood," "People in this neighborhood can be trusted," "People in this neighborhood generally don't get along with each other," and "People in this neighborhood do not share the same values." In support of the theory, Sampson et al. found that communities with greater levels of collective efficacy had lower crime rates, controlling for other factors, and that collective efficacy mediated the effects of ecological characteristics on violence.

As noted earlier, one longstanding critique of social disorganization theory centered on the fact that most studies did not include measures of the mediating concepts. After Sampson and Groves and others began to incorporate such measures, attention shifted to different issues. One issue is that some studies fail to examine the relationship between social ties and informal control, despite the fact that informal control has been traditionally theorized as an outcome of social ties. Note that only a few of the studies described here included both social ties and informal control measures, thereby not fully testing the theory.

Also problematic is the conceptual fuzziness that exists around the mediating concepts of social disorganization (Kubrin and Weitzer 2003a). It is not always clear how social ties differ from informal control or how collective efficacy is distinctive from, and truly represents an improvement over, ties and control. Conceptual fuzziness has meant that some studies use survey questions that may reflect any or all of the three concepts, depending on how you look at things. Raudenbush and Sampson (1999:2) note, "[C]ollective processes such as neighborhood social control and cohesion have rarely been translated into measures that directly tap hypothesized constructs." What is needed is for researchers to pay particular attention to developing indicators of concepts that are clearly distinguishable from each other. Moreover, they should incorporate all measures into their research design as a way to directly compare the concepts (Kubrin and Weitzer 2003a).

Measuring Crime

Critiques of measurement strategy have not been limited to the intervening measures of disorganization. Researchers also find fault with the theory's general reliance on official crime statistics. Although the selected studies mentioned here all use self-report survey data, many other studies use official crime data (e.g., Uniform Crime Reports). According to some, official records are biased (Chambliss 1999). As early as the 1930s, critics contended that systematic biases in the juvenile and criminal justice systems are what gave rise to crime differences among Chicago neighborhoods and that the "actual" distribution of crime and delinquency is more evenly dispersed throughout the city. In short, skeptics question: Do official crime rates result from actual behavior or from race and class disparities in police practices? Other theories of crime frequently use official statistics, so this concern is not specific to social disorganization theory.

Analytical Issues

Tests of social disorganization theory have uncovered important analytical issues. One of the most basic that continues to challenge researchers has to do with the proper testing of the theory. Although complete tests are more common today, many studies still only conduct partial tests. Often left out of analyses are the intervening theoretical constructs. Why might this be the case? Recall that these concepts are difficult to measure. Compared to ecological characteristics, such as poverty or racial/ethnic heterogeneity, which are often obtained from the Census, and crime or delinquency measures, which are typically taken from official crime reports, the mediating constructs do not come from any one source. Researchers capture these measures using large-scale surveys, as indicated earlier. However, collecting survey data requires a lot of manpower, is time consuming, and is very costly. In the aforementioned studies, researchers had to employ people to call households and administer the survey over the phone or go door to door asking residents to fill out paper versions of the survey. While this may not be problematic for small samples of, say, 100 residents, most of these studies have well over 4,000 respondents. You can imagine the time and energy it takes to collect all the data! It is for this reason that fully testing social disorganization theory remains an important analytical challenge, even today.

What Is a Neighborhood?

Even with time, energy, and resources to collect the data, nagging issues remain. For example, social disorganization theory operates at the neighborhood level, but many ask: What is a neighborhood? If we were to randomly ask 10 people that live in the same area to map out the boundaries of their neighborhood, how likely is it that everyone would select identical boundaries? For some, the neighborhood may be the 2 or 3 blocks surrounding their house, for others it may be up to 10 blocks, and for others still it may include everything across town. Disorganization researchers have avoided this problem by defining precisely what they mean by "neighborhood" in the survey.

More often than not, however, studies also use Census data in their analyses to measure community characteristics such residential mobility, and, according to many, the Census uses a questionable definition of neighborhoods. The Census relies on artificially drawn boundary lines to create what it calls "census tracts." Census tracts vary in size but typically contain between 100 and 4,000 residents. They are designed to be relatively homogenous in population characteristics, economic status, and living conditions so that residents in a tract are as similar as possible. For social disorganization theory, the issue is to what extent tracts are sufficient proxies for neighborhoods. An example illustrates this concern. Consider residents who live across the street from one another but are classified as living in different tracts. These residents would not be designated as "neighbors" despite their clear physical proximity. Social disorganization theorists continue to struggle with the best way to capture "neighborhood."

Spatial Dependence

A related analytical issue is raised here: Census tracts, as proxies for neighborhoods, are seldom spatially independent. First, neighborhoods that are located in proximity often share similar characteristics such as poverty levels, residential mobility patterns, and racial/ethnic composition; their likeness with each other is much greater than with neighborhoods located farther away. Second, since neighborhood boundaries are artificial (i.e., there are not walls or visible dividers that break up most census tracts), activity in one "neighborhood" (as classified by the Census) often spills into adjacent "neighborhoods." For example, residents in a given community often travel through a nearby community to go to the store, catch a bus, visit friends, or even commit crime. This means that there is a spillover effect in resident behavior from one neighborhood to the next. Both patterns described here are formally indicated by the concept of spatial autocorrelation, or the coincidence of similarity in value with similarity in location (Anselin et al. 2000:14). Spatial autocorrelation has implications for social disorganization theory since the theory operates at the neighborhood level. Researchers must ask: Controlling for other ecological characteristics, how much does crime from nearby communities influence crime in a given community? If this answer is a lot, and researchers do not control for spatial autocorrelation in their analyses, the results could be biased. The relatively few neighborhood studies that have been done so far indicate that indeed spatial autocorrelation is present and must be controlled for in analyses (Kubrin 2003; Kubrin and Wadsworth 2003; Morenoff, Sampson, and Raudenbush 2001; Rosenfeld, Bray, and Egley 1999). For a more detailed discussion about spatial autocorrelation and its implications for theory, see Baller et al. (2001).

Multicollinearity

Another issue disorganization theorists face is the strong association between many of the ecological characteristics of communities. For example, race is strongly related to economic status in this country because of inequality, segregation, and discrimination; minorities, and particularly blacks, are more likely to be poor relative to whites. This means that measures of race (e.g., % black) and socioeconomic status (e.g., poverty, median household income) are highly correlated. Other community variables are also strongly associated, including poverty and unemployment and race and female-headed households. Why should this matter? Strong correlations between measures can be problematic in regression analyses. One goal of regression analysis, as explained in Chapter 1, is to determine the effect of each variable (e.g., poverty, racial composition, divorce) on an outcome (e.g., crime), controlling for the other variables. This allows the researcher to determine each variable's independent, unique effect. But if two or more variables are highly related, it becomes nearly impossible to determine *which* of them is related to the outcome. In fact, if the correlations between the variables are high (usually above .70), this may result in multicollinearity. The problem of multicollinearity exists whenever the causal factors are highly correlated with one another, when they are, in effect, "competing" against each other to explain the variance in an outcome. While this can happen with any theory, it occurs frequently with social disorganization.

Since multicollinearity produces biased or incorrect results, researchers have had to find ways around this problem. Some choose to exclude a few community measures in the analysis so that the remaining variables are not highly correlated. This can be problematic because important measures get left out. A more popular approach uses a statistical technique called factor analysis. Factor analysis allows researchers to combine highly correlated measures into one overall measure that can be used in the regression analysis. Since many variables may be contained within this summary measure, it is up to the researcher to determine what it "represents." In nearly all disorganization studies, the same general measures tend to be highly correlated and thus are incorporated into an overarching measure: poverty, unemployment, racial composition, divorce, female-headed households, and households on public assistance. Note that each measure captures some element of economic or social disadvantage, so it makes sense that they are related. In short, disorganization researchers frequently use factor analysis to create one summary measure that they typically call "concentrated disadvantage," eliminating the problem of multicollinearity.

Reconsideration of Neighborhood Subculture

Yet another crucial analytical issue emerges from recent findings of tests of social disorganization theory. With better and more complete measures of the mediating variables, studies have reported mixed evidence that social ties affect neighborhood crime rates. For example, Elliott et al. (1996) and Warner and Rountree (1997) both find that ties matter little for social control and crime. In the latter study, while ties were directly associated with lower crime rates, they did not mediate the effect of community characteristics on crime, as the theory predicts.

Inconsistent findings have led researchers to consider other factors that may be at play. One factor is the reconsideration of the role that neighborhood subculture plays in promoting crime. We say "reconsideration" because in their discussion of the relationship between neighborhood structure and crime, Shaw and McKay (1969 [1942]) drew from many sociological traditions, including the subcultural tradition. Shaw and McKay believed that certain structural conditions could lead to the formulation of subcultures conducive to illegal activity, and they examined cultural influences on behavior—what they called the "moral order" of communities. Although Shaw and McKay's original formulation factored subculture into the community–crime equation, subsequent versions of the theory explicitly dismissed subculture. Ruth Kornhauser (1978), in particular, argued that the cultural assumptions were not a necessary component of the disorganization model. But with increasingly mixed evidence as to whether social ties matter, cultural explanations have been resurrected in some recent work. For a detailed explanation of how culture may matter for social disorganization theory, see Kubrin and Weitzer (2003a, 2003b). In sum, incorporating the role of subcultural factors is emerging as an important aspect of current research.

Modeling Dynamic Processes

Finally, one of the greatest analytical challenges for social disorganization theory has to do with modeling dynamic processes inherent in communities. Communities are not static. They change over time, with implications for social disorganization and crime. This point was fundamental for the early Chicago school theorists. One of Shaw and McKay's (1969 [1942]) most central findings was that the changing spatial distribution of delinquency in a city is the product of "larger economic and social processes characterizing the history and growth of the city and of the local communities which comprise it" (p. 14). But, despite these findings, social disorganization researchers have not adequately examined change and long-term processes of urban development (Bursik 1988:524), resulting in the field's "static conceptualization of community structure" (Sampson 1993:428). This is somewhat understandable considering the difficulty and costs associated with compiling information over an extended period of time. Collecting data for one year is difficult enough, but imagine trying to collect the data you would need to test disorganization theory over a decade. Still, there are major drawbacks to relying on cross-sectional data. It is impossible to study change in such a design, and the effects of processes such as gentrification and segregation on the distribution of crime and delinquency are difficult to detect. Findings from a small but important literature illustrate the necessity of considering dynamic models of social disorganization (Bursik and Grasmick 1992; Bursik and Webb 1982; Chamlin 1989; Kubrin 2000; Kubrin and Herting 2003; Miethe, Hughes, and McDowall 1991; Morenoff and Sampson 1997). Clearly, researchers must model change in community characteristics and crime if we are to fully understand the processes described in the theory.

Directions for Future Research

Today social disorganization theory is alive and well. Most criminological journals feature articles on disorganization theory that propose theoretical development as well as test the theory in different ways. In 1988, when Bursik published "Social Disorganization and Theories of Crime and Delinquency: Problems and Prospects," he described the theory's current state and listed the necessary changes that the theory would have to undertake to advance. Almost 20 years later, Kubrin and Weitzer (2003a) revisited these same issues in their piece "New Directions in Social Disorganization Theory." Like Bursik before them, Kubrin and Weitzer reviewed substantive and methodological deficiencies in the social disorganization literature and charted some promising new directions.

As with any perspective, much needs to be done to develop the theory's potential fully. One critical issue has to do with contemporary applications of the theory. Societal processes and shifts today are much different than in the time of Shaw and McKay and even more recent theorists; urban renewal efforts and initiatives have destroyed much of the older housing in many cities and replaced it with public housing communities; suburbanization has increased greatly with improved road access to cities; and gentrification, or the process of renewal and rebuilding that accompanies the influx of middle-class/affluent people into deteriorating areas that often displaces poorer residents, is widespread. These shifts raise questions about how well the disorganization model applies to cities in the twenty-first century. Some contend that the theory may be less applicable to contemporary America than to a bygone era (Liska 1987). Future research must address this claim.

Another new direction for future research involves whether or not to incorporate formal social control into social disorganization theory. By formal control, we mean the practices of the authorities such as the police to maintain order and enforce legal codes. While social control is central to the theory, researchers focus on informal control, essentially because it is community-based and thus hypothesized to be more central in mediating the effects of neighborhood characteristics on crime (Kubrin and Weitzer 2003a:381). On the other hand, formal control is typically exercised by institutions outside the neighborhood. Still, the neglect of formal control may be problematic for social disorganization theory because it could be important in at least two ways: (1) by directly influencing community crime or (2) by influencing residents' informal control practices (Kubrin and Weitzer 2003a:381).

Also worthy of exploration are the extra-community factors that may shape how residents "patrol" their neighborhoods. Currently, most studies focus exclusively on intra-neighborhood crime influences such as poverty, residential mobility, and so forth. Yet these community characteristics often stem directly from planned governmental policies at local, state, and federal levels as well as private investment (e.g., redlining, disinvestment from banks, public housing policy). Given this, social disorganization theory as traditionally conceptualized is hampered by a restricted view of community that fails to account for the larger political and structural forces that shape communities (Bursik and Grasmick 1993:52; Kubrin and Weitzer 2003a; Sampson and Wilson 1995:48). As Sampson (2001:102) asserts, "[N]eglecting the vertical connections (or lack thereof) that residents have to extra-communal resources and sources of power obscures the structural backdrop to community social organization." A more complete disorganization framework, therefore, would incorporate the role of extra-community institutions and the wider political environment in which local communities are embedded (see Stucky 2003 for an example of the latter). In essence, neighborhoods differ greatly in their ties to external decision makers (Guest 2000; Velez 2001) and hence in their capacity to lobby city government and businesses to keep or create jobs, repair the local infrastructure, and invest in the community, with implications for community social ties, informal control, and crime.

Some methodological new directions should comprise future research as well. First, more longitudinal studies of communities and crime are necessary to test the main thrust behind social disorganization theory fully. As stated earlier, most ecological studies of crime are done using cross-sectional analyses, which, although more practical, are problematic given that the theory is concerned with processes of change and succession in urban areas. Precious few studies in the literature have advanced a dynamic perspective of the effects of community characteristics on criminality; many more are needed.

Also essential is to incorporate more qualitative data into studies. To date, most disorganization research is quantitative. This is curious given that Shaw and McKay conducted extensive ethnographic research in Chicago. Collection of qualitative data could entail conducting interviews, surveys, and fieldwork in neighborhoods. As a good example of this sort of data collection, Sampson and his colleagues applied the method of systematic social observation (SSO) to the study of social and physical disorder in urban neighborhoods in Chicago (see, e.g., Sampson and Raudenbush 1999). One critical aspect of this method involved a field team driving through Chicago streets using a video recorder to collect data on the social activities and physical features of more than 23,000 street segments, which researchers then coded into a database. This type of data provides an excellent supplement to survey data that ask respondents to report their neighborhood conditions.

This type of data is also useful for linking neighborhood processes to the larger societal and historical context or time period. Think back to the origins of social disorganization theory and recall that the theory's development was intricately linked with what was happening in cities at the time. Chicago school researchers believed that no social fact makes sense abstracted from its historical context, a point Sampson (1993:431) asks current researchers to reconsider: "Stripped of temporal sequences of social action, human agency, social change, and local contexts, criminology has reified individuals and communities in terms of abstracted variables; old Chicago school emphasis on time and place and the fundamental insight of sociology that social behavior is interactional has been largely lost—it's time to reclaim fundamental insights by joining temporality and context with a focus on process." In sum, one final new direction for social disorganization theory involves incorporating more qualitative data to understand communities and crime better in different contexts and at varying points in history.

Discussion Questions

1. Is social disorganization a micro- or macro-level theory? Why? What are the major differences between micro- and macro-level theories?
2. Distinguish between social ties, informal social control, and collective efficacy. Why is each concept important to social disorganization theory?
3. According to social disorganization theory, how does one characterize the relationship between neighborhood conditions (e.g., poverty, residential mobility, racial heterogeneity) and crime? Is the relationship direct or indirect?

4. Why is it important to model neighborhood change in tests of social disorganization theory? What limitations result from cross-sectional analyses?

5. What is a neighborhood? How are neighborhoods typically defined in social disorganization theory? Why might this definition be problematic?

CHAPTER 5

ANOMIE AND STRAIN THEORIES

Introduction

Anomie and strain theories argue that people commit crime because of pressure or strain. Depending on the version of the theories, the pressure to commit crime can come from a variety of sources. Sometimes pressure comes in the form of not having the money to buy something a person wants or needs or being unable to secure a good job. Other times pressure comes in the form of anger brought on by perceived mistreatment by parents or teachers. Regardless of the source, anomie and strain theories are distinctive because they posit that crime results from pressure, as opposed to other factors such as biological or psychological deficiencies (Chapter 3), deviant peers (Chapter 6), or weakened social bonds to conventional society (Chapter 7). We begin with a brief discussion of the history of the concept of anomie.

Intellectual History of Anomie and Strain Theories

Merton (1968) notes that the French term "anomie," which translates literally as "normlessness," had existed since at least the sixteenth century but was brought into modern usage by Émile Durkheim in 1893 with the book *Division of Labor* (1933). The term was more fully developed in Durkheim's subsequent work in 1897, *Suicide* (1951). Durkheim observed the tremendous social upheaval of the Industrial Revolution and argued that norms for proper behavior can break down during periods of rapid social change. During these periods, when norms no longer hold their force to control behavior and regulate the passions of individuals, societies are said to be anomic. Durkheim's notion of anomie was applied to crime by an American sociologist named Robert Merton. Merton's (1938, 1968) anomie theory was based on Durkheim's work but differed in that Durkheim argued that anomie occurred during periods of change, whereas Merton saw anomie as an enduring feature of society, particularly America (Adler 1995). In addition, Merton explicitly addressed individual-level responses to anomie, whereas Durkheim focused only on macro-level differences across societies.

Modern Anomie and Strain Theories

Merton argues that societies promote goals for their citizens and norms for people's behavior in trying to achieve these goals. In America, there is a very strong focus on the goal of economic success, the "American Dream," which is defined as the commitment to the goal of material success to be pursued by everyone in open individual competition (Messner and Rosenfeld 2001a). All citizens are socialized to try to achieve economic success, as shows like *Lifestyles of the Rich and Famous* and the fascinations with Donald Trump or Bill Gates attest. At the same time, Merton notes that the social structure prevents many from becoming economically successful. So, regardless of how hard they work, some individuals can never get ahead. Anomie is a characteristic of societies, but the societal pressure to succeed creates strain on individuals. Throughout this chapter, we refer to anomie as a macro- or group-level phenomenon and strain as an individual-level phenomenon. Thus, for Merton, American society is anomic because of the strong cultural pressure to succeed economically, combined with less emphasis on the proper behavior to attain that end and limited opportunities to achieve economic success.

Merton (1968) argued that individuals respond to strain in a number of ways. He described five individual adaptations to strain based on acceptance or rejection of the goal of economic success and the socially legitimate means to achieve this goal (see Table 5.1). The most common response to strain is conformity, in which one adopts the culturally accepted goals as well as conventional means to succeed (thus the plusses under goals and means for conformity in Table 5.1). This includes those individuals who obtain legitimate jobs to secure their wealth. The adaptation most commonly linked to crime is innovation. Innovators retain the focus on success but do not feel tied to conventional means to achieve success, or the social structure blocks them from pursuing success legitimately. Thus, an innovator sells drugs to become economically successful when legitimate means to achieve economic success are unavailable. Ritualists, on the other hand, focus on following the socially acceptable means to achieve economic success. Thus, the factory worker who makes minimum wage but is proud of earning his money "the right way" would be a ritualist. Retreatists reject both the goal of success and following the socially approved means to achieve it, even if their goal of success is blocked. Merton argued that vagrants, psychotics, alcoholics, and drug addicts fall into this category. Retreatism is expected to be one of the least common adaptations. Although not typically associated with crime, retreatism could be associated with drug use, crimes committed while drunk or high, or vagrancy. Finally, rebels reject both the American Dream and supporting corporate America to achieve it. They seek to replace the

Table 5.1 Individual Adaptations to Strain According to Merton (1938)

	Goals	Means
1. Conformity	+	+
2. Innovation	+	−
3. Ritualism	−	+
4. Retreatism	−	−
5. Rebellion	±	±

American Dream with new goals and new means to achieve these goals, which in rare cases could lead to terrorist behavior. Merton noted that rebellion would likely be the least common adaptation.

Although Merton argued that the poor are most likely to experience strain, he provides little guidance on which adaptation one can expect in *response* to strain. In other words, strain may lead to conformity or criminal behavior. This is a key issue for theory testing that will be discussed further later. In short, according to Merton, America has a high crime rate because *everyone* is expected to be economically successful, combined with limited structural opportunities for people to achieve this success through legitimate means. At the individual level, crime is more likely among those who retain the focus on economic success but reject the culturally approved means to achieve it (or are blocked from pursuing success legitimately).

Following a period of relative inattention in the 1940s, Merton's anomie theory became perhaps the dominant theory of crime in the 1950s and 1960s (Burton and Cullen 1992). It was subsequently revised at both the individual and macro levels. Early revisions by Cohen (1955) and Cloward and Ohlin (1960) focused on the development of gang typologies, which were not empirically supported (for overviews, see Hoffman and Ireland 1995; Menard 1997), but had a strong influence on social policy. In particular, Cloward (1959) added the notion of *illegitimate* opportunity structures, which Cullen (1988) argues is an attempt to combine Merton's anomie theory with differential association (Chapter 6) and social disorganization (Chapter 4) theories. Although still frequently cited, few have tested Cohen (1955) or Cloward's (1959) revised anomie theories (see Hoffman and Ireland 1995, 2004; Menard 1997).

In the 1970s, anomie theory fell out of favor for several reasons, according to Burton and Cullen (1992). The first was an increasing focus on individual-level explanations of crime, especially Hirschi's (1969) social control theory (see Chapter 7) as well as the increasing use of survey methodology. Second, some early research suggested that anomie theory was not supported empirically. Early empirical tests of Merton's theory were few, were methodologically weak, and failed to capture the complexity of the theory at the individual or macro level. Although nearly thrown on the theoretical scrappile, anomie and strain theories became revitalized in the late 1980s due to a renewed focus on structural theories (see also social disorganization theory, Chapter 4) and a renewed interest in micro-level strain theories. The most prominent macro-level revision of Merton's anomie theory is Messner and Rosenfeld's institutional anomie theory (1994, 1997a, 2001a, 2001b), which is described in the next section. Following that, we outline a prominent micro-level revision, general strain theory, developed by Robert Agnew (1985, 1992, 1995a, 1995b, 1995c, 2001, 2006).

Institutional Anomie

Messner and Rosenfeld (2001a) note that Merton proposed two ways in which the social situation in America produces crime—first, by emphasizing the goal of success much more than the means to achieve it, and second, by having a high degree of inequality (discussed further later). They note, however, that Merton failed to articulate the role of social institutions in regulating behavior, namely, the economy, the polity, the family, and education. So, for example, children are socialized in how to properly behave at home by their parents but also while in school. These institutions are interrelated and each society has a unique balance among the sometimes competing interests of these institutions. In America, the economy is the dominant institution. American capitalism is extreme in its emphasis on success and innovation compared to other societies. Messner and Rosenfeld claim the economy dominates other institutions and noneconomic institutions are devalued. Other institutions accommodate to economic requirements and economic norms penetrate other institutions. Thus, the high crime rate in the United States is due to the overwhelming strength of economic institutions over noneconomic institutions. Because the economy dominates, the ability of other institutions to regulate behavior is weakened. As a consequence, crime is higher because social control is reduced. Although limited research has been done on institutional anomie theory, results are generally supportive (Chamlin and Cochran 1995; Maume and Lee 2003; Savolainen 2000).

Agnew's General Strain Theory

Robert Agnew (1985, 1992, 2001, 2006) argues that strain can come from sources other than economic failure (Cullen and Wright 1997:188). His general strain theory identifies several kinds of strain, such as the presentation of negative stimuli (e.g., getting teased at school) or the loss of positive stimuli (e.g., getting dumped by your girlfriend). Agnew claims that strain is likely to lead to "negative affective states," including anger, fear, frustration, or depression, that can lead to crime. Thus, strains create negative emotions that lead to crime. More recently, Agnew (2001, 2006) suggests that some strains are likely to lead to particular emotional responses, which then lead to criminal behavior. The conditions under which strain is expected to lead to crime are explored further later. Throughout the rest of the chapter, we distinguish Merton's strain theory from Agnew's general strain theory, referring to the former as classic strain and the latter as general strain.

Agnew (1999, 2006) also has added a macro-level component to general strain theory to account for group-level differences in crime rates. Many of the same factors that predict individual criminal behavior are expected to produce differences in crime rates. Thus, for example, higher rates of crime among the poor are due to differences in the kinds and amounts of strains the poor suffer relative to those with more money.

In sum, at the macro level, anomie theories argue that the strong emphasis on material success combined with unequal opportunities to achieve success lead to high crime rates in the United States (compared to other nations). At the individual level, strain theories argue that economic or emotional pressure pushes individuals toward crime. Anomie and strain theories have generated a large body of research, discussed later.

Concepts and Measurement Issues

Recall that one place to begin in theory testing is to identify hypotheses. Several hypotheses can be derived from anomie and strain theories (see Table 5.2). For instance, one would expect that anomic societies—those that focus more on the goal of economic success than on legitimate ways to achieve these goals—should have higher crime rates. At this point, ask yourself how you would measure the concepts necessary to test this hypothesis. How would you go about collecting data on the goals of societies and the means to achieve them? How would you characterize the "emphasis" on goals and means? No doubt, you see the difficulty of testing such a hypothesis, which ideally would involve the collection of data on the norms for success goals, the legitimate means to achieve them, and crime from a number of countries. In this way we could determine whether societies are anomic based on Merton's theory and then determine whether anomic societies have higher crime rates than those that are less anomic or do not suffer anomic conditions.

A second hypothesis would relate crime rates to the degree to which success is seen as a universal goal, combined with the lack of legitimate opportunities for all to succeed. In this case, one would expect higher crime rates in societies with a heavy focus on economic success as a goal all should strive for, especially when the means to legitimately achieve success are not

Table 5.2 Hypotheses Based on Anomie and Strain Theories

Macro-Level Anomie

1. Societies characterized by overemphasis on goals for economic success over conventional means should have higher crime rates.
2. Societies with universal success goals and nonuniversal opportunities to achieve them will have higher crime rates.
3. Crime rates will be higher when the economy dominates over other institutions.
4. Societies where the market determines individual success or failure will have higher crime rates.

Classic Strain: Merton

5. Socioeconomic class and crime are inversely related.
6. A gap between one's aspirations/goals and expectations will lead to strain.
7. Perceptions of blocked opportunities will be positively related to crime.
8. Dissatisfaction with one's current monetary situation will be related to crime.

General Strain Theory: Agnew

9. People experiencing negative life events will experience negative affective states and as a result will be more likely to engage in crime.
10. Groups with higher levels of strains and fewer resources for coping will have higher crime rates.

available to all. Here again, ask yourself how you would test this hypothesis. One could gather data on the extent to which success is seen as a universal and predominant goal. Of course, collecting this information for a number of countries would be difficult.

One might also examine differences between the rich and the poor in society as a way of capturing the extent to which legitimate success is open to more or less of the population. Various studies have shown a link between the degree of inequality and violent crime rates (Lee and Bankston 1999; Messner and Rosenfeld 1997b; Pratt and Godsey 2003; Savolainen 2000). Although consistent with Merton's theory, inequality only indicates the degree to which opportunities for success are open to all, not the universality of societal norms regarding success goals. One could imagine a society in which economic success is only expected for certain portions of society. If only some groups are expected to be economically successful, then inequality would not necessarily lead to crime, as it would be considered "natural." Many societies throughout history have had rigid class structures, in which only the nobility are expected to have wealth (e.g., France in Durkheim's era). These societies have high inequality but are not likely to be anomic because the cultural focus on success is not universal (see also Bernard 1987). By now it should be clear that the macro-level portions of Merton's theory are relatively difficult to test empirically.

For Messner and Rosenfeld's (2001a) institutional anomie theory, other hypotheses can be explored. Messner and Rosenfeld suggest the dominance of the economy over other institutions leads to a higher crime rate, which is also somewhat difficult to directly test because it requires that one collect data on the strength of various institutions within a society and relate the balance of these institutions to crime rates, preferably across a number of countries. As a consequence, researchers testing institutional anomie theory have examined several corollary hypotheses. Messner and Rosenfeld themselves (1997b) argue that homicide rates will be lower in countries that protect their citizens from the whims of capitalist markets. Thus, homicide rates are expected to be lower in countries where there is a larger social safety net to protect people from unemployment or underemployment through programs such as universal health or child care or unemployment insurance. The existence of social safety net programs is expected to reduce the likelihood that desperate financial circumstances will push people to violence. Similarly, Savolainen (2000) argues that the relationship between inequality and homicide in a country will depend on the degree to which the government provides a social safety net (see also Colvin and Cullen 2002).

Recall Merton suggested that the universal focus on economic success combined with limited opportunities to legitimately achieve success in anomic societies will produce strain on individuals. This strain can lead to a number of individual adaptations, which we outlined in Table 5.1. One major limitation of Merton's theory is that he did not suggest why people choose any particular adaptation in response to strain (if they "choose" at all; one likely doesn't choose to be laid off, for example). As a result, the theory has often been reduced to the simplistic notion that "crime results when people can't achieve monetary success through legitimate channels" (Agnew and Passas 1997:5). From this view, the strength or weakness of Merton's theory depended on whether a social class–crime relationship existed.

The relationship between class and crime has been the subject of much debate (Braithwaite 1981; Tittle 1983; Tittle and Meier 1990; Tittle and Ville-mez 1977; Tittle, Villemez, and Smith 1978). A large research literature in criminology focuses on possible links between poverty, inequality, or other aspects of the labor market and crime (Bellair and Roscigno 2000; Bellair, Roscigno, and McNulty 2003; Daly, Wilson, and Vasdev 2001; Fowles and Merva 1996; Jarjoura, Triplett, and Brinker 2002; Kelly 2000; Kovandzic, Vieraitis, and Yeisley 1998; Krivo 1996; LaFree and Drass 1996; Lee, Maume, and Ousey 2003; Messner, Raffalovich, and Shrock 2002; Shihadeh and Ousey 1998). Official statistics suggest the poor are more likely to be involved in crime, whereas most self-report studies show little or no relationship between class and crime (see Dunaway et al. 2000 for an overview). Yet most self-report research was conducted on high school samples and focused on less serious offenses. Some argue that for more serious offenses (e.g., those most likely to result in arrest and conviction) one does see a class–crime relationship (Raine 1993). Others suggest that class and crime are causally related but in conflicting ways that reduce the likelihood that correlation will be evident (Wright et al. 1999). Still others show that broader measures of disadvantage (which usually include income levels or poverty as a component) are related to crime (Krivo and Peterson 2000; Parker and McCall 1999). Although the debate may never be fully resolved, researchers came to believe that class and crime were unrelated and took this as evidence against Merton's theory.

Notice, however, Merton does not argue that class and crime are related. Merton only says the poor are more likely to *feel* strain—not that they are more likely to adapt to strain through innovation. Thus, the strength of the class–crime relationship is only relevant for Merton's theory if (a) people in all classes ascribe to the goal of economic success more or less equally and (b) people respond to strain only through innovation. While the first part of the statement can be empirically tested, the second part is highly questionable. Merton did not suggest that innovation would be a more common response to strain in the lower classes, only that strain would be more common for those with fewer resources. Therefore, studies of the purported class–crime relationship provide only a weak test of Merton's strain theory.

The other hypothesis based on Merton's strain theory that has most often been tested (especially in early studies) is that crime will be higher when there is a gap between a person's goals and her or his expectations for legitimately achieving those goals (see Burton and Cullen 1992). The question is whether this truly tests Merton's theory, since measuring the gap between goals and means only tests whether a person is experiencing strain, not how he or she reacts to it. For Merton, crime occurs based on the individual's response to strain, not in direct relation to the level of strain itself. Recall there are five individual responses to strain. Yet only two of them are expected to be related to most common crimes—innovation and retreatism, which can be associated with drug and alcohol use. Early tests of Merton's strain theory have measured strain rather than the person's acceptance or rejection of institutionally acceptable means (Burton and Cullen 1992). More recent research employs better measures of strain (Agnew et al. 1996; Burton and Dunaway 1994; Burton, Cullen, Evans, and Dunaway 1994; Cernkovich, Giordano, and Rudolph 2000; Farnworth and Lieber 1989; Jensen 1995).

As already noted, Agnew argues that Merton's theory was limited because it focused only on economic strain. Agnew claims that strain can come from several sources, which then can produce negative emotional states that lead to crime. One hypothesis that can be derived from general strain theory is that strain will produce negative emotional states. If strain doesn't produce negative emotional states, then there is no pressure that must be relieved through crime. A second hypothesis is that negative emotional states will be associated with criminal activity. In his early writing, Agnew (1985, 1992) suggested that individuals suffering from all sorts of strain would experience negative emotional states, triggering criminal responses. In recent research, Agnew (2001, 2006) suggests that particular types of strain are likely to lead to anger (discussed later), and that anger will be more likely to lead to criminal behavior. These hypotheses, although not exhaustive, provide a starting point for discussing measurement issues in research on the variants of anomie and strain theories. In this section, we consider the measurement of key concepts specified in these hypotheses, such as anomie, classic strain, general strain, negative affective (emotional) states, and crime.

Anomie

Although Merton specified both a macro- and micro-level theory, few have considered the macro-level implications of the theory (Burton and Cullen 1992). Studies of variation in crime rates based on Merton's theory are virtually nonexistent (see Cole and Zuckerman 1964 for a review), and even some of Merton's harshest critics recognize the theory has really not been subjected to empirical testing (Kornhauser 1978). In fact, the few studies that purport to be tests of anomie theory use variables representing "anomie," which are more reasonably viewed as indicators of social disorganization (Cole and Zuckerman 1964). For example, Landers (1954) classified areas as anomic if they had low rates of home ownership and large non-white populations (see also Bordua 1958; Chilton 1964), factors central to neighborhood social disorganization (see Chapter 4). The lack of studies testing Merton's macro-level arguments is likely due to the difficulty of getting relevant data to adequately test the theory, particularly at the time the theory became prominent. Tests of Merton's anomie theory ideally require information regarding norms for success goals, the means to achieve them, and crime data from several countries to determine whether anomic societies have higher crime rates.

It was not until Messner and Rosenfeld's institutional anomie theory revived the macro-level components of anomie theory that any significant tests were conducted (Chamlin and Cochran 1995; Maume and Lee 2003; Messner and Rosenfeld 1997b; Savolainen 2000). One early test of institutional anomie theory was conducted by Chamlin and Cochran (1995), who note that institutional anomie theory is not easy to test. The model suggests a complex relationship between relatively abstract concepts. For example, how does one measure the dominance of one institution over another? Because data on macro-level measures of informal social control are unavailable in the United States, they suggest a comprehensive test is impossible. Therefore, they test a hypothesis derived from the theory—the influence of economic conditions on crime will depend on the vitality of noneconomic institutions. They hypothesize that the relationship between poverty and crime will depend on the family, the church, and the polity. In particular, Chamlin and Cochran focus on the percent of registered voters that actually voted, prevalence of divorce, and religious participation. Chamlin and Cochran use state-level data in 1980 to predict robbery, burglary, larceny, and auto theft and find that poverty is not a significant direct predictor of crime, but find that, as expected, church membership, low divorce rates, and high political participation rates dampen the effect of poverty on property crime. Notice that this study compares *states* to each other rather than countries. What does this study tell us about the strength or weakness of institutional anomie theory?

Messner and Rosenfeld (1997b) conducted the first cross-national study to test their theory. They argued that homicide rates will be lower when the government does a better job of protecting people from the realities of market economies. In other words, the stronger the social safety net provided by the government, the lower a country's homicide rates will be. In a study of 45 countries, they developed a "decommodification index" to capture the degree to which governments provide social programs such as health and child care or unemployment insurance for their citizens. Consistent with their expectations, they found that countries that restrained the market through decommodification had lower average homicide rates, even after controlling for economic inequality and other factors. Also consistent with their expectations, the United States had an extremely low decommodification score and high homicide rate. Savolainen (2000) also finds support for institutional anomie in a cross-national study, noting that the effect of economic inequality on homicide is lower in countries with strong welfare states. Thus, crime depends on the relative strengths of political and economic institutions.

Maume and Lee (2003) also address the relationships among institutions in their study of homicide in 454 American counties. They include measures of voter turnout, as well as education and welfare expenditures. They find that strong noneconomic institutions reduce the impact of inequality on homicide and that this effect is strongest for instrumental homicides (i.e., homicides committed for material gain as opposed to crimes of passion). Noneconomic institutions, therefore, seem to serve as buffers against the criminogenic effects of the economy. Maume and Lee also find consistent negative effects of voter turnout on homicide.

A number of other recent studies provide evidence consistent with institutional anomie theory (Hannon and DeFronzo 1998; Messner, Rosenfeld, and Baumer 2004; Pratt and Godsey 2002, 2003; Rosenfeld, Messner, and Baumer

2001). Because institutional anomie theory is relatively new, there have only been a handful of direct tests, and a number of issues remain. First, how does one appropriately measure the strength of institutions? Ultimately a test of the theory would require measuring the strength of the economy against other institutions such as the polity, education, and the family. A second question is: Which institutions should be included? For example, Chamlin and Cochran (1995) do not include measures of education but include a measure of religious participation, although Messner and Rosenfeld (2001a) did not address religion. And what about the effects of mass media on crime? Is the media an "institution" for the purposes of Messner and Rosenfeld's theory? A third question concerns whether subnational tests of institutional anomie, in fact, test the theory. If anomie is a characteristic of societies then one must wonder to what extent studies using counties or states as the unit of analysis are directly relevant as tests of the theory. Early support for the theory at multiple levels certainly shows promise, yet more work remains.

Finally, recall that Agnew (1999, 2006) has recently developed a theory to explain variation in crime rates that essentially mirrors his individual-level general strain theory. Some refer to this as macro-level strain theory. Agnew (1999, 2006) argues that the reason disadvantaged communities have high crime rates is because of the ways in which they increase the number of individuals feeling strain and the likelihood that strain will lead to criminal responses. Such communities are likely to have many people experiencing goal blockage (poverty, low education, or low wages), the loss of positive stimuli (unemployment or divorce), and the presentation of negative stimuli (domestic abuse and incivilities). To date only a few tests of macro-level strain theory have been conducted. For example, Brezina, Piquero, and Mazerolle (2001) use the Youth in Transition survey to generate a multilevel model that includes both school (the percentage of students in a given school that are angry or frustrated) and individual-level measures of anger. The sample was a nationally representative group of 1,886 high school juniors in 87 randomly chosen schools. The dependent variables were aggressive behavior and conflict with peers. Controlling for individual-level anger, school-level anger is associated with higher conflict with peers but not aggressive behavior. Brezina et al. suggest this offers partial support for macro-strain theory.

Similarly, Hoffman (2002) examines social control, differential association, and strain theories in a multilevel model, using the National Educational Longitudinal Study. The sample consists of a nationally representative group of 10,860 tenth graders in 1,612 communities in 1990 and includes measures of stressful life events and monetary strain at the individual level and unemployment and poverty at the community level. Hoffman finds that stressful life events are more strongly related to crime when the rate of male joblessness in the surrounding community is high. Thus, community-level variables moderate the influence of individual stressors on crime.

Finally, Warner and Fowler (2003) test macro-level strain theory through interviews of 2,309 randomly sampled residents of 66 Census block groups in two Southern cities. The authors hypothesize that disadvantage should increase strain and higher levels of strain should increase violence. Measures of strain included verbal threats, feeling cheated, and having been harassed by police. The dependent variable was violent or aggressive behavior measured by the number of times in the last six months respondents had seen or heard about fights (with or without a weapon), sexual assault or rape, robbery or mugging, and spouse or partner abuse. Warner and Fowler find that neighborhood disadvantage and instability are associated with higher levels of strain and violence, controlling for neighborhood disadvantage and stability. Because research on macro-level strain theory is new, it is too early to assess the level of empirical support for the theory. More studies are necessary.

Classic Strain

A key issue in tests of Merton's individual-level strain theory is how to measure strain. Early studies of classic strain theory measured strain in terms of a goals/means disjunction, whereas recent research has considered other measures of strain, particularly the perception of blocked opportunities, dissatisfaction with monetary status, and relative deprivation (see Table 5.3).

Table 5.3 Items Tapping Measures of Classic Strain

Aspirations

1. I'd like to make a lot of money in my life (Burton et al. 1994).
2. How much schooling would you like to get eventually (Hirschi 1969)?

Expectations

3. Realistically, I don't think I will make as much money as I'd like (Burton et al. 1994).
4. How much schooling do you think you will eventually get (Hirschi 1969)?
5. In the long run, I expect to be better off financially than I am now (Agnew et al. 1996).

Perceptions of Blocked Opportunities

6. Every time I try to get ahead, something or someone stops me (Burton et al. 1994).
7. If I had connections, I would have been more successful (Burton et al. 1994).
8. I've often been frustrated in my efforts to get ahead in life (Burton et al. 1994).

Relative Deprivation

9. It bothers me that most people have more money to live on than I do (Burton et al. 1994).
10. It's frustrating to see people driving nicer cars and living in nicer homes than I do (Burton et al. 1994).
11. In general, my family is not as rich as other families in the community (Burton and Dunaway 1994).

Dissatisfaction with Monetary Situation

12. I will have enough money to live comfortably on when I retire (Agnew et al. 1996).
13. Right now I am satisfied with how much money I have to live on (Agnew et al. 1996).
14. In the long run, I expect to be satisfied with how much money I'll have to live on (Agnew et al. 1996).

In this section, we discuss the various ways that strain has been measured in tests of classic strain theory.

Burton and Cullen (1992) review nearly 50 studies testing classical strain theory from 1963 to 1991, noting that most studies have measured strain in terms of a disjunction between goals and the means to achieve them. For example, Hirschi (1969), in a survey of 4,077 junior and senior high school students in California in 1964, measures the relationship between educational aspirations and expectations, assuming that those who expect to receive less education than they aspire to will experience strain and therefore be more likely to commit delinquent acts. The aspirations measure was, "How much schooling would you *like* to get eventually" (Hirshi 1969:277). The expectations measure asked how much schooling the respondent actually expected to obtain. Hirschi then categorized the respondent's education by high school, some college, and college graduation for both aspirations and expectations. He concluded that the aspirations/expectations gap is not a significant predictor of delinquency because not many subjects experienced a gap between aspirations and expectations. In addition, those whose aspirations exceeded expectations were no more likely to be delinquent than those with identical aspirations and expectations. Interestingly, Hirschi also found that there were very few in the sample whose aspirations exceeded their expectations. Based on these findings, he rejects strain theory. Other studies using similar measures have also been largely unsupportive of strain theory (see Burton and Cullen 1992 for an overview).

Farnworth and Lieber (1989) argue that Hirschi's measurement of strain that considers only education is incorrect, suggesting a more relevant comparison is between one's *economic* aspirations and one's educational expectations. They test this argument on a sample of 1,614 mostly poor, disproportionately minority teenagers from Seattle in 1978–1979. Farnworth and Lieber test for differences between groups using alternative measures of strain and delinquency. Measures of the disjunction between economic goals and educational expectations were strongly related to both the prevalence (likelihood) and frequency of serious and minor, as well as utilitarian and nonutilitarian, delinquency. Therefore, they claim that using measures more reflective of Merton's original theory suggest greater support for strain theory.

Others suggest that measuring gaps between aspirations and expectations of any type may not be as good as measuring perceptions of blocked opportunities (see Table 5.3). Arguably this comes closer to Merton's original conception of the sources of strain in America due to legitimate opportunities not being universal. Thus, if the person perceives her or his opportunities to achieve as blocked, she or he is likely to feel strain. Burton and Cullen (1992) review studies from 1962 through 1991 and conclude that most (60%) supported strain theory when strain was measured in terms of perceptions of blocked opportunities. More recently, Burton, Cullen, Evans, and Dunaway (1994) include perceptions of blocked opportunities, gaps between aspirations and expectations, and relative deprivation using a sample of adults in a community, explicitly testing three different conceptions of strain. Burton et al. note that most prior research focuses on the gap between educational aspirations and expectations, but suggest that for adults, the gap between *economic* aspirations and expectations is probably more salient. Also, because prior research has offered support for the link between the perception of blocked opportunities and crime, they include a measure of blocked economic opportunities in the analyses. Finally, they note the classic strain model suggests that the frustration produced by lacking what others have may be criminogenic (see also Blau and Blau 1982). Therefore, *relative* deprivation would seem an important consideration. They surveyed 447 white adults in an urban Midwestern area and measure strain as a dichotomous variable, arguing that only those with high economic aspirations and low expectations are expected to feel strain. Burton et al. also include measures of blocked economic opportunities and relative deprivation that are both three-item scales (see Table 5.3). They find bivariate correlations between all measures of strain and crime, but when variables from social control and social learning theories are included, no strain variables are related to crime, suggesting that classic strain does not produce crime.

Other studies have considered relative deprivation (comparing yourself to someone else and feeling deprived). For example, Burton and Dunaway (1994) note the notion of relative deprivation could be made consistent with Merton's original theory and that it is somewhat surprising he did not explicitly incorporate it. Burton and Dunaway test relative deprivation in a sample of 264 middle class students from a Midwestern high school. Controlling for race, gender, age, parental class and school failure, relative deprivation is consistently positively related to overall crime, felonies, and drug crimes. If relative deprivation is more important than absolute deprivation (poverty), this could explain why research on the class–crime relationship has produced mixed results since all people regardless of income can feel relatively deprived depending on their reference group.

Similarly, Agnew et al. (1996) argue that the central variable in the strain model—the individual's level of satisfaction with his or her monetary status—has not been measured in prior tests of strain theory. They note that class and strain are not necessarily synonymous. Strain is most likely to be felt by those who attach high importance to monetary success and low importance to other goals, who lack legitimate means for success, and who see themselves as worse off than those to whom they compare themselves. Using a sample of 378 white adults in Cincinnati, Ohio, Agnew et al. find that dissatisfaction with current monetary situation is positively related to income-generating crime and drug use. Thus, dissatisfaction with one's monetary situation (relative deprivation) can occur at all class levels and may explain the weak findings between crime and class in past research.

In sum, research suggests that empirical support for classic strain models is greater than originally believed. Gaps between aspirations and expectations may not be relevant but perceptions of blocked opportunities, relative deprivation, and dissatisfaction with one's monetary situation seem to predict involvement in crime. It is clear, however, that most tests of classic strain have used extremely simplistic conceptions of strain. Only in the past few years have tests begun to approximate the more nuanced views of strain proposed by Merton. Yet with few exceptions (e.g., Menard 1995), these studies fail to consider the crucial element of *adaptation* to strain. Thus, nearly all studies measure strain rather than the individual response to it. In the next section, we discuss the measurement of additional sources of strain suggested by Agnew's general strain theory.

General Strain

Agnew (1985, 1992, 1995a, 1995b, 1995c, 2001, 2006) claims that economic frustration is only one type of strain that an individual can experience and that noneconomic strains may also be criminogenic. He lists three types of strains that can lead to crime. The first is being unable to achieve a goal, which would include the blocked opportunities for economic success that Merton focused on, but could also refer to noneconomic goals. The second is the removal of some positive stimulus, or losing something that is valued—for example, losing a job or being dumped by your boyfriend or girlfriend. The third is the presentation of a negative stimulus, such as being treated poorly by others. Agnew argues that any of these strains can trigger what he calls negative affective (emotional) states, which cause some people to respond in antisocial or criminal ways. The next section describes the measurement of negative emotional states such as anger, frustration, and depression in more detail. For now we focus on how strain has been measured in tests of general strain theory.

As just noted, Agnew focuses on major sources of strain that can lead to crime by causing negative emotional states. In Agnew's (1985) earliest revisions of Merton's strain theory, he focused on the inability to escape aversive or negative situations. He notes that juveniles often find themselves in environments over which they have limited control (school and family). If these environments are unpleasant (aversive), juveniles may become frustrated and try to escape or become involved in anger-based crimes. Agnew tests this argument using a nationally representative sample of 2,213 boys in public high schools in 1966 as part of the Youth in Transition study. He measures aversive home situations with a 10-item scale of parental punitiveness. He also includes a 3-item scale called mean teacher and a 23-item scale tapping school dissatisfaction. Finally, he includes a 9-item scale measuring anger. The dependent variables include a 10-item delinquency scale, interpersonal aggression, and attempts to escape school. After controlling for social control and social learning theory variables, Agnew finds that aversive family and school environments have a direct effect on delinquency, but also have an indirect effect through anger. Path models show that parental punitiveness, mean teachers, and dissatisfaction with school all contribute to higher levels of anger, which ultimately lead to greater delinquency. Agnew concludes that the inability to avoid aversive situations creates anger, which then leads to higher rates of crime and drug use.

Because Agnew realized that cross-sectional analyses such as his 1985 study cannot address causation, he developed a longitudinal test of his revisions of strain theory. Once again using the Youth in Transition survey, Agnew (1989) developed a two-wave panel model (separated by 1.5 years) that is estimated with structural equation modeling (SEM) techniques. SEM techniques combine several empirical indicators that are measured imperfectly into one underlying construct. Using SEM, one can then examine the relationships between these unmeasured underlying constructs, using the information from the measured variables. Agnew includes measures of adversity and crime but does not include measures of the intervening variable of anger. He estimates SE models with the three indicators of aversive environments from the 1985 study as indicators of adversity and the three dependent variables from the 1985 study (described earlier) as indicators of delinquency. Results suggest that adversity leads to delinquency, but the model does not explain *why* this is so because measures of anger or other negative emotional states are not included in the model.

As Agnew's revisions of Merton's strain theory evolved, he considered more events expected to produce strain. In another study, Agnew and White (1992) included additional measures of strain: negative life events (e.g., criminal victimization, parental divorce or job loss, serious illness or injury), life hassles (e.g., not getting along with friends or not having enough time to do things they want to do), negative relations with adults (e.g., parents or teachers), parental fighting, living in an unsafe neighborhood, unpopularity with the opposite sex, occupational strain, and clothing strain (e.g., lack of money for clothes). To determine whether these strains lead to crime, Agnew and White use data from the Rutgers Health and Human Development project, a longitudinal study of 1,380 New Jersey adolescents ages 12, 15, and 18 from 1979 to 1981. They include a 13-item general delinquency scale and a drug use scale. Agnew and White find that five of the strain measures are significant predictors of drug use and delinquency, but unpopularity, clothing strain, and occupational strain do not predict either. They also conduct preliminary longitudinal analyses that are supportive of the general strain theory approach.

Paternoster and Mazerolle (1994) conducted another longitudinal test of general strain theory using the National Youth Survey, which includes 1,525 children ages 11 to 17. Their strain measures include neighborhood problems, negative life events, negative relations with adults, hassles at school and with peers, and a measure of classic strain. The dependent variable was a 20-item list of delinquent behaviors in the previous 12 months. Paternoster and Mazerolle found that four of the five measures of strain (all except their classic strain measure) predict current and future delinquency, controlling for social learning and social control variables. They do not measure the intervening variables of anger and frustration, however.

Early tests of general strain theory mainly used cumulative measures of strain such as a measure of stressful life events, based on Agnew's (1992) assertion that strains are likely cumulative. Some research even showed that anticipated or vicarious strains can induce crime (Agnew 2002). Agnew (2001, 2006) now argues that only some types of strain are likely to lead to crime so global, cumulative measures will water down the effect of those crime-producing strains. Summarizing prior research, he concludes that physical and verbal abuse, parental rejection, poor school performance, and work problems are probably related to crime, whereas unpopularity and failure to achieve education or occupational success are likely not. In so doing, Agnew (2001) describes four conditions under which one would expect strain to produce crime. First, the strain is seen as unjust. Strains are most likely to be seen as unjust if they are voluntary and intentional violations of a relevant justice norm. So being robbed is more likely to be considered unjust than is losing one's wallet, even though both result in the loss of money. Second, the strain is one high in magnitude. Third, strains that are low in social control such as erratic parenting, parental rejection, secondary labor market employment, and homelessness are likely to be crime-producing. Finally, strains that create pressures or incentives for criminal responses increase the likelihood of criminal behavior. For example, teasing on the streets in the inner city is likely to create pressure to respond violently to maintain one's reputation. All four strains are expected to be equal in magnitude, and the absence of one reduces the likelihood of crime, unless the strain is extraordinarily high in magnitude or extremely unjust. Many stressful life events probably do not meet the four criteria and are therefore unlikely to be criminogenic. Based on his characterization, Agnew lists several criminogenic strains: desire for money, thrills, obtaining autonomy/masculinity, parental rejection, overly strict or erratic discipline, child abuse/neglect, negative secondary school experiences, work in the secondary labor market, homelessness, abusive peer relationships, criminal victimization, and the experience of discrimination.

Agnew (2001) suggests that researchers examine the relationships between these individual types of strain and crime, rather than considering their cumulative effects. Once the individual strains that are criminogenic have been verified, then one could presumably develop scales weighted by the relative contributions each strain would produce. He also suggests that research should examine the extent to which certain strains are more closely associated with certain crimes and whether strains are group- or age-specific. Because Agnew's specification of criminogenic strains is so recent, little research has tested this version of general strain theory. One recent test was conducted on street youth by Baron (2004). The sample included 400 mostly male respondents under age 25 in Vancouver who currently were or had experienced homelessness in the previous 12 months. Strain measures included monetary dissatisfaction, deprivation, number of months of homelessness, number of times being physically attacked or threatened, and robbery or theft victimization. Baron also measured anger through a four-item scale. The dependent variables were substance abuse and crime. Baron finds that nearly all of the individual strain measures were significantly related to crime and that anger only mediated the effect of some of these variables. Thus, Agnew appears to be correct—individual strains should be measured separately. Other recent studies also find that particular strains can be criminogenic. For example, several recent studies have linked the exposure to community violence and other stressful life events to crime (Eitle and Turner 2002; Hoffman and Cerbone 1999) and gang involvement (Eitle, Gunkel, and Van Gundy 2004). Still other research has linked child and adolescent maltreatment to crime and drug use (Benda and Corwyn 2002; Brezina 1998, 1999; Ireland, Smith, and Thornberry 2002).

In general, early research on the relationship between strain and crime suggested by general strain theory is supportive. Recently, Agnew (2001, 2006) argued that only certain types of strain are expected to lead to crime. Although it is too early to tell whether this is supported empirically, at least some direct and indirect evidence suggests that specifying the types of strain most likely to lead to crime is a worthwhile enterprise. However, the failure to include negative emotions such as anger in most early tests of Agnew's general strain theory meant these were only partial tests of the theory. Recent research has begun to consider this crucial intervening variable. In the next section, we discuss research on negative affective states such as anger, frustration, depression, and fear that are hypothesized to intervene between strain and crime.

Negative Affective States

Agnew (1992) notes that strains may cause negative emotions such as anger, depression, disappointment, or fear, but that anger is expected to be most criminogenic. Anger is expected to lead to crime because it is based on external attributions of blame, creates desire for redress/retaliation, and empowers the person. Other emotions such as depression are internally focused and tend to deempower the person.

The earliest test of general strain theory to include negative affective states is Agnew (1985). Using the Youth in Transition survey, Agnew measures anger with a nine-item scale. High scorers tend to "lose their temper easily, carry a chip on their shoulder, feel like a powder keg ready to explode, are irritated by small things, hold grudges, and 'feel like' verbally and physically aggressing against parents" (p. 158). Agnew finds that aversive events affect crime through anger. In other words, bad things happen that make people angry and they commit crimes as a result. Also using the Youth in Transition study, Brezina (1996) includes measures of anger, depression, anxiety, and resentment. He finds that strain leads to a variety of negative emotions such as anger, resentment, anxiety, and depression. He also finds that engaging in delinquency seems to (at least temporarily) reduce the negative emotions associated with strain. Thus, Brezina concludes that the study supports general strain theory because negative emotions appear to be a consequence of strain, and delinquency appears to be a coping mechanism to reduce strain. Few other studies have included measures of depression or anxiety in their tests of general strain theory (see Simons, Chen, Stewart, and Brody 2003).

Studies that include negative affective states focus mainly on anger. For example, Mazerolle and Piquero (1997) examine the role of anger in a survey of 245 male college students in 1994. Mazerolle and Piquero (p. 330) measure anger through responses to four statements: "I lose my temper easily"; "When I am angry at people, I feel more like hurting them than talking to them about why I am angry"; "When I am really angry, other people better stay away from me"; and "When I have a serious disagreement with someone, it's usually hard for me to talk calmly about it without getting upset." When these items were combined into a scale, the reliability coefficient was .78, suggesting that they all tapped a single dimension of anger. For the dependent variable, the survey describes a scenario in which a young couple is in a bar and the man goes to the restroom. When the man returns, another man is talking to his girlfriend. After exchanging words, the boyfriend hits the other male, instigating a fight. Respondents were asked to indicate the likelihood on a scale from 0 to 10 that they would have reacted similarly to the boyfriend. The survey included a cumulative measure to capture failure to achieve goals, presentation of negative stimuli, and the removal of positive stimuli. Consistent with general strain theory, Mazerolle and Piquero find that strain is positively related to anger and that anger increases the likelihood that one would indicate intentions to engage in assaultive behavior. Of course, an important question is whether the intention to engage in violent behavior is the same as actually engaging in violent behavior.

In a similar study, Mazerolle and Piquero (1998) surveyed 429 male and female students about a drinking and driving scenario, 249 males about a fighting scenario, and 186 females regarding a shoplifting scenario. Their goal was to examine the relationship between strains, anger, and a variety of illegal behaviors. They find that some types of strains are related to anger (feelings of injustice and living in a bad neighborhood) but many are not. They do not find much support for a general relationship between strain and intentions to engage in illegal activity; only intentions to engage in fighting were related to anger. The authors acknowledge, however, that the college student sample and the use of vignettes may limit the study as a test of general strain theory.

Aseltine, Gore, and Gordon (2000) also suggest that general strain theory may better account for violent crime than for nonviolent crime or drug use. In a three-wave panel study of 939 high school students in Boston, they examine the relationship between strains (family conflict, peer conflict, and negative life events), negative affective states (anxiety and anger) and crime (violent, nonviolent, and marijuana use). General strains led to anger and anxiety, which led to violent offenses but not nonviolent and drug offenses. Mazerolle et al. (2000) also found that strain was directly related to violence but not drug use or school related deviance. Contrary to general strain theory, however, Mazerolle et al. did not find that strain led to anger. In fact, their results suggest the opposite: Angry youth appeared to experience aversive situations and events leading to violence selectively. We consider the implications of this later in the chapter.

Up to this point, it has been assumed that negative affective states such as anger will automatically make criminal behavior more likely. Broidy (2001) suggests, however, that the likelihood that negative emotional states will lead to crime depends on the availability of legitimate coping strategies. Using a convenience sample of 896 college students at Northwestern in 1995, Broidy includes measures of blocked goals, unfair outcomes, stress, anger, and other negative emotions and a scale that indicates the degree of coping skills for dealing with negative life events. She documents a relationship between unjust outcomes, stressful events, and anger and finds that anger increases (but other negative emotions decrease) involvement in criminal activity. It appears that anger leads to criminal coping strategies whereas other negative emotions trigger legal coping strategies. Broidy also notes that females appear less likely to respond with anger, although when angry, females respond similarly to males. Thus the source of strain influences the type of negative affect, which in turn influences whether a legitimate or a nonlegitimate coping strategy is employed.

Capowich, Mazerolle, and Piquero (2001) argue that all previous studies of general strain theory have measured only what they call trait or dispositional anger. Trait anger refers to people that anger easily. Situational anger refers to anger in response to a particular situation. Using a scenario approach similar to Mazerolle and Piquero (1997, 1998), Capowich et al. surveyed college students and asked them to rate the extent to which a given scenario would make them angry. Scenarios included intentions to fight, engage in drunk driving, and shoplift. Similar to other studies, they found that situational anger measures related to violence but not shoplifting or drug use. In contrast, they found that generalized negative emotions predicted drug use and shoplifting (see also Mazerolle, Piquero, and Capowich 2003). As shown, although more research is necessary, recent studies suggest that anger is criminogenic under some circumstances. The key is to specify how and when anger and crime are related.

Measuring Crime

The issue of which crimes anomie and strain theories should be expected to explain has been discussed at some length. A narrow reading of Merton might suggest that only crimes for economic gain would result from strain. A broader reading suggests that both economically motivated (utilitarian) *and* nonutilitarian crimes are in the domain of the theory (Burton et al. 1994; Farnworth and Lieber 1989). Studies of anomie and strain have considered both the prevalence and the frequency of crime. Recall that few, if any, macro-level studies have directly tested Merton's anomie theory. In this section, we first discuss macro-level measures of crime used in tests of institutional anomie theory. We then discuss individual measures of crime used in tests of classic and general strain theory.

Tests of institutional anomie theory have primarily measured crime in terms of homicide, regardless of the unit of analysis, from counties to metropolitan areas to nations (Maume and Lee 2003; Messner and Rosenfeld

1997b; Savolainen 2000). Chamlin and Cochran (1995) offer one of the few tests of institutional anomie to focus on crimes other than homicide. Their dependent variable combined rates of robbery, burglary, larceny, and auto theft. Studies likely focus on homicide for two reasons. First, homicide is a serious offense that citizens and governments are legitimately most concerned about. Second, data collection systems and crime definitions are simply not compatible enough to make comparisons of most other crimes meaningful. This limitation presents a serious challenge to the generality of institutional anomie theory. It is simply not known how well institutional anomie can explain other crimes.

Individual-level studies of classic and general strain have been numerous and measure crime in a variety of ways. Burton and Cullen (1992) suggest that advocates of classic strain theory seriously consider what domain of crime to which the theory should be applied. Some argue that Merton would suggest that anomie creates strain based on economic considerations. If true, one would expect classic strain variables to be more strongly related to utilitarian (economically motivated) crimes than to "crimes of passion." Of course, this assumes that one can divide up crimes into utilitarian and nonutilitarian categories relatively straightforwardly. How does one decide whether a crime is utilitarian or not? For example, is robbery a utilitarian crime? What about a homicide that results from a fight over money that one person owes another? The distinction is easier to make theoretically than empirically.

Some tests of classic strain theory consider utilitarian crime (Agnew et al. 1996; Farnworth and Lieber 1989), others consider more general crime measures (Burton and Dunaway 1994; Burton et al. 1994; Farnworth and Lieber 1989), and still others focus specifically on drug use (Agnew et al. 1996; Burton et al. 1994; Burton and Dunaway 1994). Recent, more comprehensive tests do not suggest that classic strain measures are more strongly linked to one type of crime than another. Thus, it appears that Menard (1995) is correct: Merton's theory can explain both utilitarian and nonutilitarian crime.

Studies of general strain theory have measured violent, property, or drug offenses separately (Agnew 1989; Baron 2004) or used indices that combine these (Agnew and White 1992; Paternoster and Mazerolle 1994). Although some studies show that general strains are related to all three crime types, some evidence suggests that the theory better explains violent crime, especially when the intervening variable of anger is included in the models. Finally, several tests of general strain theory have considered *intended* actions as the dependent variable, rather than actual criminal behavior (Capowich et al. 2001; Mazerolle and Piquero 1997, 1998; Mazerolle et al. 2003). Now that we have reviewed the major concepts of anomie and strain theories, we discuss several measurement issues in the existing literature.

Summary Critique of Measurement Issues

Beginning with Merton, anomie and strain theories became one of the most popular explanations of variation in crime rates across groups and societies and, later, across individuals. Yet the previous review suggests that empirical support is not the only or even the primary criterion by which a theory becomes popular or declines in popularity (Burton and Cullen 1992). Macro-level components of Merton's theory have clearly been subjected to little testing, whereas Messner and Rosenfeld's (2001a) institutional anomie theory has been tested some. The failure to test the macro-level components of Merton's theory is perhaps understandable, given that such testing requires data on the degree to which societies focus on particular goals and means. The difficulty of obtaining such data for a sufficient number of countries is likely the reason the theory has largely gone untested. Perhaps a better approach would be to consider a qualitative study of cultural goals, norms for achieving them, and crime rates across societies. Although a few tests of institutional anomie theory have been conducted, most test only propositions derived from the theory because of some of the same difficulties faced in testing Merton's anomie theory. Therefore, proponents of institutional anomie face the challenge of finding innovative ways to test the theory. It also seems imperative to determine which institutions should be included. Although Messner and Rosenfeld (2001a) do not include religion, Chamlin and Cochran (1995) do include a measure of religious participation. Similarly, the effects of the mass media could be considered.

Most research has focused on the individual-level component of Merton's theory. The studies described here suggest that there is mixed support for the relationship between Merton's classic view of economic strain and crime. Early research, for the most part, focused on simplistic specifications of strain in terms of a disjunction between economic aspirations and expectations, but this oversimplifies Merton's arguments. Thus, evidence showing a lack of relationship between this disjunction and crime should not be grounds for discarding Merton (e.g., Agnew et al. 1996; Burton and Cullen 1992; Farnworth and Lieber 1989). More recent and sophisticated tests of classic strain have been more supportive. Yet work remains to clarify which aspects of classic strain are most strongly linked to crime, especially given one recent study that showed that the classic strain model was supported for whites but not blacks (Cernkovich et al. 2000). Another major limitation of classic strain research is the failure to consider the range of adaptations suggested by Merton, as shown in Table 5.1. The most common adaptation is conformity. The adaptation most clearly linked to crime is innovation, where one retains the goal of success but rejects institutionally accepted means for achieving it (or are blocked from legitimate success). As such, one would expect to see higher crime rates among those that (a) feel strain and (b) reject culturally accepted means of achieving them (or at least don't regard the legitimate means as necessary). Yet most researchers focus only on measuring strain and fail to include measures to capture individual adaptations to strain (one exception is Menard 1995). Part of this, no doubt, is because Merton failed to provide guidance on the conditions that would lead to particular responses to strain. But to test the theory properly one must measure adaptations to strain, not strain itself. Menard suggests it makes sense to think in terms of conventional and unconventional responses rather than the five modes of adaptation.

He finds general support for this conception of classic strain in that innovators and retreatists tend to have higher rates of criminal behavior than conformists and ritualists do.

Many also simply include objective measures of strain rather than the subjective *feeling* of strain, which is admittedly more difficult but more consistent with Merton's theory (see Passas 1997). Passas argues that the subjective feeling of strain is a necessary precursor to crime (but see Bernard 1987) and suggests that feeling strain will depend on the person's reference group. Feeling strain may be as much about the person one compares oneself to as about one's objective situation. This opens the door for measures of relative deprivation and helps free Merton from the "baggage" of the class–crime relationship.

Burton and Cullen (1992) also suggest that researchers should more fully explore the meaning of success. Agnew (1997) notes that most studies assume that people only pursue one goal and cannot adjust their expectations in light of new evidence. There are also some questions as to whether people in all parts of the social structure adopt similar goals. Poor people may adjust their expectations depending on the success of others in their reference group. Therefore more research is needed on the assumption that the goal of economic success is paramount and that individuals do not pursue multiple goals. Another question is whether strains are age-graded. Some evidence suggests that the effects of economic strain grow stronger as adolescents age (Menard 1995). Since many early tests of classic strain were conducted on high school samples, it could be that the respondents were too young to feel strong cultural pressure for economic success.

With respect to Agnew's general strain theory, some support exists for the view that a variety of crimes result from noneconomic strains, although this support is not unequivocal. Yet research including negative affective states suggests that the model explains violent crimes better than property crimes or drug use. More research is needed to compare general strain models explicitly for violent and nonviolent crimes, including measures of negative affective states. Agnew (2006) also notes that many studies combine strains in an additive fashion (i.e., more strains = more crime), but this does not allow one to determine which strains are most likely to lead to crime. Therefore, one goal of future research is to identify the most criminogenic strains. Agnew (2001, 2006) offers criteria to determine which strains are expected to lead to crime, but research has yet to evaluate these criteria.

Although originally Agnew suggested that several negative affective states could lead to crime, more recently he has focused squarely on anger, which has been the focus of much research. Studies generally find that anger mediates some of the effects of strain on crime, but many find that strains retain an independent effect on crime separate from the effect they have on one's emotions. Yet general strain theory argues that strains are criminogenic *because* they produce negative emotions. Therefore, clarification is needed on why one would expect strains to produce crime independent of the negative emotions they produce. In addition, few studies have included measures of depression or other negative affective states. Most recently, Agnew (2006) argues that anger is the primary negative affective state to consider, but some studies show a link between depression and other negative emotions and crime (Bao, Haas, and Pi 2004; DeCoster and Heimer 2001). Therefore, studies should clarify the role of depression. Agnew (2006) also notes that research has primarily measured emotional *traits* (people with tempers) rather than emotional *states* (being angry in a situation), despite the fact that the theory suggests that emotional *states* are associated with crime. Research should examine whether negative emotional states explain the effects of strains on crime and whether particular emotions are tied to particular kinds of offenses or whether some people simply are more likely to respond to given situations with anger. Finally, general strain theory suggests that coping mechanisms may blunt the impact of strains on crime, but few studies have considered such coping mechanisms (e.g., Broidy 2001).

Analytical Issues

In this section we consider how studies should be designed to test anomie and strain theories. We also consider issues of causal modeling and causal ordering of variables suggested by the theories, as well as potential alternative explanations.

Study Design

In designing a study to test anomie and strain theories, several key questions must be addressed. First, what is the proper unit of analysis? Second, what method of data collection will best capture the most relevant data for testing the theory? Third, whom should be sampled? And finally, should studies be cross-sectional or longitudinal?

Anomie and strain theories are explicitly designed to explain variation in crime rates *and* why some individuals commit crime, so the appropriate unit of analysis depends on whether one is considering the macro- or micro-level components of the theories. With respect to Merton's and Messner and Rosenfeld's anomie theories, ideally one would compare societies to each other. Anomie is clearly a property of societies, and as such, to properly test either version, one must have data from a variety of countries. Although some tests of institutional anomie theory have compared crime rates across countries, studies also have employed smaller units of analysis such as states, cities, and counties (Chamlin and Cochran 1995; Maume and Lee 2003). It is appropriate to question whether these studies test institutional anomie theory as Messner and Rosenfeld originally intended. More cross-national research is needed to test the empirical validity of institutional anomie theory. Agnew's (1999) macro-level strain theory is easier to test because it is applicable to lower levels of aggregation such as communities. Thus it would be testable in similar ways to social disorganization theory discussed in Chapter 4.

Because strain theories are meant to explain why some individuals commit crime and others don't, individuals constitute the appropriate unit of analysis.

Studies of both classic and general strain have appropriately been conducted at the individual level. Yet choosing the right unit of analysis is only the starting point for testing a theory. The next step is to consider the best strategy for collecting the data most suitable for capturing the key theoretical concepts. A variety of methods could be chosen such as observational studies, experiments, and surveys.

Although no studies use experimental methods, one could imagine experiments to consider both classic and general strain theory hypotheses. The limited relationship between the experimental setting and "the real world" no doubt accounts for the limited use of experiments in testing strain theories. The use of vignettes such as those used by Mazerolle and Piquero (1997, 1998), however, might be an interesting avenue to pursue. One could imagine setting up scenarios that vary elements crucial to general strain theory such as strain and anger and then determining whether these are related to people's stated intentions to engage in criminal behavior. Qualitative research techniques also could be used to examine the development and consequences of strain (see Agnew and White 1992; Burton and Cullen 1992). Such methods might do a better job of capturing the aspects of strain that are most relevant to crime, especially for general strain theory. Surveys simply may not capture the most important aspects of strain or the kinds most likely to lead to crime. Therefore, future research should consider the use of intensive observation or interview techniques to clarify the aspects of strain most relevant to crime.

In any event, surveys have mainly been used in tests of classic and general strain theories. This is a reasonable approach, but Agnew (2006) argues that surveys do not do a very good job of teasing out interaction effects. An interaction effect is when the influence of one variable on another depends on the value of third variable. For example, recall that Hoffman (2002) found that the influence of stressful events on delinquency depended on characteristics of the neighborhood. Both classic strain and general strain models suggest interaction effects. Therefore, if survey methods do not capture interaction effects well, then they may be biased against empirical support for these theories. Of course, if true, this limitation of surveys would be relevant to tests of several theories of crime discussed throughout the book.

Once survey methods have been chosen, the next question is whom to include in the sample. Most early tests of classic strain theory were conducted on high school samples because teens in school are easy to survey and because this age group is disproportionately involved in crime. But this choice may have implications for tests of classic and general strain theory. For classic strain it is reasonable to question whether kids in high school really feel strong pressure to succeed economically and whether this would lead to crime. Teenagers likely have other more pressing concerns such as popularity, dating, and success in school. Therefore, if Merton's version of strain doesn't manifest itself fully until one enters adulthood, then high school samples are largely inappropriate for studying the theory. A few tests of classic strain have used adult samples, but more research could certainly be done.

A similar question arises for general strain theory. Agnew focuses on the adverse events that lead to negative emotions and crime. Yet it is possible that different events will produce negative emotions for people at different stages in life. So, for example, a teenager may be angered at being brushed off by friends, whereas an adult might simply ignore the behavior. The question of whether people of all ages feel the same strains equally is an important one for general strain theory. Some research has been done on adults (Piquero and Sealock 2000; Slocum, Simpson, and Smith 2005), but most has primarily used high school or college samples. In short, more studies should consider whether the general strain model is invariant over the life course.

Another question is whether classic or general strain models are invariant across groups such as race and gender. Merton did not imply that adaptations to strain would vary by gender, but one can imagine that the experience of strain might vary by gender. This is especially likely when one considers gender role expectations for income and parenting. Women are still often seen as mothers and men are seen as breadwinners. Similarly, although the general strain model was initially gender neutral, some now suggest that different models may be needed for male and female crime (Broidy and Agnew 1997). Agnew's (2006) more recent writings suggest that higher crime rates for males may occur because males experience different kinds of strain and because men are more likely to respond with outwardly directed anger, whereas females are more likely to respond in ways that denigrate themselves. To this point, some research has shown evidence of gender differences (Agnew and Brezina 1997; Piquero and Sealock 2004), whereas other studies suggest a gender invariant process (Hoffman and Su 1997; Mazerolle 1998). Further research is needed to clarify whether and how the general strain model varies by gender.

A related study design issue has to do with whether minorities view the American Dream similarly to whites. Some evidence suggests that they may not (Cernkovich et al. 2000). Therefore, future research on classic strain needs to consider further whether models apply equally well across race, in addition to gender. To date, few studies have examined racial differences from the general strain perspective (e.g., Jang and Johnson 2003). One recent study found that discrimination experienced by African Americans is a distinct source of strain that can be criminogenic, particularly for boys (Simons et al. 2003). Here again, more research is needed that explicitly compares the experience of strain and the responses to it across different race and ethnic groups (see also Bernard 1990).

Yet another important study design issue is whether to use cross-sectional or longitudinal data. Nearly all studies of classic strain theory have been cross-sectional, but Burton and Cullen (1992) argue that this assumes that the strain process is static rather than dynamic. If strain builds over time, cross-sectional data may not capture its effects. To better test these theories, one would need longitudinal data (Menard 1995). The opposite problem exists for general strain theory. Agnew explicitly argues that strains induce negative affective states and the person responds with antisocial behavior. If anger occurs shortly after experiencing a negative life event, then one would expect a more or less instantaneous response to relieve anger. Therefore, longitudinal data may miss the relationship between strains, anger, and crime because data collection periods are typically 12 or 18 months apart (Agnew and White 1992).

Model Specification and Causal Ordering

To test a theory, the relationship between constructs must be considered, which refers to issues of model specification and causal ordering. Table 5.4 suggests several possible ways of thinking about the link between classic or general strain and crime. For example, Merton's original argument suggests that anomic societies produce strain on individuals and, in some cases, those feeling strain will reject the socially accepted means to success and turn to innovative (criminal) ways to achieve economic success. This would suggest an indirect relationship between strain and crime, which is mediated by one's response to strain. Others claim that objectively being strained leads to crime directly. Still others argue that objective strains lead to subjective feelings of strain, which lead to crime. The difference between these latter two perspectives lies in the relative importance of how the individual perceives his or her situation. Similarly, relative deprivation arguments suggest that crime is the result of feeling deprived relative to others to whom the person compares himself or herself. Thus, an issue is whether the key causal factor is objective strain or the subjective experience of strain or deprivation. For testing the theories, measuring objective strains may lead to different data collection methods than measuring the subjective experience of strain.

The more general question this discussion raises is whether anomie and strain are directly related to crime or indirectly related to crime through their influence on other factors or whether the effects of anomie or strain on crime depend on additional factors. This is an important question because it determines the variables that need to be measured to test the theory. For example, Merton suggested that innovation (crime) was only one individual response to strain but didn't specify the conditions that would lead to innovation (or

Table 5.4 Potential Relationships between Strain and Delinquency

Classic Strain

1. Strain → Rejection of Approved Means → Innovation (Crime)
2. Objective Strain → Crime
3. Objective Strain → Subjective Strain → Crime
4. Relative Deprivation → Crime

General Strain

5. General Strain → Crime
6. General Strain → Negative Affective State → Crime
7. Negative Emotionality → Strain → NAS → Crime

any other response). If Merton is correct, then properly testing classic strain theory involves measuring both objective (and potentially subjective) strains as well as the ways individuals respond to those strains. Thus, we need research to determine what makes innovation more likely than other adaptations. This is also where other factors (that then must be measured) could enter in. For example, the likelihood that strain will produce innovation could depend on whether people blame themselves or the social order for their failures. Similarly, the strength of a person's commitment to institutional norms could affect the likelihood that strain will produce crime. Thus, if a person has internalized the idea that stealing is wrong, then losing his or her job is not likely to lead to crime. The presence of delinquent friends (see Chapter 6) might also make innovation more likely in response to strain. All of these factors can influence the likelihood that strain will lead to crime, suggesting that the strain–crime relationship is conditional. The direct, indirect, or conditional nature of the relationship between strain and crime is an empirical question that needs to be resolved. Although some studies have addressed this issue (Agnew et al. 1996; Cullen 1983), more attention should be focused on resolving these questions in future research.

Similar issues arise when considering how to test institutional anomie theory. Messner and Rosenfeld (1997b) posit direct relationships between institutional anomie and crime, finding that homicides are lower in countries that have a greater social support network. On the other hand, Savolainen (2000) suggests that the influence of institutional anomie on crime is conditional, specifically that the effect of inequality on homicide depends on the strength of the welfare state. In contrast, Maume and Lee (2003) in their county-level study of homicide find minimal evidence of interaction effects, but noneconomic institutions serve as buffers in a causal sequence. The conflicting evidence on the direct, indirect, or conditional relationship between institutional anomie and crime requires further research to resolve this ambiguity.

A similar issue is germane for general strain theory. Most early tests of general strain measured only the factors likely to cause negative affective states and crime. This strategy would be adequate if the theory suggested a direct relationship between general strains and crime. More recent research has attempted to capture the nuances of general strain theory by measuring the negative affective states posited to affect crime. This is more consistent with Agnew's theory, which suggests that there is an indirect relationship between general strains and crime that is mediated by negative affective states. The relationship between general strains, negative affective states, and crime might also be conditional. For example, the likelihood that bad things happening could produce negative affective states may depend on a person's coping skills, general mental stability, or support networks. So, a well-adjusted person with a strong social support network is likely to respond very differently to negative life events than is someone with few coping skills and sources of social support. Some recent tests of general strain theory provide support for the idea that the relationship between strains, negative affective states, and crime is conditional (Agnew et al. 2002; Mazerolle and Maahs 2000), whereas others document a more direct relationship (Aseltine, Gore, and Gordon 2000). Further research should clarify which strains produce the negative affective states most likely to lead to crime and under what conditions.

Causal Order Issues

Another important issue when testing theories of crime is causal order. The discussion up to this point suggests that strains lead to crime, but the reverse may be true. In other words, strains could also be an outcome of delinquency. For example, if a person gets arrested and loses his job, he is likely to feel strain. In this case, crime would cause strain rather than the opposite. If such a relationship exists, the frequent use of cross-sectional methods to test strain theories is problematic because cross-sectional studies are unable to tell which came first, the strain or the crime. Fortunately, longitudinal studies can tease out the proper causal order of the variables, but to date few of these studies have been conducted.

A similar issue pertains to general strain theory. Mazerolle et al. (2000) argue that anger leads to strain rather than the reverse. General strain theory would say that breaking up with your girlfriend could produce anger or depression, which may lead to crime. However, if the reason that your girlfriend broke up with you is because of your temper, then negative affective states would lead to negative life events rather than the reverse. Further research is needed to tease out these causal order issues for both classic and general strain theories. Of course as we've seen from previous chapters, the need for additional longitudinal studies to determine the proper causal order is not unique to anomie and strain theories.

Potential Alternative Explanations

In determining the level of support for any theory it is important to rule out alternative explanations. With respect to strain theory, Agnew (2001) notes the difficulty of distinguishing measures of strain from measures of social control in terms of independent variables (see also Agnew 1987, 1997; Bernard 1984, 1987, 1995; Messner 1988). For example, social control theory points to many of the same factors that strain theories do. However, social control theory posits that these variables free people to follow their natural impulses to commit crime, whereas strain theory argues that these factors create pressure or strains that lead to crime. For strain theory, negative emotions lead to crime from strain, whereas control theory maintains that strains reduce the perceived costs of crime. Which theory is correct? One strategy is to examine the intervening processes (Agnew 2001). A second strategy is to control for social control theory variables and examine whether strain retains an independent effect. A third strategy is to consider apathy versus hatred. For example, if a child hates his or her parents, strain says that this will produce a more criminogenic situation than if he or she is apathetic, whereas control theory claims that apathy and hatred toward parents should both lead to crime. In any event, determining empirical support for classic and general strain theories requires that alternative explanations be ruled out (see also Konty 2005).

Research on anomie and strain theories illustrates the challenges associated with developing tests that accurately represent the complexities in theories under scrutiny. It is often difficult to get quantitative data to test particular theories fully. This is especially true for anomie theories. Perhaps a better approach would be to use qualitative methods to compare the institutional goals and means in societies, or the relative strength of economic and noneconomic institutions, and crime. Finding ways to test the full implications of anomie theories remains a significant challenge.

For studies of classic strain, many early tests failed to capture the concepts of the theory adequately. More recent and sophisticated studies have generally been supportive of the classic strain model. Yet nearly all of these are cross-sectional. Therefore, the causal effect of classic strain on crime remains an open question. There is also the issue of what group is most appropriate to sample. Merton's model is likely most applicable to adults who are in the world of work rather than kids in school. As such, more studies should be conducted using adult samples. There is also the question of whether the relationship between economic strain and crime is direct or conditional. It is plausible that it is conditional, but further research is needed to specify the conditions under which classic strains lead to crime.

General strain theory has been subjected to several tests in a relatively short period of time. Studies have generally shown that a variety of noneconomic strains influence crime, but fewer tests have measured both strain and the intervening emotional states expected to cause crime. The most recent specifications of the theory suggest that certain strains are expected to lead to particular negative emotions, which will lead to crime under certain circumstances. A few studies have tested conditional relationships between strains, emotions, and crime, but the results are somewhat conflicting. There is also the question of whether "anger people" experience situations differently, which leads to strain and crime. Most studies have examined trait anger rather than situational anger, but the theory relates situational anger to crime. Finally, studies of both classic and general strain also need additional research to explicitly consider causal order issues.

Directions for Future Research

Numerous studies have assessed anomie and strain theories born of Merton's seminal arguments. Yet until Messner and Rosenfeld's institutional anomie theory was developed, virtually all of them examined the individual-level effect of strain on crime. A few early studies tested Merton's original arguments regarding strain and crime but were methodologically weak. Therefore, the rejection of this theory was somewhat premature. More recent tests of Merton's classic views of strain suggest stronger evidence in favor of the theory. Tests of Agnew's general strain theory often indicate less favorable evidence for classic strain, but the specification of classic strain in these tests is often relatively superficial. With respect to macro-level anomie theories, no tests of Merton have been conducted, so there is no evidence to directly confirm or dispute the theory's claims. More recent tests of institutional anomie can be viewed as support for Merton's classic arguments to some extent. Yet similar difficulties arise in testing Messner and Rosenfeld's version of the theory. Perhaps the greatest challenge facing macro-level anomie theories is finding ways to provide meaningful tests of the core propositions. This will most likely entail data not currently available or employing qualitative studies. Finally, Agnew's macro-strain theory descends from the anomie/strain tradition. It is more testable because it pertains to lower levels of aggregation such as communities, and therefore offers some promise, but it should be reconciled with other anomie theories.

At the individual level, research on classic strain theory has been far less common in recent years than research on general strain theory has been. This is unfortunate because classic strain models fell out of favor for reasons that had little to do with empirical support for them. The field of criminology would benefit from paying attention to what classic strain models have to offer and engaging in serious testing of nuanced versions of the theory relative to other theories. If classic strain fails in such tests, then it might be time to consider relegating it to the criminological dustbin. Until then, we cannot fully determine what the theory offers.

In contrast, research and theory on Agnew's general strain theory have been vigorous in recent years. This line of research is robust, but it needs to tackle many of the issues we have raised throughout the chapter to become a long-term theory in the field. It seems crucial that general strain theory further specify both the conditions under which strains lead to different negative affective states and under what conditions these strains lead to crime. The recent macro-level version of the theory also seems promising because it could explain individual- and community-level differences in crime, but it is too early to tell what the ultimate utility of macro-level strain theory is without further testing.

Discussion Questions

1. What does institutional anomie theory add to Merton's anomie theory? Which theory do you think is a better explanation of crime?
2. What distinguishes macro-level anomie theories from ecological theories of crime such as social disorganization (Chapter 4)?
3. What is strain? What are the major sources of strain discussed in anomie and strain theories?
4. Is general strain theory a more convincing explanation for why individuals commit crime than classic strain theory?
5. Describe the potential direct and indirect relationships that may exist between strain and delinquency.

CHAPTER 6

SOCIAL LEARNING THEORIES

Introduction

Think about how you learned to read and write. Most likely it was because a teacher or a parent taught you. Now think about why you are not a criminal. Most of us would say we are not criminals because we were taught from an early age that it is wrong to take other people's things or to hurt people unless they are trying to hurt us. So, unlike theories that view crime as a lower-class phenomenon or produced by strain, as the previous chapter described, learning theories argue that criminal behavior is learned from others in a process similar to that which people use to learn to read and write (Vold, Bernard, and Snipes 1998).

Intellectual History of Social Learning Theories

One of the first modern-day criminologists to consider learning and crime was Edwin H. Sutherland (1883–1950). Sutherland's theory of differential association was elaborated over several editions of his book, *Criminology*, which was later revised by Donald Cressey (1955), culminating with the eleventh edition with Cressey and David F. Luckenbill (1992). One of Sutherland's main areas of research interest was white-collar crime. Focusing on law violators who were not poor led him to question the widely held assumption that crime was the result of some deficiency in the lower classes. Instead, he argued that crime is learned like any other behavior and occurs through "differential association," which will be explained in the following pages. Sutherland is considered one of the most influential theorists of modern criminology. He did not specify in detail the learning processes involved in differential association. Subsequently, Burgess and Akers (1966) and Akers (1973, 1985, 1998) reformulated differential association theory to explicitly consider how behaviors are reinforced, using modern psychological learning theories such as operant conditioning, ultimately renaming the theory social learning theory. Recently, Akers (1998) expanded social learning theory to consider how elements of social structure (e.g., neighborhood poverty, social disorganization) affect social learning. Social learning theories have been widely researched, and in this chapter we discuss a number of methodological issues in the tests of differential association and social learning theory, but we begin with a brief statement of what each theory says about why people commit crime.

Differential Association Theory

Sutherland (1947:6–7) stated his theory of criminal behavior in the nine propositions found in Table 6.1. Sutherland distinguished his theoretical position from the biological and psychological theories that dominated early criminological thought by asserting that criminal behavior, like any other behavior, was the outcome of a learning process (proposition 1). This behavior is learned through what is known as symbolic interaction, a perspective that emphasizes that learning takes place in interaction and communication (proposition 2), primarily within intimate personal groups (proposition 3). Because Sutherland comes from a symbolic interactionist perspective, the learning of definitions concerning one's behavior is crucial to the learning process. Although the people we associate with are a key factor in the learning process, our *interpretations* of their behavior and expressed attitudes (definitions) are the key to determining the probability of committing crime. Sutherland noted that we learn both how (techniques) and why (motivations) to commit crime (proposition 4). The motivation to commit crime comes from how a person views legal codes (proposition 5). Individuals who view the law positively will not commit crime. Those who view the law negatively will be more inclined to commit crime. Ultimately, whether a person commits a crime or not depends on his or her "definitions" of the law. An example of a definition favorable to crime would be, "It's okay to cheat if you can get away with it." A definition unfavorable to crime would be, "Stealing is wrong, no matter what."

According to Sutherland, a person becomes a criminal because he or she has an excess of definitions favorable to law violation (proposition 6), which can vary along four dimensions: frequency, duration, priority, and intensity (proposition 7). Frequency refers to how often one is exposed to a definition favorable or unfavorable to crime. Duration refers to the amount of time a person is exposed to a definition. Early definitions take precedence (priority) over later ones. Finally, definitions from those we are emotionally attached to are more intense than others. Therefore, definitions will carry more weight if a person is frequently exposed to them, over a long period of time, and from an early age and if they come from a significant person in their life. So, for example, the 10-year-old boy who sees his older brother smoking marijuana and hears the brother tell him it is just like drinking a beer would be more likely to smoke marijuana than he would be to abstain because some adult stranger on TV says "just say no" to drugs. Note that this is not the same thing as frequency, priority, duration, or intensity of exposure to a delinquent friend or relative. Sutherland specifically argued that it is the exposure to the *definition*, not the person.

Sutherland envisioned that there would be a formula to predict whether a person would be a criminal based on his or her ratio of definitions favorable to crime relative to his or her definitions unfavorable to crime. He also sug-

Table 6.1 Principles of Differential Association

1. Criminal behavior is learned.
2. Criminal behavior is learned in interaction with other persons in a process of communication.
3. The principal part of the learning of criminal behavior occurs within intimate personal groups.
4. When criminal behavior is learned, the learning includes (a) techniques of committing the crime, which are sometimes very complicated, sometimes very simple; (b) the specific direction of motives, drives, rationalizations, and attitudes.
5. The specific direction of motives and drives is learned from definitions of the legal codes as favorable or unfavorable.
6. A person becomes delinquent because of an excess of definitions favorable to violation of law over definitions unfavorable to violation of law.
7. Differential associations may vary in frequency, duration, priority, and intensity.
8. The process of learning criminal behavior by association with criminal and anti-criminal patterns involves all of the mechanisms that are involved in any other learning.
9. While criminal behavior is an expression of general needs and values, it is not explained by those general needs and values since noncriminal behavior is an expression of the same needs and values.

gested that definitions can vary by crime. In other words, a person could believe that shoplifting was acceptable but not armed robbery. Sutherland also believed that social groups or areas can have norms that make law violation acceptable, similar to social disorganization theory (see Chapter 4), although he preferred the term *differential social organization* (Sutherland 1947:8–9). Thus, the theory encompassed both social structural (community characteristics) and social process (learning) components. This raises the possibility of subcultural explanations for crime as different areas or groups might have different cultural beliefs regarding the law (see, e.g., Anderson 1999; Cloward and Ohlin 1960; Cohen 1955; Miller 1958). Yet the majority of Sutherland's discussion and subsequent theory focuses primarily on the social process of learning crime from others. As a consequence, this chapter will also focus on the social process aspects of the theory.

Differential association theory became one of the best-known criminological theories. Despite its popularity, some considered it untestable because its concepts were vague (Akers 1998:33). For instance, think about how you would go about measuring "definitions favorable to crime." What would you count as a definition favorable to crime? Others said the ratio of definitions favorable to or unfavorable to crime would be impossible to measure in the precise way the theory suggests (Cressey 1952). Sutherland was also criticized for failing to specify the mechanisms by which the learning of criminal behavior took place. For instance, do we learn only by seeing others' behavior directly and imitating it, or can learning occur in other ways? To address some of these limitations, several theorists have proposed revisions to the original theory of differential association (Burgess and Akers 1966; Glaser 1960; Heimer and Matsueda 1994; Jeffery 1965; Sykes and Matza 1957). The most prominent of these revisions is social learning theory.

Social Learning Theory

To help clarify the process by which criminal definitions are learned, Burgess and Akers (1966) and Akers (1973, 1985, 1998) expanded differential association to take account of advances in psychological learning principles, renaming it social learning theory. Social learning theory retains Sutherland's focus on definitions favorable to crime but specifies how they are learned. Whereas Sutherland argued that the learning of *ideas* about the law (definitions favorable or unfavorable to crime) drove criminal behavior, social learning theory argues that criminal *behaviors* can also be directly learned (Vold et al. 1998). Social learning theory relies on the psychological principle of operant conditioning, which refers to learning that takes place through responses (social or nonsocial) to a person's behavior. Akers posits that definitions favorable to crime are learned through the process of differential reinforcement. In other words, people will come to believe the definitions for which they are rewarded. Rewards can be things like social approval of family, monetary rewards, or even nonsocial rewards such as the physical high from cocaine. So, if a girl shoplifts and her friends all tell her she is cool, she is more likely to shoplift in the future. But if a girl gets caught shoplifting and her friends won't hang around with her anymore, she is less likely to shoplift in the future. According to Akers (1998), the initiation and persistence of delinquency depends on the degree to which it is rewarded:

> The probability that persons will engage in criminal and deviant behavior is increased and the probability of their conforming to the norm is decreased when they differentially associate with others who commit criminal behavior and espouse definitions favorable to it, are relatively more exposed in-person or symbolically to salient criminal/deviant models, define it as desirable or justified in a situation discriminative for the behavior, and have received in the past and anticipate in the current or future situation relatively greater reward than punishment for the behavior. (p. 50)

Social learning theory focuses on four main concepts: definitions, differential association, differential reinforcement, and imitation (Akers 1998:50). Definitions are orientations, attitudes, and rationalizations that label a behavior as right or wrong, acceptable or unacceptable. Definitions can be general (violence is wrong) or specific (fighting back to protect yourself is okay). The stronger one holds definitions that deem illegal acts as acceptable, the more likely one is to engage in them. Differential association refers to the people with whom one comes into contact. Early in life the family is the primary group. As adolescence approaches, peer influences become greater. In addition to family and friends, teachers, coaches, neighbors, authority figures, and even the media can provide models for behavior as well as rewards or punishments. Differential reinforcement "refers to the balance of anticipated or actual rewards and punishments that follow or are consequences of behavior" (Akers 1998:66–67). Behavior can be increased or decreased in several ways according to learning theory (Akers and Sellers 2004). Each is based on whether the presentation or removal of a stimulus increases or decreases the likelihood of a response. Thus, the likelihood of a response can be increased through either the introduction of a positive stimulus or the removal of a negative one. Conversely, the likelihood of a response can be decreased by the introduction of a negative stimulus or the removal of a positive one. So, for example, positive reinforcement refers to things like obtaining the approval of others, money, food, and positive feelings. To the extent that one expects or receives these things, behavior—criminal or conventional—is expected to increase. Negative reinforcement would increase the likelihood of a response by removing some unpleasant stimulus. For example, fastening your seat belt makes the buzzing stop, removing the negative stimulus. Punishments can also be positive (some unpleasant consequence follows a behavior) or negative (taking away something that is valued). An example of the former would be spanking an unruly child; an example of the latter would be when a parent takes away a favorite toy to punish a child's misbehavior.

Reinforcements and punishments also vary in amount, frequency, and probability, according to Akers (1998). A reward is more to likely reinforce a behavior if it is larger, more frequent, or more probable. Likewise, punishments are expected to reduce or prevent behavior to the extent that they are large, frequent, or probable. Note that deterrence theory suggests that the same effects of "swift, severe, and certain" punishments (see Chapter 2). Thus, criminal behavior is more likely to the extent that one expects large, frequent, or likely rewards or infrequent, unlikely, or small punishment. Similar to Sutherland, Akers predicts that a person's criminal or law-abiding behavior will be most like that of his or her close friends or family because these are the most frequent and regular sources of reinforcement.

The other major reason that our behavior tends to be similar to that of family and friends is imitation. Imitation refers to behavior that is modeled by observing others. For example, seeing an older sibling roll a marijuana joint and smoke it would provide a behavior that could be modeled. Akers argues that imitation is probably more important for the initiation of a behavior than its persistence. In any event, social learning theory suggests that imitation and social reinforcement are the two processes that explain why our behavior is usually most similar to that of friends and family.

More recently Akers (1998) has revised and expanded social learning theory to consider the role of social structure in crime. As noted earlier, Sutherland and Akers' earlier revisions focused mainly on the explanation of individual-level crime differences. In 1998, Akers proposed that social learning theory should explicitly be integrated with macro-level theories of crime. He argued that the elements of social structure considered in other macro-level crime theories such as class, race and ethnicity, gender, age, and marital status all provide the general learning contexts in which the social learning principles of differential association, definitions, differential reinforcement, and imitation operate. So a poor inner-city teen living in a crime-ridden neighborhood will be more likely to be exposed to, and model, delinquent definitions and behaviors than will a rich kid from a rural farming community. Because very little research has tested Aker's social structure and social learning (SSSL) theory (e.g., Lanza-Kaduce and Capece 2003), we will not discuss it here.

To summarize, all social learning theories posit that criminal behavior is the product of learning just like conforming behavior. Sutherland claimed that crime is the result of one learning more definitions favorable than unfavorable to crime. Akers' social learning theory also considers learning but shifts the focus somewhat to argue that criminal behavior is learned through reinforcement. Social learning theories suggest that criminal behavior is learned from other people through a process of differential association. It is important to keep in mind that differential association and social learning are closely related theories but they retain some differences. Throughout this chapter common points and differences between the two theories will be discussed.

Concepts and Measurement Issues

Sutherland argued that crime is learned in communication with others (mainly family and friends) and is the result of having an excess of definitions favorable to crime. These statements permit us to generate several hypotheses that can be tested (see Table 6.2). Whether these hypotheses are supported or not in empirical research will help determine whether we should accept social learning as a cause of criminal behavior.

One hypothesis is that individuals are more likely to commit crime when they spend time with other individuals who commit crime. For children and adolescents, this is likely to mean their friends. In fact, one of the most consistent findings in studies of juvenile crime is that delinquents are more likely to have delinquent friends (Warr 2002). The exact meaning of this finding will be discussed later. Fewer studies have examined the links between family and crime (e.g., Ardelt and Day 2002; Cernkovich and Giordano 1987; McCord 1991; Poole and Regoli 1979; Warr 1993a; Zhang and Messner 1995), which is somewhat surprising given Sutherland's argument that the family is one of the major sources of learned definitions. Similarly, one would expect that a person is more likely to be delinquent if he or she is exposed to definitions favorable to crime by family or friends, particularly if those definitions are longstanding (duration), are frequent, begin early in life (priority), and come from respected sources (intensity). In addition, Sutherland would predict that the association with delinquent definitions or behavior precedes delinquency rather than follows it. We can therefore hypothesize that association with delinquent peers or family will come before delinquency rather than after it.

Akers' social learning theory suggests additional hypotheses. Akers states that criminal behavior is more likely to occur if it is reinforced, so one would hypothesize that crime is more likely if the person believes it will be rewarded (and not punished). Thus, one would expect a girl to shoplift if she thinks her

Table 6.2 Hypotheses Based on Differential Association and Social Learning Theory

Differential Association

1. A person is more likely to commit crime if he or she has delinquent friends.
2. A person is more likely to commit crime if family members commit crime.
3. A person is more likely to commit crime if he or she has more frequent, early, intense, and longstanding exposure to definitions favorable to crime than unfavorable to crime.
4. Association with definitions favorable to crime precedes delinquency.

Social Learning Theory

5. A person is more likely to commit crime if he or she believes the behavior will be rewarded.
6. Those who are rewarded for criminal behavior are more likely to commit crime again.
7. Those who are punished for criminal behavior are less likely to commit crime again.
8. A person is more likely to commit crime if he or she sees others committing crime (imitation).

friends will approve and refrain from it if she thinks they will disapprove. Social learning theory also suggests that seeing others commit criminal activity would provide behavior that can be modeled. One who sees family or friends engage in criminal activity is therefore more likely to engage in this behavior himself through imitation. Although not an exhaustive list of the hypotheses that have been or could be studied, this gives us a reference point to discuss some of the major measurement issues in research on social learning theories.

Let us now consider how to measure the key concepts in differential association and social learning theories. This step is crucial because if the theoretical concepts are not measured adequately, then it is hard to know if negative results are due to bad theories or bad measures of concepts in theories. One longstanding criticism of differential association theory is that Sutherland did not specify the content of definitions favorable to crime. In other words, he never specifically described what constituted favorable or unfavorable crime definitions. Therefore, a critical issue is how to measure the constructs in the theory. In this section, we discuss some of the major concepts to be measured, including crime, definitions and differential association, differential reinforcement, and imitation and describe how they have been operationalized in empirical studies.

Definitions

Differential association theory states that people will commit crime when they hold definitions favorable to crime. From a measurement standpoint, an important issue is the question of what definitions can be considered favorable or unfavorable to crime. Many beliefs would likely be neutral regarding crime. For instance, a person's preference for coffee with or without sugar would likely be unrelated to definitions favorable or unfavorable to crime. Because Sutherland provided minimal guidance, researchers have chosen a number of ways to resolve this issue. Some have attempted to provide specific content to the definitions. Most notably, Sykes and Matza (1957) developed "techniques of neutralization," arguing that most definitions favorable to crime reduce the wrongfulness of, or neutralize, crime rather than make it appear like morally upstanding behavior. Table 6.3 lists Sykes and Matza's five techniques of neutralization. Denial of responsibility is when the person claims that the acts were not his or her fault or were accidents, and therefore he or she shouldn't be held accountable. For example, one could say, "My family was starving so I had to steal the food." Denial of injury is when the person denies that the acts are harmful or wrong and is encompassed in statements like, "I was just borrowing the car" or "Boys will be boys." Denial of victim neutralizes the wrongness of the act by claiming the victim had it coming or by ignoring the rights of some absent victim such as a big corporation. Thus, it is acceptable to steal from Wal-Mart because it makes billions of dollars each year. Condemnation of the condemner means that the person sees the world as a corrupt place and he or she is only committing crime to get by. This shifts the blame from the person to the system. Finally, appeal to higher loyalties refers to a situation in which the person claims that some things are more important than the law, such as providing for family or backing up a friend. An example would be a gang member claiming, "I had to back up my posse." For research on these techniques, see Agnew 1994; Ball 1968; Dabney 1995; Hollinger 1991; Minor 1980, 1981, 1984; and Scully and Moralla 1984.

Another method for determining what constitutes favorable and unfavorable definitions is simply to generate a number of statements about the law, police, and crime and ask the degree to which people agree or disagree with such statements. For our purposes, the question is to what extent these questions accurately measure what it is they are trying to measure (construct validity). Table 6.4 includes a few examples of both general and specific statements that have been used to tap definitions favorable or unfavorable to crime. For instance, using the Richmond Youth survey, Matsueda (1982) and Matsueda and Heimer (1987) include six general statements regarding respect for the police ("Policemen try to give all kids an even break"), general respect for the law ("It is all right to get around the law if you can get away with it"), and some of what Sykes and Matza (1957) would describe as neutralizing definitions ("Most things people call delinquency don't really hurt anyone"). Others include more specific definitions, such as, "How morally wrong is illegal gambling, marijuana smoking, theft, or assault?" (Tittle, Burke, and Jackson 1986).

Table 6.3 Techniques of Neutralization

---

1. Denial of responsibility
2. Denial of injury
3. Denial of victim
4. Condemnation of the condemner
5. Appeal to higher loyalties

Table 6.4 Examples of Definitions Favorable or Unfavorable to Crime

General Definitions (Matsueda 1982)
1. Policemen try to give all kids an even break.
2. Most things that people call delinquency don't really hurt anyone.
3. It is all right to get around the law if you can get away with it.
4. I have a lot of respect for the police.
5. To get ahead you have to do some things which are not right.
6. Suckers deserve to be taken advantage of.

Specific Definitions
1. How morally wrong is each of the following: illegal gambling, tax cheating, $5 theft, $50 theft, marijuana smoking, assault (Tittle, Burke, and Jackson 1986)?
2. What is your attitude toward using marijuana (Akers and Lee 1999)?
3. It takes many years for the bad health effects from smoking (Akers and Lee 1996).
4. Sales of cigarettes should be outlawed (Akers and Lee 1996).

An important question is whether definitions favorable to crime are general or specific. If a person believes *any* law violation is okay, will he or she believe all law violations are okay? From the standpoint of testing theories, this is an important issue because if definitions are general then it doesn't matter which crimes we select. If definitions are crime specific, then we must measure them specific to the crime we are considering; otherwise, finding no association between our measures of definitions and crime could simply mean we didn't ask the right questions. For example, if definitions are general, then a person who thinks smoking marijuana is acceptable would be more likely to think any drug use or even violent crime such as robbery is acceptable. Conversely, if definitions are specific, then a person could believe burglary was acceptable but robbery was wrong. A person might agree that, "It is okay to steal little stuff from big corporations" but disagree that, "Stealing stuff from other people is okay as long as no one gets hurt." The real question is how that person would respond to general questions regarding stealing. People's general attitudes can contain inconsistencies and ambiguities. Therefore, one must be cautious about using general items to tap definitions. Jackson, Tittle, and Burke (1986) suggest that definitions may be crime specific. If this is the case, then empirical support for social learning theories may be less likely to the extent that items tapping general definitions are not as strongly related to criminal behavior as more specific ones are. In general, tests of Akers' social learning theory more consistently link specific definitions to specific behaviors (see Table 6.4 for examples).

It is important to remember that Sutherland predicted crime only when one has an *excess* of definitions favorable to crime. So to truly test the theory, one would need to figure out what definitions are favorable and unfavorable to crime, measure *all* of them, and then calculate a ratio, remembering, of course, to weight the definitions by frequency, duration, priority, and intensity. This is widely recognized to be extremely difficult, if not impossible (Matsueda 1988).

Researchers have, however, resolved the issue of how to measure the excess of definitions in a number of ways. For instance, Matsueda (1982) uses structural equation modeling (SEM) in his test of differential association against social control theory using the Richmond Youth data originally used by Hirschi (see Chapter 7) to validate social control theory (see also Matsueda and Heimer 1987). Matsueda argues that if one thinks of definitions as being on a single continuum from most favorable to most unfavorable then conceivably they could be measured using one underlying construct with several empirical indicators (which SEM permits). The definitions used to measure this underlying construct are listed in Table 6.4. Matsueda finds that these six indicators statistically capture one underlying construct, which he labels "definitions favorable to crime." He also finds that definitions entirely mediate (account for) the effects of the social control variables (e.g., parental supervision, peer attachment) included in the model. Differential association and Hirschi's social control theory are often tested against one another because they both focus on individual differences in crime and point to similar variables such as family, friends, and beliefs. In one reanalysis, however, Costello and Vowell (1999) suggest that Matsueda's formulation of control theory was incomplete. Using variables they claim are truer to Hirschi's social bond concept, they find that the effects of the social bond and delinquent peers on delinquency are not mediated by definitions and are, in fact, stronger than the effects of definitions. They conclude that social control theory is supported over differential association theory.

Orcutt (1987) takes a different approach. Orcutt asked college students to characterize their opinions on marijuana from highly positive to highly negative. He then divided the students into three groups: negative, neutral, and positive. He also asked them to list how many of their friends used marijuana. He found that the effects of one's definitions on marijuana smoking depended on both the number of friends who used and whether one's definitions toward smoking marijuana were positive, neutral, or negative. Those with positive definitions of marijuana smoking were more likely to use it as the number of friends using it increased. Similarly, the proportion of those saying they had neutral definitions who smoked it also increased as the number of friends who smoked marijuana increased. This effect was much weaker, however. Nearly all of the respondents with positive definitions and four friends who smoked marijuana used it, compared to only about half of those with neutral definitions and four friends who smoked marijuana. Those with negative definitions were less likely to use marijuana, even if their four closest friends used it. Thus, the likelihood of use depended both on one's definitions and on the number of peers who smoked.

In trying to capture the excess of definitions favorable to crime, most researchers assume that as pro-crime definitions increase, anti-crime definitions decline or remain constant, so as pro-crime definitions increase the ratio of criminal to conforming definitions must be increasing. In other words, think of a cup. If the cup can only hold so many definitions, more of one would automatically mean less of the other. At issue is whether definitions are a zero-sum game, as this way of measuring them suggests, or whether one can hold both criminal and noncriminal definitions, applying one set in some circumstances and another in other circumstances.

As already noted, Sutherland claimed that learning related to crime also included skills and techniques. Few studies have included measures of skills and techniques on the assumption that most individuals have the skills necessary to commit crime. Studies have assumed the skills necessary to commit crime are essentially the same as those required for law abiding-behavior. Some recent research suggests this assumption might be incorrect. For instance, in a study of theft and drug sales among 390 homeless youths in Toronto, McCarthy (1996) found that differential association transferred important skills and techniques, which he calls tutelage. He suggests his results call for a broader interpretation of what is learned from deviant peers to include skills and techniques. More research should probe the degree to which skills and techniques are integral to learning across the various types of crime. One can certainly imagine instances in which skills are likely to be critical (e.g., safecracking) and others in which skills are minimal (e.g., vandalism).

Finally, a related question is whether Sutherland accurately described the sources of definitions. The theory suggests that family and friends will be the most common sources of definitions. While few studies have included both measures, some research suggests that peer influences are stronger than parental influences (Bruinsma 1992; Griffin and Griffin 1978). Social learning studies to date have not examined whether other potential sources such as the media also influence definitions favorable to crime. More research should probe these issues. Another related issue is the "stickiness" of definitions. If definitions are relatively permanent once developed then they could be fairly strong predictors of behavior. Yet if this is so, then children born to law-abiding parents would be unlikely to change the definitions learned from their parents simply by being exposed to delinquent peers. Alternatively, if exposure to delinquent peers causes changes in attitudes and behaviors then it seems that definitions would likely have less explanatory weight.

In general, research supports the notion that definitions favorable to crime are related to criminal behavior as social learning theories predict. Oddly, some studies claim to be tests of differential association but include no measures of definitions (Dull 1983; Erickson, Crosnoe and Dornbush 2000). Given that some studies have suggested that definitions are crime-specific and others find that general definitions are predictive of criminal behavior, it seems that tests of the theory should include both general and specific definitions. A related issue is that studies have generally failed to measure definitions unfavorable to crime, yet Sutherland clearly argued that both favorable and unfavorable definitions are important. Hence, developing questions to tap definitions unfavorable to crime is a critical step in clarifying the role of definitions. One could generate a statement such as, "It is wrong to steal" and then ask the degree to which respondents agree or disagree with such a statement. If respondents agree that it is wrong to steal but also agree that sometimes, "It is alright to get around the law if you can get away with it," then focusing only on definitions favorable to crime would suggest false support for the theory. In sum, questions tapping both favorable and unfavorable definitions should be included in separate questions within the same survey.

Differential Association

Recall that Sutherland argued that definitions are learned in a process of differential association. The finding that delinquents are more likely to have delinquent friends is one of the most robust in all criminological research (Agnew 1991; Warr 2002). Differential association theory argues that this is due to the effect friends have on a person's definitions favorable to crime. Akers' social learning theory contends that this is also due to the ability of friends to provide models and reinforcement for behavior. Simply finding that delinquents have delinquent friends, however, is not by itself support for social learning theories. For instance, one could alternatively argue that delinquents seek out other delinquents. So, instead of friends causing delinquency it could be that "birds of a feather flock together" (Glueck and Glueck 1950; Gottfredson and Hirschi 1990; Sampson and Laub 1993). In this section we discuss how delinquent peers have been measured and whether the research on delinquent peers supports social learning theories. In particular, we explore some key questions regarding delinquent peer associations: Do delinquent peers cause delinquency, or do "birds of a feather flock together"? Is it the behavior of peers or their attitudes and beliefs that affect delinquency? Does the nature of the group to which one belongs or the strength of the relationship with peers matter for delinquency?

Numerous studies have examined the delinquent peer association issue. As we have stressed throughout the book, one important question centers on how the construct is measured. Most studies measure the number of delinquent friends or the frequency of friends' delinquent acts (Agnew 1991). For example, Thornberry et al. (1994) use the Rochester Youth Development Study (RYDS), which asked respondents how many of their friends in the last six months had committed delinquent acts of varying seriousness. The response categories ranged from most to none. Similarly, Matsueda and Anderson (1998) used data from the National Youth Survey (NYS) and asked respondents how many of their friends had committed major theft, minor theft, or burglary. Response categories included none, very few, some, most, and all. Also using the NYS, Agnew (1991) distinguished between the number of minor and serious delinquent friends. Minor delinquency of friends included destruction of property, theft of less than $5, and hitting or threatening to hit someone. More serious delinquency of friends included breaking into a car or building to steal something, selling hard drugs, and theft of more than $50. In general, studies of delinquent peers find strong effects (see Thornberry and Krohn 1997 for an overview). Youth who have delinquent friends are more likely to be delinquent themselves. Delinquent peers have a strong and independent effect on delinquency, and this effect operates directly as well as indirectly through influencing pro-criminal definitions.

Another major issue in delinquent peer studies is the effect of peer approval on delinquency. Is a teen more likely to commit crime if he or she believes that his or her friends approve? From a methodological standpoint, this issue offers an opportunity to determine whether social learning theories operate as Sutherland suggests or whether Akers' model is superior. Recall that Sutherland argued that we learn to commit crime because our friends suggest that it is acceptable. Thus, according to differential association theory, the effect of peer approval is to increase our definitions favorable to crime, which then leads to crime. Here, the influence of peer approval would be indirect by influencing definitions favorable to crime. For social learning theory conversely, the actual or potential reaction of peers is an important element to consider separate from the learning of pro-criminal definitions. If peer influences operate only indirectly by increasing pro-criminal definitions, then Sutherland's model would be a better fit. If peer approval retains a direct influence apart from creating pro-criminal definitions, then Akers' model is better supported.

The concept of peer approval has been measured several ways. Agnew (1991) used the NYS data, which measures peer approval by asking how the respondents' close friends would react if they stole something worth less than $5 or worth more than $50, sold hard drugs, hit or threatened to hit someone, destroyed property, or broke into a vehicle to steal something. Response categories ranged from strongly approve to strongly disapprove. Thornberry et al. (1994) used data from the RYDS and measured "peer reactions" to six delinquency items from skipping classes to armed robbery. Response categories included, "Say it was okay," "Say nothing," and "Say it was wrong." Finally, some studies include measures of "peer pressure" capturing the negative side of peer influence (Agnew 1991; Reed and Rountree 1997). For instance, Agnew (p. 57) created a six-item scale including questions such as, "You have to be willing to break some rules if you want to be popular with your friends" or "It may be necessary to break some of your parents' rules in order to keep some of your friends." The results of these studies are mixed. Agnew reports that friends' delinquency has a stronger effect on delinquency when the person feels pressured to commit delinquency, especially serious offenses. He also reports that youth are substantially more likely to feel pressure to commit acts of both minor and serious delinquency when they have some or many delinquent friends. Reed and Rountree, on the other hand, found no effects of overt peer pressure on substance abuse using the 1977–1979 NYS. Thus, they conclude that the commonly held view that youth are pressured into using drugs is wrong.

Studies on peer influence raise one of the thorniest methodological issues in tests of social learning theory. Most studies ask one person to describe his or her perceptions of the attitudes of his or her friends. Thus, there is no direct measure of the friend's attitudes, only the person's interpretation of them. Studies suggest that this may overestimate the impact of peers on delinquency. One reason for this may be what Jussim and Osgood (1989) call "projection," or the tendency to believe that the people we like also think the way we do. In other words, if Sara likes Jessica, she will tend to overestimate the degree to which they agree on things. One solution to this problem is to obtain direct measures of peer attitudes. Jussim and Osgood control for projection effects in a study of matched pairs of incarcerated juveniles who described each other as their best friends. It was thus possible to know what Johnny thought about crime (own attitudes), what his friend Jimmy thought about crime (peer attitudes), and what Johnny thought Jimmy thought about crime (projection). Jussim and Osgood find that people dramatically overestimate the similarity of their own views to others' views. The effect of peers on delinquency, therefore, is often overstated in studies that ask Jimmy what Johnny's attitudes are. Other studies using this matched-pair technique also find similar effects (Aseltine 1995). Despite the overestimation of peer influence in many previous studies, Thornberry and Krohn (1997:222) conclude that peer association "remains a strong and significant predictor of respondent behavior."

The other major issue with peer influence studies is raised by Gottfredson and Hirschi (1990:157), who argue that rather than measuring friends' delinquency, the researcher is actually capturing the respondents' own delinquency because teen crime is often committed in groups. In other words, if we ask whether Joe has committed vandalism and whether Joe's friend has committed vandalism, Joe may be remembering the same incident for both questions. From a methodological standpoint, this would mean that measures of peer influence would be artifacts of bad measures, suggesting that with proper measures of self and peer delinquency we would find no association. Several studies have examined this question, with mixed results. Warr (1993b), Thornberry and Krohn (1997), and Thornberry et al. (1994) argue that measures of delinquent peer behavior are not simply another measure of one's own delinquency while other research suggests there may be some merit to Gottfredson and Hirschi's claim. Matsueda and Anderson (1998) find that the effect of delinquency on peers is actually stronger than the effect of peers on delinquency. Similarly, Zhang and Messner (2000) find there is significant overlap between the respondents' own reported delinquency and that of her peers. To further investigate Gottfredson and Hirschi's claim, Zhang and Messner include measures of the *parents'* perception of delinquent peers. Parental perceptions of delinquent peers exerted a significant influence, net of prior delinquency. They thus conclude that some of the reported delinquent peer association is simply capturing the youth's own delinquency but that some of the reported delinquent peer effect remains. As such, Gottfredson and Hirschi appear to be only partially correct.

Another important question is whether the attitudes and beliefs of peers or the behavior of peers is more closely related to delinquency. Sutherland suggests that the attitudes of friends are important, whereas Akers claims that both attitudes and behavior are critical (recall the discussion on imitation). Assessing whether peer attitudes or behavior is more closely related to

delinquency can help us determine whether the original differential association theory is correct or whether Akers' social learning theory adds a critical
dimension.

Research generally suggests that the behavior of delinquent friends is more
important than their attitudes are (Agnew 1991; Johnson, Marcos, and Bahr
1987; Warr and Stafford 1991). Warr and Stafford found that the behavior of
peers had a stronger influence on delinquency than peer attitudes did and
that when the two disagreed, behavior was more important than attitudes.
How do we interpret this finding? It would seem to suggest that Sutherland's
exclusive focus on the transmission of definitions is too narrow. Perhaps
Akers' social learning theory is better supported by such a finding. Recall that
Akers argues that delinquent peers provide behavior that can be imitated or
modeled. It could also be that delinquent peer behavior creates opportunities
for what Briar and Piliavin (1965) call "situational inducements." If that were
the case, then we would only expect to find that delinquent peers increase
group offending, not solo offending. In other words, if one only reacts to peer
pressure or opportunities to show off, then delinquent peers should only be
associated with that person's group offending. But a recent study by Hochstetler, Copes, and DeLisi (2002) found that the influence of delinquent peers
remained even in the case of solo offending. The authors suggest that this
supports differential association because situational inducements or direct
peer pressure could not be present in the case of offenses committed alone.
Hence, while there is evidence that peer behavior is a strong influence, it also
appears that attitudes independently influence behavior.

Another important issue when considering the effect of delinquent peers is
whether the characteristics of the relationship matter. Does the effect of delinquent peers depend on how close the friends are? In methodological terms,
the issue is whether the effects of delinquent peers are conditional or unconditional. If the effect of delinquent peers is like a germ, then any exposure
would likely lead to criminal behavior. If the effect depends on the strength of
the relationship, then the degree to which delinquent peers lead to increases
in the youth's own delinquency will depend on the strength of that relationship. Research suggests that the strength of the relationship with one's
peers does matter (Agnew 1991; Warr 1993b, 2002). Agnew finds that delinquent peers had a stronger effect on delinquency when the respondent
spent more time with, and was more attached to, delinquent friends, felt they
approved of delinquency, and felt pressure to engage in delinquency. And
recall Orcutt (1987), who found that the effects of one's definitions on marijuana smoking depended on both the number of friends who used marijuana
and whether one's definitions toward smoking marijuana were positive,
neutral, or negative. Finally, Warr (1993b) found that the duration of one's
friendships with other delinquents affected the likelihood that one would
become delinquent. He argues that friendships with other delinquents tend to
be "sticky"—once acquired, they are not easily lost. Warr (1993b) also discovered that more recent friendships had a stronger impact than early ones,
which runs counter to the idea of priority but is consistent with the idea that

recent friendships are more salient. Therefore, the peer–delinquency relationship appears to be conditional.

A similar question can be asked with respect to the nature of the groups to which one belongs. Clearly, most teens do not spend time with only one peer. It seems reasonable, therefore, to wonder whether characteristics of the peer group condition the effect of delinquent peers. Research suggests that it does. Haynie (2001) argues that the degree to which delinquent peer groups will influence behavior depends on the structure of the peer group to which one belongs (see also Haynie and Payne 2006). She focuses on network density, or the degree to which all group members know each other, as well as centrality, or the degree to which an individual has relationships with other members of the network. She also focuses on popularity, arguing that the behavior of popular group members will be more like that of the group because they have the most to lose in terms of social status. Haynie uses the Adolescent Health survey to measure these network characteristics. Popularity is measured as the number of times the respondent is mentioned by others in the school. Density is the number of ties listed in the respondent's network as a proportion of the number of possible ties. Note that this study avoids the problem associated with asking indirect questions about people's friends by asking direct questions and then drawing friendship networks from the survey respondents directly. Haynie finds that the effect of delinquent peers is stronger when group network structure is more dense or cohesive. Using the same dataset, in another study she also finds that the proportion of delinquent friends in a person's network is more strongly related to the respondent's delinquency than is the absolute amount of delinquency committed by group members (Haynie 2002). She claims that this provides support for Sutherland's notion of a ratio of definitions affecting behavior.

Haynie's network approach could also provide a way of considering the relationship between gangs and crime. Although there is a long tradition of research on gangs, only a few social learning studies consider gang membership and delinquency (Brownfield 2003; Winfree, Mays, and Vigil-Backstrom 1994; Winfree, Vigil-Backstrom, and Mays 1994). Thornberry et al. (2003) examine the causes and consequences of gang involvement in the RYDS, and find that socioeconomic disadvantage and social learning account for involvement in gangs. They also find that gang involvement strongly facilitates delinquency. In particular, they discover that delinquency rates are higher during active gang involvement than before or after. Finally, they find that the duration of gang involvement is directly related to the rate of criminal activity. These results are consistent with a social learning approach.

Few would dispute the idea that gangs could be characterized as delinquent peer groups. Yet some would argue that they are qualitatively different from nongang delinquent peer groups (Thornberry et al. 2003). It could be that gangs represent unique social environments for peer approval and pressure, as well as opportunities for criminal activity. Or it could be that gangs simply represent one extremely dense form of a peer social network. Using the network approach it would be possible to examine whether gangs are unique (and therefore must be modeled separately) or whether they are simply an extreme form of a delinquent peer group. This issue should be explored in future research.

Differential Reinforcement

Akers' social learning theory suggests that crime will be more likely when it is reinforced, such as when a girl who shoplifts gets away with it and her friends show approval. The theory maintains that people with the most control over rewards will have the greatest influence on one's behavior. Akers contends that most reinforcement is social, coming from other people. If you think about it, this makes sense. Most of what we do comes from the way we expect others to react. A husband buys flowers for his wife in anticipation of the smile she will give him (positive reinforcement) or her forgiveness for forgetting to take out the trash (negative reinforcement). Even things that are nonsocial such as money are mainly important to us because they are social symbols. The theory does allow that some reinforcement can be nonsocial. The degree to which reinforcement is social or nonsocial is explored later.

Most social learning studies include some measure of reinforcement. Table 6.5 provides examples of survey items used to tap reinforcement. In general, research supports the idea that those who believe their behavior will be viewed positively are more likely to engage in crime. For example, in the first major "test" of social learning theory Akers et al. (1979), using a sample of more than 2,400 middle and high school students in three Midwestern states, found that both alcohol and marijuana use were more likely when the teen believed that the reactions of friends and parents would be positive. The full models of alcohol and marijuana use, which contain all of the social learning concepts (imitation, differential association, differential reinforcement, and definitions), explained 68% of the variation in marijuana use and 55% of the variation in alcohol use. Krohn et al. (1985) confirmed that differential reinforcement mediates the relationship between association with delinquent peers and adolescent smoking in a longitudinal study of students. Consistent with social learning theory, the reason association with delinquent peers matters for crime is that it increases the anticipated or actual rewards for criminal behavior. This finding was also confirmed in a study of alcohol consumption for 1,093 high school students in Maryland, Oklahoma, and Arkansas (Benda 1994). Benda noted, however, that the reinforcement variables accounted for only a small amount of the variation in alcohol use when other variables (including those representing social control theory) were included in the model.

Because the concept of differential reinforcement is relatively broad, it has been measured in a variety of ways. Some measures focus on the respondent's expectations about whether others will approve or disapprove of the behavior. For example, Krohn et al. (1985) include measures of the most likely reaction of the respondent's father, best friend, and others the person's age to his or her smoking. Response categories ranged from strongly supportive to very much against.

Other studies measure differential reinforcement in terms of the expected consequences or rewards. In a study of police misconduct, Chappell and Piquero (2004) ask about the specific consequences that would follow if a police officer engaged in misconduct that was discovered. Response categories ranged from verbal reprimands to termination. It would seem that measures of differential reinforcement that focus on the actual or expected consequences from criminal behavior are better suited to distinguishing the concept of reinforcement from that of beliefs. To illustrate, consider the question, "What is the more likely reaction of your father to smoking?" from Krohn et al. (1985). Isn't this just another way of asking whether the father defines smoking favorably or unfavorably? Of course, statistical techniques allow one to test whether different survey questions are tapping the same underlying construct. More research is needed to identify the areas of conceptual overlap and the distinction between definitions and reinforcement.

It is also problematic that some studies consider both the positive and negative consequences of criminal or deviant behavior (Akers and Lee 1999; Akers et al. 1989; Krohn et al. 1985), whereas others consider mainly the negative consequences (Chappell and Piquero 2004; Skinner and Fream 1997). Because learning theories specify that both positive and negative consequences can influence criminal behavior, it seems essential to include measures that tap both positive and negative consequences.

One important question is whether the reinforcement of criminal behavior is primarily social or whether nonsocial reinforcement is also an important predictor of criminality. Recall that nonsocial reinforcement refers to things like the physical effects of drugs or the "rush" from risky behaviors. Research

Table 6.5 Items Used to Tap Akers' Concepts of Reinforcement

Krohn et al. 1985

1. What is the most likely reaction of your father to your smoking?
2. What is the most likely reaction of your best male (female) friend to your smoking?
3. What is the most likely reaction of others your own age to your smoking?
4. Smoking makes one look sophisticated.
5. Smoking makes one look like an adult.

Chappell and Piquero 2004

6. If another officer engaged in this behavior and was discovered doing so, what if any discipline do you think would follow?

Akers et al. 1989

7. Does alcohol use mainly effect your social relationships and enjoyment in a positive negative or balanced way?
8. What is the usual reaction of _____ when you drink?
9. Are the physical effects from drinking mainly positive, negative, or balanced between the two?

suggests that the effects of nonsocial reinforcers may be greater than initially posited in Akers' social learning theory formulation. Previous researchers have claimed that the effects of drugs can be nonsocial (Wood et al. 1995). Similarly, Wood et al. (1997) argue that violent crimes can produce a neuro-physiological high in criminals that can reinforce and maintain a criminal career. Of course, social learning theorists believe the interpretation of these physical sensations as positive or negative is likely based on past social experiences, and therefore in a larger sense is "social," even if not directly so (Akers 1998; see also Becker 1953). Brezina and Piquero (2003) find evidence of this. Using a sample of 1,600 high school students, they report that social learning factors such as peer beliefs regarding alcohol and marijuana influenced the likelihood that respondents would experience intrinsic rewards. They conclude that Akers (1998) may be correct, that even "nonsocial" reinforcements may be influenced by social learning and that isolating nonsocial reinforcement is difficult.

Imitation

Finally, imitation (sometimes called modeling) is simply engaging in a behavior after observing others perform similar behaviors (Akers and Sellers 2004). Table 6.6 lists some examples of questions used to measure imitation. Skinner and Fream (1997), in a study of computer crimes by college students, asked about the sources of learning of five crimes. They questioned how much respondents had learned about crime from family, teachers, books, television and movies, and computer bulletin boards. Response categories ranged from learned nothing to learned everything. Their results showed that imitation had inconsistent effects across the five crimes. Generally, fewer studies of social learning have included imitation than differential reinforcement. This may be due, in part, to the findings of Akers et al. (1979), who showed that imitation had the weakest effect of the social learning variables tested. Similarly, Akers and Lee (1999) dropped imitation from their models because it had minimal effects on marijuana use.

Others argue that imitation is likely more important for the initiation of criminal behavior than the maintenance of it (Reed and Rountree 1997:170). It may also be that imitation effects are not often documented because they are likely very similar to the measures of differential association. Think about the way differential association is typically measured (i.e., how many of your close friends engage in criminal behavior?). One is most likely to know that a friend engages in criminal behavior because they witness it. Thus, although

Table 6.6 Items Used to Measure Akers' Concept of Imitation

1. My best male friend smokes (Krohn et al. 1985).
2. My best female friend smokes (Krohn et al. 1985).
3. How many of the people you admire (parents, friends, other adults) have you observed using alcohol (marijuana) (Akers et al. 1979)?

conceptually distinct, the two may be empirically similar. Consistent with this, Krohn et al. (1985) found that the correlation between their measures of differential association and imitation was .63, indicating they might be tapping the same underlying dimension.

Of course, a large body of research has examined imitation outside the context of peers. Much of this research considers the effects of media violence on aggression and violence, particularly among children. Generally, the findings indicate that violence begets violence (for a discussion, see Akers 1998). The mixed findings on the role of imitation indicate that this concept should be reworked or removed. Studies either need to develop measures that capture imitation's independent influence or should exclude it from social learning models.

Measuring Crime

Tests of social learning theories have measured the dependent variable of crime in several ways. This is partly because neither differential association nor Akers' social learning theory contain any scope conditions that limit them to particular types of crime. Thus, the theories should be able to explain any type of criminal behavior, and Akers (1985) expands this to include all *deviant* behaviors as well. Studies have focused on such disparate behaviors as cheating among college students (Vowell and Chen 2004), police misconduct (Chappell and Piquero 2004), and even alcohol consumption among the elderly (Akers and Cochran 1985). Studies of Akers' social learning theory have most often focused on relatively minor forms of crime and deviance such as smoking (Akers and Lee 1996; Krohn et al. 1985; Massey and Krohn 1986) and drinking and drug use (Krohn et al. 1996; Sellers and Winfree 1990). This is likely due to the fact that self-report surveys are more suited to minor forms of crime and deviance and less able to adequately measure more serious offenses. A few studies have focused on serious offenses such as rape (see Akers 1998:Chapter 10). Future research, however, needs to specifically address the social learning process in serious crime if learning theories are to be considered as a general explanation across all crimes.

Most studies include indexes that combine a number of criminal and delinquent behaviors. Jensen (1972) and Matsueda (1982) use a delinquency scale that includes six items: theft of less than $2, theft of items between $2 and $50, theft of items worth more than $50, driving a car without permission, vandalism, and battery. Short (1957) uses an 11-item index including the same theft items but also includes skipping school, driving a car without a license, buying wine or beer, drinking wine or beer, being placed on probation at school or expelled, sexual intercourse, stealing a car, and running away from home. Bruinsma (1992) includes a scale of 15 items (which he doesn't specify clearly other than to say that they are property crimes and common activities of juveniles), whereas Miller and Matthews (2001) employ Mazerolle's (1998) scale of 24 items. Alarid, Burton, and Cullen (2000) use a scale of 35 items (15 property crimes, 9 violent crimes, 11 drug crimes) based on Elliott and Ageton

(1980). On the one hand, general support for social learning theories across these dependent variables lends support to the idea that it is a "general" theory of crime (i.e., wide in scope). On the other hand, variation in results across studies could be the result of measuring the dependent variable differently, rather than limitations underlying the theory.

The use of scales to measure delinquency raises important issues. Most studies treat criminal activity as a continuous variable like age rather than as a dichotomous variable like gender. Therefore, they are measuring crime frequency. This means that increases in crime are considered to be linear. In other words, going from 0 crimes to 1 is statistically the same as going from 1 to 2 or from 19 to 20. Is this assumption reasonable? Or would it make more sense to treat criminal activity as an all-or-nothing concept—either you have committed crime or you haven't. If this is the case, then entirely different statistical techniques must be used with potentially different results.

Related to this is the issue of crime types. As illustrated, many studies include property and violent crimes in one index (Matsueda 1982; Matsueda and Heimer 1987; Miller and Matthews 2001). Based on the scope of the theory this makes sense. Social learning theories are intended to explain all types of crime. But if social learning theories explain property but not violent crime, then including them both in the same index could lead to misleading results. A few studies do separate the dependent variable by crime type. Jackson, Tittle, and Burke (1986) examine marijuana smoking, assault, tax cheating, $5 and $50 theft, and illegal gambling in separate equations.

Or consider the dependent variable in Orcutt's (1987) study of differential association and marijuana use. He disaggregated the dependent variable into two categories. The nonuser group included those who had never tried marijuana and those who had tried it but not gotten high. The user group included only those who had tried it *and* gotten high. As such, some of the people in the "nonuser" group had committed a crime but were classified with those who hadn't. This may have been reasonable in the context of the study, which focused on becoming a self-identified "user" of marijuana, but it could raise problems as a test of differential association because the theory predicts that criminal behavior (even trying marijuana once) will be the result of an excess of definitions favorable to crime. This is problematic because some of the individuals that Orcutt identified as "noncriminal" would be considered "criminal" by other researchers, introducing error into the measurement of the dependent variable. This makes it less likely that one would find a relationship between definitions and crime.

Summary Critique of Measurement Strategy

In general, the research discussed here is consistent with learning theories of crime, yet a number of methodological issues somewhat limit our confidence in these findings. First, only a handful of studies include all of the relevant factors, such as one's own definitions and the behavior and definitions of peers and family. Social learning is said to involve the learning of an excess of definitions favorable to crime from others. Therefore, complete tests require the measurement of the subject's own attitudes as well as those of others, namely family and friends. Essentially, we need to know if the attitudes of the delinquent mirror those of family or friends because if not, it would be difficult to argue that they were learned from these others. Unfortunately, not all studies measure peer attitudes and fewer include measures of familial attitudes. In fact, some claim to be tests of differential association without even measuring attitudes at all!

But even if studies included all the relevant variables tapping perceptions of family and friends' beliefs, the question would still remain as to how accurate the person's perceptions are. Psychological research suggests that we systematically misperceive the attitudes of others we like to be more similar to our own (Heider 1958; Sherif and Hovland 1961). This tendency could explain apparent similarities between a delinquent's attitudes and those of her peers. A few studies have avoided this issue by asking the friend's responses directly rather than using the indirect measure of perceived attitudes (Aseltine 1995; Huizinga, Weiher, and Esbensen 1992; Kandel 1978). These studies generally find that peer influences remain important predictors of delinquency, even if somewhat overstated in studies using indirect measures (Thornberry and Krohn 1997). More studies employing direct measures of friends' definitions would increase confidence that previous results aren't artifacts of people's psychological misperceptions.

As noted earlier, one difference between differential association and social learning theories is the concept of differential reinforcement. Although Sutherland suggested that crime was learned, he did not specify the mechanisms by which this learning occurred. Akers identifies the concepts of differential reinforcement and imitation as the mechanisms by which learning occurs. Studies have generally supported the inclusion of differential reinforcement, suggesting that Akers' social learning theory adds an important dimension to Sutherland's original formulation. Yet many studies include survey items that appear to be rephrased questions regarding peer or parental definitions. Some have focused on the actual rewards or consequences following criminal behavior, but studies of social learning theory need to distinguish carefully between beliefs and reinforcement or the theory essentially becomes a restated version of differential association. Studies have been less supportive of imitation. This may be because items measuring imitation overlap with differential association or it may be that imitation is not a particularly strong determinant of criminal behavior. Again, better measures need to be developed or imitation should be dropped from the model.

Finally, most studies consider minor crimes or deviant acts that are not illegal. The existing studies make a fairly convincing argument for the explanatory power of social learning models for drinking and drug use, especially by teenagers. However, these may be the most inherently social of deviant/illegal behaviors. It is less clear whether social learning accounts for more serious behaviors such as robbery or homicide because so few studies include such behaviors (e.g., Heimer 1997). Recent research has begun to widen the range of behaviors examined through the lens of social learning, but firmer conclusions on the scope of social learning theories await further research.

Analytical Issues

In this section we discuss study design issues as they apply to social learning theories. As with any theory, the choices one makes regarding how to design the study can have tremendous consequences for the degree of confidence one can have in a theory's empirical adequacy. When tests of theories are strong methodologically, we can have more confidence in the conclusions they reach. When they are weak, we don't know whether the results are due to the theory or how the theory was tested (recall the opening story of the Ph.D. candidate in Chapter 1). This is especially the case when our findings do not support a theory. If the methods used to test the theory are weak, we cannot ascertain whether the failure was in the test or the in the weakness of the theory. In this section, we consider general study design, sample selection issues, causal mechanisms and causal ordering, and potential alternative explanations.

Study Design

In a test of any theory one must consider how best to capture data on the theoretical concepts. Although Sutherland considered the notion of differential social organization, he noted that others were doing good work on the structural and cultural levels and so chose to focus on the social psychological aspects of crime (Cohen, Lindesmith, and Schuessler 1956). Similarly, until Akers' SSSL theory explicitly considered elements of social structure, social learning theory was (and still is) primarily a theory of individual learning and behavior. Therefore, it makes sense that researchers would choose individuals as the unit of analysis.

Once one has chosen the appropriate unit of analysis, it is necessary to consider how best to collect the data necessary to capture key theoretical concepts and to test the major hypotheses under consideration. Although a few studies use experimental methods (Andrews 1980), most tests of social learning theories employ survey methods. One could also imagine the use of qualitative research to examine the key concepts of social learning theories. In fact, some of Sutherland's early research consisted of in-depth studies of white-collar criminals (Sutherland 1937, 1940, 1949). Unfortunately, few studies have assessed learning theories of crime using qualitative methods, but such an approach, despite its drawbacks, could yield insights into learning not available through survey methodology. In any event, the research style most often used in testing social learning theories has been survey research. This seems a reasonable choice because one of the key variables of interest— definitions favorable or unfavorable to crime—refers to the attitudes of the individuals being studied. At this point, given the choice to use survey methods, whom should researchers survey?

Sample Selection

Nearly all tests of social learning theories have been conducted using self-report surveys, mostly on middle and high school students (Akers and Lee 1996, 1999; Akers et al. 1979; Benda 1994; Matsueda 1982; Matsueda and Heimer 1987) or college students (Griffin and Griffin 1978; Lo 2000; Miller and Matthews 2001; Orcutt 1983, 1987; Skinner and Fream 1997). A few studies have examined other populations, notably the elderly (Akers and Cochran 1985) and police officers (Chappell and Piquero 2004). And only a handful have focused on convicted offenders (Alarid, Burton, and Cullen 2000; Andrews 1980; Winfree, Mays, and Vigil-Backstrom 1994). The choice of school-based samples is partly a matter of convenience and partly a conscious one. Studies have shown that crime varies by age, increasing rapidly during the teenage years and declining sharply in adulthood (Gottfredson and Hirschi 1990; Hirschi and Gottfredson 1983). Therefore, samples of teenagers are likely to capture those most involved in crime. Yet it may be that students in school are not necessarily the ones researchers are interested in studying. Besides children that are ill, the students most likely *not* in school on a given day are those who are truant, have dropped out of school, or are in a juvenile detention facility. This raises the issue of sample selection bias. If the sample systematically excludes cases in ways that are related to the dependent variable (crime), then the statistical conclusions one reaches can be wrong. In this case, the causes of crime may be different for serious criminals (who are not as likely to be in the sample) than for minor offenders (who are more likely to be included). We could arrive at incorrect conclusions about the causes of crime if we base our studies only on school samples.

Existing research has generally been supportive of social learning theories regardless of the sample used. For example, research on convicted offenders supports social-learning theories (Alarid et al. 2000; Andrews 1980; Winfree, Mays, and Vigil-Backstrom 1994). Alarid et al. tested differential association against social control theory using 1,158 male and female first-time offenders sentenced to a residential boot camp in Texas. Although both theories received some support, differential association received more consistent support across gender and crime type. But more work is needed to increase confidence in the generality of social learning theories by applying them across diverse populations. Specifically, more research should be conducted across gender. Many tests of differential association have focused on samples that included only males (Matsueda 1982; Matsueda and Heimer 1987). If the differential association process works similarly for boys and girls then this is not a problem. Some research, however, suggests that the effects of differential association vary by gender. Heimer and DeCoster (1999) found that boys were more likely to associate with delinquent peers, and Erickson et al. (2000) found that boys were more susceptible to the influence of delinquent peers than were girls. And DeCoster (2003) argues that social learning of gendered roles explains why girls are more likely to respond to stressful events through depression whereas boys are more likely to become delinquent. One must, therefore, consider both males and females to determine if the social learning process is invariant across gender. Given dramatic differences in delinquency rates among boys and girls, this seems a crucial step in future research.

Model Specification and Causal Ordering

One basic tenet of research noted in Chapter 1 is that in order to conclude confidently that one variable causes another we must show that the two are correlated and that the purported cause (in this case, definitions) comes prior to the supposed effect (crime). Differential association and Akers' social learning theory both posit that crime is the result of learning, primarily through exposure to criminal definitions or behavior. This suggests a dynamic process, or one that occurs over time. Yet most research on social learning theories is cross-sectional. Cross-sectional research can test a number of elements of differential association. Consistent with theoretical predictions, existing research has shown that delinquents are more likely to have delinquent peers and that delinquents are more likely to have definitions favorable to law violation. From a methodological standpoint, however, showing that two variables are correlated is only the first step; to establish that one causes the other we need longitudinal data (data over time).

Some studies, particularly tests of Akers' social learning theory, have used longitudinal data. Most have focused on smoking (Akers and Lee 1996; Krohn et al. 1985; Massey and Krohn 1986), drinking (Sellers and Winfree 1990), or drug use (Krohn et al. 1996). Longitudinal studies generally find support for social learning theories. Sellers and Winfree examine the support for Sutherland's differential association in a two-wave panel model (two time points) of drinking behavior among 675 junior and senior high school students. In this study, the dependent variable was the frequency of alcohol use in the last six months. Response options included no use, 1–2, 3–5, 6–9, 10–19, 20–39, and 40 or more times. Sellers and Winfree document support for the effect of differential association with drinking peers and pro-drinking definitions on later drinking. In other words, their results support the causal sequence of differential association theory. They also find that drinking among middle school students is more affected by peer beliefs and behavior than is high school students' drinking. They suggest this is because attitudes are less well formed among middle than among high school students and, therefore, middle school students are more susceptible to peer influences. They also find that adults have minimal inhibiting effects on alcohol use among the students in the sample. In fact, anti-drug messages from adults may actually *increase* drinking behavior by inducing rebellion.

Another longitudinal study by Krohn et al. (1985) investigated the initiation and continuation of adolescent cigarette smoking. They collected three waves of data on students attending two junior high schools and one high school. Questionnaires were administered to 1,068 students in the spring of 1980, 1981, and 1982. The dependent variable was the frequency of cigarette smoking, and independent variables tapping differential association, definitions, reinforcement, and physical effects were included. The study examined initiation and maintenance of smoking separately. Although many of the social learning variables were significant predictors of smoking initiation, they only accounted for about 3% of the variation in beginning smoking from time 1 to time 3. Social learning theory does a much better job in the maintenance model, explaining about 41% of continued smoking among those who smoked throughout the study.

Another longitudinal study by Akers and Lee (1996) examines the social learning theory model for smoking behavior among 454 middle and high school students in Iowa. They include measures of differential association; differential reinforcement; and definitions in the first (time 1), third (time 2), and fifth year (time 3) of a five-wave panel study. The authors validated the self-reported smoking of the respondents by testing saliva samples for nicotine residue. They found that nicotine residue levels closely matched the self-reported frequency of smoking, suggesting that self-reported smoking is a valid measure of smoking in this survey. Akers and Lee found support for the social learning model. Social learning variables accounted for 33% of the variation in smoking at time 2 and 31% of the variation in smoking at time 3. Thus, longitudinal studies seem to support social learning theories for smoking, drinking, and drug use. Of course, some might argue that the dependent variables in these studies are relatively minor forms of criminal behavior that are particularly likely to exhibit social influences.

A few longitudinal tests of social learning theories also consider other kinds of criminal behavior. Heimer (1997) examines how definitions affect violent crime among high school students using the NYS. Although she includes other measures such as parenting styles and social structural variables such as socioeconomic status, race, and neighborhood crime, her models include definitions favorable to violence as the most proximate cause of violent behavior. The dependent variable is a 10-item scale including hitting parents, teachers, or others; using physical force on parents, teachers, or others; physically attacking others; carrying weapons; gang fighting; and sexual assault. Heimer finds that definitions favorable to violence explain nearly one third of the variation in violent behavior, controlling for previous violence. She concludes that the relationship between social structural factors such as socioeconomic status and crime is largely explained by the learning of pro-violent definitions, which supports the social learning approach. A few other longitudinal studies have also found support for social learning theories as part of integrated theories (Hayes 1997; Massey and Krohn 1986).

Testing social learning theories using longitudinal data is also necessary to determine whether the variables are related to each other in the order that the theories suggest (causal order). Table 6.7 lists several different ways that delinquent peers may be related to delinquency (see also Stafford and Ekland-Olson 1982:168; Strickland 1982). For social learning theories, specifying the exact nature and meaning of the delinquent peer association is crucial. Sutherland claims the reason delinquent peers will have an effect on a youth's

delinquency is because they influence the youth to have an excess of definitions favorable to crime (Table 6.7, hypothesis 1). Others might argue that the
correlation only appears because delinquent peers provide an opportunity for
delinquency (Table 6.7, hypothesis 2). Or Akers would claim that delinquent
peers provide an opportunity for reinforcement or approval of delinquent
behavior. The Gluecks (1950) and Gottfredson and Hirschi (1990) would argue that we pick friends like ourselves, and delinquents pick delinquent
friends (Table 6.7, hypotheses 3). Or it may be that getting in trouble cuts
off relationships with nondelinquent friends as delinquents become stigmatized (see labeling theory, Chapter 8). Longitudinal data are necessary to test
whether the variables suggested by social learning theories—definitions,
differential association, and crime—are related in the way that the theory
suggests (see Stafford and Ekland-Olson 1982; Strickland 1982). Longitudinal
data also allow us to distinguish between differential association and social
learning theory models. Sutherland clearly suggested a unidirectional model,
which led from differential association to definitions to delinquency. Most
studies of Akers' social learning theory have considered only a unidirectional
causal sequence from differential association to differential reinforcement to
delinquency.

Some have suggested that a unidirectional causal model may be too simplistic (Thornberry and Krohn 1997; Thornberry et al. 1994). Again, one of the
most consistent findings in criminological research is that delinquents have
friends that are delinquent, but there are several possible explanations for this
correlation. The question remains: Do we learn crime from criminal friends
(social learning model), or do "birds of a feather flock together" (social control
model)? In reality, both observations may be true. Several studies have found
that the main variables in social learning theories are reciprocally related.
Associating with delinquent friends appears to increase delinquency, which
leads to spending more time with delinquent friends. Using three waves of the
RYDS, Thornberry et al. (p. 75) find that "[a]lthough delinquency is influenced
by peer associations and delinquent beliefs, it also influences those associations and beliefs to create behavioral trajectories toward increasing delinquency for some youths and toward increasing conformity for others." Thus,
friends cause delinquency, but delinquency affects the likelihood of having
delinquent friends. Krohn et al. (1996) find similar relationships for drug use
using five waves of the RYDS. And Thornberry and Krohn (1997: 228) arrive at
similar conclusions: "Overwhelmingly, the studies that have formally tested
bi-directional effects have found support for bidirectional effects." Recall also
that Matsueda and Anderson (1998) document a reciprocal relationship between delinquent peers and delinquency, although they note that the effect of
delinquency on the likelihood of delinquent friends is stronger than the effect
of delinquent friends on delinquency.

From the standpoint of evaluating social learning theories, these studies
suggest that the glass is half full. On the one hand, learning mechanisms
and pro-criminal definitions appear to be related to crime. On the other hand,
the process seems to be more complex than simply to claim that learning

Table 6.7 Hypothesized Relationships between Delinquent Peers and Delinquency

1. Delinquent Peers → Definitions Favorable to Crime → Delinquency
2. Delinquent Peers → Opportunity → Delinquency
3. Definitions → Delinquent Peers → Delinquency
4. Delinquency → Definitions → Delinquent Peers

definitions precedes criminal behavior. Sutherland's unidirectional causal model, therefore, is too simplistic. Direct tests of Akers' social learning theory typically model a unidirectional causal sequence as well, which is also too simplistic in light of the reciprocal effects found in studies such as Thornberry et al. (1994) and Krohn et al. (1996). Yet Akers (1998:120–121) acknowledges that there can be reciprocal effects. If this is the case, theoretical discussions as well as tests of social learning theory need to include these reciprocal effects more explicitly.

Research on social learning theory underscores many of the thorniest issues in measuring crime and illustrates the reality that we cannot always get what we want. As noted, most social learning studies use cross-sectional self-report surveys. Such designs can never adequately test the theory, which inherently involves processes over time. The maxim "correlation does not equal causation" applies here. Cross-sectional designs also cannot tell us whether the relationship between the variables specified in the theory is correct. Do delinquent peer associations precede or follow crime? Do definitions come first, or do we rationalize our behavior afterward? Is differential association a global concept that captures all learning processes? Similarly, the choice of populations to sample from has constrained our confidence in social learning theory. We do not know with certainty if the theory explains serious violent crime for adults because so few studies include such crime measures or samples. Finally, there is the question of whether delinquency leads to delinquent friends, delinquent friends lead to delinquency, or both. The research to date clearly finds that unidirectional models are not supported by the evidence. Akers acknowledges the reciprocal nature of the relationships, but more work remains to specify how the differential association concept fits into a reciprocal model, if at all.

Directions for Future Research

A large body of research has been conducted on differential association and social learning theory. Most findings are consistent with this approach, and social learning theories have earned an important place among individual explanations of crime. Yet several key issues remain. First, research generally shows that definitions favorable to crime are related to crime and deviance (see Akers 1998 for an overview). Of course, it is not surprising that criminals would hold attitudes more favorable to law violation. The critical issue, and one that has not been adequately tested, is which comes first—the attitude or the behavior. Future research must employ modeling strategies that more closely match the dynamic processes of these theories. True support for social learning theories requires that we show that people learn criminal attitudes from family and friends (or elsewhere) and then commit crime.

The ambiguity of terms in Sutherland's original statement and subsequent revisions should also be addressed. To the extent that concepts are vague, they become a moving target. Failure to find support for the theory could simply mean one hasn't asked the right questions. Relatedly, more work needs to be done to clarify which definitions are most strongly related to crime and whether these definitions are general or crime specific. We also need more information on how definitions are acquired and whether the frequency, duration, priority, and intensity of definitions are all equally important dimensions affecting the strength of definitions favorable to crime. Although early research suggested support for the modalities with respect to delinquent friends (Short 1957, 1958), because of the difficulty in measuring them, recent theoretical tests have more or less ignored the weighting of definitions. At least some research, however, suggests that recent friends have more influence than early ones (Warr 1993b). Social learning theories also have not addressed the "stickiness" of definitions. Presumably once a person has developed a set of definitions it would seem unlikely that he or she would change them simply because they associate with people with different views. If definitions are changed easily, it seems unreasonable to give them the causal weight that social learning theories do. Social learning theories also need to do a better job of explaining desistance from crime. Recent research (Laub and Sampson 2003; Sampson and Laub 1993) suggests that criminals can desist from crime, yet current versions of learning theories do not adequately account for desistance patterns. Additionally, the question arises whether differential association is a global measure that encompasses all other learning concepts. If it is, then Sutherland's original formulation would seem to be all that is necessary. If not, then the appropriate placement of the concept in models must be clarified (Krohn 1999).

As noted earlier, the association of crime with delinquent/criminal peers is one of the most consistent findings in criminological research (Akers 1998; Warr 2002). This finding, however, does not indicate the superiority of social learning theories. There are several plausible explanations for such a finding. Some would argue this relationship exists because like-minded individuals seek each other out. Others would suggest that delinquent peers provide an increased opportunity for delinquency. Recent research on this issue seems supportive of a social learning explanation. Agnew (1991) finds that the quality of one's relationship with delinquent peers mediates the strength of the delinquent peer–delinquency association (see also Haynie and Payne 2006). Research must continue to clarify the role of delinquent peers and peer networks.

Research must also clarify the role of parents and siblings because failure to include measures of family definitions could mean that definitions come from this source and then individuals choose delinquent friends based on this. If so, the "birds of a feather" conclusion would be wrong since definitions actually cause choice of friends who would later influence definitions. Similarly, more studies should examine the effects of media influences on definitions. We also need to know more about whether and how the social learning processes differ by gender and race. Existing studies show gender and race differences in crime. The question is to what extent social learning theories can account for these differences. Some research has addressed this issue (DeCoster 2003; Erickson et al. 2000; Haynie and Payne 2006; Matsueda and Heimer 1987; Mears, Ploeger, and Warr 1998), but more work remains.

Finally, some suggest that the concepts from Hirschi's social control can be combined with social learning concepts (Conger 1976; Erickson et al. 2000; Marcos, Bahr, and Johnson 1986; Massey and Krohn 1986). Massey and Krohn's model, which includes elements of the social bond and social learning, would seem to be a good candidate. Thornberry's (1987) interactional model is another possibility. Criminologists have longed struggled to link macro-level processes with individual-level processes. It would seem that Akers' SSSL provides an opportunity to further this cross-level integration of theories (see Chapter 10 for more on theoretical integration). Tests of SSSL have begun (Lanza-Kaduce and Capece 2003), but more work remains (see Morash 1999 and Sampson 1999 for critiques of SSSL).

Discussion Questions

1. What are the major concepts of social learning theories?
2. What does Akers' social learning theory add to Sutherland's differential association theory?
3. Beyond peers, where might individuals, particularly youth, acquire definitions both favorable and unfavorable to crime and deviance?
4. What types of samples are predominantly used in tests of social learning theory? Is this a strength or weakness of the theory? Why?
5. Compare and contrast social learning theories with micro-level strain theories, discussed in Chapter 5. Which offers a more convincing argument for understanding crime and delinquency? Why?

CHAPTER 7
♦

CONTROL THEORIES

Introduction

Should I or shouldn't I? A teenage boy has the opportunity to go to a party where he knows there will be drugs. He has heard that using drugs is a wild experience that can be fun. Should he go or shouldn't he? Or consider the girl who would really like the latest CD of her favorite recording artist but does not have the money to pay for it. She thinks it would be relatively easy to steal the CD and is attracted to the idea of taking a risk. Should she or shouldn't she?

We have all faced such dilemmas sometime in our lives. A behavior that we know is wrong or illegal is also very attractive. Yet most of the time, most of us will not participate in the behavior. Why would we not participate in behavior that is attractive to us? This is precisely the question that social control theory addresses.

An underlying assumption of social control theory is that deviant behavior is attractive because it is exciting, rewarding, fun, or the most efficient way to achieve other ends. Given this assumption, control theorists see no need to explain why people commit deviant behavior; they participate in deviant activities because they are attracted to them. The real issue is: Why would people not participate in those activities? Why would people not do something that was fun, rewarding, exciting, or an efficient means to a desired end?

The answer to this question from a social control perspective is that something constrains or prevents the individual from participating. There are many potential constraints on our behaviors. For example, we might not want to disappoint our parents or jeopardize our future. We might abstain because we believe that rules and laws are necessary and the state has the right to define what is proper or improper behavior. We might have developed an ability to control our impulses and desires. Different theories that fall under the social control perspective umbrella are distinguished from one another by the source of the constraint. However, all control theories share the assumption that deviant behavior is attractive, and, therefore, explanations must center on why individuals do not commit deviant behavior rather than on why they do commit it. Before we examine the specific perspectives that share these assumptions, it is important to review the intellectual roots of the theory.

Intellectual History of Social Control Theory

Travis Hirschi (1969), who has been most influential in promoting social control theory, attributed the intellectual source of his ideas to the work of Émile Durkheim. As was briefly discussed in Chapter 5 (anomie and strain theories), Durkheim was a nineteenth-century European sociologist who grappled with the question of how, given the changes brought about by the Industrial and French Revolutions, society could reestablish social order. Durkheim's concepts of social integration and social regulation form the basis on which social control theories are built.

Durkheim did not clearly define social integration, but from the examples he used it is evident that he was referring to how individuals and groups are attached to society and social institutions. Such attachment allows individuals to find meaning in life and prevents them from acting out of purely individual interests. Durkheim (1951:210) stated, "the bond that unites them with common cause attaches them to life and the lofty goal they envisage prevents their feeling personal troubles so deeply." This passage is from Durkheim's book *Suicide*, in which he applies a sociological analysis to the seemingly individualistic behavior of taking one's own life. As an example of this principle, Durkheim observed that people with children had lower rates of suicide than did people without children. He explained this in terms of social integration: Parents feel a sense of attachment and responsibility toward children, providing a meaning and purpose for their lives. This attachment protects them from taking their own lives, even if they are experiencing great difficulties.

In addition to the forces of social integration constraining individuals from deviant behavior, society also provides norms by which people's behaviors are regulated. Durkheim assumed that people had insatiable desires and that a function of cultural norms was to place a cap on those desires. A society that could not effectively do this was said to be in a state of anomie (ineffective norms). In a state of anomie, deviant behavior would be more likely. Using another example from Durkheim's analysis of suicide, married men (even without children) have lower suicide rates than do unmarried men. Durkheim assumed that men had insatiable sexual desire that included the desire for a diversity of partners. Marriage places a cap on their sexual desires and lowers the potential for the frustration that may be created by trying to realize those desires.

Social integration and social regulation, according to Durkheim, are necessarily related. Social regulation enhances social integration. Rules of conduct make people feel integrated or more attached to the group or institution, which becomes a more meaningful part of their lives. For example, Durkheim suggested that religious denominations with rituals and dogma (e.g., Catholicism) integrate their members into the church more effectively than do denominations without such rituals (e.g., Protestantism). He also maintained that social regulation is only effective if people feel integrated into the group or institution. If one does not care about the group, why would he or she adhere to its rules?

The concepts of social integration and social regulation play central roles in social control theories. Although social disorganization theory (Chapter 4) evolved into what Kornhauser (1978) called a "mixed model" containing elements of social control, cultural deviance, and strain theories, initially it was a "pure control model" (Kornhauser 1978:51). The source of constraint is the social integration of the neighborhood: How much do neighbors interact? How supportive are they of one another? How tied to neighborhood organizations are they? The more socially integrated the neighborhood, the more effective it is in exerting informal social control to regulate behavior. Because we have already reviewed social disorganization theory, we only mention it here to note that some scholars include it within the social control perspective (Kornhauser 1978; Krohn, Thornberry, Collins-Hall, and Lizotte 1995). In this chapter, we focus on two varieties of control theory, both of which were developed by Travis Hirschi: social control theory (Hirschi 1969) and self-control theory (Gottfredson and Hirschi 1990). Although these two perspectives are related to one another through their common intellectual heritage and architect (Hirschi), they are distinct and have generated their own research agendas. We therefore present the substantive arguments, concepts and measurements, and analytical issues separately for each perspective.

Social Control Theory

The publication of Hirschi's book *Causes of Delinquency* in 1969 had a major impact on the examination of why youth commit delinquent behavior. It is not that Hirschi's ideas were unique. Indeed, the focus on the importance of social institutions such as the family and school had been previously examined empirically (Glueck and Glueck 1950) and incorporated into theoretical perspectives aimed at explaining delinquency (Nye 1958; Reckless 1961; Reiss 1951). In addition to avoiding some of the logical errors in this prior work, Hirschi clarified the assumptions on which notions of social control were based and provided a concise statement of the theory. Hirschi also presented an empirical examination of his theory, providing scholars with a reason to further examine the theory along with a methodological roadmap identifying how to proceed.

Hirschi begins by stating that delinquent acts occur when an individual's bond to society is either weakened or broken (Hirschi 1969:16). The weakening of the social bond frees the individual from the constraint that the bond exercises on that person. Once freed from that constraint, the individual can, but not necessarily will, commit delinquent behavior. Thus, the weakening of the social bond is a necessary but not sufficient reason for deviant behavior.

For Hirschi, the social bond is composed of four elements: (1) attachment to others, (2) commitment to conventional activities or goals, (3) involvement in conventional activities, and (4) belief in the rules of society. When the elements of the social bond are strong, there is little likelihood that individuals will commit deviant behavior. However, when one or more of the elements is weakened or broken, individuals are freed from conventional constraints and deviant behavior becomes more likely. Let us briefly examine how Hirschi conceptualized the elements of the social bond.

Attachment to Others

In a general sense, attachment refers to the affection that characterizes a relationship between people. Hirschi stated that the bonds established in close relationships to conventional others will act as a deterrent to crime because the individual will take these relationships into account before committing a crime. Attachment to parents is the most obvious source of social control, particularly among youth. A good relationship with parents will result in parents having a psychological presence even when the child is out of their direct control. How many times have you considered what your parents would think of your activities if they found out about them? In some cases, you probably did not engage in those activities because of your concern for the relationship you had with your parents.

A strong emotional bond between child and parent will also facilitate the child seeking the parents' opinions about activities. This communication process will decrease the probability that the child will ignore the opinion of his or her parents when contemplating misbehavior. Indeed, Hirschi stated that the extent and quality of communication between children and their parents are as important as affection in deterring crime. The inverse relationship between attachment to parents and delinquency should hold up even if the parents are unconventional because even unconventional parents will espouse conventional values when dealing with their children.

Hirschi hypothesized that attachment to peers would have the same constraining impact as attachment to parents. This would be the case even if those peers commit delinquent behavior. Hirschi claims that the idea that delinquents have close relationships with peers who are delinquent (see social learning theories, Chapter 6) is a myth. Rather, delinquents are less likely to have close relationships with their peers and are less likely to identify with them. As we will see when we examine the research on social control theory, this hypothesis has been called into question.

The other component of attachment that Hirschi addressed is attachment to school. Along with attachment to parents and peers, attachment to school shares the notion that the quality of the relationship between the student and either the institution of the school or its representatives (teachers) will make the student consider the potential consequences if he or she commits a delinquent act. A student who does not like school or has poor relationships with teachers is freed from the constraint that school achievement typically places on delinquent behavior.

Commitment to Conventional Lines of Action

Hirschi suggested that the desire to achieve conventional goals and the pursuit of those goals constrained delinquent behavior because delinquency potentially makes the achievement of these goals more difficult. Hirschi identified three "career lines" to illustrate this concept: educational, occupational, and passage to adult status. Commitment to educational and occupational status constrains youth from delinquency because they would not want to jeopardize their quest for achievement. You, for example, have shown a commitment to a conventional goal by virtue of your enrollment in a college class. You (or your parents) have spent a substantial amount of money and you are investing time both in and out of the class to pursue your educational goal. Would you want to jeopardize all of that by being arrested for a felony? You might have future goals in mind as well. You might want to attend law school and eventually become an attorney. Getting in trouble with the law might undermine these goals. Indeed, a criminal record might be problematic for acquiring a well-paying job. Such concerns might be considered and are expected to decrease the probability of committing illegal acts.

Hirschi's reference to "passage to adult status" in the context of commitment is more difficult to comprehend. Passage to adult status refers to adolescents who enter into the adult world prematurely. Dropping out of school before graduating, teen pregnancy or parenthood, and being employed while still attending high school are examples of premature passage to adult status. Adolescents who face this situation are, in one sense, adults, yet in another sense they are still children. The result, according to Hirschi, is a high rate of delinquency. Clearly, passage to adult status is different than commitment to conventional lines of action. Its effect is to increase rather than decrease delinquency. Moreover, premature acquisition of adult status cannot be considered "conventional" according to societal values. It, therefore, does not appear to be consistent with Hirschi's overall argument.

Involvement in Conventional Activities

Involvement in conventional activities represents the time dimension of commitment. The notion that "idle hands are the devil's workshop" (Hirschi 1969:187) suggests that adolescents not involved in conventional activities (e.g., playing sports, going to school, doing homework) are free to deviate. Stated alternatively, if adolescents are committed to conventional activities and spend their time pursuing those interests, they will be less likely to commit delinquent behavior. Consider the teenager who participates in practice for the play after school, gets home around 6:30 p.m., and then does homework until 10 p.m. When does he or she have time to get into trouble?

The problem with this concept that even Hirschi (1969:190) recognized is that delinquency actually takes very little time. Thus, time spent in conventional activities will only deter delinquency if that time is indicative of a commitment to a conventional pursuit. Given this, it becomes difficult to measure involvement separately from commitment, and some researchers have suggested integrating the two concepts into one (Krohn and Massey 1980).

Belief

What we believe concerning the law or other rules that are intended to govern our behavior is one reason why we behave the way we do. Social learning theory (Chapter 6) suggests that people learn definitions favorable and unfavorable to the violation of the law and will commit delinquent behavior if they learn more definitions favorable to violation than unfavorable to violation. In most of the work on this theory, the focus has been on the learning of definitions favorable to the violation of the law.

For control theorists, it is the *absence* of effective beliefs that forbid or discourage delinquency, which allows for such behavior to occur. A control theorist contends that there is variation in the degree to which people believe in the moral validity of the law. People vary on the degree to which they believe that lawmakers have the right to make and enforce laws or that their parents have the right to set standards of behavior for them. Those who do not have a strong belief in the moral validity of the law or the rules set by their parents are not as constrained by them and, therefore, are more likely to violate those standards. Note that the emphasis is not on the moral correctness of specific behaviors but rather on the general set of rules. A person might obey a law despite not agreeing with the specific content of the law because he or she believes that the state has the right to make and enforce laws.

Social control theory suggests that when one or more of these elements of the social bond are weakened or broken, individuals are freed from the constraints of the bond and are more likely to commit delinquent behavior. This applies to all four elements; if teenagers' relationships with their parents deteriorate, if they are not committed to acquiring a higher education, if they are no longer involved in conventional activities, or if they do not believe in the moral validity of the law, they are more likely to engage in delinquency. The elements of the social bond are also hypothesized to be related to one another. For example, if teenagers are less attached to their parents, it is expected they will be less committed to conventional goals. The youth who does not have a strong bond with his or her parents will be less likely to share their interest in the pursuit of conventional goals and will be less concerned about living up to their parents' expectations.

It also follows that the more the overall social bond is weakened, the more probable is delinquent behavior. The individual who has a troubled relationship with his or her parents and is not involved in conventional activities would be more likely to commit delinquent behavior than would the individual whose bond to conventionality is weak in terms of only one of these elements.

Hirschi did not specify a formal causal order among the elements of the social bond. He did, however, claim that the element of attachment to parents occupies a central role in the theory and implied that attachment should be

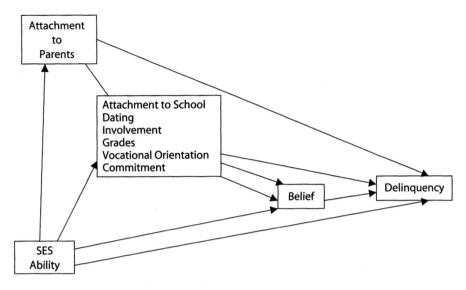

Figure 7.1 Complex Model of the Social Bond.

considered causally prior to the other elements. Other researchers have concurred that attachment to parents should be considered causally prior to the other elements of the social bond. Thus, weak attachment to parents should lead to less commitment and involvement in conventional arenas and to a weaker belief in the moral validity of the law. Moreover, some have suggested that commitment and involvement should be antecedent to belief (Wiatrowski, Griswold, and Roberts 1981). Figure 7.1 depicts the causal order suggested by Wiatrowski and colleagues. This is a reasonable interpretation of the causal order implied by Hirschi.

An argument could be made that the relationship between some of the elements is reciprocal in nature. For example, if lower attachment to parents leads to youth being less committed to conventional goals, the lower commitment to conventional goals may, in turn, lead to more problems with parents. We will consider this and other related issues after we discuss how the concepts in social control theory have been measured.

Concepts and Measurement Issues

The structure of social control theory is rather straightforward. Four concepts are all predicted to be inversely related to delinquent behavior. However, the picture is more complicated since, for some of the concepts, alternative measures reasonably reflect their meaning. For example, attachment could be measured by questions asking about the quality of the relationship between parent and child or the degree to which the parent supervises the child. As stated earlier, Hirschi (1969), in an empirical examination of his theory, provided a beginning point for discussing these alternative measures.

The concept that has received the most attention in the research literature and has generated the greatest number of alternative measures is attachment to parents. Hirschi provided five separate measures of this concept reflecting different aspects of parenting and the child–parent relationship. He included measures of supervision, emotional attachment, intimacy of communication flowing from the child to the parent (and a separate indicator measuring communication flowing from the parent to the child), identification with the parent(s), and parental disciplinary techniques. With the exception of the scale measuring disciplinary techniques, these measures are computed separately for mothers and fathers. All of the measures, excluding identification with mother or father, have multiple items that are incorporated in scales or indices, although Hirschi did not report their reliability coefficients (which indicate the degree of overall relationship among the items in the scale).

Hirschi measured parental supervision with a two-item index, asking children whether their parent knew where they were and with whom when away from home. If children think their parents know where they are and with whom they are interacting, parents will have a "psychological presence" that should constrain adolescents from doing something wrong. Hirschi found that supervision by both father and mother were inversely related to self-reported delinquency. Subsequent measures of this dimension similarly operationalized have generated similar zero-order (correlational) relationships (Kempf 1993; Krohn and Massey 1980; Wiatrowski et al. 1981).

The affectional bond between parent and child is the most commonly measured construct from Hirschi's theory. Hirschi had two measures of affection: affectional identification and intimacy of communication. Affectional identification is a single-item measure asking the child if he or she would like to be the kind of person their mother or father is. Intimacy of communication is divided into two separate indices, one in which the communication flows from the child to the parent and the second in which the communication flows from the parent to the child. The former includes two items that ask whether the child shares thoughts and feelings with the parent and how often they talk about future plans, while the latter asks the child whether the parent explains reasons for rules, helps explain other things the child does not understand, and explains how he or she feels to the child. The latter measure is often subsumed under a broader concept referred to as positive parenting, identifying appropriate or recommended parenting practices.

In terms of criteria that social scientists typically use to evaluate measurement techniques, Hirschi's measures were problematic. The number of items he used to measure each concept (often only one) is limited. And Hirschi, despite claiming that the items in an index were closely related, did not provide information on the strength of relationships. Nevertheless, at the zero-order level, all items were related to self-reported delinquency in his study.

The measurement of attachment to parents has developed along a number of different dimensions. Instruments measuring the affectional tie between child and parent have been expanded to include more items, and their measurement structure has been more thoroughly examined than what was found in Hirschi's original work. One example of such measurement strategies is the use of the Hudson scale (Hudson 1982), briefly discussed in Chapter 1. The scale contains items that can be used to measure the child's perception about their relationship to the parent or the parent's perception about the relationship he or she has with the child. The questions ask about how well they get along, trust, and understand one another; get angry or violent toward one another; enjoy or are proud of one another; and wish that the other was more like others (parents or children) they know. The scale has excellent measurement properties with reliability coefficients typically exceeding .80 (recall the scale ranges from 0 to 1, with scores closer to 1 indicating higher reliability). It was later adopted by the Denver, Pittsburgh, and Rochester studies as part of the Causes and Correlates of Crime and Delinquency three-site study (Smith, Weiher, and Van Kammen 1991). In most research using the scale, it is found to have a moderate but significant relationship with delinquency (Smith and Krohn, 1995). The size of the relationship has been found to vary, however, depending on whether the parent or child is asked the questions (Smith and Krohn 1995).

Other dimensions of parenting in addition to the affectional tie between parent and child, supervision, and communication have also been occasionally incorporated into the measurement of attachment. For example, the type and consistency of discipline have been examined, as well as positive parenting (offering verbal and tangible rewards for proper behavior) (Smith and Krohn 1995). Although these measures may be related to attachment to parents, they are better conceptualized as measures of effective parenting.

One of the more interesting methodological developments has been the increased use of observational techniques to measure aspects of the parent–child relationship (Simons, Stewart, Gordon, Conger, and Elder 2002; Stewart and Simons 2006; Stewart, Simons, and Conger 2002; Stewart, Simons, Conger, and Scaramella 2002). The use of these techniques has become more prevalent with the development of videotaping, making the recording of parent–child interaction easier than in the past. Typically, researchers provide the parent and child with some task to accomplish and record the interaction that takes place as they attempt to finish the task. Tasks such as putting a puzzle together or cleaning up toys after the child has played with them can be used to observe how the parent interacts with the child and how the child responds to the parent. Does the interaction evidence any hostility? Does the parent use appropriate strategies to elicit cooperation from the child? Does the parent verbally reward the child? Is there a display of affection between the child and parent? The videotapes are then coded by trained researchers along a number of dimensions (e.g., affection between the parent and child). The development of the codes and the ability for researchers to employ these codes in a uniform manner is a key part of this measurement strategy.

Observational measures of the parent–child relationship have been used to predict which youth will exhibit delinquent behavior with some success. These measures have been used both by themselves and in conjunction with survey measures. Conger et al. (2002) found that when measured by a combination of observational and survey methods, attachment to parents is a strong predictor of antisocial and delinquent behavior. The advantage of these measures is that they do not rely solely on the reporting of the parent or child but reflect how the participants interact. Observational measures are also quite useful with young children who may have difficulty understanding survey questions posed to them.

Commitment to Conventional Action

Travis Hirschi centered his examination of commitment to conventional action on the educational arena. He used a few different measures of educational commitment, all of which were inversely related to delinquent behavior.

Hirschi began by exploring the relationships between educational aspirations and expectations and delinquency. Aspirations and expectations gauge how committed a person is to the goal of getting an education (ranging from less than high school education to college graduate). Hirschi found that responses to both the question of whether individuals would like to get a college education and whether they expect to obtain one are negatively related to delinquency. Hirschi also examined whether youth whose aspirations exceeded their expectations of obtaining a college education would be more, rather than less, likely to commit delinquent behavior, as some versions of strain theory would suggest (see Chapter 5). He found that those boys whose aspirations exceeded their expectations were no more likely to be delinquent than were boys who had expectations consistent with their aspirations.

Hirschi also used a measure of grade point average (GPA) and an index of achievement orientation to measure commitment to education. The index of achievement orientation contained items tapping how hard youth try in school and whether good grades are important. The assumption is that trying hard on schoolwork is an indicator of commitment to education as is the outcome of that effort, GPA. Neither of these directly measures commitment to an educational goal, but both are reasonable estimates and fall within the general concept of commitment to conventional action. Hirschi found that both GPA and the achievement index are inversely related to delinquent behavior.

Subsequent examinations of social control theory use similar measures. GPA continues to be used as an indicator of commitment, as does educational aspirations. Scales similar to, but more extensive than, Hirschi's achievement index have been developed to provide a better assessment of how youth feel about school (e.g., Cernkovich and Giordano 1992). To some extent, these measures tap not only commitment but also Hirschi's notion of attachment to school. They include questions about how much the youth likes school, whether it is boring, whether he or she does his or her homework, and whether he or she tries hard (Thornberry, Lizotte, Krohn, Farnworth, and Jang 1991). The scales generally demonstrate high inter-item reliability and are moderately successful in predicting delinquent behavior (Cernkovich and Girodano 1992; Thornberry et al. 1991). See Maddox and Prinz (2003) for a review of the school bonding literature.

Education is not the only arena of conventional action to which youth can be committed. Hirschi assessed the impact of expectations concerning jobs desired. Youth who aspired to professional as opposed to manual jobs had lower rates of delinquency regardless of their expectations. Most examinations of social control theory do not include this measure or other indicators of job or career commitment, primarily because most youth do not have the type of jobs (if they have one at all) to which one would expect them to be committed. Youth tend to have part-time or temporary as opposed to full-time permanent jobs. Research that has extended the investigation of antisocial behavior into young adulthood and beyond has had to develop measures to assess job or career commitment. One way this has been done is to generate items that are analogous to the school commitment scale and reword them to make them applicable to the work arena. For example, one Rochester Youth Development Study (RYDS) scale includes items similar to those found in the school commitment scale, such as liking one's job or being bored with it. Items such as doing extra work to improve success at the job and caring if one gets fired are also included. As more studies extend the research design to cover the years from adolescence to adulthood, commitment in other areas of life will have to be measured.

One issue that Hirschi did not explore is commitment to religion. Clearly this has been examined in other literature, but it is typically referred to as religiosity, that is, the degree to which individuals are committed to their religious beliefs and/or their church. Religiosity has been measured in a number of ways. One is simply to ask respondents how religious a person they are. While this is straightforward, it does not address dimensions of commitment to religion that one might want to incorporate (e.g., how often respondents read religious material, pray, let religious beliefs influence everyday decisions, discuss religion with other people, and watch or listen to religious programs). Generally, items measuring commitment to religion are better predictors of delinquency than are items that simply ask whether a person is a member of a church or synagogue or what his or her denomination is (Chard-Wierschem, 1998).

Involvement

Involvement is the time dimension of commitment. Presumably, if you are committed to a goal or activity you will spend more time pursuing it. The more time you spend in conventional activities, the less time you have available to participate in delinquent behavior. Hirschi (1969) used time spent doing homework as a measure of involvement in the conventional institution of the school. He found that it was strongly related to delinquency. But note how similar this is to the question about how hard one works to do well in school, which Hirschi used as a measure of commitment. It does not appear that these two measures are either conceptually or empirically distinct. Hirschi admitted it may not be necessary or even possible to measure involvement separate from commitment. To capture involvement, he also included a more general measure that asked youth if they felt like there was nothing to do (time on one's hands). He found a weak relationship between this measure and delinquency.

Other researchers have expanded the measurement of involvement to include participation in conventional arenas including religion, community organizations, extracurricular school activities, and clubs. Overall, the relationships between these measures and delinquency are relatively weak or nonsignificant when entered in an analysis that also includes commitment measures.

Belief

The concept of belief has been measured in a number of different ways. Recall that Hirschi (1969:198) stated that social control theory is not concerned with beliefs that cause delinquency but rather with the absence of beliefs that forbid delinquency. Therefore, some of the items that are used to measure differential association theory's concept of definitions favorable to delinquency would not be appropriate to measure the beliefs. For example, questions tapping whether respondents think it is okay to steal, assault, vandalize, and so on would not adequately reflect Hirschi's concept.

How then should we measure beliefs? Let us examine the measures Hirschi used. He argued that lack of respect for the police is indicative of lack of respect for the law. To ensure that answers to the question concerning whether respondents have respect for the police were not a result of contact with police, Hirschi examined the relationship between this item and delinquency for those respondents who did not have previous police contact. He found the expected inverse relationship between respect for the police and delinquent behavior. Hirschi also claimed that if expediency was the only reason for not committing a crime, youth would be more likely to commit a crime if they think they can get away with it. To examine this, he used a question asking whether it was all right to get around the law if one could get away with it. Again, he found support for the hypothesis.

The other belief measures that Hirschi used were a series of questions intended to measure Sykes and Matza's (1957) concept of techniques of neutralization. Recall that this has also been used as a measure of definitions favorable to the violation of the law (see Chapter 6). The techniques of neutralization can be interpreted as ways in which people cognitively suspend their beliefs in conventional values. Hirschi views them in this way not for initial delinquent acts but for subsequent acts. He maintains that these beliefs are formed after the initial behaviors and can serve to increase the probability of future acts. Hirschi included questions concerning denial of responsibility, denial of injury, denial of the victim, and condemnation of condemners.

On the whole, the items that Hirschi used to measure his belief concept are problematic. While the single items used to measure respect for the police and getting around the law come close to the meaning of belief in that they reflect some dissatisfaction with the law and its agents, these are single items with weak measurement properties. Moreover, it is not clear just what role techniques of neutralization measures have in Hirschi's theory. If they are only useful for addressing the continuation of criminal behavior, as Hirschi seems to suggest, their contribution is necessarily limited. Indeed, their role in addressing continued criminality is also not clear given the cross-sectional design of Hirschi's study.

Subsequent research has measured the belief concept in a number of ways. Krohn and Massey (1980) used three items representing belief in parental norms, legal norms, and belief in the value of education. In a later study, Massey and Krohn (1986) measured belief with three other scales, the first two of which were comprised of items asking how wrong it is to use different types of drugs. They admitted these items did not conform to Hirschi's notion that beliefs should not be tied to any specific behavior, but these were the only items identified by factor analysis to be included in a scale. Three items that were not identified as belonging in the scale by this statistical method more appropriately measured the belief concept. They were appropriateness of parental rules, duty to obey the law, and the appropriateness of laws against teenage smoking. Massey and Krohn used these items despite a relatively low alpha coefficient of reliability (.54).

Wiatrowski et al. (1981); Marcos, Bahr, and Johnson (1986); and Agnew (1985) constructed belief scores intended to measure the more general concept of beliefs. Wiatrowski et al. used a scale comprised of items assessing attitudes toward truthfulness, lying, cheating, and helping friends. They attempted to incorporate items that assessed guilt in doing something wrong, but the scale did not have acceptable reliability and was dropped from the analysis. Marcos et al. also recognized that a general belief measure was appropriate. They developed a conventional values scale comprised of four items including the importance of following rules and obeying the law, the acceptability of stealing under specified circumstances, and attitudes toward sneaking into a movie or ballgame without paying. Marcos et al. did not report the reliability of the scale. Finally, Agnew's measure included items asking respondents if it is good to be honest and avoid things like cheating.

While Kempf (1993) reports that there is a substantial similarity in the way the concept of beliefs has been measured, it must be noted that some researchers have measured the concept by asking about respondents' attitudes toward specific forms of delinquent behavior. For example, Agnew (1991), using the National Youth Study data, includes a deviant beliefs measure comprised of items asking how wrong it is to engage in specific delinquent acts. Again, Hirschi stated that this type of measure is more consistent with the notion of definitions favorable to the violation of law from a differential association. We now turn our attention to the various analytical issues in testing social control theory.

Analytical Issues

There have been numerous empirical examinations of social control theory. Kempf (1993) identified 71 studies that specifically tested Hirschi's version of the theory from 1970 to 1991. In addition, many other studies have incorporated one or more measures of the elements of the social bond into their research. If it is not the most frequently researched theory, it is certainly one of the two or three most frequently researched. As such, a number of analytical issues could be examined. We limit our discussion to two of the most important: cross-sectional versus longitudinal research and the role of peers.

Cross-Sectional versus Longitudinal Analysis

Early studies of social control theory, including Hirschi's own research, were limited to cross-sectional designs in which the elements of the social bond were measured at the same time as the behavioral outcome (e.g., crime or delinquency). We first take a brief look at illustrative results from the cross-sectional studies and then compare those results to those from longitudinal analyses.

Hirschi (1969) was primarily concerned with demonstrating that each element of the social bond was significantly related to delinquency rather than attempting to examine how well the combined effect of the elements could predict behavior. He therefore relied primarily on zero-order relationships (i.e., correlations) between a measure of an element and self-reported delinquency. The results from these analyses indicate that the elements of the social bond are all related to delinquency. Because he was not particularly concerned with the relative effect of the social bond measures, his use of multivariate analysis was quite limited. Hence, not only is it difficult to determine how each element fared relative to the others but it is also impossible to know how well the elements combined to explain the variance in delinquency.

Krohn and Massey (1980) performed a multivariate regression analysis incorporating 10 variables designed to measure attachment, commitment, and belief. They assessed how well these variables explained four indices of deviant behavior: marijuana and alcohol use, minor delinquency, hard drug use, and serious delinquency. The purpose was to determine if social control theory accounted equally well for deviance at different levels of seriousness. They found that the collective bond measures accounted for between 18% and 29% of the variance in the deviance measures. Social bond variables were more successful in explaining less serious deviant behavior (alcohol and marijuana use and minor delinquency) than hard drug use and serious delinquency. A commitment scale indicating how important it was for respondents to participate in seven different conventional activities and a measure of GPA had the strongest effect on three of the four deviance scales. Belief measures had the largest effect on alcohol and marijuana use. Krohn and

Massey explain the greater effectiveness of social control theory in explaining less serious offenses by suggesting that the theory is intended to account for the release from constraints, not the embeddedness in the delinquent activity. It makes sense that the theory better predicts less serious behavior.

Wiatrowski et al. (1981) used one wave of the Youth in Transition data to assess social control theory. After creating scales from the individual questionnaire items, they examined a model that incorporated 11 variables measuring the four components of the social bond. They found that the 11 items accounted for 32.5% of the variance in a seven-item scale of delinquent behavior. Variables measuring attachment to parents, school commitment, involvement, and beliefs were all significantly related to delinquency in the hypothesized directions. Peer attachment, however, was not a significant predictor. Although they did not have longitudinal data, they identified a causal model suggested by the theory (see Figure 7.1). The model suggests that socioeconomic class and educational ability are directly related to delinquency and indirectly related through parental attachment, commitment, involvement, and belief. Parental attachment is related to delinquency only indirectly through the four commitment and involvement variables and belief. The commitment and involvement variables have both direct and indirect effects (through belief) on delinquency. Belief is directly related to delinquency. Acknowledging that this model could not be adequately tested without longitudinal data, the findings were consistent with the predicted relationships.

To properly test a model such as that suggested by Wiatrowski et al. (1981), longitudinal data are needed. Cross-sectional analysis does not allow one to determine which variables are a cause or a consequence of other variables in the model. For example, the model purports that if one holds conventional beliefs, he or she will be less likely to participate in delinquent behavior. However, it is equally plausible that participating in delinquent behavior increases the probability that one will hold less conventional beliefs. To adequately address such a model, one needs to be able to separate out belief and delinquent behavior in time.

Robert Agnew (1985) was one of the first researchers to use longitudinal data to examine Hirschi's theory. Interestingly, Agnew used the same data set that Wiatrowski et al. (1981) did—the Youth in Transition data. Whereas Wiatrowski and colleagues only used one wave of the data to be consistent with how Hirschi had conducted his analysis, Agnew used the first two waves of the data. Agnew first examined the cross-sectional relationship using eight of the variables contained in the earlier Wiatrowski et al. study. His findings were similar in that the variables accounted for a moderate amount of the variance in a total delinquency scale (29%) and a small amount of the variance in a serious delinquency scale (15%). Note that this is consistent with Krohn and Massey's findings indicating that social control theory better accounts for less serious than more serious delinquency.

When Agnew incorporated the second wave of the data, he used Wave 1 measures of the social control variables to predict the Wave 2 measures of delinquency. To properly estimate the impact of Wave 1 social control variables on Wave 2 delinquency, Wave 1 (prior) delinquency had to be included in the equation. Essentially, the analysis addresses the question of whether Wave 1 social control variables can predict the *change* in delinquency that occurred between Wave 1 and Wave 2.

Agnew found that, when examined over time, the social control variables had a weaker effect on the change in delinquency than the cross-sectional effects he reported. This would be expected given the separation in time of the measures of the two variables. What surprised Agnew, however, was just how weak those effects were. Only three of the social control variables (grades, dating, and belief) were significantly related to Wave 2 delinquent behavior. Moreover, he reported that the social control variables were able to explain only between 1% and 2% of the variance in delinquency at Wave 2. Agnew suggests that part of the reason why these measures do not account for the change in delinquency is that there is a great deal of stability in delinquency over time: Adolescents who commit delinquency at the beginning of tenth grade (Wave 1) are highly likely to continue to commit delinquency at the end of eleventh grade (Wave 2), leaving little variance to be explained by social control variables. Agnew also notes that other research (LaGrange and White 1985) found that the impact of social control variables tends to diminish as adolescents enter the later teenage years. Wave 2 measures of delinquency were collected when most of the respondents were age 17 or older. Of course, an alternative explanation for the findings is that social control variables may have little causal effect on delinquent behavior, even though they are significantly correlated (remember, correlation is not necessarily causation).

Agnew's findings are consistent with most longitudinal studies of social control theory. Parental attachment has been found to have at best a weak effect when examined within a longitudinal framework (Agnew 1991; Elliott, Huizinga, and Ageton 1985; Massey and Krohn 1986; Paternoster and Iovanni 1986). Similar conclusions have been documented regarding commitment and involvement (Agnew 1991; Elliott et al. 1985; McCarthy and Hoge 1984; Paternoster and Iovanni 1986). The results regarding belief are mixed, with some studies reporting a moderate impact on delinquency (Burkett and Warren 1987; Massey and Krohn 1986; Paternoster and Iovanni 1986) and others reporting no effect (Agnew 1991; Elliott et al. 1985; Paternoster 1988). It would appear that Agnew's (1985) conclusion that "cross-sectional studies have greatly exaggerated the importance of Hirschi's social control theory" (p. 58) reflects the consensus found in longitudinal studies of the theory.

The Role of Peers

One way to address the weak longitudinal relationship between social control variables and delinquency is to consider mediating variables that might intervene between social control and delinquent behavior. Recall that Hirschi's theory is explicitly amotivational; that is, the weakening of the elements of the social bond frees one to commit delinquency, it does not cause one to. Hence, some have suggested adding a reason for committing delinquency to social control theory, hypothesizing that the weakening of the elements of the social bond is indirectly related to delinquency through a variable that provides a motivation for the youth to misbehave. The most considered candidate to play that mediating role has been associating with delinquent peers. Associating with delinquent peers is one of the key variables used in tests of differential association theory (see Chapter 6). The assumption is that if one hangs out and is friends with peers who are involved in delinquency, he or she will be more likely to be delinquent.

This is not the role that peers play in Hirschi's theory. Recall that he argued that attachment to others would *constrain* one from delinquent behavior. He further suggested that the relationships among adolescents who engage in delinquent behavior would not be intimate. He therefore predicted that those adolescents who were closely attached to their peers would be less likely to engage in delinquency. For Hirschi, the observed cross-sectional relationship between having delinquent friends and one's own delinquency was more the result of people who engage in a particular type of behavior seeking out and interacting with others who also engage in that behavior. For example, if a youth enjoys playing soccer, he or she seeks others who also play the sport. This youth may not necessarily be influenced by, or may not necessarily learn how to play, from those other kids. Hirschi's position on the role of peers has been controversial and largely unsupported. Attachment to peers has not typically been shown to be a constraint on delinquent behavior (Agnew 1985). There is overwhelming support for the importance of having friends who are delinquent (Krohn, Thornberry, Rivera, and LeBlanc 2001; Warr 2002), as much of the literature on differential association theory indicates.

Some researchers have suggested that we need to recognize that Hirschi was wrong about peers and that the theory should be modified to incorporate peers as a deviance-enhancing, rather than deviance-constraining, force. Marcos et al. (1986) examined an integrated model (see Figure 7.2) that included parental, educational, and religious attachment; conventional values; and drug-using friends to predict drug use. All of the social control variables were hypothesized to be related to having drug-using friends. Having drug-using friends and the control variables, except for parental attachment, were hypothesized to lead to drug use. In additional analyses, Marcos and colleagues examined the viability of the model for explaining alcohol use, cigarette smoking, marijuana use, and the use of amphetamines and depressants (in separate models). Although there were differences in the findings across the different drugs, the general theoretical model was supported.

Massey and Krohn (1986) also suggested that a measure of friends' behavior be incorporated with social control measures to explain adolescent deviant behavior. They had the advantage of data collected over three time periods so they could separate the variables over time and examine the causal structure of their model. They included attachment to parents, attachment to

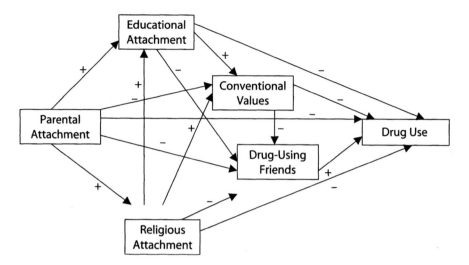

Figure 7.2 An Integrated Bonding/Association Model of Drug Use.

peers, a measure of family smoking, respondent smoking, and socioeconomic status (SES) at Time 1; a measure of commitment, belief, and the number of deviant friends at Time 2; and respondent smoking at Time 3. They found significant effects of SES, family influences, attachment to parents, and Time 1 smoking on both commitment and belief at Time 2. Commitment and belief were, in turn, significantly related to peer smoking at Time 2. Only smoking at Time 1, commitment, association with friends who smoked, and attachment to peers had significant direct effects on smoking at Time 3. Attachment to peers increased rather than decreased the probability of smoking at Time 3, contrary to what Hirschi had hypothesized. Overall, their model accounted for 58% of the variance in Time 3 smoking.

Agnew (1991) used two waves of the National Youth Survey to examine a longitudinal model similar to that developed by Massey and Krohn (1986). However, Agnew employed a more sophisticated data analytic strategy (structural equation modeling), providing a better estimate of the relative effects of social control and differential association measures on delinquency. The technique is too complicated to detail for our current purposes. Agnew found that parental attachment and school attachment at Time 1 were not directly related to delinquent behavior at Time 2. Only commitment had a constraining effect on Time 2 minor delinquency, while delinquent peers and deviant beliefs increased the probability of delinquency. Parental and school attachment were only indirectly related to delinquency through commitment. School attachment was indirectly related to delinquency through commitment and delinquent beliefs. Agnew (1991) concludes by suggesting that the social control variables "have only a weak effect" and that his findings "raise further doubt about the importance attributed to Hirschi's theory as an explanation of general delinquency among adolescents" (p. 150).

Directions for Future Research

When you first learned about how social control theory explained why an adolescent would refrain from committing delinquent behavior, did it seem like a plausible explanation? For many of us, this theory is appealing because it does seem to make intuitive sense. We do not engage in delinquency because we care about what our parents will think, because we have long-term goals and short-term activities in which we are involved, and because we believe in conventional values.

Social control theory is also appealing because it can account for other findings in regard to delinquent and criminal behavior. For example, we know that the prevalence rate for delinquency is highest during the ages of 15–17. How would you account for that using the concepts and hypotheses from social control theory? The teenage years are a time when youth are in the process of learning to become independent from their parents. Parents, while recognizing that their children must become independent, still want to protect them from mistakes. Often this tension between children and parents causes strife in their relationship, thus weakening the element of attachment. As adolescents acquire more independence and develop additional commitments in the conventional system (e.g., college or a full-time job), delinquency rates go down. The prevalence of delinquency continues to decrease as youth become young adults. Researchers who have examined this process typically attribute the continual decline in the prevalence of crime to the formation of different, albeit strong, bonds, such as establishing one's own family, continuing one's education, or beginning a career (Kandel and Yamaguchi 1987; Sampson and Laub 1993; Yamaguchi and Kandel 1985).

Social control theory does not link criminal behavior directly to social class or race, unlike many of the theories that we discuss in this book. For example, traditional strain theory (Chapter 5) assumes that delinquent and criminal behavior is disproportionately a lower-class phenomenon. In this perspective, strain is caused by a failure to achieve monetary or status success because of socioeconomic disadvantage. In social control theory, there is no necessary reason why members of one social class or race/ethnicity should be more likely to have weak or severed elements of the social bond. Thus, the theory is equally applicable to middle-class as well as lower-class people.

Despite these advantages, equivocal empirical support for the theory is problematic. While the cross-sectional studies document significant relationships between most measures of the social bond and deviant behavior, longitudinal studies largely fail to support the notion of a direct causal link between the elements and deviance. There is some support for a direct relationship between commitment and delinquency or drug use, but attachment and belief are, at best, only indirectly related to behavior. Moreover, when examined within a longitudinal research design, measures of the social bond elements explain only a relatively small amount of the variance in deviant behavior.

Despite the disappointing longitudinal results, theorists and researchers have not abandoned the insights of Hirschi's theory. Rather, they have suggested that the elements of the bond are important in the causal process that leads to deviant behavior because they increase the probability of people forming deviant beliefs and associations with deviant peers. The development of models that integrate the elements of the social bond with some motivational variable, such as delinquent peers, will continue to be the way in which social control measures are used in future research.

Moreover, the ideas contained in the theory have been successfully used to account for desistance from crime in adulthood. As more longitudinal studies over longer spans of the life course are available, better indicators of adult social bonds will be devised and employed to account for why some individuals no longer commit crime while a minority of others continue to do so. Identifying the factors that lead to desistance may very well be social control theory's most important and enduring contribution.

Self-Control Theory

It is not often that a scholar known for being the chief proponent of one theoretical perspective adopts a different, albeit related, theoretical perspective. This is precisely what Travis Hirschi has done. In conjunction with Michael Gottfredson (Gottfredson and Hirschi 1990), Hirschi coauthored a book entitled *A General Theory of Crime* in which what is known as self-control theory is developed.

The main premise of their theory is straightforward: Self-control accounts for a difference in the extent to which people are vulnerable to temptations. It is "the barrier that stands between the actor and obvious momentary benefits crime provides" (Hirschi and Gottfredson 1993:53). You probably have been in a situation with a friend where both of you were tempted to do something that was illegal. Maybe it was using drugs or shoplifting a CD from the music store. One of you may have proceeded to do it while the other resisted the temptation to reap the immediate benefits of the behavior because of concern for the longer-term consequences. Social control theory would attribute the criminal behavior to a weak social bond. Alternatively, Gottfredson and Hirschi would view the individual who did not give in to temptation as having high self-control, whereas the individual who committed the illegal behavior would be seen as having low self-control.

How do you determine if a person has low self-control? Gottfredson and Hirschi claim you can identify characteristics of the people who commit crime from the nature of crime itself. They state, "[C]riminal acts provide immediate gratification of desires" (Gottfredson and Hirschi 1990:89). Therefore, people who commit criminal acts have a "here and now" orientation, as opposed to the ability to defer gratification, a characteristic of those with high self-control. Identifying the other characteristics of criminal acts as being easy or simple, exciting, risky or thrilling, having meager long-term benefits, requiring little skill or planning, and resulting in pain or discomfort for the victim, Gottfredson and Hirschi deduce that people with low self-control tend to be "impulsive, insensitive, physical, risk-taking, short-sighted, and non-verbal" (p. 90).

Gottfredson and Hirschi posit that self-control is developed or not developed early in life. Importantly, they go on to suggest that once an individual's level of self-control is developed, it is stable throughout his or her life. So, if you were an impulsive risk taker as a child (low self-control), you would exhibit the same tendencies as an adult. Although the level of criminal offending may vary for a person at different ages because of other contingencies like having a job and so on, the person who had low self-control will always have a greater propensity to commit crime than will the person with high self-control. This assumption allows the theory to account for the stability in criminal offending. By stability in offending, we simply mean that a person who commits crime at a young age is more likely to commit crime at an older age compared to the person who did not commit crime at a young age. A more direct way of stating this is that the best predictor of future criminal behavior is past criminal behavior.

As just noted, self-control develops very early in a person's life. Subsequently, the influence of new friends or family and other sources of socialization that occur after a level of self-control has developed will have minimal impact on one's level of self-control. Again, the difference in self-control levels among people will be stable regardless of later events or situations. Those later influences may impact the probability of criminal behavior so that the person who acquires a well-paying job may not be as likely to commit criminal behavior as he was during his teenage years, but he will still have low self-control that may be manifested in other noncriminal behaviors (e.g., going to a casino and gambling, practicing unsafe sex, driving without a seatbelt).

Gottfredson and Hirschi consider their perspective a "general theory of crime" because they assert that the theory, and more specifically the concept of self-control, applies to all types of behavior where an inability to resist the temptation of an immediate benefit might come into play. Because they characterize most criminal acts in this way, their theory is meant to apply to a wide variety of criminal (and noncriminal) behaviors. Indeed, one of the advantages of their theoretical perspective, they claim, is that it explains the versatility of crime. Criminals tend not to be specialists; if they commit one type of crime, they are likely to commit other types as well. In fact, Gottfredson and Hirschi suggest that criminals are also likely to engage in other noncriminal risky behaviors such as smoking, drinking, speeding, and so on. These are important and far-reaching claims for the impact of low self-control. In short, low self-control is believed to be a stable characteristic in a person's life that increases the probability of his or her committing a wide variety of both criminal and noncriminal risky behaviors. So how do we develop self-control?

Gottfredson and Hirschi suggest that the major cause of low self-control is ineffective child rearing. Much parenting is done to suppress impulsive behavior and teach children the consequences of their acts. How many times did your parents say to you, "Think before you act," or claim that you would be sorry if you acted in a certain way? Gottfredson and Hirschi contend that parents also teach their children to be sensitive to the feelings and rights of others. Young children are admonished not to take another child's toy and are told not to call another child names because it would make him or her feel bad.

More specifically, Gottfredson and Hirschi identify three necessary conditions for adequate child rearing in order to teach the child self-control. Parents must monitor the child's behavior. For adequate monitoring to take place, the parent must care about the child. Hence, attachment of the parent to the child is an important precondition for adequate supervision. It is also recognized that some criminal behaviors are easier to monitor than others, a partial explanation for why the prevalence of some deviant activities is higher than for others.

The second aspect of effective parenting is recognition of deviant behavior when it takes place. According to the theory, some parents do not recognize behavior that evidences a lack of self-control. For example, some parents allow their children to watch too much television or to stay home from school when they do not feel like going.

Once recognized, parents must punish deviant acts. Gottfredson and Hirschi are not suggesting harsh punishments. In fact, they recognize that the most effective punishment may simply be the expression of disapproval. However, they do claim that parents who punish too leniently, or too harshly, foster a lack of self-control.

Other family-related factors such as parental criminality, family size, single-parent families, and mothers who work outside the home play a role in generating low self-control to the extent that these factors have an impact on effective parenting. For example, parents who have criminal records are assumed to have low self-control. Their lack of self-control makes them less effective parents. Gottfredson and Hirschi (1990:101) state, "If criminal behavior is oriented toward short-term rewards, and if child-rearing is oriented toward long-term rewards, there is little reason to expect parents themselves lacking self-control to be particularly adept at instilling self-control in their children." Family size, single-parent families, and mothers working outside the home have an impact to the extent that they contribute to parent(s) not having the time to devote to supervising the child. Gottfredson and Hirschi recognize that if provisions for supervision can be made, these conditions should not impact self-control.

What about the school as an arena in which the child can learn self-control? Gottfredson and Hirschi recognize that the school has a positive effect in this respect. However, the school is not seen as being as effective as it should be in modern-day society. This is because the same families that are ineffective in child rearing do not support their child in school-related activities. The school then plays only a secondary role to the family in generating self-control.

Ineffective child rearing at young ages results in a failure on the part of the child to learn how to resist the temptations of immediate gratification. This lack of self-control is manifested by a number of markers, including being impulsive, insensitive, physical, risk-taking, short-sighted, and nonverbal. The level of self-control, once established, will be relatively stable throughout a person's life. Therefore, people with low self-control, as opposed to those with high self-control, will continue to have low self-control throughout their lives. Because most deviant activities, including legal and illegal behaviors, are the result of failing to resist temptations, low self-control explains a wide variety of deviant acts.

Concepts and Measurement Issues

Gottfredson and Hirschi's theory has generated much debate and criticism. While there have certainly been questions about just what they meant by self-control, when it is established, and how much it can change over the life course, the primary controversy regarding the empirical investigation of the theory is just how researchers measure the concept of self-control.

Controversy concerning the measurement of self-control arose from Hirschi and Gottfredson's (1993:49) assertion that "the best indicators of self-control are the acts we use self-control to explain: criminal, delinquent, and reckless acts." This statement appears in a commentary on two research articles that used different approaches to measure self-control. Hirschi and Gottfredson find the approach used by Keane, Maxim, and Teevan (1993) to be particularly appealing. Keane and colleagues attempt to explain driving under the influence of alcohol with a number of measures that are related to drinking and/or driving behavior. They used data from the Ontario Survey of Nighttime Drivers (Province of Ontario 1988), a survey of drivers that had passed by sites along highways and were pulled over by the police for the purpose of participating in the survey. In addition to filling out a brief questionnaire, drivers were given a breathalyzer test. On the questionnaire, respondents were asked if they used their seatbelts. They were also asked to state their opinion on what percentage of drivers who were legally impaired would be stopped by police. These two questions were used to assess risk-taking behavior. To measure impulsiveness, the surveyors asked drivers if anyone had tried to discourage them from drinking and driving. If someone had tried to discourage them but they drove under the influence anyway, the researchers inferred that the drivers were impulsive. Pleasure seeking was measured by a question regarding the number of drinks they had consumed in the past seven days. Finally, respondents were asked if they thought they were intoxicated. If they did and drove anyway, it would be an indicator of lack of self-control.

Note that all the questions used to tap self-control deal specifically with either risky driving (failure to use seatbelts) or drinking. Critics of this approach suggest that to predict risky driving (driving while intoxicated) with other measures of risky driving (failure to use seatbelts) is tautological; essentially, it amounts to saying that if someone is a risky driver he or she will be a risky driver. It is neither surprising nor theoretically interesting that

Keane et al. find support for their hypotheses. Hirschi and Gottfredson (1993) recognize that some may not find this research convincing, so they suggest that independent indicators of self-control can be used. They suggest indicators such as "whining, pushing, and shoving (as a child); smoking and drinking and excessive television watching and accident frequency (as a teenager); difficulties in interpersonal relations, employment instability, automobile accidents, drinking and smoking (as an adult)" (p. 53). Since these behaviors are not criminal, they are logically independent from crime and any relationships found cannot be considered a matter of definition. The Achenbach externalization scale has frequently been used to assess antisocial behavior in early childhood (Achenbach 1991, 1992). Using this scale has the clear advantage of identifying low self-control not only independent of delinquent behavior, but also prior to the time when most youth begin to exhibit criminal or delinquent behavior.

The alternative method of measuring self-control is to assume that self-control represents underlying personality traits that can be measured through self-reports about what respondents are like. Grasmick, Tittle, Bursik, and Arneklev (1993) took this approach and developed a 24-item scale representing six components of low self-control: impulsivity, the preference for simple tasks, risk seeking, physical activities, self-centeredness, and having a temper (see Table 7.1). For example, impulsivity is measured by four items including statements like, "I often act on the spur of the moment without stopping to think." Although they provide measures of six different components of self-control, Grasmick et al. suggest the theory argues that self-control is a unidimensional latent trait that should be measured by combining the components into one scale. They examine this assumption through a series of factor analyses, concluding there is some support for Gottfredson and Hirschi's unidimensional trait argument.

It would seem that Grasmick et al.'s approach has a number of advantages over Keane et al.'s approach. Grasmick et al.'s measure specifically taps the underlying dimensions identified by Gottfredson and Hirschi. It does so by asking about tendencies that are behaviorally generic; that is, they are not tied to any one type of deviant behavior. Moreover, they clearly avoid the tautology problem that is inherent in Keane et al.'s approach. So why do Hirschi and Gottfredson prefer Keane et al.'s approach?

Hirschi and Gottfredson identify two reasons why they prefer the behavioral approach over the trait approach. They suggest that their theory predicts that self-report responses will be less valid the more a respondent lacks self-control, both because of his or her unwillingness to participate in surveys and the greater tendency for those lacking self-control to lie. Since the Grasmick et al. approach requires respondents to self-report both their general attitudes and behaviors and their specific participation in crime, whereas Keane et al. only self-report on the independent variable measures, Hirschi and Gottfredson prefer the latter.

Hirschi and Gottfredson also have a substantive or theoretical reason for not opting for the trait approach. They are concerned that this approach

Table 7.1 Low Self-Control Scale Items

Item

Impulsivity

I often act on the spur of the moment without stopping to think.
I don't devote much thought and effort to preparing for the future.
I often do whatever brings me pleasure here and now, even at the cost of some distant goal.
I'm more concerned with what happens to me in the short run than in the long run.

Simple Tasks

I frequently try to avoid projects that I know will be difficult.
When things get complicated, I tend to quit or withdraw.
The things in life that are easiest to do bring me the most pleasure.
I dislike really hard tasks that stretch my abilities to the limit.

Risk Seeking

I like to test myself every now and then by doing something a little risky.
Sometimes I will take a risk just for the fun of it.
I sometimes find it exciting to do things for which I might get in trouble.
Excitement and adventure are more important to me than security.

Physical Activities

If I had a choice, I would almost always rather do something physical than something mental.
I almost always feel better when I am on the move than when I am sitting and thinking.
I like to get out and do things more than I like to read or contemplate ideas.
I seem to have more energy and a greater need for activity than most other people my age.

Self-Centered

I try to look out for myself first, even if it means making things difficult for other people.
I'm not very sympathetic to other people when they are having problems.
If things I do upset people, it's their problem not mine.
I will try to get the things I want even when I know it's causing problems for other people.

Temper

I lose my temper pretty easily.
Often, when I'm angry at people I feel more like hurting them than talking to them about why I am angry.
When I'm really angry, other people better stay away from me.
When I have a serious disagreement with someone, it's usually hard for me to talk calmly about it without getting upset.

implies that self-control is a personality concept that predisposes people to crime. They remind us that a fundamental assumption of their theory is that people are not specifically predisposed to crime, but develop self-control at an early age primarily because of child-rearing practices.

Neither of Hirschi and Gottfredson's criticisms of the trait approach is compelling in our view. Both the behavioral approach of Keane et al. and the trait approach of Grasmick et al. rely on self-reports. If Hirschi and Gottfredson are correct about respondents with low self-control providing less valid information in self-report studies, it would seem they would be particularly likely to lie on the types of measures that Keane et al. use to tap self-control. More information on the potential bias of self-report studies in assessing self-control hypotheses must be presented to justify Hirschi and Gottfredson's assertion.

Their assumption that treating self-control as a personality concept is problematic because it implies that self-control predisposes people to crime is also not convincing. It is just as logical to suggest that having the attributes contained in Grasmick et al.'s scale makes it difficult for people to control their behavior, putting them in a position, but not necessarily motivating them, to commit criminal acts. This interpretation of an observed relationship between Grasmick et al.'s self-control measure and criminal behavior is consistent with the control assumptions that Hirschi and Gottfredson propound.

Most researchers prefer to use a trait-based scale similar to Grasmick et al. In an extensive review of published research on self-control theory, Pratt and Cullen (2000) identified 94 studies. Of these studies, 82 used an attitudinal measure of self-control whereas only 12 used a behavioral-based measure. The most common attitudinal measure was the Grasmick et al. scale. What was particularly surprising about Pratt and Cullen's review is that, in terms of the strength of the relationship between self-control and deviant behavior, it did not matter whether an attitudinal or behavioral measure was used. The average relationship between attitudinal measures and deviancy was .257 and for behavioral measures it was .277, a difference that was not statistically significant.

Analytical Issues

Gottfredson and Hirschi make some strong claims for their general theory of crime that go well beyond the prediction that measures of self-control will be significantly related to criminal behavior. They suggest that self-control should be equally capable of explaining a range of deviant behaviors and that it should do so equally well for people with different demographic characteristics (e.g., sex, race, class, age). Gottfredson and Hirschi also suggest that the effect of variables from competing theories (e.g., delinquent peers, elements of the social bond) should not be significant once a measure of self-control is included in the analysis. Furthermore, because self-control is considered a stable characteristic that once established early in life does not change, Gottfredson and Hirschi claim that longitudinal research should not obtain different results than cross-sectional research.

What does the research demonstrate regarding these hypotheses? First, we reiterate that measures of self-control, whether behavioral or attitudinal, are consistently related to criminal behavior. Pratt and Cullen (2000) point out that the average size of the relationship between self-control measures and criminal behavior that they observed in their review of 94 studies compares very favorably to reviews of concepts from other theoretical perspectives. They conclude that the average effect size they observed "would rank self-control as one of the strongest known correlates of crime" (Pratt and Cullen

2000:952). Is this strong effect size documented regardless of the type of deviant or criminal behavior studied? Pratt and Cullen conclude that it is. Looking at studies that examined crime versus those that examined analogous behaviors, they find that the average relationships are significant for both, with those for analogous behaviors being somewhat larger.

More recent studies are consistent with Pratt and Cullen's conclusions. Jones and Quisenberry (2004) examined a range of problematic behaviors including risky driving, risky sex, pathological gambling, academic dishonesty, and thrill and adventure seeking. The latter measure is distinguished from the others in that it contained behaviors not typically considered antisocial but that still should be predicted by self-control. The scale included mild forms of thrill and adventure seeking (e.g., playing a contact sport) and more extreme forms (e.g., skydiving). The Grasmick et al. scale was used to predict these behaviors. Jones and Quisenberry found strong support for Gottfredson and Hirschi's claim that self-control is significantly related to a wide variety of problematic behaviors, including both antisocial behavior and socially acceptable thrill or adventure seeking.

Benda (2005) examined how well self-control predicted four measures of deviant behavior (alcohol use, drug use, property crime, and violent crime) among a sample of 3,335 public high school students. He found that both behavioral and cognitive measures of self-control were significantly related to all four forms of deviance. The behavioral measure, not surprisingly, was more strongly related to deviance than was the cognitive measure.

Generality across Different Subgroups

Gottfredson and Hirschi not only assert that their theory applies to most forms of deviant behavior but also claim that it can account for such behavior equally well across different subgroups. If males have higher rates of criminal behavior than females, it is because they have lower self-control. There are two implications of their position. First, the relationship between self-control measures and deviant behavior should be similar across different subgroups. Second, if you remove the effects of self-control by statistically controlling for it, the relationship between sex and crime should no longer be significant. A similar hypothesis would apply to differences across other subgroups such as race or ethnicity. Tittle, Ward, and Grasmick (2003:426) state that the interpretation of the main demographic facts about crime and deviance is the strongest implication of self-control theory.

In their review, Pratt and Cullen (2000) found that the nature of the sample did not have a significant effect on the average relationship documented between self-control and deviant behavior. There were some differences in the size of effects across subgroups, but these differences were not significant. Benda's (2005) results differ from Pratt and Cullen's conclusion. He found that, for males and females, the relationship between self-control and deviant behavior did differ depending on the type of deviant behavior examined. For example, he found that the relationship between alcohol use and self-control was stronger for males than it was for females. This finding is inconsistent with the logic of Gottfredson and Hirschi's theory.

Tittle et al.'s (2003) results are more supportive of the generality assumption in self-control theory. As expected, measures of self-control were significantly negatively related to deviant behavior for both males and females. For only one of the four different measures of deviance (an index asking respondents whether they anticipate committing any of several different forms of misbehavior) was the difference in the relationship between self-control and deviance different for females and males (the relationship was stronger for females).

A more rigorous method for examining Gottfredson and Hirschi's assertion of the generality of their theory is to determine if a measure of self-control can explain away the relationship between sex and crime. If the reason why males commit more crime than females is because they have lower self-control levels, then by statistically controlling for self-control when examining the relationship between sex and crime, the initial relationship should change from being statistically significant to nonsignificant.

Both Benda (2005) and Tittle et al. (2003) examine whether measures of self-control mediate the relationship between sex and deviance. Both studies find that, although the relationship between sex and deviance is reduced, it remains significant. It is important to recall that both studies used behavioral and cognitive measures of self-control. These findings suggest that Gottfredson and Hirschi overstated their claim for the effectiveness of self-control in explaining relationships between demographic variables and deviant behavior. Clearly, self-control can account for some of this relationship, but it does not account for all of it. To fully explain the relationship between sex and deviance, we need to identify additional explanatory variables.

Incorporating Other Theoretical Variables

Perhaps the most ambitious claim that Gottfredson and Hirschi make for their concept of self-control is that variables from other theories will not contribute significantly to the explanation of deviant behavior once self-control is accounted for. Essentially, they suggest that self-control is not only a necessary but also a sufficient explanation of deviant behavior; if you know an individual's level of self-control, you do not need to know whether the person has friends who are delinquent, whether the person has limited opportunities, and so on, to explain his or her behavior.

Pratt and Cullen (2000) conclude from their meta-analysis that "Gottfredson and Hirschi's claim that variables from social learning theory should not contribute significantly to the amount of explained variation in crime after self-control has been held constant is unsupported by the data" (p. 948). Findings consistent with this conclusion have been reported in other studies as well (Chapple 2005; Gibson, Schreck, and Miller 2004; Winfree and Bernat 1998). Wright, Caspi, Moffitt, and Silva (1999) assessed whether social bonds mediated the relationship between self-control and delinquency. They found that self-control was largely mediated by measures of the social bond. Longshore, Chang, and Messina (2005) reached a similar conclusion. Thus, although self-control is an important variable in explaining delinquent behavior, it is not the only important variable. Indeed, it may not even be the most important variable.

Longitudinal versus Cross-Sectional Design

For all theories, the effect of most independent variables will lessen as the time increases between when the independent variable is measured and when the dependent variable (e.g., delinquency) is measured. This makes sense when you consider that most factors in people's lives have an immediate impact and, as time passes, the effect either wears off or people adjust to the effect. Gottfredson and Hirschi, however, view self-control as a stable characteristic that should not change over time. They therefore assert that the effect of self-control should not vary even when the time between measuring self-control and delinquency does. A corollary of this assertion is that we do not need to perform longitudinal analysis to determine the causal impact of self-control on delinquency. Once again, there does not appear to be much support for this assertion. Pratt and Cullen (2000) compared a limited number of studies that used longitudinal and cross-sectional designs. Based on their analysis, they concluded that the effects of self-control variables were significantly lower when examined longitudinally than when examined cross-sectionally.

Directions for Future Research

If all of the claims that Gottfredson and Hirschi have made regarding self-control theory were supported, we would certainly say it was a most "elegant" theory. By the term elegant, we are referring to a theory that can explain, in an intuitively appealing manner, a number of different facts about crime and deviance with relatively few concepts and propositions. Unfortunately, as we have seen in our review of the empirical studies, many of the claims the authors make for the generality of self-control are either not supported or are only partially supported.

So, where does that leave us in our assessment of the contribution of self-control theory to the explanation of crime and deviance? As suggested earlier, the notion that we can account for deviant behavior by identifying the degree to which people have a propensity to control their own behaviors is intuitively appealing. Does it not make sense that engaging in crime is a reflection of being less able to control your own behavior compared to other people? And it would seem that the markers of low self-control, such as a tendency to take risks and being impulsive, are reasonable indicators of low self-control.

The empirical studies of self-control theory are supportive of the relationship between self-control, measured either behaviorally or cognitively, and a variety of types of deviant behavior. Given the similarity in results, using both types of measures, and given the potential for falling into a tautological trap when using behavioral measures, we see no reason why future research should not use cognitive instead of behavioral measures.

Gottfredson and Hirschi also provide an explanation for how low self-control is developed early in childhood. As in other control theories, the family—and, more specifically, parenting—is an critical factor. For Gottfredson and Hirschi, the story ends there. Levels of self-control are established early in life, and the relative differences in those levels remain stable thereafter. Research, however, has demonstrated that later factors are also important in accounting for subsequent delinquent and criminal behavior (Sampson and Laub 1993; Laub and Sampson 2003). Some of these factors mediate the relationship between self-control and later behavior, suggesting an indirect rather than direct effect of self-control. The conclusion we derive from this is that self-control is an important predictor of delinquent behavior that should be taken into consideration when explaining delinquency and crime. However, other variables need to be incorporated, both as antecedents and consequences of self-control, to understand how self-control contributes to the explanation of crime and delinquency.

Have you noticed we have reached similar conclusions regarding both social control and self-control theories? Both are intuitively appealing, identifying factors that make sense as predictors of deviant behavior. It is logical that youth who are less tied to conventional others, conventional goals and activities, and conventional beliefs would be more likely to be delinquent. It also is logical that individuals who have not formed an ability to control their behaviors would be more likely to engage in all forms of deviance. The research literature has confirmed that these variables provide a partial answer to why we commit crime. But for both perspectives, it is important to recognize that additional processes are involved. To the extent that proponents of the theories are willing to accommodate these other processes, the concepts will continue to play an important role in future theoretical developments. However, to the extent that proponents of the theory adhere strictly to some of the overarching assumptions suggested by Hirschi and by Gottfredson and Hirschi, theoretical developments involving these concepts will be limited.

Discussion Questions

1. What is the difference between social control and self-control? According to their respective theories, how is each related to crime and delinquency?
2. Some have suggested that social control theory should incorporate concepts from other theories, most notably, the concept of delinquent peers from differential association theory. How might the concept of delinquent peers fit into the control framework? In your opinion, does this improve the theory?
3. Because Hirschi was primarily concerned with demonstrating that each element of the social bond (attachment, commitment, involvement, and

belief) was related to delinquency, his analyses were primarily corre-lational in nature. What limitations result from such analyses?

4. What is the problem with measuring self-control by asking survey respondents if they've committed a list of varying crimes in the last year? What is a better method for measuring self-control?

5. Given the methodological and analytical issues pertinent to each the-ory, is social control or self-control a more convincing explanation of crime in your opinion? Why?

CHAPTER 8

LABELING THEORY

Introduction

Consider the following anecdote:

> Sam is an old guy who likes to drink beer and smoke pot. All his life, he has carried with him a can of beer and a pipe. In 1920, the Eighteenth Amendment was passed and Prohibition began. During this time, it was illegal to consume alcohol in the United States. The day after Prohibition passed, Sam was arrested, brought to court, and sentenced to prison for alcohol consumption. The pipe was of no concern because marijuana use was legal in 1920. Sam served his sentence and was released in 1938. He was delighted to discover that Prohibition had been repealed in 1933, and stepped back on to the street with his beer and pipe. He was, of course, immediately arrested and thrown back in jail for possession of marijuana, as marijuana was made illegal in 1937.

Think for a minute about Sam. How can we understand his behavior? What is the cause of his criminality? How would other micro-level theories such as differential association (Chapter 6) or social control (Chapter 7) explain Sam's behavior? As you may have guessed, these perspectives are not very effective. We could better understand Sam's criminality by focusing not on his behavior but rather on societal *reaction* to his behavior. Societal or audience reaction to behavior is a critical component of labeling theory. Labeling theorists ask: (1) What is defined as deviance? and (2) Who is defined as deviant? In answering these questions, the theory addresses larger issues such as: Who makes the laws in the first place? Is breaking the law the most important criterion for being a criminal? Are all people who break the law criminals? Questions about the origins of law set labeling apart from other criminological theories that take for granted how laws come to exist.

Like many other criminological theories, labeling theory is a product of its times—the 1960s. This decade was a turbulent era in U.S. history highlighted by the civil rights movement, the Vietnam antiwar movement, and the women's movement. Against this backdrop, sociologists began critically to question traditional views of society, including those of crime (Adler, Mueller, and Laufer 1991:177). For the first time in history, some criminologists turned attention away from theories that explained crime based on characteristics of offenders or of the social structure. Instead, they focused on the ways in which people and institutions respond to crime and criminals. They set out to demonstrate that people become criminals because of what others with power, especially those in the criminal justice system, do. These "critical" criminologists largely rejected the consensus model of crime on which earlier theories were based.

In this social climate, these theorists, many of whom were labeling theorists, began to explore how and why certain acts were defined as deviant or criminal and others were not. They viewed criminals not as inherently evil persons engaged in inherently wrong acts but rather as individuals who had a criminal status conferred upon them by the criminal justice system and community at large. This view contrasts sharply with earlier theories that assumed deviants could be separated from nondeviants and deviance from nondeviance based on intrinsic characteristics. As evident in previous chapters, traditional criminological theories adopt an "absolutist" approach, meaning that deviance is considered inherent in behavior. In contrast, labeling theory adopts a "relativist" definition, assuming that nothing about a given behavior automatically makes it deviant. In other words, deviance is not a property of behavior but rather the result of how others regard that behavior. As such, criminal acts themselves are less significant than the social reaction to them (think back to Sam). One of labeling theory's biggest proponents, Howard S. Becker (1963:9), notes, "Deviance is not a quality of the act the person commits, but rather a consequence of the application by others of rules and sanctions to an 'offender.' The deviant is one to whom that label has successfully been applied; deviant behavior is behavior that people so label."

As will become increasingly apparent throughout the chapter, labeling theory considerably broadens criminologists' investigations of crime. Whereas other theories focus on what causes criminal behavior, labeling theory—by arguing that criminality is not intrinsic in an act or in a person who commits an act—moves beyond the etiological question. It also broadens the study of crime by directing attention to the role of the state in the production of crime and deviance (Paternoster and Iovanni 1989). Previously, criminologists had not been interested in the study of the state, typically considered a field of inquiry for political scientists or political sociologists. But labeling theorists observed that the state essentially creates crime by deciding that some behaviors are so harmful or injurious that they deserve to be called "criminal."

This and the following chapter ("Conflict Theory") discuss the major critical perspectives on crime. Although critical perspectives differ in many respects, they all consider the definition of crime "problematic," meaning that the definition of a behavior as a crime and the defining of individuals as criminals need to be explained. In explaining how these definitions originate, critical perspectives emphasize the concept of power and inequality based on differences in power. The theories maintain that behaviors by people or groups with power are less likely to be labeled crimes than behaviors by those without power. In this chapter we focus on labeling theory.

Intellectual History of Labeling Theory

The intellectual roots of labeling theory can be traced, in part, to symbolic interactionism theory in sociology (Paternoster and Iovanni 1989:362). "Symbolic interactionism" refers to the idea that meaning arises in social interaction, through communication using language or symbols (Blumer 1969). According to George Herbert Mead (1934), Charles Horton Cooley (1902), and other symbolic interactionist scholars, an individual's identity and self-concept, cognitive processes, values, and attitudes exist only in the context of acting, reacting, and changing in social interaction with others (Akers and Sellers 2004:136). Alternatively stated, our conception of ourselves is shaped by our interaction with others. In this sense, social order is an outcome of interaction and negotiation between members of society.

With respect to labeling theory, symbolic interactionism implies that the labeling or appraising of individuals by others affects one's identity. A critical concept in symbolic interactionism is the "looking-glass self" (Cooley 1902), in which our self-concepts are reflections of others' opinions of us. What others think of us is communicated, in part, by applying labels to us (e.g., mother, athlete, criminal, drug addict). We define ourselves in response to the ways that others have labeled, defined, and reacted to us. We come to learn that we are friends or enemies, attractive or ugly, funny or serious, and overweight, skinny, or just right, and often treat ourselves accordingly. We view ourselves from the perspectives of others and we take into account how they have treated us to develop a sense of who and what we are as a result (Curra 2000). In short, symbolic interactionism provides a general behavioral theory from which the specific propositions of labeling theory are derived.

One of the earliest statements on labeling theory was provided by historian Frank Tannenbaum in *Crime and the Community*, published in 1938. In his study of juvenile street gangs, Tannenbaum described the process by which a delinquent youth is created. He began by noting how breaking windows, climbing onto roofs, and playing truant are all normal parts of the adolescent quest for excitement and adventure. He then described how local merchants and others in the community may consider youth who engage in these behaviors a nuisance. According to Tannenbaum, this conflict between the youth and the community sparks the beginning of the process by which the "evil act" transforms the youth into an "evil individual," followed by efforts to separate him or her from conventional society. Given a delinquent label, these youth begin to think of themselves in the way they have been characterized. Tannenbaum maintained that it is the process of labeling, or the "dramatization of evil," that locks a mischievous youth into a delinquent role. He (1938:19–20) notes, "The process of making the criminal, therefore, is a process of tagging, defining, identifying, segregating, describing, emphasizing, making conscious and self-conscious; it becomes a way of stimulating, suggesting, emphasizing, and evoking the very traits that are complained of."

The first systematic analysis highlighting the effects of labeling on deviant behavior was by Edwin M. Lemert, whose 1951 book, *Social Pathology*, many consider the original version of labeling theory. Lemert's work was critical because he carefully outlined the sequential stages in the labeling process (discussed later). But it was the publication of Howard S. Becker's book *Outsiders* in 1963 that placed labeling theory at the center of theories of crime and deviance (Akers and Sellers 2004:138). Becker analyzed the history of marijuana laws in the United States. He described the historical context by which rule creators labeled marijuana use as deviant through the Marijuana Tax Act of 1937. According to Becker, the Federal Bureau of Narcotics started a moral crusade against marijuana use in response to public sentiment, reflected in the Protestant ethic of individual responsibility where actions taken solely for the purpose of pleasure were frowned upon. To negatively label marijuana use, the Federal Bureau of Narcotics saturated the media with stories of marijuana-crazed Mexican immigrants, children out of control, and marijuana-induced rape. Becker argues that these media accounts facilitated new legislation to criminalize the drug and provide the Bureau with money and power. Becker's work, building on the foundation of symbolic interactionist theorists along with Tannenbaum and Lemert, launched labeling theory into mainstream criminology.

Labeling Theory

Labeling theory is often referred to as the "societal reaction" perspective (Gove 1980). According to the theory, without societal reaction, deviance would most likely remain sporadic and unorganized. Societal reaction is what causes deviance to stabilize into a deviant career. Why is this? Because once it becomes known that an individual has engaged in deviance, he or she can be labeled (e.g., "thief," "whore," "junkie") and segregated from society. This process of segregation creates "outsiders" (as Becker [1963] called them), or societal outcasts, who may turn to other outcasts. As society begins to view these individuals as deviant and respond accordingly, the deviants can internalize their labels and react to society's response by continuing to engage in the behavior now expected of them.

As implied by this explanation, labeling theory focuses its attention on the *process* of criminalization. It is a sequential theory, or perspective in which factors that explain initial involvement in crime or deviance are not necessarily factors that explain continued or systematic involvement. The labeling process is described next.

The Labeling Process

The basic assumptions of labeling theory are discussed in Lemert's classic work, *Social Pathology* (1951). Lemert claimed that there are two kinds of deviant acts: primary and secondary. Primary deviance, or what Scheff (1963:439) also termed "residual deviance," occurs when an individual violates norms without viewing himself or herself as being involved in a deviant social role.

This form of deviance, which can arise from diverse sources, including genetic, physiological, psychological, and sociological origins, is ignored or rationalized and transitory. In other words, prior to public labeling, deviants' violations of the law are thought to be unorganized, inconsistent, and infrequent. As such, these acts typically do not alter an individual's self-concept. With societal reaction and labeling, however, the deviance changes in form and function. Once a label is attached to a person, sporadic deviance can stabilize into a deviant career. Secondary deviant acts, therefore, are those that result from the change in self-concept brought about by the labeling process. Secondary deviance sets in after the community has become aware of an individual's primary deviance and has labeled the individual (e.g., "criminal"). Secondary deviance is thus produced when individuals engage in behavior that they would not have otherwise done had they not been labeled "deviant."

According to Lemert (1951), the sequence of interaction leading to secondary deviance is as follows: (1) primary deviation, (2) social penalties, (3) further primary deviation, (4) stronger penalties and rejection, (5) further deviation, (6) crisis reached in the tolerance quotient, expressed in formal action by the community stigmatizing the deviant, (7) strengthening of the deviant conduct as a reaction to the stigmatizing and penalties, and (8) ultimate acceptance of the deviant social status and efforts at adjustment on the basis of the associated role. In practical terms, the labeling process looks something like this:

1. A youth commits a deviant act, or primary deviation, such as stealing something from a neighbor.
2. There is an informal social reaction—the neighbor gets angry.
3. The youth continues to break rules (primary deviations) by vandalizing the neighbor's car or stealing additional items.
4. There is increased but still informal social reaction; the neighbor tells the youth's parents.
5. The youth commits a more serious act; he is caught shoplifting (still a primary deviation).
6. There is now a formal reaction; the youth is charged and adjudicated a "juvenile delinquent" in juvenile court.
7. The youth is now labeled "delinquent" by the court and "bad" by the neighborhood, his family, conventional peers, and others.
8. The youth begins to think of himself as "delinquent"; he joins other unconventional youths engaging in similar bad behaviors.
9. The youth commits another yet more serious deviant act (secondary deviation), robbing a local grocery store with members of a gang.
10. He is returned to juvenile court, has more offenses added to his record, is cast out further from conventional society, and adopts a deviant lifestyle. (Adler et al. 1991:180)

Perhaps you are wondering how one's identity can transform so dramatically as a result of being labeled. How do people become involved in a sustained pattern of deviance following labeling? What are the causal mechanisms central to the labeling process? These are best understood by considering the various effects of labeling on individuals.

The Effects of Labeling

There are three ways that the labeling of deviant behavior can lead to secondary deviation: by altering one's self-concept, by limiting one's range of conventional opportunities, and by encouraging movement into a deviant subculture. Each path reinforces the others, leading to greater involvement in crime and deviance for the labeled individual.

Regarding altering one's self-concept, people who violate the law, are arrested by the police, and are tried in court may alter their self-perceptions and come to think of themselves as criminals or deviants. Schwartz and Skolnick (1962) argued that processing juveniles through the legal system, for example, produces a permanent negative effect on their self-concept. And research by Bliss (1977) found that delinquents in detention had the most negative self-concepts, followed by delinquents on probation, while nondelinquents had the most positive self-concepts. Along these lines, court appearances have been referred to as "status degradation ceremonies" in which people accused of violating the law are recast as unworthy persons and given a new identity as a result of being labeled (Garfinkel 1956). Being officially labeled in court can produce a self-fulfilling prophecy, so that people behave in ways consistent with their altered self-concepts.

Schur's (1971:69–81) concept of "role engulfment" applies here. He argues that when deviant labels are applied, persons being labeled tend to get "caught up" in the deviant role, organizing their identities and activities around that role. That is, one who is role-engulfed both thinks of himself or herself and is thought of by others in terms of the deviant identity and acts accordingly. This is because an individual's self-concept is a product of many influences including the reactions of others. Of course, the effects of labeling vary depending on who is being labeled. While the label can affect a person's self-concept, the individual can also reject or fight the label (Paternoster and Iovanni 1989:376). In other words, the opinions of others are sometimes incorporated into the self-concept but those opinions may also be rejected as inconsistent with a person's idea of himself or herself (Davis 1961; Scimecca 1977). There is also support for the idea that labels matter more for some groups than others. One study found that the self-concepts of lower-class white delinquents appear to be more influenced by appearance in juvenile court than are the self-concepts of other delinquents (Ageton and Elliott 1974). Another study demonstrated that labeling was related to secondary deviance (drug use) among males but not females (Ray and Downs 1986). In short, according to labeling theory, self-concepts are constructed in an active way. Identity is not fixed. Rather, one's self-concept is formed and re-formed in an interactive process where the individual is reflexive, role-playing, and negotiating his or her identity (Akers and Sellers 2004:137).

Even if one's self-concept does not change as a result of labeling, a person may experience difficulty in relationships with parents, friends, teachers, or potential employers. Thus, a second possible effect of labeling is a reduction of opportunities for, and harm to the social relationships of, people labeled by the criminal justice system. As Becker (1963) noted, labeling deviants denies them the ordinary means of carrying on routines of everyday life open to most people (e.g., securing a job, finding a partner, calling upon friends for help), and because of this, deviants of necessity must develop illegitimate routines. This notion is supported by Schur's (1971) concept of "secondary elaboration," by which he meant that the effects of the labeling process become so significant that individuals who want to escape from their deviant groups and return to the conventional world find it difficult to do so. Schur views the experiences of members from the gay and drug cultures as illustrative of this. The strength of the label, once acquired, tends to exclude such people permanently from mainstream culture. Schur found that involvement in activities that are disapproved of can lead to more participation in deviance than one had originally planned, thereby increasing the social distance between the labeled deviant and the conventional world.

A good example of when this can happen is with respect to finding employment. How likely are employers to want to hire ex-convicts for a job, even if they served their sentence without incident? According to research, the answer is "not very likely." There is now ample evidence that job opportunities become restricted once potential employers learn about a person's trouble with the law (Davies and Tanner 2003; Erickson and Goodstadt 1979; Schwartz and Skolnick 1962; Western 2002). This research finds that a criminal record presents a major barrier to employment (Pager 2003:937). In fact, even the knowledge that a job applicant has been acquitted of charges seems to make some employers less willing to offer him or her a job (Schwartz and Skolnick 1962). In short, labeling can segregate individuals from conventional realms even in the absence of physical obstacles such as incarceration (Matsueda 2001:226).

Finally, in addition to the effects of labeling on self-concepts and social relationships, labeling can push people into subcultures where they learn criminal motives and skills from peers (see social learning theories, Chapter 6). Tannenbaum (1938) noted that a juvenile delinquent's isolation forces him into companionship with other children similarly situated and this group (in some cases a gang) becomes his means of escape, his security. Once contact is initiated with members of a subculture, the learning process described by differential association theory may increase law-violating behavior (see Bernburg, Krohn, and Rivera 2006). Joining a deviant subculture provides the individual with rationalizations, motives, and attitudes that support deviant behavior, consistent with differential association theory.

Figure 8.1 illustrates labeling theory in schematic form. As shown, primary deviation can lead to the labeling of the rule breaker, which can affect an individual's self-concept and opportunities and drive the person into a subculture. In the subculture, the individual may undergo a change in self-concept

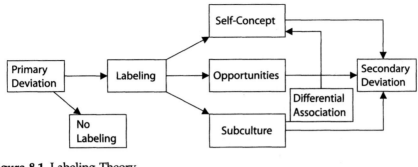

Figure 8.1 Labeling Theory
(*From Conklin 1992:296*)

through differential association with other deviants. In these ways, the labeling process may amplify deviant behavior, leading to secondary deviation.

Note that the emphasis is generally on formal (e.g., criminal justice system) as opposed to informal (e.g., parents, friends, neighbors) labeling. This emphasis reflects, in part, the history of the theory (Paternoster and Bachman 2001). For example, Garfinkel (1956) discussed the conditions that contributed to successful labeling. Recall his discussion of labeling events as "status degradation ceremonies," after which one's status shifts from that of nondeviant to deviant. Garfinkel claimed that these ceremonies are most effective in changing one's status when they are formal, that is, when they involve an institutionalized ceremony such as a public trial. We discuss the role of informal labeling later on in the chapter.

Classic Studies of Labeling Theory

Empirical investigations of labeling theory have been carried out by researchers in many disciplines using a variety of research methods. A number of early studies found support for the effects of labels on subsequent deviance. Research by Wenz (1978), for example, reported that informal labeling by parents and close friends increased the probability of suicide attempts among youth. And Aultman and Wellford (1979) employed variables from several competing theories including anomie, control, and labeling theories and found the variables reflecting labeling by parents and teachers were most closely related to delinquency. Much early research on labeling theory was qualitative in nature. Two classic qualitative studies are described here.

D. L. Rosenhan (1973) designed a clever study to examine the difficulty people have in shedding labels, in this case, the label of mentally ill. He decided the best study approach was from the inside of mental institutions through participant observation. Rosenhan had his graduate students committed to different mental hospitals by complaining they were hearing voices (a symptom commonly linked to schizophrenia). The hospital staff did not know the pseudopatients were actually part of a field experiment. Beyond the alleged symptoms and a falsification of name and occupation, the important events of the pseudopatients' life histories were presented as they had actually occurred. Upon admission to the hospital, Rosenhan instructed the students to act normal. They were not to act crazy in any way (in fact, Rosenhan told them that acting normal was the only way they could get out!). Despite not doing anything out of the ordinary, the pseudopatients remained hospitalized for an average of 19 days (one was hospitalized as long as 52 days), their sanity was never detected, and upon release they retained the deviant label—their schizophrenia was said to be in remission, implying that it could resurface. At no time during their hospital stay was the legitimacy of their schizophrenic label ever questioned.

Rosenhan's findings suggest that once an individual is labeled with a disorder, the label can be difficult to shed. Everything the pseudopatients said and did was understood from this premise; normal behaviors were overlooked entirely or misinterpreted. For example, minor disagreements became deep-seated indicators of emotional instability, boredom was interpreted as nervousness or anxiety, and even the act of writing on a notepad (students were instructed by Rosenhan to keep a journal) was seen by the staff as a sign of deeper psychological disturbance. Rosenhan did not conclude that staff members were incompetent or dishonest; rather, they were doing their jobs effectively. He reasoned that the labels were so powerful that they profoundly affected the way information was processed. Had the same behaviors been observed in a different context, without the perceptual effects of the label, they no doubt would have been interpreted in an entirely different fashion.

Another study by Leslie Margolin (1992) focused on the opposite side of the labeling coin by considering the perspective of the persons doing the labeling. In her work she demonstrates how a criminal label—that of "child abuser"—is constructed by caseworkers and becomes attached to accused individuals, in this case, babysitters of young children. Through her analysis of 120 official records, Margolin shows how social workers "prove" that babysitters committed child abuse. In describing this process, she notes that the victims, or children, are almost always viewed as credible witnesses. She finds that the suspects or babysitters, alternatively, are considered noncredible witnesses, their testimony taken seriously only when they agree with the allegations against them. Margolin also finds that social workers develop several methods for simplifying the labeling process as it became reflected in official records. For example, hitting that resulted in an injury was always treated as if it indicated the intent to injure. Margolin's study underscores the role of those in power in the labeling process.

Theoretical Critiques of Labeling Theory

After the publication of Becker's (1963) work, along with others, the concept of labeling diffused from academic circles to policy circles, and eventually to everyday public discourse (Matsueda 2001:238). Regarding public policy, labeling theory supported the view that we should decriminalize "victimless crimes" because they were not especially harmful and because defining and then reacting to them as crimes could have the unintended result of actually increasing crime (Schur 1965). Some labeling theorists extended this position to a general attitude of "radical nonintervention" (Schur 1973). In short, labeling theory provided support for the decriminalization, diversion, and deinstitutionalization movements (Sheley 1991).

But while efforts were underway to place labeling at the forefront of criminological theory, questions and criticisms about the theory began to emerge. A common one had to do with primary deviance. Critics asked: Why do people engage in primary deviance? What causes these original acts or violations? According to critics, labeling theory fails to explain primary deviance and thus ignores the effects of family, peer relationships, neighborhood composition, and other forces on crime and deviance. At the heart of this criticism is the claim that the theory is deficient because it does not address the root cause of crime (Davis 1972).

This criticism is best countered by one of labeling theory's strongest proponents. Becker (1963) explains that labeling is intended not as a theory of causation but rather as a perspective, a way of looking at human activity, which expands traditional research to include the process of formal social control. Labeling theory is "not so much interested in the person who commits a deviant act once as in the person who sustains a pattern of deviance over a long period of time, who makes deviance a way of life, who organizes identity around a pattern of deviant behavior" (p. 290). The debate about what labeling theory does, or ought to do, has major consequences for analyzing and testing the theory, a point discussed later in the chapter.

Another question often raised by critics is: Where is human agency? They question the overly passive role labeling theory has assigned to offenders. According to Akers (1968), the impression is sometimes given that people are passive participants in the labeling process—they seldom fight back, reject, deny, or otherwise negotiate their self-identities. Because of this, critics argue that labels identify real behavior rather than create it, pointing out that some criminals have a long criminal history, despite never having been apprehended, officially labeled, or stigmatized (Mankoff 1971). They further support this claim with findings from research on individuals who choose deviance as a way of life. Most check forgers, marijuana users, and embezzlers adopt deviant careers without labeling ever occurring (Tittle 1975:404). In short, labeling theory ignores the possibility of genuine commitment to deviance on the part of the rule breaker; theorists are so intent on the reaction to behavior, they completely neglect the fact that someone has defied the conventions of society or broken the law (Gibbs 1966).

Finally, some theorists, particularly conflict theorists (see Chapter 9), believe that labeling theory has not gone far enough in its censure of the system. They claim the labeling approach concentrates too heavily on "nuts, sluts, and perverts," the exotic varieties of deviants who capture the public imagination, rather than on the "unethical, illegal, and destructive actions of powerful individuals, groups, and institutions of our society" (Liazos 1972:111). They claim that more attention be directed toward the powerful in society who formulate the law and apply the labels. Thus, these critics have chastised labeling theorists for not developing a political theory of society to augment the theory of labeling individuals (Matsueda 2001:231).

Concepts and Measurement Issues

Labeling may be one of the most difficult theories to empirically test, in large part due to the conceptualization of key concepts (Paternoster and Iovanni 1989:360). Before we discuss measurement and analytical issues in testing labeling theory, let us first review the theory's major concepts.

Most of the concepts are identified in Figure 8.1. Recall that the labeling process begins with a deviant act, or primary deviance, which is the violation of a norm by chance or for unexplained reasons. These initial norm violations or crimes typically have little influence on the individual and are quickly forgotten. In essence, primary deviance is nonpatterned acts.

An important assumption is that a significant contributor to continued deviance is how individuals who initially violate norms are treated by law-makers, police officers, judges, psychiatrists, and others who have the power to affix the label of "deviant." In some cases, public labeling does not follow primary deviance; in other cases it does. But what constitutes labeling? How is labeling defined? This is difficult to answer because a label is intangible and not easily identifiable. One cannot see, feel, or touch a label. There is no concrete behavior that constitutes "being labeled." Thus, although the labeling of behavior is central to the theory, there is no formal definition of labeling. The consequences of this for testing the theory are discussed in the following sections.

Regardless, when labeling follows primary deviation, according to the theory, there is a greater probability that subsequent deviance will occur. Deviant behavior that is a product of the labeling process is called secondary deviation. Secondary deviance is a persistent form of deviance around which people organize their lives. It differs from primary deviance in that it is the product of the interactions between those committing deviance and those reacting to it. As Lemert (1967) notes, secondary deviance "refers to a special class of socially defined responses which people make to problems created by the societal reaction to their deviance" (p. 40–41). He later explains, "When a person begins to employ his deviant behavior or a role based upon it as a means of defense, attack, or adjustment to the overt and covert problems created by the consequent societal reaction to him, his deviation is secondary" (p. 75–76).

Three other concepts are central—self-concept, opportunity structure, and subculture. These concepts reflect the mediating factors or processes responsible for the relationship between labeling and secondary deviation. These concepts help explain why labeling is likely to influence subsequent acts of crime or deviance. First, recall that labeling can affect one's self-concept. Self-concept refers to the ways in which people describe themselves (Felson

2000). A self-concept is determined by the answer to the question: Who am I? According to labeling theory, people typically think of themselves in line with what others think based on the roles they occupy (e.g., sex, age, race, occupation). Most relevant for labeling theory is the notion that the way individuals think of themselves has an impact on how they behave, inducing the association between a deviant label and secondary deviance.

Second, labeling can diminish an individual's access to legitimate opportunities to achieve success. In American culture, where success is typically measured by money, status, and power (recall strain theory, Chapter 5), individuals are expected to achieve success through legitimate avenues, such as getting an education, working hard, and finding a well-paying job. According to labeling theory, however, such opportunities may become limited once an individual is labeled deviant. As a result, labeled individuals are more likely to engage in subsequent deviance given the challenges they face in legitimately attempting to achieve culturally defined success. These individuals come to see illegitimate opportunities, such as crime, as more viable options.

A third mediating concept is subculture. A subculture is a social group with shared characteristics that distinguish it in some way from the larger cultural group or society in which it is embedded. Here we are referring to a group of people whose behavior has features that set it apart from the wider, dominant culture of the society. But such groups are considered subcultures rather than cultures in their own right because they retain links to, and features of, the wider culture. A subcultural group can develop around any number of social activities (family, work, education, religion, geographic region, etc.). Labeling theory posits that labeling can push individuals into criminal subcultures, which become their means of escape, security, and place of acceptance. It is in a criminal subculture where individuals learn motives and skills from peers, which can influence secondary deviance.

One final concept deserves review—master status. Although we occupy many roles and statuses, the master status is our most important status. It is the identity that others come to best know and judge us by. According to Becker (1963), being labeled deviant or a criminal becomes one's master status. Think back to the study by Rosenhan where graduate students acting as pseudopatients were labeled "schizophrenic" upon admission into mental hospitals. Recall how hospital staff interpreted personality traits and behaviors—even mundane ones—within the confines of the label. For these pseudopatients, being mentally ill was their master status.

Labeling as an Independent and Dependent Variable

How have theorists measured these concepts? What challenges have they faced? How successful have they been in their efforts? And how has measurement of these concepts affected their ability to document empirical support for the theory? Before we answer these questions, an important general point about measurement is warranted. Unlike other theories discussed in this book that clearly specify the independent and dependent variables, labeling theory is less clear.

Labeling as:

Dependent Variable (Effect):
Individual and Community Characteristics, Social Distance, Visibility → Labeling

Independent Variable (Cause):
Labeling → Secondary Deviance

Figure 8.2 Labeling as a Dependent and Independent Variable

As shown in Figure 8.2, labeling theory treats labels as both a dependent variable (effect) and an independent variable (cause) (see Paternoster and Iovanni 1989). It views labels as the dependent variable when it attempts to explain why certain behavior is socially defined as wrong and certain persons are selected for stigmatization and criminalization (e.g., the mentally ill, the poor). In other words, labeling is treated as the dependent variable when the theory is concerned with explaining why certain people come to be labeled deviant or criminal and others do not. According to the theory, a person is labeled primarily as a consequence of several factors, including the power or resources of the individual, the social distance between the labeler and the labelee, the tolerance level in the community, and the visibility of the individual's deviant behavior (Paternoster and Iovanni 1989:373). As Becker (1963:12) notes, "The degree to which an act will be treated as deviant depends on who commits the act and who feels he has been harmed by it."

Alternatively, labeling theory treats labels as the independent variable when it hypothesizes that discrediting labels can cause a continuation of criminal behavior. The label as an independent variable is used to address the question: What are the long-range consequences of being labeled deviant? The critical issue, of course, is whether or not the societal reaction leads to secondary deviance. As discussed in the following section, while there is some empirical support for labeling as a dependent variable (where labels come from) (see Paternoster and Iovanni 1989:369–375) there is relatively little for labeling as an independent variable (cause of deviance) (Akers and Sellers 2004:135; Paternoster and Iovanni 1989:364).

Measures of Labeling and Self-Concept

As with any criminological theory, a number of measurement issues exist. One of the most problematic has to do with the central concept of labeling itself. Many studies use weak and oftentimes questionable measures of labeling. Some studies don't even precisely specify how they measured labeling, giving only general information about their methods. For example, the only information provided about how perceived labeling was measured in Schneider and McKim (2003) is, "The concept . . . is operationalized in five questions constructed to investigate if the probationer perceived to be stigmatized. Here, probationers are asked about their assessment of how employers, family, the community, law enforcement and friends see them as a result of their probation" (p. 21). The authors provide neither the exact questions nor the choices of response so that the reader can discern how perceived labeling was measured.

Most frequently, studies use what amount to proxies of labeling. The most common measures reflect contact with criminal justice officials—the police through arrests, the courts through sentencing, and correction officers through probation. For example, one study uses a single measure of parole officer's assessment of recidivism risk (high or low) as evidence of labeling (Kronick, Lambert, and Lambert 1998). Another study also uses a single measure that reflects "whether a youth had a record for a juvenile-status and/ or adult law violation" (Palamara, Cullen, and Gersten 1986:93). And Johnson et al. (2004) measure labeling using criminal justice system involvement as a proxy; in a survey respondents were asked to indicate how often during the preceding year they had been arrested, placed in juvenile detention or jail, gone to court, or been placed on probation. They find that controlling for a host of other factors, criminal justice system involvement is associated with criminal continuity, supporting the theory's basic proposition (p. 18) (see also Bernburg, Krohn, and Rivera 2006). But these measures are one step removed from the real thing. Is criminal justice system involvement a sufficient proxy for labeling? Do being arrested, tried in court, and sentenced accurately capture the labeling process? Is formal processing through the system indicative of labeling for all violators?

A discerning reader should question the accuracy and preciseness of the above-mentioned measures. Unfortunately, it is difficult to determine the validity of these measures because as noted earlier, the theory offers no precise definition of what constitutes labeling. As a result, labeling's theoretical imprecision leads to insufficient clarity regarding key concepts (Gove 1980; Wellford 1975). In short, the unclear definition of labeling has led to poor operationalization of this concept in many studies.

Similar problems have occurred with measuring other theoretical concepts. According to some, a major obstacle to empirically verifying labeling theory is the self-concept variable (Adams et al. 2003:173). Most self-concept studies have relied on global measures of self-esteem instead of focusing on the adoption of a deviant self-concept. This is problematic because an individual can have a negative self-concept and yet have high self-esteem (Adams et al. 2003:173). Other studies don't directly measure self-concept but instead use crude proxies, such as placement in a noncollege track in high school, to assert they are tapping into "negative self-image" (Lotz and Lee 1999). The question remains: Are these valid measures of self-concept?

Some studies have been more successful in operationalizing labeling theory's key concepts. For example, to examine how one's self-concept is related to delinquency, Matsueda (1992) used data from the National Youth Survey, which conducted personal interviews to collect self-reports of delinquent behavior, parents' reported appraisals of their child, and youths' reflected appraisals of themselves from the standpoint of parents, friends, and teachers. The content of the appraisals cluster on four dimensions: (1) sociable, measured by "well-liked" and "gets along well with others"; (2) "likely to succeed"; (3) distressed, measured by "often upset" and "has a lot of personal problems"; and (4) rule violator, measured by "gets into trouble" and "breaks rules" (Matsueda 1992:1591). Matsueda found support for labeling theory. Reflected appraisals of self are determined by parental appraisals and prior delinquency; further delinquency is affected by reflected appraisals of self as a rule violator; and reflected appraisals mediate much of the effects of parental appraisals, prior delinquency, and other variables on delinquency.

In another study, Adams et al. (2003) incorporated measures of formal and informal labeling of youths to create a combined measure of the effects of societal reactions. The formal labeling variable reflected the extent to which youths had been stigmatized by being processed through the juvenile justice system and in contact with other social control agencies. The variable was operationalized by the juveniles' responses to the following questions, coded $0 =$ no and $1 =$ yes:

1. Have you ever been taken into custody by the police?
2. Have you ever been required to attend an adjudicatory hearing?
3. Have you ever been on court-ordered probation?
4. Have you ever been on court-ordered parole?
5. Have you ever been on house detention?
6. Have you ever had to pay a fine?
7. Have you ever had to pay restitution?
8. Have you ever been in a temporary holdover?
9. Have you ever been sent to counseling?
10. Have you ever been sent to counseling with your parents?

Scores on this index ranged from 0 to 10, with high scores reflecting high levels of negative formal labeling. To measure perceived negative informal labeling, respondents were asked to identify the labels that best reflect the perception of them from the perspective of three groups of significant others—parents, teachers, and peers. The descriptive contrasting adjectives were (1) cooperative or troublesome, (2) good or bad, (3) conforming or deviant, (4) obedient or disobedient, (5) polite or rude, and (6) law-abiding or deviant. Positive descriptors were coded as 0, neutral descriptors as 1, and negative descriptors as 2. Scores for each index ranged from 0 to 12, with higher scores indicating greater perceived negative labeling of the self from the perspectives of others. Clearly the combined negative self-concept measure is an improvement over previous ones because it asks youth specifically about deviant labels by others, incorporates multiple measures of labeling (breadth), and incorporates informal as well as formal labeling (scope). In line with the theory, Adams et al. found that formal labeling increases delinquency, controlling for age, race, and gender of the youth. With respect to informal labeling, only labeling by teachers was found to be a significant predictor of delinquency.

Despite these studies and a handful of others (e.g., Downs and Robertson 1990; Ray and Downs 1986), most research on labeling theory fails to precisely measure the concepts. Unfortunately, such imprecision has major consequences for researchers' ability to show empirical support for the theory. Remember from Chapter 1 that without valid measures we cannot be confident about a study's empirical findings.

Analytical Issues

Is Labeling Theory a Theory?

Several analytical issues also confront labeling theory, the most important of which is whether labeling theory should even be considered a theory at all. Some ambivalence exists in the criminological community as to whether it is actually a theory in the strictest sense of the word (Gove 1980; Hagan 1974; Meade 1974; Tittle 1980; Wellford 1975). This ambivalence stems from two arguments: (1) Labeling theory is not strictly testable, and (2) the studies that do "test" whether labels cause subsequent crime or deviance report little empirical support. Let's discuss each of these in detail.

Regarding the theory's testability, in place of research that is grounded in the empiricist branch of sociological positivism—sophisticated statistical analyses, for example—the labeling perspective stresses field research and participant observation (Schur 1971; Warren and Johnson 1972:70–71). Think back to the landmark studies of Rosenhan (1973) and Margolin (1992), which are based on interviews and participant observation. The goal of these approaches is to produce "sensitizing observations" to "deal with" deviance and to consider the perspective of those who were so labeled (Becker 1967; Schur 1971:22–27).

Not surprisingly, criminologists, most of whom are trained in the positivist tradition, have criticized labeling theory's research methods. Positivists argue that the goal of criminology, like the goal of science generally, is to develop theoretical propositions about phenomena such as deviant and criminal behavior that can be tested with data. The results are then used to reformulate the original theories to improve them (Gibbs 1966:9; Tittle 1975:161). Critics have deemed labeling theory "mushy" and unscientific and have rejected the perspective because it offers no testable hypotheses (Davis 1972:459–460; Hirschi 1975:198; Tittle 1975:159, 175; but see Paternoster and Iovanni 1989). In short, some believe that labeling theory should not be called a theory because it is "a collection of 'sensitizing' notions or a broad perspective about deviance and criminality rather than an explicit set of concepts and propositions" (Gibbons 1994:83).

In response, labeling theorists have argued that they are being criticized for not offering a causal explanation when a central goal of their perspective is to enlarge the scope of theory beyond the causal issue. Labeling theorists contend that they have been held to a view of science that is limited to the empiricist branch of positivism (Scheff 1974:444), yet most are not interested in predictive statements about deviance or in hypothesis testing (Schur 1969:316; for an exception, see Lemert 1981:299). Others suggest that it is appropriate to view the labeling perspective as a theory when theory is defined more broadly as "an attempt to make sense out of observations" (Shoemaker 1996:204).

Although some labeling theorists reject empiricism, research has indeed "tested" the perspective. Critics contend, however, that the findings are not favorable, that the preponderance of evidence shows little or no support for the theory (Hagan 1974; Hirschi 1975; Tittle 1975; Wellford 1975). For example, research shows that the deviant/criminal behavior precedes and creates the label more than the label creates the behavior. And the majority of self-image research on juveniles finds that official labeling does not increase deviant self-images, as the theory predicts (Barkan 1997). Other self-image research finds that a "juvenile delinquent" self-concept does not result in more behavior problems than a "popular teenager" self-concept (Chassin and Young 1981). Moreover, most studies find that when prior offenses and personal and social characteristics are held constant, official labels make little difference in the development of a stabilized deviant career or in the continuation or cessation of deviant behavior (Akers and Sellers 2004:157; Ray and Downs 1986:171). Finally, among those with the same level of primary deviance, those who are not labeled are just as likely as those who are to develop deviant careers (Akers and Sellers 2004:141). Collectively, concerns of theory testing and causality have led some to conclude that although the labeling perspective "is useful in directing our attention to social processes that may, under some circumstances and for some kinds of people, reinforce tendencies to violate the law . . . it is not yet a fully developed and empirically tested theory of crime and delinquency" (Conklin 1992:297).

In response, Paternoster and Iovanni (1989:360) have argued that the lack of empirical support has more to do with how labeling theory has been tested than with the theory's basic assumptions: "Unfortunately, empirical tests of the labeling perspective have been conducted with rather inelegant formulations of a complex theory. Such research often is based on simplistic, nonconditional hypotheses that even the most staunch proponent of the labeling doctrine would support only with substantial qualification." They further argue that the effect of labeling is indirect (e.g., through alteration of one's self-concept, a reduction in opportunities, movement into a deviant subculture) and that such indirect effects can be discerned only through a fully and properly specified causal model (p. 382). They claim by identifying the intervening links, which existing research has not successfully done, the relative explanatory power of labeling will be enhanced. Along these lines, it may be the case that the effects of labeling may be observable only when individuals not labeled (control group) are compared with labeled individuals (experimental group), something else that existing research has not yet done.

The Predicted Effects of Labeling

Related to the issue of causality is another concern about the theory's claim regarding the predicted effects of labeling. Recall that audience reaction in the form of labeling is at the heart of the explanation. Labeling is what causes, in large part, secondary deviance. Indeed, Tannenbaum (1938:21) has noted that the dramatization of evil "plays a greater role in making the criminal than perhaps any other experience" and that a person labeled deviant "becomes the thing he is described as being." For many, however, the effects of labels are overstated. The deviance-enhancing effects of labeling do not occur as frequently as labeling theorists propose (Akers and Sellers 2004:141). Mankoff (1971) notes that labeling undoubtedly plays an important role in the generation of career deviation but is probably not as crucial in the process as some proponents claim. Of issue, then, is whether societal reaction to rule-breaking is a necessary and sufficient condition for career deviance. Labeling certainly can be debilitating, but it need not be.

Potential Alternative Explanations

As we have noted in previous chapters, it is necessary to rule out alternative explanations before researchers can claim that one variable is the cause of another. While it is argued that labeling contributes to a deviant self-image, a competing perspective—deterrence theory (see Chapter 2)—claims instead that official reaction increases the offender's perceived risk of arrest and aversion to punishment. Thus, according to deterrence theory, in some cases official reaction in the form of labeling may actually serve to *decrease* future behavior, a finding supported in the literature (again, see Chapter 2). A crucial next step for labeling theorists, therefore, is to identify and contrast those conditions that make labeling debilitating from those that do not. Theorists must determine when official reactions (labels) increase crime and deviance (in line with labeling) compared to when they reduce future criminality (in line with deterrence). As Tittle (1975:407) suggests, whether sanctions create further deviance may depend on characteristics of offenders. Being punished may differentially affect the futures of people with different SESs, ages, sexes, races, and power. Moreover, characteristics of sanctions themselves are an important determinant of whether future rule-breaking results. Finally, research on mediating conditions such as structured opportunities, interpersonal relationships, and self-concept may be useful for understanding why labeling is found to increase future norm violations in some studies, decrease it in others, and have no effect in still others (Liska 1987:144). In short, a fundamental task is to specify the conditions under which one or the other outcome is likely and then build an integrated theory that incorporates those contingencies (Tittle 1975). This has been achieved, to some degree, in John Braithwaite's (1989) reintegrative shaming theory, which is discussed in the following section.

Longitudinal Study Design

A final analytical issue has to do with the proper testing of labeling theory. Labeling theory focuses its attention on the *process* of criminalization, an interactive process that culminates over time. Quantification of such a process requires either the use of a simultaneous equation technique (which accounts for causality in both directions using cross-sectional data) or, more ideally, analysis of longitudinal data (Ray and Downs 1986:171). But how many studies actually use simultaneous equation techniques or employ longitudinal data? The answer is that relatively few do (for exceptions, see Bernburg et al. 2006; Davies and Tanner 2003; Hagan and Palloni 1990; Johnson et al. 2004; Palamara et al. 1986; Ray and Downs 1986). One recent exception is a study by Bernburg et al., who examine the short-term impact of formal criminal labeling (e.g., involvement in the juvenile justice system) on involvement in deviant social networks (e.g., gangs) and increased likelihood of subsequent delinquency. Recall that movement into deviant subcultures following labeling is one way in which secondary deviance can occur. Using measures from three successive time points, the authors find that juvenile justice intervention positively affects subsequent involvement in serious delinquency through involvement in deviant social groups, namely, street gangs. Bernburg et al. are able to properly model these relationships given their multiwave panel dataset, which includes measures at varying time points (e.g., delinquency at waves 1, 2, and 3). But most labeling studies do not have data over time or employ such techniques. As such, the research is limited in terms of the conclusions that can be drawn. Most problematic is that studies cannot disentangle the direction of causality between deviant/criminal behavior and labels. While this constitutes a shortcoming, it is important to point out that such a shortcoming exists for nearly all other criminological theories discussed throughout the book.

Directions for Future Research

The labeling perspective had its heyday during the 1960s, generating dozens of studies, essays, and books. Because various attacks have reduced the theory's popularity, it was downgraded from a theory to a perspective, and by the late 1970s, even as a perspective it had lost much of its appeal (Sheley 1991). Akers (1994:137) notes, "It no longer generates the interest, enthusiasm, research, and acceptance it once did as a dominant paradigm two or three decades ago."

Despite these pessimistic assessments, efforts to revise the theory are currently underway. Given the inconsistent evidence regarding the effects of official labeling, some recent work has begun to return labeling theory to its symbolic interactionist roots by addressing the negative effects of informal labeling by social networks of friends, relatives, and loved ones (Adams et al. 2003; Link and Cullen 1983; Link et al. 1999; Matsueda 1992; Paternoster and Iovanni 1989; Ray and Downs 1986; Schneider and McKim 2003; Wellford and Triplett 1993). Even though critics claim the theory overstates the effects of official labeling, this recent research finds that refocusing the theory to incorporate unofficial labeling provides valuable insight into the social processes leading to deviance and crime.

Other researchers have abandoned the hypothesis of labeling as deviance-causing. Instead, they have reemphasized the need to identify and describe how the labeling process itself takes place. Triplett (2000), for example, explains how the theory provides a framework for characterizing society's emerging reaction to juvenile delinquency in terms of labeling, predicts what the effect of labeling will be, and encourages us to think about how we can respond to juvenile delinquency in a way that avoids the negative effects of labels.

The most prominent revision is proposed by John Braithwaite in *Crime, Shame, and Integration* (1989). Braithwaite sets out to answer the fundamental question: When is a label likely to have the effect of producing a criminal self-concept and future criminal behavior, and when is it likely to have the opposite effect of preventing crime (recall the previous discussion about labeling causing or deterring future crime)? He claims that shaming is central to this question. Braithwaite defines shaming as social disapproval, which has the "intention or effect of invoking remorse in the person being shamed and/or condemnation by others who become aware of the shaming" (p. 100).

Braithwaite identifies two types of shaming, disintegrative (which involves no attempt to reconcile the shamed offender with the community) and reintegrative (which is followed by efforts to reintegrate the offender back into the community through words or gestures of forgiveness or ceremonies to decertify the offender as deviant) (p. 100–101). He argues that disintegrative shaming is more likely to cause future deviance; stigmatization will lead to higher rates of crime and deviance by increasing the likelihood of subcultural association and by insulating offenders from future attempts at shaming. Reintegrative shaming, however, is likely to deter recidivism. It can be accomplished through societal rituals or gestures of forgiveness or, even better, through ceremonies to decertify the offender as deviant. Braithwaite correctly points out that the United States has a surplus of ceremonies to confer deviant status on people but few to no ceremonies allowing people the opportunity to exit the deviant role. Although relatively few studies have explicitly tested these ideas, Braithwaite's ideas offer the promise to fully reinvigorate the labeling tradition in contemporary criminology.

Whatever the future of labeling theory, it has altered the way criminologists think about crime and deviance. Although other theories recognize that social control techniques which publicly identify and stigmatize individuals can have unintended consequences, only labeling theory gives deviant social labels a central role in the commission of future deviant behavior and in the development of a deviant career (Akers and Sellers 2004:155). Labeling theory reminds us that we must always have a clear understanding of exactly what is considered deviant and who gets to designate it as such.

Discussion Questions

1. Unlike most other criminological theories that adopt an absolutist approach to studying crime and deviance, labeling theory adopts a relativist approach. What does this mean? How do the two approaches differ?
2. Why does official labeling produce secondary deviance for some individuals? What are the proposed three mechanisms described by the theory?

3. In research study designs, labeling can be both an independent and dependent variable. What is an example of a research question related to labeling as an independent variable? What is an example of a research question related to labeling as a dependent variable?
4. Why do some argue that labeling is not a theory at all? How do proponents of labeling respond?
5. Labeling theory focuses its attention on the *process* of criminalization. What are the implications of this for designing an ideal study? What kind of data and research models best address this aspect of the theory?

CHAPTER 9

CONFLICT THEORY

Introduction

Why do some behaviors get defined as criminal while others do not? Why are robbery, vandalism, and drug use considered crimes but not air pollution, exploitation of the poor, and deficient medical treatment? Why are some crimes punished more harshly than others, despite comparable harm? These questions are of critical importance for conflict theory, a macro-level perspective closely aligned with labeling theory (see Chapter 8). Like labeling, conflict theory has its roots in the questioning of values. Yet while labeling theorists and traditional criminologists focus on crime and the criminal, including the labeling of the criminal as such by the system, conflict theorists question the nature of the system itself (Adler, Mueller, and Laufer 1991:186). Conflict theory goes a step beyond labeling theory in identifying those who selectively decide, in the first place, what conduct should be singled out for condemnation.

At the heart of conflict theory is a concern with social inequality. Theorists contend that to understand crime requires an examination of the power relations within society and their respective roles in defining crime. According to the theory, those who control the resources determine what behaviors are defined as crimes. In a capitalist system, for example, criminal law is believed to reflect the will of the economic elite (e.g., large corporations with power). The elite impose their definitions of crime and deviance upon those who lack power. The starting point of analysis, therefore, is an understanding of the economic organization of society and the impact of that organization on law formulation and violation. Here is where conflict theory diverges from traditional theories of deviance, which are essentially nonstructural and ahistorical. Theories that locate the source of crime in factors such as biological or personality traits (see Chapter 3), family structure (see Chapter 7), peer influences (see Chapter 6), and social disorganization (see Chapter 4), among others, share a common flaw according to conflict theory—they attempt to understand deviance apart from historically specific forms of political and economic organization. Because of this, deviance is typically viewed as episodic and transitory, rather than as the outgrowth of long-term structural conditions (Spitzer 1975:407).

The main ideas behind conflict theory stem directly from the perspective's characterization of law formulation. Note that most theories reviewed in this book (excluding labeling) adopt a consensus perspective of law. According to this perspective, laws reflect values shared by the community—common beliefs about what is good, right, just, important, or at least excusable (Vold, Bernard, and Snipes 2002:227). Consensus-based explanations stress the positive functions of law and view it as necessary in modern society to maintain social order. Law and the criminal justice system are thus designed to benefit all members of society.

In challenging these notions, conflict theorists question: If the criminal law supports the collective communal interest, why do many people deviate from it? Why is there conflict over so many issues? And why are some behaviors considered criminal at one point in time but not at others? Conflict theorists observe that diversity and lack of uniformity, not commonality of values, are the hallmarks of society. They also note the relativity of norms to time and place; possession of marijuana, prostitution, and gambling, for example, all have been legal at some times and in some places and illegal at other times and in other places.

For these reasons, the theory adopts a conflict perspective of law. Theorists argue that laws do not exist for the collective good; they instead represent the interests of specific groups that have the power to get their wishes enacted (Adler et al. 1991:186). Law is a key part of the struggle in society between the powerful and the powerless. To preserve their position at the top, the powerful use law to control the powerless, enacting legislation that supports their interests by designating as criminal any behavior that might threaten their standing. In this vein, Chambliss (1999:22) reminds us, "Conflicts that are the basis of legal changes are not fought by equals." As a result, those who hold economic and political resources will inevitably see their interests and ideologies more often represented in the law than will others. For conflict theorists, then, the study of crime begins with the sociology of law: "the study of the institutions which create, interpret, and enforce the rules that tolerate and encourage one set of behaviors while prohibiting and discouraging another" (Chambliss 1999:18). Accordingly, "The criminal law is . . . first and foremost a reflection of the interests and ideologies of the governing class—whether that class is private industry or state bureaucracy. Only secondarily, and even then only in minor ways, does the criminal law reflect the value-consensus, the public interest, or the sifting and weighing of competing interests" (Chambliss 1999:21).

Conflict theory and its offshoots have been variously termed "critical," "new," "radical," "dialectical," "socialist," and "Marxist" criminology. All of these essentially adopt a Marxian approach (see later) to the study of law and crime (Barkan 1997:232), although there are differences in many versions of conflict theory that warrant attention, as discussed in the following section.

Intellectual History of Conflict Theory

Conflict theory lies at the heart of the "conflict tradition" in sociology, which goes back to the work of German social philosopher and political activist Karl

Marx (1818–1883) and his collaborator Friedrich Engels (1820–1895). In *Communist Manifesto* (1848), Marx and Engles argued that all aspects of social life, including laws and crime, are determined by the economic organization of society. In particular, Marx viewed the history and development of any society, but particularly capitalist society, as a reflection and outcome of class struggle. He described the most important relationship in industrial, capitalist society as that between the bourgeoisie, who own the means of production (e.g., businesses and factories), and the proletariat, or the workers who labor for them. According to Marx, society is organized in a hierarchical fashion with the state representing not the common interest but that of the bourgeoisie.

In his work, Marx did not discuss crime at length or its relation to the economic system, although two of his arguments have been particularly important in later Marxist theories of crime (Vold et al. 2002:251–252): First, Marx argued that it was essential to human nature that people be productive in life, yet in industrialized capitalist societies, the large number of unemployed individuals meant that many were unproductive and therefore demoralized, leading to crime and vice. Marx referred to these individuals as the "lumpenproletariat." Second, Marx contested the commonly held belief that people collectively joined in a social contract for the common good, with law representing common interests. Marx argued that this view denied the fact that the unequal distribution of wealth in a society produced an unequal distribution of power.

Marx and his collaborator, Engels, also wrote about the function of law in capitalist societies, which, they argued, helps the ruling class in at least two ways: (1) by emphasizing and preserving private property, almost all of which belongs to the ruling class, and (2) by giving everyone various legal rights and thus appearing to provide equal justice for all. In promoting an appearance of equality, the law pacifies the powerless by making them satisfied with the status quo and obscuring the true nature and extent of their oppression (Barkan 1997:232). These fundamental points provide the basis for conflict theory in general, and a Marxist theory of law and justice in particular.

Conflict Criminology

Conflict theory was long established in the field of sociology (see, for e.g., Ralf Dahrendorf [1959]) before it became popular as an explanation of crime and justice. This did not occur until the 1930s, when Thorsten Sellin (1938) introduced a theory of crime focusing on the conflict surrounding conduct norms, or cultural rules that require certain types of individuals to act in certain circumstances. Sellin distinguished between homogeneous societies, where conduct norms are enacted into law and reflect consensus, and more complex societies, where there are competing norms from different cultural groups.

Roughly 20 years later George B. Vold (1896–1967) presented a group conflict theory of crime in *Theoretical Criminology*. Vold (1958) argued that individuals band together in groups because they are social animals with needs best served through collective action, and that these groups continuously struggle to maintain, or improve, their standing in ongoing competition with other groups (Vold et al. 2002:228–229). The result is that society is in a constant state of conflict and, more importantly, that the processes of lawmaking and crime control directly reflect this conflict between interest groups: "The whole political process of law making, law breaking and law enforcement becomes a direct reflection of deep-seated and fundamental conflicts between interest groups and their more general struggles for control of police power and the state" (Vold 1958:339).

Building on these ideas, Austin Turk (1969) proposed a theory of criminalization that attempted to describe "the conditions under which... differences between authorities and subjects will probably result in conflict, [and] the conditions under which criminalization will probably occur in the course of conflict" (p. 53). According to Turk, criminality is a social status based on how an individual is perceived, evaluated, and treated by legal authorities. Criminal status is determined by those whom he calls the "authorities," or the dominant class of decision makers. Through the use of power, criminal status is imposed on "subjects," or the subordinate class. Turk identified several types of power that authorities use to control the lower classes, including economic, political, police or war, diversionary, and ideological power. He further explained that this process works in such a way that both authorities and subjects learn to interact with each other as performers in their dominant and submissive roles, resulting in "social norms of dominance" and "social norms of deference." Conflict arises when some individuals refuse to accept the existing order and challenge the authorities. Law breaking, then, becomes a measure of the stability of the ruler/ruled relationship (Adler et al. 1991:186–188).

Marxist Criminology

While conflict theory continued to gain prominence in American sociology and criminology during the 1960s, by the mid-1970s some theorists began to shift toward embracing Marxist or "radical" approaches that were viewed as synonymous with, or closely related to, Marxist theory (Akers and Sellers 2004:217). Like conflict theory more generally, Marxist theory views inequality in power as causally related to crime. But while conflict theory largely ignores the sources or origins of power, Marxist perspectives are centrally concerned with this issue (Vold et al. 2002:248). They focus squarely on the relationship between the owners of the means of production and the workers under capitalism as the root cause of crime, in line with Marx's ideas discussed earlier. Although these theorists share the central tenet of conflict theory, that laws are created by the powerful to protect their own interests, they disagree with conflict theorists regarding the quantity of forces competing in the power struggle.

Marxist work on law and crime is often categorized according to whether it embraces "instrumental," "structural," or "dialectical" Marxist views.

Instrumental Marxism considers the ruling class to be a small, unified group that uses the law to dominate the poor and advance its own interests. As Quinney, a key proponent of this view, wrote, law "is an instrument of the state that serves the interests of the developing capitalist ruling class" (Quinney 1977:45). Instrumental Marxists, therefore, view street crime as a form of political rebellion by the poor, or "crimes of resistance" (Quinney 1977) arising from the frustration and hostility caused by inequality. Instrumental Marxists believe that crime would greatly diminish if the United States (and other capitalist nations) were to become socialist, where individuals are more cooperative and altruistic.

Structural Marxists generally consider these views too simplistic (Beirne 1979:380; Chambliss 1999; Chambliss and Zatz 1993). If law were just a means of oppression, they ask, how do we explain civil liberties, health and safety measures, unemployment insurance, and other legally mandated benefits for the working class? Structural Marxists claim that the ruling class is not as unified as instrumental Marxists believe. Instead, members often disagree over important issues and compete among themselves for political and economic resources. Chambliss (1999:22) notes, "The starting point . . . is the recognition that modern, industrialized society is composed of numerous social classes and interest groups who compete for the favors of the state. The stratification of society into social classes where there are substantial (and at times vast) differences in wealth, power, and prestige inevitably leads to conflict between the extant classes. It is in the course of working through and living with these inherent conflicts that the law takes its particular content and form." Still, structural Marxists recognize that the state must be "relatively autonomous" to ensure the long-term interests of capitalism, in part by providing legal rights and other benefits that help convince the public of the fairness of the existing order. In this sense, legal and political victories by the poor are ultimately a sham, since in the long run they preserve capitalist interests.

Dialectical Marxists criticize the structural approach for ignoring the possibility of real, not just sham, legal victories by the poor. They agree that the ruling class does use the law against the powerless, but also recognize that the law often restricts what the ruling class is able to do. In other words, the "rule of the law" in democratic societies limits the use of excessive extralegal power.

Critical Criminology

Several other varieties of conflict theory have appeared in recent decades. Collectively referred to as "critical theory," these include feminist criminology, left realism, and peacemaking criminology (Akers and Sellers 2004). These viewpoints are critical in that all of them, to varying degrees, attack mainstream criminologists for their "scientific" pretensions, or assumptions about an objective and stable reality that can be captured by conventional quantitative methods (Gibbons 2000:xxviii). Although space precludes a full discussion of each of these perspectives, we do outline the major ideas behind feminist perspectives, given that they have become increasingly central in the field. For more information on left realism, see Young (1997) and Lea (1987), and for more information on peacemaking criminology, see Pepinsky and Quinney (1991).

Feminist Perspectives

Generally, feminist perspectives have sought "to draw more attention to the unique concerns of girls and women and to highlight the ways in which gender inequalities structure criminal and noncriminal options, definitions of self, and processes of social control" (Giordano, Deines, and Cernkovich 2006:20). Feminist contributions to criminology can be roughly divided into two phases, the first beginning in the late 1960s and the second in the late 1980s (Daly and Maher 1998:2). In the early phase, Bertrand (1969) and Heidensohn (1968) were two of the first to criticize the omission of women (and girls) from theories of crime and delinquency. They and others at the time questioned whether general crime theories could be applied to women's or girl's deviance. They also noted that while class, race, and age occupied central roles in criminological theory, gender did not. They eschewed the prevailing claim that a focus on gender is unimportant because there are so few women criminals and questioned, "Where are the women and women's experiences?" During this early phase, scholars critiqued criminological theories for failing to consider gender differences or for characterizing women in sexist ways, and researchers began to conduct empirical analyses of women's experiences as law breakers, victims, and workers in the criminal justice system (Daly and Maher 1998:2).

In the later phase, feminist work in criminology closely paralleled developments in broader feminist theory during the 1980s. Topics of concern for researchers included problematizing the term "women" as a unified category, acknowledging that women's experiences are often constructed by legal and criminological discourses, revisiting the relationship between sex and gender, and reflecting on the strengths and limitations of constructing feminist truths and knowledge (Daly and Maher 1998:3).

The critical issues considered during both of these phases continue to occupy a central role in research today. As feminist criminology has grown in prominence, so too have the themes expanded to cover wide-ranging topics in the study of gender and crime. Feminist readings in crime and justice cover topics as diverse as violent offending by females (Koons-Witt and Schram 2004), the war on drugs and incarceration of mothers (Bush-Baskette 2004), masculinity and homicide (Polk 1998), female onset and desistance from crime (Giordano et al. 2006), fighting between girls (Miller and Mullins 2005), neonaticide and infanticide (Gartner and McCarthy 2005), changes in the gender gap in crime and women's economic marginalization (Heimer 2000), and the representation of gender in mainstream criminology journals (Sharp and Hefley 2007), to name a few.

Particularly relevant for this chapter, one type of feminist theory, radical feminism, focuses on the plight of women under capitalism, arguing that male domination has been the norm and women have been subjected to it in the home, workplace, and street. The central concept is that of "patriarchy," originally used by sociologists like Max Weber to describe social relations under feudalism but later used by others (e.g., Kate Millett) in the 1970s to refer to a form of social organization in which men dominate women (Vold et al. 2002:271). According to Millett (1970), patriarchy is established and maintained through sex-role socialization and the creation of core gender identities, through which both genders come to believe that men are superior to women. Men dominate women in social situations including within contexts that could lead to crime and violence (e.g., the family). In short, "radical feminism views all systems of domination, including those based on class, as extensions of the underlying politics of male supremacy" (Paternoster and Bachman 2001:262). From this brief description it should be clear that radical feminism specifically, and feminist criminology generally, share fundamental assumptions with Marxist and conflict theories in understanding the causes of crime.

Conflict Theory

Conflict theory is based on several primary assumptions that are relevant to all aspects of society, not just crime. These include:

1. Competition over scarce resources (e.g., money, leisure, power) is at the heart of social relationships. Competition, not consensus, is characteristic of these relationships.

2. Inequalities in power and rewards are built into social structures.

3. Groups that benefit from any particular structure strive to see it maintained.

4. Change occurs as a result of conflict between competing interests rather than through adaptation. It is often abrupt and revolutionary, not evolutionary.

Because of these assumptions, conflict theory provides an explanation of both law formulation and law violation unlike other perspectives examined in this book. For theorists, in addition to asking, "Why do some people commit crimes and others do not?" it is equally important to ask, "Why are some acts defined as criminal while others are not?" (Chambliss 1975a). The two are considered to be inextricably linked.

On the Content and Operation of Criminal Law

According to conflict theory, "Although law is supposed to protect all citizens, it starts as a tool of the dominant class and ends by maintaining the dominance of that class. Law serves the powerful over the weak.... Yet we are all bound by that law, and we are indoctrinated with the myth that it is our law" (Quinney 1974:24). The reality of law is that it is a set of resources for which people contend and with which they are better able to promote their own ideas and interests against others (Turk 1976). Criminal law, more specifically, is used by the powerful to designate as deviant any group that threatens the existing order. In other words, behaviors are defined as criminal because it is in the interests of the ruling class to so define them. Conflict theorists, however, do allow for some societal consensus with respect to which behaviors are "criminal": "In many cases there is no conflict whatsoever between those in power and those not. For most crimes against the person, such as murder, assault, and rape, there is consensus throughout society as to the desirability of imposing legal sanctions for persons who commit these acts. It is also true that laws are passed which reflect the interests of the general population and which are antithetical to the interests of those in power" (Chambliss 1969:10).

On the Nature of Crime

Given their position on the nature of law, it should not be surprising that conflict theorists adopt a definition of crime as a social situation—as a set of relationships—rather than as an act or behavior under specific legal definition. Recall the questions at the beginning of the chapter. Why is the air polluter not arrested and tried for doing bodily harm? Or the business owner who exploits the worker by paying substandard wages? Or the doctor whose negligence causes severe harm or even death to a patient? According to the theory, "The reality of crime—that is, the acts we label crime, the acts we think of as crime, the actors and actions we treat as criminal—is *created:* It is an image shaped by decisions as to *what* will be called crime and *who* will be treated as a criminal" (Reiman 1999:26). Crime, in other words, is a political phenomenon. What gets defined as criminal is the result of a political process within which rules are formed that prohibit or require people to behave in certain ways (Chambliss 1999:23).

So what causes crime? Traditionally, the answer has been sought in the study of "the criminal." Think about the theories reviewed so far (excluding labeling theory). The sources of crime are believed to reside in the person who violates the law (e.g., he or she is not acting rationally, has weak bonds to conventional society, has strong associations to deviant peers). This emphasis has meant that criminal law and political theory have been largely ignored and that criminologists have not treated crime as a product of the authority that defines behavior as criminal (Quinney 1974:27). Along these lines, conflict theorists maintain that behaviors common among society's disadvantaged (e.g., the poor, minorities) have a greater likelihood of being called "crime" than those activities in which the powerful participate. Reiman (1999) posits, "The fact is that the label 'crime' is not used in America to name all or the worst of the actions that cause misery and suffering to Americans. It is primarily reserved for the dangerous actions of the poor" (p. 25).

As an example, consider the criminal justice system's response to street crime (e.g., assault, robbery, burglary) compared to white-collar crime, or the pursuit of illegal financial gain or law breaking to minimize or avoid financial losses (e.g., fraud, bribery, embezzlement). Conflict theorists assert, and most of us would agree, that street crime has been and currently is portrayed as "the crime problem" and thus the target of major legal efforts, including crackdowns, sweeps, and harsher penalties. Alternatively, white-collar crime is often not considered "real" crime and is rarely targeted by criminal justice efforts. Yet white-collar and corporate crime, it turns out, have a great financial impact on taxpayers, consumers, employees, and society. The general public loses much more from price-fixing, monopolistic practices, consumer deception, and embezzlement than from all the property crime in the FBI's Index combined (Reiman 1999:29). It has been estimated that economic losses due to white-collar crime, broadly defined, may exceed $1 trillion annually in the United States alone (Schlegel 2000). Losses to workers and investors as a consequence of the collapse of Enron were estimated at up to $50 billion (Greider 2002). By even the most conservative estimates, the annual financial losses due to white-collar crime are in the hundreds of billions of dollars, a figure that dwarfs financial losses attributable to conventional forms of property crime such as burglary.

Conflict theorists further point out that corporate crime does not merely consist of financial offenses. Hundreds of thousands of people die each year as a result of corporations' actions or failure to act. Some estimate that in the United States, corporate crime is 13.5 times more deadly than homicide (Kappeler, Blumberg, and Potter 2000). "We have as great or sometimes even greater chance of being killed or disabled by an occupational injury or disease, by unnecessary surgery, or by shoddy emergency medical services than by aggravated assault or even homicide" (Reiman 1999:29). By some estimates, more than 30,000 Americans die annually from work-related diseases and accidents and nearly 3 million workers suffer other significant physical harm in the workplace (Reiman 2004). If one accepts such estimates, the American labor force is more vulnerable to injury from corporations than from conventional offenders, with much of the injury being avoidable.

Conflict theorists claim the prevailing, narrow view of what constitutes crime is not limited to the general public. Criminologists are equally guilty, having devoted most of their research attention to conventional forms of crime and violence. This has resulted in what Liazos (1972) called our fascination with "nuts, sluts, and perverts." As a result of researchers' obsession with street crime, Liazos notes, little attention is paid to the unethical, illegal, and destructive actions of powerful individuals, groups, and institutions. He argues that discussions of violence treat only one type—dramatic and predatory violence committed by (typically) the poor and minorities against persons or property. He further points out that because institutional violence is carried out quietly in the normal course of events, the sociology of deviance does not consider it central subject matter. In effect, this bias is rooted in the very conception and definition of the field.

What this collectively suggests is that powerful entities in society all too often have been able to shield themselves in various ways from being labeled criminals and from becoming involved in the criminal justice system, although, as suggested earlier, many of their activities can be characterized as criminal by virtue of violations of international law, human rights protocols, or laws of the state itself. "Yet these far more costly acts are either not criminal, or if technically criminal, not prosecuted, or if prosecuted, not punished, or if punished, only mildly" (Reiman 1999:29). Today our prisons are filled with drug and street offenders, yet is far from clear that, on balance, they have inflicted more harm than have corporate executives and others who hold legitimate occupational statuses. Yet few corporate offenders go to prison for their actions.

Conflict theorists suggest at least two consequences of this: First, as long as so much concern and anger about violent crime is directed toward the activities of conventional offenders, such as "street criminals," it is deflected from the harm inflicted by the rich and powerful. Rather than focusing on the capitalist class or the economic system, the focus is directed toward members of the underclass. Of course, this diversion is necessary if social order is to be maintained and reproduced and if the lower classes are to remain powerless. Gordon (1976:208) states, "If the system did not effect this neutralization, if so many poor were not trapped in the debilitating system of crime and punishment, then they might otherwise gather the strength to oppose the system which reinforces their misery." Thus, criminalization of the poor negates their potential "for developing an ideologically sophisticated understanding of their situation...and by incarcerating them it is made difficult for them to organize and realize their ideas" (Pearce 1976:81).

A second consequence is that the public is led to believe that the criminal justice system is protecting them against the gravest threats to their well-being when, in fact, it is protecting members against only some threats and not necessarily the gravest ones (Reiman 1999:30). Reiman (2007) contends that Americans continue to tolerate gentle treatment meted out to white-collar criminals, corporate price fixers, industrial polluters, and political-influence peddlers, while voting to lock up more poor people faster and longer, indicates the degree to which they harbor illusions as to whom is most threatening. He further notes that the most important benefit derived from the current classification of crime is that it paints the picture that the threat to middle-class Americans comes from those below them on the economic ladder, not those above.

In sum, conflict theorists argue that crime is a reality that exists primarily as it is created by those in society whose interests are best served by its presence (Chambliss 1975a). For this reason, "Much, if not most, crime continues to victimize those who are already oppressed...and does little more than reproduce the existing order" (Quinney 1977:103). These points help explain why theorists have little interest in discovering the "motivation" for crime or in trying to understand the reasons why some people commit crimes while others do not (Paternoster and Bachman 2001:254).

The main ideas of conflict theory in terms of the content and operation of criminal law, the nature of crime, and the consequences of crime for society

Table 9.1 Six Propositions on the Social Reality of Crime

Proposition 1 (definition of crime): Crime is a definition of human conduct that is created by authorized agents in a politically organized society.

Proposition 2 (formulation of criminal definitions): Criminal definitions describe behaviors that conflict with the interests of the segments of society that have the power to shape public policy.

Proposition 3 (application of criminal definitions): Criminal definitions are applied by the segments of society that have the power to shape the enforcement and administration of criminal law.

Proposition 4 (development of behavior patterns in relation to criminal definitions): Behavior patterns are structured in segmentally organized society in relation to criminal definitions, and within this context persons engage in actions that have relative probabilities of being defined as criminal.

Proposition 5 (construction of criminal conceptions): Conceptions of crime are constructed and diffused in the segments of society by various means of communication.

Proposition 6 (the social reality of crime): The social reality of crime is constructed by the formulation and application of criminal definitions, the development of behavior patterns related to criminal definitions, and the construction of criminal conceptions.

can be summarized by Quinney (1970), who offered six propositions on "the social reality of crime" (see Table 9.1).

The Implications for Crime Control and Criminal Justice Policy

For conflict theory, the role of the state in capitalist society is to defend the interests of the ruling class. Crime control becomes a major device in that defense. The ruling class is not in direct control of the legal system but must operate through the mechanisms of the state, including the government, administration, military and police, and judiciary. Steven Spitzer (1975) described how crime control is necessary to maintain and reproduce the existing social order. He introduced the idea of problem populations, or populations in society who threaten the established order. Problem populations consist of "social junk" and "social dynamite." Social junk, or the costly but relatively harmless burden to society, represent a failure, inability or refusal of a group to participate in roles supportive of the capitalist society (e.g., the homeless, those on welfare, the mentally ill). Social dynamite represent the more youthful, alienated, and politically volatile problem population who pose real threats because they directly challenge the social order (e.g., revolutionaries, Black Panthers, feminists). Both social junk and social dynamite constitute problem populations that pose a threat to capitalist order and therefore must be managed or controlled. Spitzer claims that state controls are usually designed to regulate and contain, rather than eliminate, social junk, whereas active intervention and control are required for social dynamite. To control these problem populations, the state uses the criminal justice system, welfare system, mental health agencies, and other systems: "[C]rime control in capitalist society is accomplished through a variety of institutions and agencies established and administered by a governmental elite, representing ruling class interests, for the purposes of establishing domestic order" (Quinney 1974:16).

Empirical Research on Conflict Theory

As stated earlier, conflict theory is interested in both law formulation and law violation. Studies of the theory, therefore, range in focus to include development of criminal laws by those in power, bias and discrimination in the criminal justice system, differential crime rates of the powerful and the powerless, and the relationship between rulers and the ruled (Adler et al. 1991:189). According to Akers and Sellers (2004:200–201), among these foci are four types of empirical studies that attempt to evaluate the validity of conflict theory as an explanation of criminal law and crime (see Table 9.2). We discuss each of these in turn.

One type examines the influence of interest groups on legislation, administrative regulations, and court decisions. It may involve research on law making during early historical periods or on law and policy in more contemporary times. A variety of studies have investigated the background and nature of group conflict in the formulation of laws on theft (Hall 1952), vagrancy (Chambliss 1964), alcohol (Gusfield 1963), drugs (Beckett and Sasson 2000; Duster 1970; Galliher and Walker 1977; Tonry 1995), smoking (Troyer and Markle 1983), kidnapping (Alix 1978), juvenile delinquency (Hagan and Leon 1977; Platt 1969), computer crimes (Hollinger and Lanza-Kaduce 1988), and other areas of crime-control policy. These studies identify the various powerful groups involved in influencing the enactment of the law and the establishment of public policy.

A classic historical example of this type of study is Joseph R. Gusfield's 1963 *Symbolic Crusade*, which details the origins and dynamics of the temperance movement during the late 1800s and early 1900s. Gusfield finds fault with most studies that have examined the movement from an economic standpoint in explaining why, at one point in time, it was illegal to drink alcohol in the United States. Gusfield contends that this singular approach ignores important aspects about determining why the movement took place. He prefers instead to understand the movement as a symbolic attack of one group on another. In this context, Gusfield examines the relationship between temperance attitudes and conflicts between divergent subcultures in American society. He describes

Table 9.2 Four Types of Empirical Studies of Conflict Theory

Research on the influence of interest groups on legislation, administrative regulations, and court decisions

Research on public opinion agreement or disagreement about what behaviors are disapproved of and how strongly

Research on the relationship between the presence of threatening social groups and its impact on crime control efforts within a geographic area

Research on the exercise of discretion in applying the law against accused law violators two groups that were directly in conflict. On one side were the nondrinkers—the social elite and middle-class, rural, native American Protestants who adhered to a culture in which self-control, industriousness, and impulse renunciation were praised. For this group, sobriety was virtuous and viewed as necessary for social acceptance and self-esteem. On the other side were the drinkers—the urban, secular, generally Catholic, mostly immigrants who rejected the social status, as well as political power, of the leadership. Gusfield explains how the former group was slowly losing power to the latter group and, as a result, sought to reestablish their position through coercive action in the form of the temperance movement and more punitively, Prohibition: "Coercive reform became the dominating theme of Temperance. It culminated in the drive for national Prohibition. The Eighteenth Amendment was the high point of the struggle to assert the public dominance of old middle-class values. It established the victory of Protestant over Catholic, rural over urban, tradition over modernity, the middle class over both the lower and upper strata" (Gusfield 1986:7). In line with conflict theory, Gusfield's study of Prohibition demonstrates how behaviors (in this case, the consumption of alcohol) that disrupt or threaten the position of the privileged are the ones most likely to be labeled criminal. Although this sort of conflict over drinking is no longer apparent today, there are several examples of current social problems for which opposing groups (with conflicting interests) are battling in order to assert their moral opinions on the rest of society: gun control, abortion, cigarette smoking, gay marriage, and violent video games, to name just a few. Empirical evidence in this respect is quite strong for conflict theory.

A second type of study identified by Akers and Sellers (2004) includes research on public opinion regarding what behaviors are disapproved of and how strongly. If, as conflict theory predicts, laws do not reflect the common interests of the public but are enacted to protect the interests of the powerful, then we should witness little congruence between the social and legal definitions of wrongdoing and penalties. In other words, we would not expect to find consensus among the general population as to which behaviors should be criminal and which should not, if conflict theory is accurate. Moreover, an "implicit assumption has been that if group-linked variations in public rankings were found that diverged from the penalties imposed by criminal statutes, this would signal a way in which the criminal law is used unjustly by some groups to impose their interests and values on others" (Hagan and Albonetti 1982:331).

Collectively, research in this tradition has failed to find substantial group-linked differences in public perceptions of crime seriousness. The majority of studies find that those acts defined by criminal law as the most serious, offenses with the most severe penalties (e.g., murder, rape, robbery, assault) constitute the same ones that citizens agree are most heinous and threatening to society. Violent personal crimes are rated the most serious, with drug offenses not far behind and property offenses ranking lower in terms of seriousness. Offenses to public morality and order (e.g., gambling, prostitution, public drunkenness) rank the lowest (Pease et al. 1975; Rossi et al.

1974; Wellford 1975; Wolfgang et al. 1985). It has also been shown that these seriousness rankings correlate with the severity of sentences received by convicted offenders (Blumstein and Cohen 1980). This literature, therefore, does not appear to support conflict theory's proposition on the nature of law.

Some studies, however, do find sizeable variation in the average opinion for certain kinds of behavior and for favored levels of punishment (Jacoby and Cullen 1998; Miethe 1982; Warr, Gibbs, and Erickson 1982). An interesting study by Hagan and Albonetti (1982) on race, class, and perceptions of criminal *injustice* in America finds (1) that blacks are more likely than whites to perceive injustice; (2) that regardless of race, members of the surplus population (e.g., unemployed) are more likely than members of other classes to perceive injustice; and (3) that class position conditions the relationship of race to the perception of injustice with divisions between the races being most acute in the professional managerial class. A follow-up study by Hagan, Payne and Shedd (2005) continues to document racial variation in perceptions of injustice. As such, the literature does not support a pure consensus model of law and justice, lending some support to conflict theory.

The afore-mentioned studies generally examine law formulation, but conflict theorists also focus on law violation and enforcement. These latter topics constitute Akers and Sellers' (2004) third and fourth categories. In particular, a third type of study assesses the relationship between the presence of threatening social groups (e.g., racial minorities, the poor, young males) and crime control efforts within a geographic area. According to the theory, as minority populations increase in size and power, majority populations exercise ever-increasing social control over these populations to maintain the status quo. "Indeed,... stratification is so important to the vitality of the advantaged that they will pressure legislators to enact repressive measures intended to control groups considered volatile and threatening" (Petrocelli, Piquero, and Smith 2002:2). In other words, the relative size and distribution of minority populations are critical for understanding the application of punishment (Chiricos and Crawford 1995:286).

The primary approach in this research is a macro-level focus on the demographic composition of an area (e.g., its economic status, racial composition) and various measures of punitiveness (e.g., arrest, sentencing, incarceration). For example, one study by Jacobs, Carmichael, and Kent (2005) found that death sentences for blacks were greater in states with more African Americans, controlling for the crime rate, the unemployment rate, state political ideology, and whether judges face partisan elections. They also found that death sentences for blacks were most common in states with large black populations that had a history of repeated lynching. These findings support conflict theory's contention that "if criminal punishments are shaped partly by the menace of a racial underclass whose members have much to gain from violence used to take goods from the privileged, a harsh punishment such as the death sentence should be more likely where such threats are most severe" (Jacobs et al. 2005:657).

In another study, Behrens, Uggen, and Manza (2003) perform event-history analysis using Census data from 1850 to 2002 and document a strong and consistent relationship between racial threat (as measured by the percentage of nonwhite state prisoners) and laws restricting felon voting rights. Specifically, they find that states with larger shares of African Americans behind bars have been more likely to adopt broad statutes forbidding convicts and ex-convicts from the voting booth, controlling for region, timing, economic competition, partisan political power, population composition, and incarceration rates. A number of other studies find evidence for the racial threat hypothesis (Bridges and Crutchfield 1988; Chamlin 1989a, 1989b; Crawford, Chiricos, and Kleck 1998; Garofalo 1980; Holmes 2000; Jackson and Carroll 1981; Johnson 2005; Liska, Chamlin, and Reed 1985; Liska, Lawrence, and Benson 1981; McGarrell 1993; Mosher 2001; Myers and Talarico 1987; Sampson and Laub 1993; Ulmer and Johnson 2004; but see Britt 2000; Kautt 2002; Petrocelli et al. 2002; Ulmer 1997). A related literature finds similar class effects, primarily reflected in the positive relationship between income inequality or unemployment levels and various amounts and forms of social control (Box and Hale 1985; Brenner 1976; Chiricos and DeLone 1992; Greenberg 1977; Hochstetler and Shover 1997; Inverarity and Grattet 1989; Inverarity and McCarthy 1988; Jacobs 1979; Jacobs and Britt 1979; Jacobs and O'Brien 1998; Jankovic 1977; Kent and Jacobs 2004; Lessan 1991; Liska and Chamlin 1984; Liska et al. 1985; Sorenson, Marguart, and Brock 1993; Yeager 1979). The effects of inequality and employment, however, are far from consistent (Arvanites 1993; Liska 1987:80, Liska and Messner 1999:195–196; McGarrell 1993:8) and there are some important limitations of this research (Chiricos and DeLone 1992), which we discuss later in the chapter.

Finally, a fourth category of study, which determines the exercise of discretion in applying the law against accused violators, is the most frequently conducted type of study on conflict theory (Akers and Sellers 2004:202). In this literature, theorists argue that criminal justice decisions from arrest through conviction are biased against less powerful individuals. Theorists assert that the social threat presented by the underclasses affects the decision making of criminal justice officials, who ultimately use their discretionary power to impose more punitive responses on powerless offenders (and more lenient responses on offenders belonging to powerful groups) (Akers and Sellers 2004:199). An example of such an assertion is provided by Chambliss (1969), who maintains:

> The lower-class person is (1) more likely to be scrutinized and therefore to be observed in any violation of the law, (2) more likely to be arrested if discovered under suspicious circumstances, (3) more likely to spend the time between arrest and trial in jail, (4) more likely to come to trial, (5) more likely to be found guilty, and (6) if found guilty, more likely to receive harsh punishment than his middle or upper-middle counterpart. (p. 86)

In testing these notions, conflict theorists propose that criminal justice decision making will be based more on extralegal variables, or status characteristics, such as offender race, class, and gender, than on relevant legal variables such as the defendant's offense, prior criminal history, and so on, despite the notion that "principles of Anglo-Saxon justice should not permit nonlegal variables like race and social class to affect the severity of dispositions" (Thornberry 1973:90). A wide body of literature supports these contentions; studies find that the lower classes and minorities are more likely to be watched by the police, arrested in suspicious circumstances, held in jail rather than released on bail, tried in court, found guilty, and given harsh sentences, controlling for several legally relevant factors (Albonetti and Hepburn 1996; Bontrager, Bales, and Chiricos 2005; Chiricos and DeLone 1992; Demuth 2003; Hagan, Bernstein, and Albonetti 1980; Lizotte 1978; Swigert and Farrell 1977; Wooldredge and Thistlethwaite 2004; but see Bernstein, Kelly, and Doyle 1977; Chiricos and Waldo 1975).

Now that we have reviewed the types of conflict studies, we are ready to evaluate the concepts used in the theory, to assess their measurement, and to determine the various analytical issues involved in testing conflict theory.

Concepts and Measurement Issues

The key concept in conflict theory is power. "Power" is derived from the Latin *potis*, meaning "able." "Power is the basic characteristic of social organization" (Quinney 1970:11) and is a "relational attribute involving comparative differences in resources" (Jacobs and Britt 1979:405). Conflict theory maintains that power is most frequently used to enact or enforce laws against those populations who represent the greatest threat to the existing order. Thus, the concept of threat (or perceived threat—see Sampson and Laub 1993:290) is also central. Threat is generally described as the actual or perceived potential of a minority group to pose a realistic challenge to political or economic control (Hawkins 1987:735). But who or what constitutes the greatest threat to the elite control? According to the theory, the lower classes do; for this reason, the concept of social class is fundamental.

Social class refers to the hierarchical distinctions between individuals or groups in societies or cultures. Schools of sociology differ in how they conceptualize class. One distinction is drawn between analytical concepts of social class, including the conflict tradition, and the more empirical traditions that note the correlation of income, education, and wealth to social outcomes without necessarily implying a particular theory of social structure. In criminology, several theories identify the concept of social class as vital to their explanation (e.g., strain, social disorganization), yet social class is conceptualized in a unique way in conflict theories in general, and Marxism in particular. Marx defined class in terms of the extent to which a group has control over the means of production. As such, classes are not conceived as "above" or "below" one another but instead are viewed as a set of structural relationships mainly constitutive of the social and technical relationships of production and exchange (Beirne 1979:377; Hagan and Albonetti 1982:334). For Marxists and other conflict theorists, there are several class-related concepts, including economic inequality and segregation, as well as several traits typically used to define social class, including income level, poverty, unemployment, and educational level, all of which are discussed in further detail in the following sections.

Economic inequality, or the unequal distribution of economic assets and income between groups in society, is one of the most important class-related concepts. It is critical because according to the theory, inequality both produces more crime and provides a "target population" (e.g., the poor) for crime-control efforts. "Because conflict theorists . . . hold that the state's monopoly of violence is controlled by those who benefit from inequality, it follows that the control agents of the state should be more likely to use extreme force when economic inequality is most pronounced" (Jacobs and Britt 1979:403). In other words, greater differentiation due to economic inequality creates a pool of potential targets for punishment (McGarrell 1993:13; Spitzer 1975).

For most theorists, class and race cannot be treated as separate dimensions of inequality. Rather, race and class are considered part of the same system and need to be understood through an analysis of the system as a whole: "[R]ace relations are seen as distinctive products of the development of world capitalism. Both racism and capitalism developed together reinforcing one another in a single, exploitative system" (Bonacich 2000:319). But race and ethnicity are also important in their own right, not only to the extent to which they link to class. The poor are not treated equally badly; rather, some are treated worse than others (Liska and Messner 1999:186). The overarching point is that societies characterized by extensive economic (class) and social (gender, race, ethnicity) inequalities will have higher levels of crime than will more equal societies. In this sense, "a society gets the type and amount of crime it deserves" (Lynch and Stretesky 2001:273).

Economic and racial inequalities are also responsible, in part, for creating "surplus" or "problem" populations (Spitzer 1975), another fundamental concept. Surplus populations, consisting of social junk and social dynamite, pose threats to the established order either because they constitute a drain on societal resources (junk) or because they seek to radically alter existing conditions (dynamite). Thus, surplus populations must be managed and controlled, typically through increasing amounts of social control.

A final central concept is that of crime control and, in particular, law making and enforcement. The conflict perspective assumes an uneven distribution of self-interests in crime control and an uneven distribution of power to implement self-interests into social policy (Liska 1987:77; Quinney 1974). Theory and research focus on how these distributions of power come into being, persist, and influence law making and enforcement, primarily by examining arrest, sentencing, and incarceration rates. The bottom line is that law enforcement tends to process and punish most harshly those with less, rather than more, political and economic power (Vold et al. 2002:241) as well as those who pose the greatest threat to the existing order.

As you may have figured out, most of these concepts are broad and complex, and therefore pose a challenge for theorists to operationalize and measure. Next we consider how successful researchers have been at this task.

One of the most common criticisms of conflict theory is that it is nearly impossible to empirically test, in part because the concepts are not well-defined. Liska (1987:78) notes that "major concepts, like interest and threat, are not clearly defined and are rarely measured" in studies. Let's consider a few examples of the measurement of concepts from tests of conflict theory to determine whether Liska's criticism is warranted.

Social Class

We'll start with social class. "Although the concept of class is central to conflict theories of crime and criminal justice, little attention has been given by conflict criminologists to the actual operationalization of this concept" (Hagan and Albonetti 1982:333). Probably more than any other concept, social class has been operationalized differently across studies, with no emerging consensus on the best way to measure it. Studies typically use one of several measures including an individual's income level, poverty status, unemployment status, or educational level. But does one's income level truly represent the social class to which he or she belongs? One could make little money at a job but be wealthy because of stocks or family inheritance. Likewise, one could have a high income but be poor because of debt. And what about unemployment? Are people who are retired and choose not to work "unemployed," therefore representing those in the lower classes? Essentially, do these measures accurately or comprehensively reflect one's social class, especially in light of how class is conceptualized in conflict theory? It appears there is some incongruence in the theory's substantive definition and the various measures employed in studies. At the very least, studies should combine measures of income, education, and occupation to create a more comprehensive class measure (see Chiricos and Waldo 1975:758). Unfortunately most include only one, typically income, assuming that the concept of class is unidimensional. Still, even studies that combine measures may not truly tap into the aspects of social class most relevant to conflict theory.

Not all studies suffer from this problem. A good example is found in Hagan and Albonetti (1982), who examine whether perceptions of criminal injustice vary across different social classes and races. Hagan and Albonetti offer a suitable definition of social class, one that is informed by Marxism. They maintain that classes are to be defined in relational rather than gradational terms based on "their social relation to one another, with each class representing a common structural position within the social organization of the relations of production" (p. 334). They use three conceptual criteria—ownership of the means of production, relationship to the means of production, and relationship to labor power—to distinguish four class positions: (1) employers, (2) the professional-managerial class, (3) the working class, and (4) the unemployed workers (the surplus population). According to Hagan and Albonetti (pp. 336–337), implicit in this measure "is a use of the concept of class that is closer to the purposes of Marx than are the recent quantitative studies of income inequality." We agree.

Threat

Let's consider another fundamental concept—threat (or perceived threat). Threatening people or threatening acts are expected to result in greater levels of social control according to conflict theory. But how have theorists measured threat in their studies? Ideally, this concept should be measured directly, possibly through surveys that question people about their perceptions and beliefs of threatening people and acts. Yet researchers almost always measure threat indirectly through structural conditions *assumed* to threaten elite interests. Typically, macro-level studies use the crime rate as an indicator of the presence of threatening acts and a variety of measures to capture the presence of threatening people, including percentage poor (Liska and Chamlin 1984; Petrocelli et al. 2002), percentage unemployed (Jacobs et al. 2005; McGarrell 1993; Petrocelli et al. 2002), percentage black or non-white (Jacobs and Britt 1979; Jacobs et al. 2005; Johnson 2005; Liska and Chamlin 1984; Petrocelli et al. 2002; Stolzenberg, D'Alessio, and Eitle 2004), economic inequality as measured by the Gini coefficient (Jacobs and Britt 1979; Liska and Chamlin 1984; McGarrell 1993), and degree of racial segregation, typically measured as the Dissimilarity Index (which measures the relative separation or integration of groups across all neighborhoods of a city or metropolitan area) (Liska and Chamlin 1984). Note that none of these directly measures threat. Therefore, if one wants to claim that the finding that cities with more racial minorities have higher arrest rates is supportive of conflict theory, one must accept the assumption that "percent non-white" in an area equates with threat.

Surplus or Problem Populations

Similar assumptions must be made about other concepts in conflict theory given that they, too, are measured indirectly. Consider the concept of surplus or problem populations, populations that must be managed, typically through formal social control such as the prison or welfare system. How might one go about measuring the presence of problem populations? In most cases, a measure of unemployment (percent unemployed) serves as the sole proxy for surplus or problem populations (Chiricos and DeLone 1992:426; see, e.g., Hagan and Albonetti 1982:334; Lessan 1991; McGarrell 1993:14). Although researchers claim that "increases in unemployment expand the pool of surplus labor" and "increased unemployment should lead to an increase in the incarcerated population" (McGarrell 1993:14), note again that this measure only indirectly captures the presence of problem populations in an area.

An additional problem for studies on surplus/problem populations is their reliance on official measures of unemployment—measures typically derived from the Census. In a comprehensive review of the literature, Chiricos and DeLone (1992) explain why these measures may be problematic in studies: "[I]t is important to remember that 96 percent of the findings of a relationship [between unemployment and punishment] are based on official measures of unemployment which, as is widely known, underestimate the amount of labor surplus by as much as one half." They claim, "Moreover, these official measures do little to capture dimensions of 'social dynamite' so central to this issue. In fact, only 7 percent of the relationships actually involve age, race, or gender specific measures of even official rates of unemployment" (p. 431). Here Chiricos and DeLone underscore the necessity of disaggregating unemployment rates by age, race, and gender to truly test the idea that the relationship between unemployment and imprisonment will be strongest for young, minority males, consistent with the social dynamite argument.

According to some, using indirect rather than direct measures of central concepts yields weak tests of conflict theory and does not rule out alternative explanations (a point discussed in greater depth later). Liska (1987:78) notes, "research examines the extent to which the level and distribution of acts (e.g., civil disorders) and people (e.g., percentage unemployed and percentage nonwhite) *assumed* to be threatening to the interests of the ruling class affect various forms of crime control. Yet it is not clear theoretically, how the level and distribution of these acts and people generate a threat to the interests of the ruling class and how that threat leads to specific forms of crime control" (emphasis added).

Along these lines, little consideration has been given to accurately pinpointing the specifics of these relationships. For example, researchers contend that a high percentage of non-whites creates a perceived threat of crime, but what constitutes a high percentage: 30%? 50%? 80%? Liska and Chamlin (1984:384) note, "a relatively large culturally dissimilar group constituting 20%–30% of the population may be perceived as posing a substantial threat and as a problem of social control." How did the authors arrive at these figures? Unfortunately, they do not discuss this in their study. One final measurement problem related to testing the threat hypothesis is that "race conflict is frequently conceptualized as a proxy for class conflict" (Liska and Messner 1999:207), which suggests that conflict theory places more emphasis on class over race and other forms of conflict, despite the "realization today that race plays a role independently of class" (p. 207). In other words, race and class measures are not interchangeable and should be included separately in analyses.

Not surprisingly, fuzzy measurement, particularly the use of indirect measures of concepts, has potentially serious implications. One has to do with the characterization of the collective literature on conflict theory. According to some, this literature is not well defined and integrated: "Studies are categorized by the substantive forms of crime control (imprisonment, arrests, lynching, and police size), rather than by theoretical propositions. Researchers studying imprisonment are criminologists interested in prisons, and researchers studying lynching are specialists in race relations or collective behavior. Conflict theory is employed to guide research loosely and to interpret findings, and explanatory variables are selected because they are readily accessible and/or are generally amenable to a conflict interpretation" (Liska 1987:78).

More importantly, perhaps, problems in the measurement of central concepts have had implications for theory testing and development. According to Liska (1987:83), the definitions of terms used by conflict theorists frequently yield tautological propositions; for example, "law formulation and enforcement, thought to be explained by ruling class interests, are frequently used to infer those interests in concrete historical cases in either the short (Quinney 1977) or the long (Beirne 1979) term." The consequences are serious. Because of loose linkages, research on crime control, although directly relevant to the theory, has not had much feedback on conflict theory: "the theory has not grown and developed as a result of this research; instead, the research has been merely used to illustrate the theory" (p. 83). Because of tautological propositions and other related problems, "conflict theory is frequently able to explain everything and predict nothing" (p. 86), a point discussed in greater depth in the next section.

Analytical Issues

Conflict theory has several analytical issues that make empirical testing of this perspective quite difficult. As a result, some believe that the literature is characterized by too many ideas and not enough systematic research and that most empirical studies are illustrative of, but do not actually *test*, the theory (Liska and Messner 1999:208). These have been longstanding criticisms. In his 1975 Presidential Address to the Society for the Study of Social Problems, Stanton Wheeler commented on the state of literature on conflict theory, pointing out that "the emergence of conflict theory and the rediscovery of Marx may perhaps move us in a new direction...but it is my strong impression that the achievements have been more rhetorical than anything else, that whatever their value in changing our conception of crime, they have not led to new and fresh empirical inquiry" (Wheeler 1976:527). Liska (1987:82, 85) has also noted, "The conflict theory of crime control consists of a set of loosely interrelated and ideologically charged ideas. Conflict theorists, particularly Marxists, have not been overly concerned with theory construction and testing." The result, for some, is that the theory "is a perspective rather than a well formulated theory with testable hypotheses. Neither the work of Quinney nor that of Chambliss and Seidman, the principal architects of the perspective, represents a theory per se" (Hawkins 1987:722). Unfortunately, this complaint continues to surface; among some, conflict theory is viewed as not much different today than when it was developed in the 1960s and 1970s (Liska and Messner 1999:206, 208).

Untestability

A more disillusioned criticism is that instead of being theoretical in nature, strands of conflict theory consist of philosophical and political statements about what society should be and how the system ought to operate (Akers and Sellers 2004:239–240; Greenberg 1993:6–10; Liska and Messner 1999:207). It has also been suggested that the goal of some conflict theorists is to challenge the hegemony of modern scientific thought, to dethrone and replace it with linguistically based nonscientific views that recognize "a need to advance a progressive agenda favoring disprivileged people" (Schwartz and Friedrichs 1994:222). In other words, according to some, conflict theorists focus "more on a critique of the shortcomings of other criminologists than on offering an alternative explanation of crime" (Akers and Sellers 2004:237). This does not sit well with those who contend that "however persuasive the logic or appealing the ideology of such an argument, its validity and scientific utility require that it be formulated as testable research hypotheses which can direct the accumulation of relevant empirical evidence" (Chiricos and Waldo 1975:754; see also Hawkins 1987:721).

Some strands of conflict theory are particularly susceptible to this criticism. Akers and Sellers (2004:239) note, for example, "The empirical validity of left realism...has not been established. The question is what theory of crime and/or criminal justice is proposed by left realists that can be tested?" They also state, "Peacemaking criminology does not offer a theory of crime or of the criminal justice system that can be evaluated empirically. It may be possible to construct a testable, parsimonious, and valid theory from peacemaking criminology, but at this point it remains a philosophy rather than a theory" (p. 241). In addition, Marxist theory has been criticized for stating tautological propositions and dogmatic ideology rather than providing a testable theory of law making and enforcement. For some, there is little in Marxist theory of law and criminal justice that is empirically testable (Akers and Sellers 2004:220–221).

A related point is that conflict theory is really a theory of law formulation and application, rather than law violation. In this sense, the theory does not explain crime, it simply identifies social conflict as a basic fact of life and as a source of discriminatory treatment by the criminal justice system of groups and classes that lack power (Adler et al. 1991:188). In line with these criticisms, research that explicitly tests conflict hypotheses of criminal behavior is quite rare, and the dearth of such studies means that the validity and scope of the theory have not been adequately tested (Akers and Sellers 2004:210–211).

Responses to these criticisms have varied. Beirne (1979), for example, directly challenges the empiricist critique of Marxist theories of law and crime and takes issue with those who do not properly differentiate Marxist theory from conflict theory more generally—the latter being a perspective that, Beirne argues, is positivist in nature and seeks to determine "mechanistic causation" (p. 376), unlike Marxist theory. In his comment, Beirne demonstrates the positivistic nature of conflict theory when he cites Jacobs (1978:515), who notes, "[I]nstead of seeing the law as an impartially administered codification of shared norms, conflict theorists hold that the criminal statutes are created and enforced according to the wishes of those with power." According to Beirne, the rigidity of the causal structure of this argument, whose logic is almost identical to that held by positivist criminology, is underscored by the related assertion that "the more there are differences in economic resources and economic power, the more one can expect that the criminal codes will be administered in a way that pleases monied elites" (Jacobs 1978:516). Beirne further notes that the corollary of this assertion, in turn, extends the causal chain to the argument that "when sanctions are imposed, the most severe sanctions will be imposed on persons in the lowest social class" (Chambliss and Seidman 1971:451). For Beirne, the concern is that "conflict theory was generally so vague in its basic assumptions, and so wide-ranging in its scope, that it might easily incorporate (or co-opt) a variety of different perspectives, including Marxism, within the compass of its structure" (p. 377). In the second half of his paper he seeks to demarcate the causal structure of Marxist propositions on law and crime from the causal structure of conflict theories. Beirne stresses that Marxist theory did not develop from any sector of mainstream sociology but rather arose, largely, from Marxist philosophy and theories of the capitalist state. In this sense, the logical structure of Marxism is not causal but relational. Hence, "much of the empirical evidence directed towards the assessment of Marxist propositions is either grossly misdirected or else inadvertently supports them" (p. 378).

Lack of Empirical Validity

A different issue often raised by critics is that the theory's basic explanation for crime is too simplistic. This is particularly the case in the Marxist view of capitalist society as criminogenic (Mankoff 1978; Adler et al. 1991:193). If the Marxist view is valid, then crime should be high in capitalist societies and low in socialist societies. Yet this is not always the case. For starters, crime exists in noncapitalist societies, in some cases at high rates. Furthermore, if there is something inherently criminogenic in a capitalist mode of production, then all capitalist societies should have similar crime rates, which should be higher than those found in any socialist system. This is also not the case. The United States, Japan, Germany, Great Britain, and virtually all other industrialized nations, including the social welfare capitalism such as that found in Scandinavian countries, as well as most of the developing nations, are more or less capitalist. Yet they have widely varying crime rates, some of which are lower and others of which are higher than the rates that prevailed under communist rule (Akers and Sellers 2004:230–231). Given this, it is too simplistic to argue that capitalism is the root cause of crime.

This criticism extends beyond Marxist views, however. Scholars challenge, "We cannot explain the criminal behavior of those who violate . . . broad values and norms as simply acting on behalf of some group interest in conflict with the dominant view. Of course, groups conflict and values clash in the enactment of laws, but it does not necessarily follow that most crime is simply the result of a continuation of that conflict beyond legislative battles" (Akers and Sellers 2004:211). In support of this argument, critics charge that the vast majority of crime cannot be explained as behavior reflective of group conflict, in part because it is commonly recognized that most crime is intra-group— committed by members within a group against one another (e.g., black-on-black crime), rather than inter-group (black-on-white crime). These critics do concede that conflict theory accurately applies to some crime types, including politically or ideologically motivated acts, but they contend that most crimes, typically street crimes such as homicide, assault, robbery or burglary, do not fit the theory's model (Akers and Sellers 2004:211).

Competing Explanations

In addition to these larger questions about the empirical validity of the theory, a variety of analytical issues arise related to each type of conflict study. For example, Vold et al. (2002:242) note:

> Conflict criminologists generally are able to demonstrate that broad patterns in crime and criminal justice are consistent with the arguments and predictions of their theories. But other possible explanations also exist for the same crime patterns. The major problem with testing conflict criminology is distinguishing between conflict explanations and the other possible explanations.

Nowhere is this more the case than with testing the threat thesis. According to the theory, when minority populations pose an increasing threat to the status quo, the level of social control should increase. Studies that examine this notion commonly test hypotheses such as that an increase in the African-American population in a city will result in an increase in the hiring of more police officers, or generate more arrests for blacks, or lead to harsher sentences for blacks, and so on. A positive association between percent minority and these outcomes is typically viewed as support for conflict theory. But as Vold et al. point out, "non-conflict explanations are also compatible with the same findings" (p. 243). For example, increases in arrests or harsher sentencing may stem from pressure from fellow victims for greater control, not from the elite who view minorities as a threat to existing order. In short, research has not been able to distinguish the threat hypothesis from nonconflict interpretations of the same findings.

Extralegal Effects

The fourth type of conflict study, research on the use of discretion in applying the law against accused violators, has its fair share of issues as well. Most studies of this kind determine the extent to which extralegal factors (e.g., race/ethnicity, socioeconomic status, age) play a role in criminal justice outcomes, including arrest, conviction, and sentencing, controlling for relevant legal factors. Theorists maintain that they can claim support for conflict theory if a study finds that extralegal factors operate above and beyond legal factors. But critics question: What exactly constitutes evidence in favor of conflict theory? Must extralegal variables account for all of the variation, most of the variation, or only some of the variation in outcomes? Do race, class, gender, and age effects above zero, regardless of level, constitute evidence in favor of conflict theory? In short, at issue is the extent to which extralegal variables must account for differences in outcomes to constitute support for conflict theory (see Akers and Sellers 2004:202).

A related issue has to do with the theory's basic assumption that any effect of extralegal variables can be attributed to bias and discrimination against accused violators, as opposed to some other phenomenon (again, an issue of not being able to rule out competing explanations). For example, it is true that minorities are overrepresented in almost all stages of the criminal justice system. But one must question if this is due to their race/ethnicity or to the fact that they commit more serious crimes and/or have more prior arrests than nonminorities do (see Blumstein 1982). While most studies control for these two legally relevant factors and still find extralegal effects, it may be the case that other legal variables omitted from the study are, in fact, responsible for the observed race effect. In other words, the study may only document extralegal effects because important and related legal variables such as victim characteristics or crime type have not been properly controlled or accounted for (Hawkins 1987:724–731). To support conflict theory, research must demonstrate that people are treated differently *based on* their race or social status, given equivalent legal conditions. In essence, to find empirical support for conflict theory a study must properly control for all relevant legal variables to determine if the extralegal variables have a true independent effect on criminal justice decisions.

Taking these points into consideration, one can make several conclusions about the literature on extralegal effects: (1) Criminal justice decisions are based more on legally relevant, neutral, and nonbiased legal factors than on extralegal factors; (2) when legal variables are controlled, differences in arrests, court outcomes, and the severity of sentencing by race, class, sex, age, and ethnicity either disappear or are reduced to small, statistically insignificant levels; and (3) the influence of extralegal variables, when present, tends not to produce large differences in typical outcomes; in other words, even when studies find independent effects of extralegal variables, such effects are fairly small (Akers and Sellers 2004:203–204; see also Chiricos and Waldo 1975:766; Hagan 1974; Hagan and Albonetti 1982:331; Kleck 1981; Walker, Spohn, and DeLone 2000). Collectively, this suggests little support for conflict theory's proposition that the powerless, because of their status, are more likely to be subject to punishment in the criminal justice system.

Still, evidence exists that extralegal factors—race and class in particular—matter in important ways above and beyond legal factors (Bishop and Frazier 1996; Bridges and Steen 1998; Paternoster 1991; Steffensmeier and Demuth 2000, 2001). And scholars point out that although extralegal effects at any given stage may be small, successive decision points result in a "cumulative" effect for individuals (Vold et al. 2002). The total effect of race on sentencing, for example, includes the effect of race on earlier decision points such as making bail, hiring an attorney, and so on. As such, the total effect of race on sentencing may actually be quite large. This recognition provides support for conflict theory, and the accumulation of effects has been particularly well documented in studies on the processing of juveniles (Bishop and Frazier

1996, 1988; Krisberg et al. 1987; Liska and Tausig 1979; McCarthy and Smith 1986; Pope and Feyerherm 1990).

It is also the case that research on disparities focuses almost entirely on formal decision-making points, thereby ignoring racial, ethnic, and class disparities in informal and unauthorized actions taken on the street (Akers and Sellers 2004:207). It may be that racial and class biases are found in the patterns of police patrols, citizen harassment, stop and search, use of excessive force, and other actions taken by the police in the community, which is generally supported in a small but important literature (Jacobs 1979; Jacobs and Britt 1979; Rubenstein 1973; Westley 1972), particularly on racial profiling (for reviews, see Ramirez et al. 2000 and Engel et al. 2002).

So how to make sense of the extensive literature on selective enforcement? We argue that it can be summed up in this way: "In most research, the more serious the offense, the more likely it is that decisions will remain neutral on race, class, and other status characteristics of the offender. Discretionary decisions are more apt to produce such disparities in minor offenses. There appears to be some racism, sexism, and class bias in the system, but they have a relatively weak effect on actual arrest, conviction, and sanctioning outcomes. In sum, whatever effect extra-legal factors may have operates in a subtle, complex fashion, rather than in a direct, unequivocally discriminatory manner" (Akers and Sellers 2004:205; see also Chiricos and Crawford 1995; Chiricos and Waldo 1975:768; Liska and Messner 1999:200).

Directions for Future Research

Where does conflict theory stand today? And how relevant is the theory in an era in which increasing attention is given to white-collar crime and criminals? Do the theory's basic assumptions still hold true? The answer, in part, is that problems and setbacks continue to exist. As noted earlier, critics claim that the theory today is not much different than it was 30 years ago (Liska and Messner 1999:206). In particular, critics still complain that the theory does not define its major concepts well, which poses difficulty for testing. If this problem is to be eliminated, "conflict theorists must define clearly what is in the interests of different social categories, such as capitalists and labor, whites and blacks, and males and females in order for researchers to observe whether there is a correspondence between these interests and power, and the law" (Liska and Messner 1999:207).

There is another part to this answer, however. Despite problems and setbacks, conflict theory is alive and well today. Its presence is particularly felt in two areas of research, which are currently hot-button topics for criminologists. First, it is the theoretical framework most commonly employed in studies of racial profiling by the police. Although a relatively new topic for empirical inquiry, "the results from most reported racial profiling studies indicate that minorities are stopped, searched, and sometimes ticketed at rates that exceed those for Whites when compared to some benchmark population" (Petrocelli et al. 2002:5; see also Lamberth 1997; Zingraff et al.

2000). Support for racial profiling is consistent with conflict theory's notion that (perceived) problem populations—in this case, minorities—are subject to greater levels of social control.

Second, conflict theory provides an appropriate framework for understanding dramatic increases in the crime control industry in the last two decades, particularly with respect to the "war on drugs." In *Malign Neglect*, Michael Tonry (1995) presents a conflict-oriented interpretation of the "war on drugs," arguing, "crime and drug control policies were a deliberate effort to destabilize black communities" (p. 38). Whatever your position, it is hard to argue with a commonly recognized fact associated with the drug war: that racial disparities in drug arrests and sentencing are due, in part, to disparities in laws for crack and powder cocaine. The original guidelines created by the United States Sentencing Commission (USSC) for crack and powder cocaine resulted in a penalty ratio of 100 to 1 (possession of 1 gram of crack cocaine would yield the same sentence for a defendant as would possession of 100 grams of powder cocaine). Given that blacks more frequently use crack cocaine and whites more frequently use powder cocaine, this has resulted in vastly different sentence lengths by race. After years of reviewing and evaluating their guidelines, in 1995 the USSC recommended to Congress that the sentencing disparity be reduced, arguing that the two drugs were pharmacologically identical but that the sentencing disparity resulted in minority offenders serving much longer sentences. Members of Congress, however, rejected the recommendation, which was the first time since the USSC's inception in 1984 that Congress acted against a recommendation. Although the USSC has repeatedly suggested that the disparity be reduced to at least 20 to 1, no changes have been made. Conflict theorists would argue that this is no accident. Rather, as young black males (the typical users of crack cocaine) continue to pose a threat to the existing order, they will continue to experience heightened levels of social control. Indeed, little will change until the economic organization of society changes, whether that means reducing poverty or inequality or fundamentally altering the capitalist economic structure.

Discussion Questions

1. Why are power relations within society, especially those related to class differences, so fundamental to conflict theory? Does the theory predict that more unequal or less unequal societies will have greater crime rates? Why?

2. Think about a current social problem (e.g., gun control, abortion, immigration). According to conflict theory, how will this problem ultimately be resolved?

3. What are the four types of conflict studies in the literature? Which set of studies has received the least empirical support?

4. Define the concept of social class, which is fundamental to conflict theory. What are some of the problems with how researchers have measured social class in their studies? How might these problems be remedied?

5. Identify some of the analytical issues in studies that attempt to determine the extent to which extralegal factors (e.g., race, ethnicity, socioeconomic status) play a role in criminal justice outcomes, including
arrest, conviction, and sentencing. On the whole, what can one conclude about this literature?

CHAPTER 10

INTEGRATED THEORY

Introduction

To integrate or not to integrate? This has been one of the most debated questions by scholars in criminology over the last three decades. The debate formally began in the 1970s when Elliott, Ageton, and Cantor (1979); Hirschi (1979); and Short (1979) presented arguments for and against theoretical integration in a special issue of the *Journal of Research in Crime and Delinquency*. Ten years later, the debate came to a head in Steven Messner, Marvin Krohn, and Allen Liska's edited 1989 book, *Theoretical Integration in the Study of Deviance and Crime*, which was published following a conference on the problems and prospects of theoretical integration. Today, the dialogue continues. While there are still vocal opponents of integration, most notably Travis Hirschi, over the years numerous voices have called for theoretical integration in one form or another (Barak 1998; Bernard and Snipes 1996; Elliott et al. 1979; Pearson and Weiner 1985). Scholars agree that a main goal in any field of study, criminology included, is theoretical development. But what is the best way to develop theories and move the field forward? As we already noted in Chapter 1, there are several ways to advance theory: "Theoretical development takes place through explicating, testing, and modifying a single theory, through competition of rival theories, and through theoretical integration" (Akers and Sellers 2004:286).

This chapter explores how theoretical development in criminology has been influenced by theoretical integration. After describing the different forms of theoretical integration, we examine several perspectives that serve to illustrate some of the issues raised. As we have done in prior chapters, we assess the measurement and analytical strategies employed. However, because we are dealing with integrated theories that combine concepts from perspectives already reviewed, our discussion of measurement issues will be limited to those concepts not already covered in prior chapters.

Intellectual History of Integrated Theory

As just noted, three procedures are used to evaluate and develop theory: (1) theoretical falsification, (2) theoretical competition, and (3) theoretical integration. Each of these, to varying degrees, has shaped theoretical development in the field of criminology.

With falsification, researchers want to know: Does the theory have empirical validity? Theories are evaluated on "the extent that they can be shown to harmoniously exist with or be hostile to a set of known facts or with a set of predictions that the theory makes" (Paternoster and Bachman 2001:303). If a theory cannot account for known facts (e.g., crime is disproportionately committed by men) or if its predictions are not empirically borne out, it is falsified. Falsification helps determine which theories should remain viable and which should be discarded. Because science places a high value on empirical accuracy, the process of empirical verification and falsification seems a reasonable basis on which to evaluate theory.

In practice, however, falsification rarely determines which theories remain and which are abandoned, at least in the social sciences. You have probably noticed that all of the theories discussed in this book have been falsified, in some respects, due to lack of empirical confirmation in studies. At the same time, all of the theories have received some empirical support. The result is that each theory is able to explain some but not all of the known facts of crime, and some but not all of its predictions will be found to be true (Vold, Bernard, and Snipes 2002:314). As a result, "it has been rare that a criminological theory has been completely dismissed by those in the discipline because it lacks empirical validity" (Paternoster and Bachman 2001:304).

To date, the most common approach to evaluating theory in criminology has been theoretical competition or opposition, which has been depicted quite favorably in the literature on the philosophy of science (Hempel 1966:25–28; Stinchcombe 1968:27–28). Theoretical competition involves directly testing theories against each other. The key word here is competition, or the logical, conceptual, or empirical comparison of two or more theories (Akers 1999). Theoretical competition is concerned with the empirical validity of one theory compared with others. The nature of this strategy is to keep different theories competing against one another to discard erroneous or extraneous theories and more fully develop promising ones. In this sense, theoretical competition forces a theory to advance by explicitly developing itself (e.g., offering testable propositions, clearly defining the concepts) rather than concerning itself with other theories, as in the case of integration.

In short, theory competition is considered "an efficient and economical means of hypothesis testing, and it has informed much research and theorizing on the causes of crime and deviance" (Liska, Krohn, and Messner 1989:3). Despite this, the number of theories of crime has grown, rather than diminished, over the years. Most criminologists would agree that there are too many criminological theories, and new ones continue to appear on the scene with astonishing frequency (Bernard and Snipes 1996:301). Moreover, "despite all the theory and research in criminology, the field lacks a unified conceptual framework" (Pearson and Weiner 1985:116).

For some, this suggests that theoretical competition has largely failed (Elliott 1985). Elliott, Huizinga and Ageton (1985) claim that theory competition has resulted in the acceptance or semi-acceptance of a number of theories, each of which can explain only 10–20% of the variance in criminal behavior (see also Liska et al. 1989:5). For others, the current abundance of criminological theories has impeded scientific progress (Bernard 1991). Theory is supposed to direct research and to accumulate its product into a coherent, understandable framework, but "the failure to accomplish this is one reason why criminology research has tended toward a million modest little studies that produce a million tiny conflicting results" (Bernard and Snipes 1996:302; see also Wolfgang, Figlio, and Thornberry 1978:4). Given this, some scholars advocate theoretical integration as the key to developing more powerful theories of crime and delinquency.

Over the years, several definitions of theoretical integration have surfaced. Integration consists of "the combination of two or more pre-existing theories, selected on the basis of their perceived commonalities, into a single reformulated theoretical model with greater comprehensiveness and explanatory value than any one of its component theories" (Farnworth 1989:95). "Theoretical integration can be defined as the act of combining two or more sets of logically interrelated propositions into one larger set of interrelated propositions in order to provide a more comprehensive explanation of a particular phenomenon" (Thornberry 1989:52). "The goal of theory integration is to identify commonalities in two or more theories to produce a synthesis that is superior to any one theory individually" (Akers and Sellers 2004:268). As you can see, theoretical integration has the goal of fusing together closely related theories in an effort to reduce the number of explanations. Integration is also appealing because it offers a more comprehensive explanation through the assumption that there are multiple causes of crime (Elliott 1985).

To a certain extent, every theory "integrates" at least some previously existing theories in new arguments (e.g., Cloward and Ohlin [1960] incorporate differential association theory into their revision of Merton's anomie theory—see Chapter 5). The real issue here is the degree of integration. One of the earliest systematic attempts at producing a truly "integrated theory" was by Elliott, Ageton, and Cantor (1979) and later by Elliott, Huizinga, and Ageton (1985), who combined strain, social control, and social learning perspectives into a single explanatory paradigm. Elliott et al. claim that none of these theories alone explain delinquency as well as their combined model. For example, social control theory, even according to Hirschi himself, underestimates the importance of delinquent friends and overestimates the significance of involvement in conventional activities, a miscalculation that stems from the assumption of "natural motivation" to delinquency. If such natural motivation could legitimately be assumed, delinquent friends would be unnecessary, and involvement in conventional activities would curtail the commission of delinquent acts. In driving home their point, they argue that "it is one thing to be a social isolate with weak bonds to conventional peer groups and another to be highly committed to and integrated into a delinquent peer group" (Elliott et al. 1979:15). For more on this issue, see Chapter 7.

According to Elliott et al., there are two primary paths to juvenile delinquency: (1) weak bonds to conventional society (social control) lead to exposure and commitment to delinquent groups (differential association), which in turn leads to delinquency; and (2) strong bonds to conventional society (social control) may be conditioned by experiences that attenuate those bonds (strain), and this may lead to exposure and commitment to groups involved in delinquency (differential association). Whereas control theory focuses on the strength of conventional socialization (strong or weak bonds), learning theory is concerned with its content (norms favoring conformity or deviance). Elliott et al. claim an individual can form strong or weak bonds to conventional or deviant social groups. Deviant behavior is most likely to result when an individual has strong bonds to deviant groups and weak bonds to conventional groups; alternatively, deviant behavior is least likely when one has strong bonds to conventional groups and weak bonds to deviant groups. Thus, in the first part of their integrated theory, low social control is considered causally prior to strong delinquent bonding.

In the next stage of their theory they integrate strain. Strain is expected to occur before bonding to conventional and delinquent groups occurs. Elliott et al. theorize that strain will have direct effects on delinquent behavior, but more importantly, that it will influence delinquency primarily by affecting conventional and delinquent bonding. In their integrated model, they also include other factors that may influence conventional bonding, including social disorganization (see Chapter 4). A simplified version of their integrated model is presented in Figure 10.1.

Elliott et al. (1985) find support for their integrated theory using data from the National Youth Survey. They found no direct effects of strain and social control measures on delinquency. Most importantly, they documented that variation in delinquency was attributed to the most proximate source in their model: bonding to delinquent peers. More recent research also reports modest support for Elliott et al.'s integrated theory (Menard and Elliott 1994).

Since Elliott et al.'s theory in the late 1970s, dozens of other integrated models have been proposed. All of the theories reviewed in the previous chapters have been subjected, in some way, to integration with other theories. Later in the chapter we describe the varying ways that criminological theories have been integrated, as well as discuss four examples of integrated theories that are well known in the field.

Integrated Theory

Before we can review examples of integrated criminological theories, we must first come to agreement as to what constitutes integration. Earlier we provided several definitions of theoretical integration, but in this section we consider how two or more theories can actually be integrated. What counts as integration? When scholars describe theoretical integration, each usually has a slightly different idea about what that process entails. In other words, there is no one way to integrate theories of crime and deviance. Let's explore some of the different ways theories have been integrated in criminology.

To start, an important distinction is between interdisciplinary and intradisciplinary theoretical integration. Interdisciplinary integration occurs when

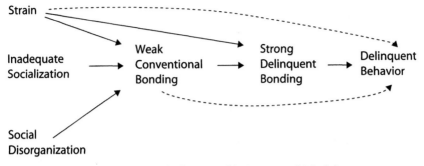

Figure 10.1 Simplified Version of Elliott et al.'s Integrated Model.
(*Reprinted from Bernard and Snipes 1996:311*)

theories from different disciplines are integrated, such as from psychology and sociology or biology and sociology. This type of integration is rare, mostly because researchers work within their own disciplines and are not as familiar with theoretical ideas or studies outside their discipline. Moreover, incompatibility on basic assumptions about human behavior is more likely to result across, rather than within, disciplines. Despite this, in this chapter we review one of the most popular and successful attempts at interdisciplinary integration—the life-course perspective, which combines elements of biological and psychological perspectives with elements of sociological theory.

Intradisciplinary theoretical integration is much more common. This form of integration occurs when theories within a discipline are integrated, such as conflict and labeling or social control and social learning theories. Because intradisciplinary integration has dominated theoretical integration in criminology, we review two examples of this type of integration—interactional theory and power-control theory.

Theoretical integration can also vary in terms of the level of analysis. Each theory discussed in this book is either a micro-level or macro-level theory. Again, micro-level theories, such as labeling or social control, attempt to explain the behavior of individuals. These theories assess why one individual is more or less likely to engage in crime or deviance compared to another. Conversely, macro-level theories focus on explaining variation in rates of crime or deviance across groups (e.g., the poor, as in conflict theory) or geographic units (e.g., neighborhoods, as in social disorganization theory).

Along these lines, theoretical integration can be within-level, for example, integrating micro-level (e.g., biological and rational choices theories, as in Wilson and Herrnstein 1985) or macro-level (e.g., conflict and social disorganization, as in Bursik 1989) theories. Some within-level attempts at integration include several theories. For example, Charles Tittle (1995, 1997, 1999) draws on deterrence and rational choice, strain, social learning, and social control theories to characterize crime as a result of an imbalance of control. And John Braithwaite's (1989) theory of reintegrative shaming combines labeling, subcultural, opportunity, social control, and social learning theories (see Chapter 8).

Less common but also possible, integration can be cross-level, such as when micro- and macro-level perspectives are joined. In most cases, combining macro- and micro-level theories reflects an attempt to explain both structural and processual factors associated with crime. Using social learning theory as an example, Akers (1989:28) notes, "The burden of ... structural theories is to indicate what kinds of situations and structures lead to deviant behavior. But none of them adequately specifies the *process* by which social structure shapes the behavior of individuals.... They propose something about the structure of learning environments likely to produce deviant behavior, but they do not specify *how* they do so. Thus, social learning is complementary to, not competing with, the structural theories. By conceptualizing the deviance-producing environments as setting up conditions that have an impact on individual conduct through the operation of the learning mechanisms, we can begin to integrate structural and processual explanations of deviant behavior." In short, cross-level integrated theories emphasize the influence that larger structural forces have on individuals and their actions (Paternoster and Bachman 2001:306). In this chapter, we review a cross-level theory, power-control theory, which combines conflict (macro-level) and social control (micro-level) perspectives to understand delinquency.

In addition to this, Liska et al. (1989) suggest two main types of theoretical integration, conceptual and propositional. Conceptual integration involves determining those concepts that have similar meanings in different theories and merging them into a common language (Einstadter and Henry 2006:316). Concepts from one theory are shown to overlap in meaning with concepts from another theory, and thus can be merged. A common example of conceptual integration involves social learning and social control theories. Consider social control theory's concept of belief in conventional norms and laws, which strengthens one's bond to conventional society. It is argued that the belief concept can be absorbed into the more general social learning concept of definitions favorable or unfavorable to crime and delinquency (see Chapter 7). The social learning integration of differential association and reinforcement principles (see Chapter 6) is another an example of conceptual integration (Akers 1989:27). If done improperly, attempts at conceptual integration can "distort, even transform, the original concepts" (Lanier and Henry 2004:342). For a fully developed model based on conceptual integration, see Pearson and Weiner (1985), who convert 13 theories into 12 constructs.

In contrast to conceptual integration is propositional integration, which involves linking separate theories by a given principle. Propositional integration relates propositions from different theories by showing, for example, how two or more theories make the same predictions about crime, even though each begins with different concepts and assumptions (e.g., both anomie and conflict theory predict higher crime rates in the lower class). This is a more formal effort at integration because it entails linking the propositions, and not just the concepts, of two or more theories into a new theory. As Paternoster and Bachman (2001) note, "The key word is 'linking'—to be considered theoretical integration, rather than simply usurpation, a propositionally integrated theory must actually meaningfully connect or relate the propositions of different theories into the new theory" (p. 307).

There are three ways to integrate theoretical propositions. First is side-by-side or horizontal integration. Here one theory is assumed to explain one component of crime and other theories explain other components of crime. The integrated theory is simply the sum of the components. This approach involves deciding which theories best explain which types of deviants (e.g., by social class, race) or which types of crime (e.g., violent, white-collar). A good example is the recent developmental theory, which focuses on distinct types of offenders: the life-course persistent offender and the adolescent-limited offender, which are created by two different causal processes. One causal process is biological and psychological in nature, while the other is sociological. We discuss this integrated theory in detail later. See also Gibbons and Farr (2001) as a good illustration of side-by-side integration.

A second type of propositional integration is end-to-end or sequential integration. In this approach, theories are combined in such a way that the independent variables (the cause) in one theory are linked to another so that they become the dependent variable (the effect) in the integrated theory. In this way, the concepts of two or more theories provide a causal chain or sequence. Think of various theories "kicking in" at different stages of the explanation (Einstadter and Henry 2006:316). End-to-end integration is developmental because it proposes a causal order across propositions of the various theories to be integrated (Bernard and Snipes 1996:307). Elliott et al.'s (1979) theory described earlier is a perfect example of end-to-end propositional integration in that independent variables from one or more theories (e.g., strain) are positioned causally prior to concepts from other theories (e.g., social control, social learning). See also Bursik (1989) and Colvin and Pauly (1983) for examples of sequential integration.

Finally, up-and-down or deductive integration constitutes a third type of propositional integration. Deductive integration involves identifying a higher level of abstraction or generality that encompasses some of the parts of two or more theories within it. Stated alternatively, this approach raises the level of abstraction of one theory, such that its components merely follow from the conceptually broader theory (Bernard and Snipes 1996:308). As Liska and Messner (1999) note, "This can be done by recognizing that theory A contains more abstract or general assumptions than theory B and, therefore, that key parts of theory B can be incorporated within the structure of theory A. Or, it can be done by abstracting more general assumptions from theories A and B, allowing parts of both theories to be incorporated in a new theory C" (p. 219). A good example of deductive integration is Burgess and Akers' (1966) integration of Sutherland's differential association theory with their own behaviorally based social learning theory. Overall, this type of integration is rarely attempted in the social sciences.

These three types of integration can be applied equally well to micro-, macro-, or cross-level integration. To sum up, "propositional integration involves combining previously formed theories, and conceptual integration involves demonstrating that several concepts from different theories all relate to a more abstract concept" (Bernard and Snipes 1996:316).

Finally, an alternative approach related to integration is theoretical elaboration, proposed by Thornberry (1989). Thornberry's theoretical elaboration is viewed as a compromise that lies somewhere between integration and opposition. Elaboration involves the logical extension of a particular theory, in an attempt to improve its explanatory power. Rather than starting with multiple theories and attempting to reconcile their differences to generate a comprehensive model, theoretical elaboration explicitly starts with a particular theory. Specifically, elaboration aims to revise and expand a theory based on empirical evidence that better explains the reasons for crime or delinquency. The blending of theory does not begin at the start, but rather once the contrary evidence is introduced. This allows the theory to develop with the observed evidence as opposed to a rigid structure of integrated expectations. Essentially, in the process of elaboration, the theorist is concerned with maximizing the explanatory power of a particular theory without the attendant concern of reconciling differences across theories. Unlike integration, elaboration does not value the melding together of differing theories as an end in itself; it values the incorporation of differing perspectives only selectively, and only if they offer a clear advantage to our efforts to explain crime and delinquency.

Thornberry (1989:59) describes a model that has been elaborated: (1) It is likely that propositions have been added, deleted, combined and reordered to offer a better explanation of delinquency; (2) the basic assumptions have probably been reevaluated and possibly altered to allow for the inclusion of propositions from differing perspectives; (3) the structure of the theory, including temporal ordering of concepts and the type of relationships permitted, may well have changed; and (4) it is likely that when this process is played out over time from the point of view of a number of different focal theories, the overall result will be the blending together of originally different and competing theoretical models into a more general body of explanatory principles. In turn, this will require fundamental changes in the theories of origin as the elaborated models replace them.

To reiterate, in elaboration, the theorist is concerned with how well the theory can be explained without merging crucial differences in theories. The researcher is also able to borrow ideas from other theories without being obligated to institute them in their final theory. Finally, in this approach, the goal is oriented toward maximizing the power of a single theory, whereas in integration it is toward reconciling differences across theories.

In sum, researchers can use several methods to integrate theory (for an overview of types of theoretical integration, see Liska et al. 1989:5–17). Regardless of which approach is practiced, the end result must have certain components to reflect a successfully integrated theory. Thornberry (1989:54) claims that integrated theories must contain four general elements. The first is a set of basic assumptions about the model. The propositions and concepts of the new theory will be based on these beliefs. Second, the theory must account for the level of explanation at which it functions (e.g., macro- or micro-level). Third, there has to be a set of logically interrelated propositions within all of the merging theories, which enables them to fuse without contradicting one another. And fourth, there must be an underlying structure that influences how the propositions are interrelated.

All of the theories reviewed in this book have played a role in theoretical integration over the last several decades. Attempts at theoretical integration and empirical tests of integrated theories abound. In the next section, we provide four examples of integrated theories and include a discussion of the various concepts involved as well as their measurement.

Integrated Developmental Theories

Although we could present at least two dozen attempts at theoretical integration in this chapter, we have chosen to focus on four that are representative of the various efforts in the field: life-course theory, interactional theory, age-graded theory of informal social control, and power-control theory. The first three are considered integrated developmental theories, so we discuss them together. We begin with Terrie Moffitt's life-course theory (Moffitt 1993, 1997) because it is explicitly an interdisciplinary integration and features two distinct causal chains by which youth come to offend.

Life-Course Theory

Moffitt begins with the observation that there are two distinct types of offenders. A small group of offenders begin their problematic behavior at a very young age and continue to behave in antisocial ways throughout their lives. Moffitt labels this group life-course persistent (LCP) offenders. Most individuals who commit delinquent behavior, however, do not start their antisocial behavior early in life but rather onset during their teenage years. Moffitt suggests that this later group of adolescence-limited (AL) offenders have a much shorter span of time when they are offending, as they generally cease engaging in criminal behavior as they move out of their teenage years. Beyond the duration of their antisocial careers, the LCP and AL youth are also distinguished in that the former engage in much more serious criminal behaviors than do the latter. Based on the distinct differences in the type and duration of delinquent careers, Moffitt argues that two different explanations are needed to account for why some people are persistent offenders while others limit their delinquent behavior to the adolescent years.

As just noted, LCP youth begin their antisocial behavior very early in life. Moffitt therefore suggests that we need to look for the roots of such behavior soon after birth, or even before. Among the factors Moffitt identifies are physical anomalies in neural development. Neuropsychological deficits lead to poor verbal and executive functioning such as self-control, temperament, and impulsivity. These, in turn, are related to childhood emergence of anti-social behavior.

The link between early problematic temperament and antisocial behavior is due to two processes involving the youth's parents. First, Moffitt suggests that the basis of some of the problematic behaviors may be genetically linked. That is, the parents of children who have problematic temperaments or are impulsive are likely to be temperamental or given to impulsive behavior themselves. In addition to providing an environment conducive to further problematic behaviors, parents of children with neurological and executive dysfunctions are also likely to have inconsistent parenting styles. For example, because of their own executive dysfunctions parents may not be capable of disciplining their children on a consistent basis.

In addition to the possibility of a genetic link between neurological and executive dysfunctions, Moffitt recognizes that the temperamental behavior of children may, in and of itself, elicit dysfunctional parenting. Were you ever in line at the grocery store when the child in front of you began to cry and scream because he wanted the candy displayed at the counter? The parent tries to calm the child down and tell him that he may not have the candy but the child persists until, finally embarrassed, the parent gives him the candy to keep him quiet. The reaction of the desperate parent only reinforces the child's temperamental behavior and can eventually lead to an escalation in antisocial behavior.

Children who have problematic temperaments and have not been effectively parented are likely to continue to experience problems in other areas of their lives. The child who acts up may experience problems in school and have difficulty making friends. The child experiences difficulty in learning conventional prosocial alternatives to antisocial behavior and is likely to become involved in a deviant lifestyle. For example, the increased difficulty that the child has in school may result in failure to attain a level of reading and math skills necessary to pursue conventional behavior. With conventional options limited, the youth may later turn to alternative and illegal means of making a living. As Moffitt (1993:682) states, "If a child who 'steps off on the wrong foot' remains on an ill-starred path, subsequent stepping-stone experiences may culminate in life-course-persistent antisocial behavior. For life-course-persistent antisocial individuals, deviant behavior patterns later in life may thus reflect early individual differences that are perpetuated or exacerbated by interactions with the social environment, first at home, and later at school."

The theory predicts that a rather small percentage of those who offend will fall into the LCP category. Delinquent behavior among other youth will occur only during the adolescent years. Moffitt's explanation for this behavior revolves around her observation that there is an increasing maturity gap when youth are no longer children but have not attained the status of an adult. This gap has increased in length because of a decreasing age of puberty coupled with an increasing need for education and training. Teenagers want to have sexual relationships, have their own spending money, be autonomous from their parents in their decision making, and have the respect that adults are often given by virtue of their status.

Faced with the maturity gap, AL teenagers may observe that the LCP youth are more likely to have achieved some of those desired goals. For example, LCP youth may be more likely to have sexual relationships at younger ages, acquire money or material goods through illegal activities, and disregard parental authority. Moffitt posits that AL youth learn delinquent behavior through mimicking the behavior of LCP youth because they see it as their entrée into adulthood. Moffitt points out that LCP youth, after being ostracized in their preteenage years, move to influential positions in the peer social structure during adolescence.

AL youth do not have the same or as serious deficits as LCP youth do. Therefore, as AL youth age, more legitimate adult roles become available to them. The probability of sexual relationships increases, they get part-time or full-time jobs, and parents gradually allow them to make more of their own decisions. Thus, the motivation for delinquency decreases. Moreover, AL youth have something to lose if they are caught for illegal behavior. Given that the maturity gap no longer poses a problem and they do not suffer from severe deficits, their behavior gradually conforms to the norms of conventional society.

In sum, the clear emphasis in Moffitt's theory is on early neurological and temperament factors that distinguish LCP offenders from AL offenders. LCP offenders exhibit problematic behavior early in life and have longer and more serious careers than other offenders. Their deficits lead to a cascading series of problems that limit opportunities in conventional arenas and increase the probability that they will become embedded in deviant networks. AL offenders delay their antisocial behavior until their teenage years. They begin at this developmental stage because of the maturity gap faced by adolescents who are seeking adult privileges such as sexual relationships, spending money, and the ability to make their own decisions. Limited by constraints placed on them by parents and other adults, they mimic the behavior of LCP offenders, who have broken free of such restraints earlier in their lives. Not strapped by the deficits of LCP offenders, AL offenders will eventually cease their delinquent behavior as those privileges previously denied are slowly granted with their transition into young adulthood.

Interactional Theory

True to his emphasis on theoretical elaboration (see earlier), Thornberry has continually extended his theory to take into account not only empirical findings but also opportunities to research individuals at different developmental stages. He first articulated his theory in his 1987 article "Toward an Interactional Theory of Delinquency." Thornberry discusses the limitations of control and learning theories and suggests an integrated approach that incorporates both in an effort to better explain delinquent behavior. Thornberry lists three limitations with these existing approaches. First, they have unidirectional causal structures. That is, they do not account for reciprocal effects or for the fact that while association with delinquent peers is likely to influence delinquency, for example, delinquency is also likely to influence the likelihood that youth will spend greater time with delinquent peers. Second, control and learning theories are nondevelopmental. That is, they do not take into account that criminal influences vary by age and at different stages of the life course. And third, both assume consistent causal effects regardless of an individual's position in the larger social structure. Yet social class, race, and neighborhood characteristics affect the strength of one's bonds to conventional society as well as association with delinquent peers.

Thornberry offers his interactional model as an alternative that attends to these limitations. His model addresses the question: "How are traditional social constraints over behavior weakened and, second, once weakened, how is the resulting freedom channeled into delinquent patterns?" (Thornberry 1987:866). He begins with the assumption that a primary cause of delinquency is the weakening of bonds to conventional society but also argues there should not be the taken-for-granted assumption that the reduction of control directly leads to delinquency. Social constraints merely free up behavior; delinquency still depends greatly upon an interactive process in which the behavior is learned, performed, and reinforced. In other words, "adolescents interact with other people and institutions and ... behavioral outcomes are formed by the interactive process" (p. 864). The weakening of controls remains significant because it allows for weaker ties to society and thus a wider range of behaviors from youth, but there still must be an interactive setting for youth to engage in delinquency (e.g., the deviance has to be learned, performed, and reinforced, usually in the setting of delinquent peers). Here, the youth is able to develop delinquent beliefs and behaviors, as differential association predicts.

In specifying his model, Thornberry focused on five concepts and their interrelationships (see Figure 10.2). Three are from control theory (attachment to parents, commitment to school, and belief in conventional values), while two are from social learning theory (associations with delinquent peers and adopting delinquent values). Thornberry focused explicitly on juvenile delinquency as the outcome. Because the theory is developmental, he offers three models that correspond to different stages in the life course (e.g., early, middle, and late adolescence), although these models are relatively similar (Bernard and Snipes 1996:315). According to Thornberry, attachment to parents and commitment to school both directly influence delinquent behavior, such that the greater the bonding, the smaller the probability of engaging in delinquency. Belief in conventional values is affected by both attachment and commitment and affects delinquent behavior indirectly through its reciprocal influence on behavior. Delinquent behavior, in turn, negatively influences attachment and commitment (and belief, indirectly through attachment).

The larger social structure factors in when Thornberry argues that one's position in society will influence one's delinquent involvement. Children from lower-class families, relative to their middle-class counterparts, should be less bonded and more likely to form delinquent values, have delinquent friends, and engage in delinquency.

Thornberry (1987) does not stray too far from Hirschi in his definition of concepts from social control theory. Attachment to parents is defined as the emotional relationship between the parents and adolescent. It includes communication, parenting skills, and any relationship conflicts. Commitment to school is how the youth succeeds in school, the perceived importance of education, attachment to teachers, and participation in school activities. This represents the youth's stake in conformity. The belief in conventional values is his or her devotion to middle-class values such as education, financial success, personal occupation, and other similar virtues. Association with delinquent peers signifies the level of attachment to the youth's peers, how the peers perceive deviance and act deviant, and how they reinforce these values to the youth. Delinquent values are how delinquent behavior is accepted and how willing the youth is to act delinquently. Last, delinquent behavior is the outcome variable.

Thornberry's interactional perspective provides the theoretical basis of the Rochester Youth Development Study (RYDS). The RYDS is a longitudinal panel study. The first phase of the study sampled 1,000 youth who were at high risk for serious delinquency and one of their parents or guardians. The study continued to follow up the original 1,000 adolescents through to the age of 30. This necessitated the extension of the theoretical explanation to account for the continuation or cessation of criminal behavior through the adult years. The RYDS also studied the children of their original sample, those as young as 2 years of age. The theory then had to be elaborated to account for early childhood problematic behavior. Let us examine these elaborations.

In their elaboration of interactional theory, Thornberry and Krohn (2003) incorporate explanations of both early childhood antisocial behavior and criminal behavior after the teenage years. The major premises of the theory remain the same in that the focus is on the reciprocal relationships among the

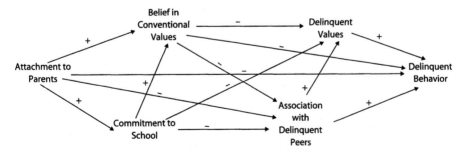

Figure 10.2 A Typical Recursive Causal Model of Delinquency. (*Reprinted from Thornberry 1987:868*)

social bond, peer-related variables, structural adversity, and antisocial behavior. However, to account for antisocial behavior beginning in childhood, like Moffitt they recognize the importance of negative temperamental qualities and neuropsychological deficits as well as parents' inability to monitor and reward prosocial behaviors or effectively punish antisocial behavior. These deficits are coupled with structural adversity that leads to an accumulated disadvantage. Thornberry and Krohn state, "very early onset offending is brought about by the combination and interaction of structural, individual, and parental influences. Extreme social adversity contributes to both parenting deficits and negative temperamental qualities in the child; in turn, both attributes, and especially their interaction, greatly increase the likelihood of early onset offending" (p. 295).

Children who have not exhibited antisocial behavior at these very young ages may onset during the years in which they are in elementary school. Thornberry and Krohn suggest that at these ages it is unlikely there is an intense coupling of temperament, parenting, and structural adversity. Negative temperament is deemphasized as a cause of antisocial behavior at these ages. Rather, the effect of growing up in families and neighborhoods marked by poverty and disorganization on parenting and on increasing access to deviant opportunity structures, including delinquent peers and gangs, are seen as likely causes of antisocial behavior. As stated earlier, as youth go through their teenage years, the family becomes less important while the school context and peer groups become more important.

Whether individuals commit criminal behavior after their adolescent years depends on several processes and, in some cases, a combination of them, according to Thornberry and Krohn. For example, those individuals who engaged in delinquent behavior at very young ages are likely to continue to be involved in crime into their adult years because of the extreme deficits they faced in childhood and because it is likely those deficits will persist.

Another factor that can lead to adult criminality is experiencing "precocious transitions." Precocious transitions are transitions that take place earlier in the life course than what is normatively expected. We generally expect a son or daughter to complete their high school education before leaving the birth home, getting married, having children of their own, and working full time. If the order and timing of the events are not consistent with this pattern, it can lead to increased difficulty in succeeding in the conventional adult world. The high school dropout and the teenage parent have more hurdles to scale than do those who have completed their education and delayed having children. Experiencing these precocious transitions is linked with adult criminality (Krohn, Lizotte, and Perez 1997; Thornberry, Krohn, Lizotte, Smith, and Tobin 2003).

In sum, interactional theory has been elaborated to take into account the period of time from early childhood through adulthood. Through the process of elaboration, Thornberry and then Thornberry and Krohn have generated a complex theory that begins with what appears to be an elaboration of social control theory and ends with a multidisciplinary, multilevel explanation of problematic behavior.

You probably have noted many similarities between Moffitt's life-course and Thornberry and Krohn's interactional theories. They are both developmentally specific, they both incorporate early childhood deficits such as temperament, they both emphasize the importance of parents and peers, and they both recognize that many of these factors are reciprocally related.

Although there are several important differences between the two theories, the most important is expressed in Moffitt's (1993) opening paragraph when she states that, "The central tenet of this article is that temporary versus persistent antisocial persons constitute two qualitatively distinct types of persons. In particular, I suggest that juvenile delinquency conceals two qualitatively distinct categories of individuals, each in need of its own distinct theoretical explanation" (p. 674). Thornberry and Krohn, alternatively, argue that there are not two distinct types of offenders. Rather, it is a matter of how severe and coupled are the causal factors that increase or decrease the probability of early onset and later continuation of criminal offending.

An Age-Graded Theory of Informal Social Control

Sampson and Laub (2005), who developed their age-graded theory of informal social control, summarized the three major tenets of their theory in the following manner:

> The first is that structural context is mediated in fundamental respects by informal family and school social controls, which in turn explain delinquency in childhood and adolescence. The second theme is that there is strong continuity in antisocial behavior running from childhood through adulthood across a variety of life domains. The third theme is that informal social control in adulthood explains changes in criminal behavior over the life span, independent of prior individual differences in criminal propensity. In our view, childhood pathways to crime and conformity over the life course are significantly influenced by adult social bonds. (p. 167)

The processes that cause delinquent behavior for Sampson and Laub are similar to those hypothesized by Thornberry (1987). The emphasis is on the role of the family in exercising both relational control (through attachment) and instrumental control (through monitoring and supervision). Those processes are theorized to be affected by the social structural location of the families. Ineffective informal social control during childhood and adolescence can lead to delinquent behavior and set in motion a cascading series of events that further embed the individual in delinquent and criminal behavior. Thus, there is strong continuity in antisocial behavior. An important point of divergence between Sampson and Laub's explanation and that of Thornberry is that their theory downplays the role of peers as a cause of delinquency whereas in Thornberry's theory, peers play a major role.

Although Sampson and Laub suggest there is strong continuity in antisocial behavior from childhood to adulthood, they specifically reject Moffitt's contention that there is a group of individuals who, because of their criminal propensity in early childhood, are LCP offenders. Rather, Sampson and Laub emphasize the role that informal social control can play in adulthood in terms of changing the trajectory of antisocial behavior. More specifically, they argue that life events such as getting married, having children, securing a full-time job, joining the military, and so on can reestablish the social bond with conventional society and change behavior accordingly. This can happen regardless of one's criminal propensity and delinquent behavior evidenced in childhood and adolescence. Benson (2002) characterizes this insight as the distinguishing feature of their theory.

Concepts and Measurement Issues of Integrated Developmental Theories

As you may have noticed when reading about the three integrated developmental theories, most of the concepts that are integral to the theories have been discussed in other chapters of this book. For example, all three theories incorporate dimensions of parenting as key components of their explanations. We have discussed parenting in relation to social control theory (Chapter 7). The use of concepts to which you have previously been introduced should not be surprising because these theories are intentionally comprised of parts of other theories.

You may have also observed that these theories are more complex than most that we have discussed up until now. As explicitly developmental theories, they attempt to account for the inception of delinquency and its continuation, or cessation, from childhood through the adult years. They take into account the many changes that occur throughout the life course and try to assess how different factors are more or less important at different stages in one's life. While this complexity may be required of integrated developmental theories, it makes it difficult, if not impossible, for the theories to be fully tested within a single analysis (see the discussion on analytical issues later). This has resulted in researchers dividing these theories into parts so they can empirically examine them. Because of overlap in the three theoretical perspectives, the discussion of many of the concepts in previous chapters, and the complexity of the theories, we orient our discussion of the research to parts of these theories that are either emphasized or that offer a unique contribution to our understanding of antisocial behavior.

Moffitt's unique contribution to our understanding of delinquent behavior and its continuity is her concept of LCP offenders. This relatively small group of offenders begins antisocial behavior at very young ages and persists in serious crime longer than do other offenders. She emphasizes the causative role in neuropsychological deficits in such areas as temperament, speech, motor coordination, impulse control, attention span, and language and reasoning. Prior to Moffitt presenting her argument, not much attention was focused on these concepts. This is largely because most scholars who study delinquency in this country have a sociological or social-psychological background and do not have the expertise to incorporate and measure many of the concepts central to Moffitt's theory. Moreover, to examine whether early neuropsychological indicators predict LCP offending, a data set that follows individuals from their very early years through adulthood is required. Relatively few data sets have measures of neuropsychological variables over an extended age span.

Moffitt and her colleagues (Moffitt, Caspi, Rutter, and Silva 2001) have acquired such data in a study known as the Dunedin Multidisciplinary Health and Development Study. The study is a longitudinal investigation of a cohort of individuals born between 1972 and 1973 in Dunedin, New Zealand. Perinatal data were collected at delivery and individuals were followed up every two years from the age of 3 to 30. The data set is impressive not only for the vast array of measures it includes but also for its very high retention rate (97%).

The Dunedin study includes a number of neuropsychological measures. At age 3, each child was examined by a pediatric neurologist to assess motility, passive movements, reflexes, facial musculature, foot posture, and gait (Moffitt et al. 2001). Intelligence was measured at age 3 by the Peabody Picture Vocabulary Test; at age 5 by the Stanford Binet Intelligence Scales; and at ages 7, 9, and 11 by the Wechsler Intelligence tests—all standardized intelligence tests frequently used by psychologists. Note that the type of test changes to take into account the developmental stage of the child. The Burt Word Reading Test, which assessed the degree to which children could recognize words, was administered at ages 7, 9, and 11. Finally, heart rate was measured at ages 7, 9, and 11 as well.

In addition to these indicators, Moffitt et al. (2001) collected data on child behavioral risk predictors, including temperament and hyperactivity. Temperament was measured by both parental reports and by observations made by psychological examiners. The parental measure consisted of simply asking mothers whether their child was easy or difficult to manage. In addition, 3- and 5-year-olds were observed by trained psychological examiners over a 90-minute session in which they participated in cognitive and motor tasks. The examiners rated the child, generating a measure that indicated how irritable, negativistic, inattentive, and emotional he or she appeared. Hyperactivity was measured with a well-known scale—Rutter Child Scales (Rutter, Tizard, and Whitmore 1970). These scales are created from responses by parents and teachers assessing the child's level of hyperactivity.

It should be noted that the collection of these diverse measures required medical staff and psychologists trained in the administration of standardized intelligence tests and in the assessment of children's behavior and emotional states. We have only mentioned the neuropsychological, emotional, and early behavioral measures that comprise this data set. Of course, Moffitt et al. (2001) included a number of other more standard parent, peer, and school-related variables, which are measured in a manner consistent with what we have already reviewed. The results of analyses using these measures have been reported in a number of research studies. We offer a brief summary of the findings.

Research from both the Dunedin study and other data sets has clearly supported the hypothesis that early evidence of neuropsychological deficits, learning disabilities, and emotional and behavioral problems predict later delinquent behavior. For example, IQ is related to later delinquency (Denno 1990; Moffitt 1990a; Moffitt, Gabrielli, Mednick, and Schulsinger 1981; White, Moffitt, Earls, Robins, and Silva 1990). This relationship holds even when other potential delinquency predictors such as socioeconomic class, race, and academic attainment are controlled (Lynam, Moffitt, and Stouthamer-Loeber 1993). Moffitt (1997) has summarized her research on other neuropsychological deficits by stating, "[T]he link between neuropsychological intellectual impairment and antisocial outcomes is one of the most robust effects in the study of antisocial behavior" (p. 19).

In addition to intellectual deficits, cognitive deficits such as inattention, impulsivity, aggression, and poor judgment have also been linked to delinquent behavior (Lynam et al. 1993; Moffitt 1990b). Moffitt, Lynam, and Silva (1994) found that conduct problems and hyperactivity at ages 3 and 5 predicted stability of self-reports of delinquency through the ages of 13 to 18. Moffitt (2003) suggests that the interaction between neuropsychological deficits and family adversity (e.g., parents who suffer from the same deficits, poor parenting) interact to create a particularly strong effect on later delinquency. One should not get the impression that findings supportive of her theory come only from the Dunedin study. Piquero and Moffitt (2005) cite a number of studies using data sets from both the United States and other countries that have generated similar results. Clearly, the early predictors of delinquency that Moffitt has identified are important factors in the process of generating persistent, serious delinquent behavior.

The concepts in Thornberry's interactional theory are derived primarily from social control and differential association theory, and we have covered these in other chapters. The unique contributions of Thornberry's (and later, Thornberry and Krohn's) approach is his emphasis on the hypothesized developmental differences in the impact of certain factors, the hypothesized reciprocal relationships among the variables, and the emphasis on the importance of precocious transitions in the continuity of criminal behavior from adolescence to adulthood.

In one of the first studies that is a partial test of interactional theory, Thornberry, Lizotte, Krohn, Farnworth, and Jang (1991) test the relationships among the two bonding concepts—attachment to parents and commitment to school—and delinquency over the life course. The researchers use data from the RYDS, a prospective longitudinal study of 1,000 high-risk youth from Rochester, New York, that began in 1988. To measure attachment to parents, they use an 11-item scale adapted from Hudson's Child's Attitude Toward Mother Scale (Hudson 1996). This scale measures adolescents' perceptions of warmth, liking, and the absence of hostility between themselves and their parent or primary caretaker, including questions such as, "You get along well with your parent?"; "You feel that you can really trust your parent?"; "You think your parent is terrific?"; "You have a lot of respect for your parent?"; "Your parent is too demanding?" For all questions, respondents are asked how often they would agree with these statements: never, seldom, sometimes, or often. According to Thornberry et al. (1991), the questions all tap the underlying construct of attachment to parents, which is empirically confirmed. Coefficients of reliability (e.g., Chronbach's alpha) are quite high for these measures (e.g., > .80) across all three waves of data.

Commitment to school reflects a 10-item scale measuring whether students like school, how well they do in school, and how hard they work on their schoolwork. It is comprised of questions such as, "Since school began this year, you like school a lot?"; "You do poorly at school?"; "Homework is a waste of time?"; "Sometimes you do extra work to improve your grades?"; "You don't really belong at school?" Respondents are asked to indicate how strongly they agree or disagree with these statements: strongly disagree, disagree, agree, strongly agree. Like attachment to parents, commitment to school has high scale reliability for all three waves.

Finally, 29 questions on delinquent behavior and drug use are included in the survey. The items are derived, in part, from the National Youth Survey and range from running away from home to using a weapon to trying to hurt someone, forging a check, or selling different drugs.

Thornberry et al. (1991) find general support for interactional theory. Most important, perhaps, they find support for the reciprocal relationships between social bonding and delinquency. They note, "Commitment to school and delinquent behavior are involved in a mutually reinforcing causal relationship over time. Low commitment increases delinquency, and delinquency, in turn, reduces commitment to school. Reciprocal effects for these variables are quite stable over the three waves of this panel model" (p. 29).

In another study, Thornberry, Lizotte, Krohn, Farnworth, and Jang (1994) examined the relationships among associations with delinquent peers, peer reactions, delinquent beliefs, and delinquent behavior over time. The measures of delinquent peers and delinquent beliefs are consistent with those used in prior studies of differential association theory. Delinquent peers was measured with an eight-item scale asking how many of the youth's friends committed delinquent acts that ranged in seriousness from skipping classes to armed robbery. Cronbach's alpha of reliability ranged from .86 to .89. Questions that asked respondents to indicate how wrong it was to commit the same type of delinquent acts were combined into a scale to measure delinquent beliefs. The scale has a reliability ranging from .78 to .86. Thornberry et al. also introduced a measure of peer reactions intended to capture how friends would perceive their illegal behavior. This scale contained six items (alphas ranged between .80 and .83). They used the same delinquency index as in their earlier study.

The results from the study support two central premises of interactional theory. First, delinquent behavior and delinquent peers are reciprocally related over time. Associating with delinquent peers leads to an increase in delinquent behavior. Committing delinquent behavior, in turn, leads to associating more with delinquent peers. Second, the role of delinquent beliefs increases as youth become more embedded in a delinquent network. Krohn, Lizotte, Thornberry, Smith, and McDowall (1996) extended the analysis to five years, focusing on drug use instead of delinquent behavior, and arrived at similar conclusions.

Interactional theory views the transition from adolescence to adulthood as a critical juncture in the life course. Youth who make successful transitions at the prescribed time and in the right order (marriage before children) are more likely to be successful. Those making precocious transitions (leaving school before graduating) place themselves at a disadvantage to succeed in adulthood. Krohn et al. (1997) examined four types of problematic transitions: teenage pregnancy (females) or impregnating someone (males), teenage parenthood, dropping out of school, and moving out of the family of origin's home before graduating from high school. These were measured by asking respondents whether they experienced any of these things.

Krohn et al. (1997) were interested in whether teenage drug use increased the probability of these precocious transitions and whether experiencing these precocious transitions led to continued drug use in young adulthood. By taking advantage of the longitudinal RYDS data set, they were able to find support for both hypotheses for both the male and the female respondents in their study. In their book on gangs, Thornberry et al. (2003) determined that the effect of being a gang member on both shorter-term (precocious transitions) and longer-term (young adult employment, educational attainment, and adult crime) outcomes was similar to what their earlier work had found regarding alcohol and drug use.

As stated earlier, Sampson and Laub's most important theoretical contribution is their emphasis on why some individuals who committed crimes in their teenage or young adult years do not continue to do so through the life course. They were able to investigate this question using a unique data source. Sheldon and Eleanor Glueck (1950) wrote a book entitled *Unraveling Juvenile Delinquency* based on the analysis of longitudinal prospective data they collected on 1,000 boys at ages 14, 25, and 32. The sample was purposively selected to acquire 500 boys who had been officially identified as delinquent and a matched (on age, race/ethnicity, IQ, and low-income residence) sample of 500 boys who were officially nondelinquent. Sampson and Laub (1993) reconstructed and augmented the data set, extending the analysis. Subsequently, they went back and reinterviewed the sample of delinquents when they were 70 years old (Laub and Sampson 2003). While some of the data are retrospective and therefore problematic, the age span that the data set covers makes it an invaluable resource.

Sampson and Laub's (1993) results are consistent with what Thornberry and colleagues found. Delinquency sets in motion a variety of impediments to successful transition into adulthood in the spheres of work and partner relationships. This "cumulative disadvantage" undermines potential social bonds that might otherwise have emerged in the adult years (e.g., stable marriage, successful career), increasing the chances of continued offending. What was especially important in their findings was the impact of informal social controls that were formed in later teenage or adult years. Job stability and marital attachment in adulthood were significantly related to changes in the trajectory of crime. Those individuals who were able to establish strong marriages or have stable jobs, despite the cumulative disadvantages caused by their delinquent behavior, were most likely to stop offending. The results from quantitative analysis of interview data were confirmed by their examination of case histories.

They continue this line of inquiry in their later analysis (Laub and Sampson 2003) based on retrospective interviews with the original sample when they were 70 years of age. They summarize their findings by suggesting that the "turning points" (e.g., marriage) in these men's lives involve: "(1) New situations that knife off the past from the present; (2) New situations that provide both supervision and monitoring as well as new opportunities of social support and growth; (3) New situations that change and structure routine activities; (4) New situations that provide the opportunity for identity transformation" (Sampson and Laub 2005:172).

Summary Assessment of Developmental Theories

The three theories offer slightly different approaches to explaining the development of delinquent behavior, while at the same time substantially overlapping in the types of factors and processes that are hypothesized to take place. Each perspective offers different emphases. Moffitt's theory focuses primarily on the early neuropsychological factors that interact with family functioning to lead to persistent criminal behavior. Thornberry's theory emphasizes the need to take into account how the relationships among predictor variables may change as youth go through developmental changes. Additionally, the theory draws attention to the impact that delinquent behavior itself has on those processes, forming reciprocal relationships that increase the probability and level of such behavior. Finally, Thornberry, unlike Moffitt, recognizes that even for those individuals who begin early in life to commit delinquent behavior, behavior can change, depending on events and relationships that occur at different developmental stages. It is this latter point that Sampson and Laub have been particularly effective in articulating. Focusing on turning points, they argue that certain changes in one's life can significantly alter their pattern of later behavior. Sampson and Laub focus particularly on marital and family relationships and employment and careers.

Each perspective requires longitudinal data to assess. Each perspective also requires extensive and diverse measures to test the derivative hypotheses. To the credit of the theorists, all have either collected the necessary data or, in the case of Sampson and Laub, supplemented an already existing data set. Numerous studies have supported many of the propositions of each theory. However, the theories are complex and involve many different concepts and specify different processes for different developmental stages. This makes it difficult to provide any comprehensive examination of the theoretical argument for any of these perspectives. Certainly we can confidently state that there is enough support for each perspective that encourages their continued examination. But, as we discuss in the "Analytical Issues" section later in the chapter, the complexity of the theories may be problematic.

We now turn to a theory that does not emphasize the developmental aspect of delinquent behavior. Rather, power-control theory is included as representing an explicit integration of macro- and micro-level theories of behavior.

Power-Control Theory

The fourth example of integrated theory we present is John Hagan's power-control theory. We selected this theory not only because some of the substantive contributions that it makes are different than the developmental theories just discussed but also because it is an excellent example of cross-level integration. It explicitly combines a social structural argument with social process variables.

The key to understanding power-control theory is Hagan's assumption that family relationships, specifically those between males and females within the family, reflect the roles that mothers and fathers occupy in the work force. Hagan and his colleagues begin by introducing two concepts, power and control, suggesting that power focuses on macro-structural issues of relations of dominance over the means of production, while control focuses on micro-structural issues of relations of dominance in the family (Hagan, Gillis, and Simpson 1985). They integrate these two concepts to explain the relationship between gender and delinquency. Control within the family is used to explain the relationship between gender and delinquency, while power outside the family (defined in terms of class) is used to explain why relationships between gender and delinquency vary across different class groups. The presence of power and the absence of control contribute to the individuals' freedom to deviate.

If you have a sibling of the opposite sex, did he or she seem to have more freedom to go out, stay out late, and be in unsupervised places than you did? Typically girls will answer this question with a yes while boys will say no. It is commonly believed that parents monitor their daughters more than their sons. Hagan et al. (1985) suggest that the freedom to deviate is related to class position. In our society, males have a higher class position than do females. Hence, this is mirrored in the exercise of family control, where sons are given more freedom than daughters. In addition, mothers are more likely to be the instruments of control than are fathers since, because of their relative status, they are more likely to be in the home. Hagan et al. further argue that males will be even more likely to be free to deviate in the most powerful classes. They hypothesize that males, because of their privileged status relative to females, will acquire a greater taste for risk and think that their risk for getting caught is lower than will females.

Families vary in terms of their adherence to a patriarchal structure. Historically, patriarchal families mirrored the dominant role that males played in the work force. Fathers went to work while mothers were more concerned with domestic chores, including the rearing of children. In these family structures, mothers are more likely to be the instruments of control while daughters are more likely to be the objects of control. Sons have greater freedom to engage in risky behavior and, therefore, are more likely to be delinquent than are daughters.

Some families are more egalitarian than others. In these families, decision making is more equally shared between the mother and the father. Again, according to Hagan (1989), this reflects the roles that fathers and mothers play in the work force. With women entering more jobs that include supervisory responsibilities, relationships within the family are changing accordingly. As the relations between the mother and father become more egalitarian, the differences in the freedom provided sons and daughters are reduced. Hence, girls raised in egalitarian families are more likely to acquire a taste for risk taking and are more likely to commit delinquent behavior than are girls raised in patriarchal families.

Power-control theory generates a number of intriguing hypotheses. In general, boys are more likely to be appreciative of risk-taking activities and to commit delinquent behavior than are girls. This difference should be particularly apparent in patriarchal families. The type of family structure (patriarchal versus egalitarian) should reflect the type of roles that fathers and mothers occupy in the work force. If these roles generate a more egalitarian family structure, then the differences between risk-taking attitudes and activities (including delinquency) between boys and girls should be less than the differences observed in families that are patriarchal.

Concepts and Measurement Issues of Power-Control Theory

Power-control theory provides an innovative explanation of the differences in male and female delinquency. It is innovative in that it focuses on the authority relations evident in the work force as a predictor of the type of control exercised in the home. Most theories of delinquency that include parents' position in the work force focus only on the relative socioeconomic status (e.g., lower to upper status) of the family or some dimension of disadvantage (e.g., poverty). While the incorporation of authority relations is intriguing, it makes the task of testing the theory more difficult. To appropriately measure this concept, questions concerning whether parents are in a position of authority over others in their jobs must be asked. Few data sets have included these types of questions, so some of the research on power-control theory either does not include a major component of the theory or uses a measure that does not adequately reflect it (Hagan et al. 1985).

In one of the more successful attempts, Hagan et al. (1985) used data from 458 adolescents in the Toronto metropolitan area to test the theory. To acquire data on the relational class measures, they included a telephone interview with the parents of the target subjects. They asked parents the following four questions: (1) Is the head of your household currently working full time? (2) Does the head of your household currently work for himself/herself or for someone else? (3) Are there any people who work for him or her or are paid by him or her? (4) Does the head of your household supervise anybody as part of his or her job? From these questions they classified respondents into employers, who own the means of production, control employees, and buy labor; managers, who do not own but control subordinates and sell their labor; workers, who do not own, do not control others, and do not sell their labor; and the surplus population, who are nonowners with no control over others and are unable to sell their labor (unemployed).

Hagan et al. (1985) used this classification to examine common forms of delinquent behavior (as opposed to more serious delinquency). Their rationale for focusing on common forms of delinquency was stated in theoretical terms. The theory suggests that the presence of power and absence of control lead to cognitive processes in which actors evaluate their tastes for risk and their perceptions of getting caught. They argue that the calculation of tastes for, and perceptions of, risk is more likely to favor common delinquency than more serious forms of crime. They use a six-item scale asking how often in the past year youth have done things ranging in seriousness from taking items worth less than $2 to taking items over $50.

Hagan et al. (1985) found that being from the employer class and being male is positively related to self-reported delinquency. More importantly, they found that the difference in the effect of gender on delinquency is reduced as the analysis moved from the employer class to the surplus population, supporting the major premise of power-control theory. They also incorporated the intervening variables of taste for risk (measured with a two-item scale of responses to the statements "I like to take risks" and "The things I like to do best are dangerous"), risk perception (measured with a three-item scale asking about perceptions of getting caught for different misbehaviors), and parental controls to determine if the theory correctly identifies the reasons for the observed pattern between class and delinquency. They found that parental controls (supervision) mediate the relationship between class and delinquency. In particular, it is maternal rather than paternal control that is most important.

Hagan (1989) extended the analysis of power-control theory by taking into consideration the relative positions of fathers and mothers in the work force. He posited that if their positions were unbalanced, where the father was in the command class and the mother was either in the obey class or was unemployed, it would increase the disparity in male and female delinquency. Using the same dataset, he found that more maternal controls are found in the most patriarchal households (father in command class, mother in obey class or unemployed). The disparity in parental controls of sons and daughters was also greater in patriarchal households than in egalitarian or female-headed households. Patriarchal households also exhibited a greater disparity between sons and daughters in tastes for risk, perceived risks, and delinquent behavior. Overall, strong support is found for the theory.

Measuring class in a manner consistent with Hagan's argument is absolutely critical to the examination of power-control theory. Because of the difficulty in finding data sets that have asked the appropriate questions on position in the work force, some research has focused on the theory's other hypotheses regarding gender, parental control, taste for risk, and risk perception. However, other theoretical perspectives can comfortably incorporate such predictions. What makes Hagan's theory distinct is the claim that family power and control reflect the relative positions of mothers and fathers in the work force. Akers and Sellers (2004) acknowledge this, stating, "Without an empirically viable 'power' component . . . power-control theory becomes little more than an extension of social control theory to explain gender differences in crime" (p. 256). Therefore, we focus only on those studies that incorporate an appropriate class measure.

Singer and Levine (1988) specifically set out to replicate Hagan et al. (1985). They collected data on 705 youths and their parents and used measures of class, maternal and paternal control, taste for risk, perceived risk, and delinquency that were identical (or very similar to) those used by Hagan et al. They found little support for the hypotheses derived from power-control theory. Indeed, many of the results were in the opposite direction. For example, differences by gender were greater in balanced households as opposed to unbalanced households. Singer and Levine offer possible explanations for their failure to replicate Hagan et al.'s results. They recognize their data were collected 10 years after Hagan collected his. By then, the feminist revolution of the 1970s had taken hold. Singer and Levine's data were also collected from a sample in the United States, whereas Hagan's sample was located in Canada. While Singer and Levine could not determine whether these differences explain the discrepancy in the results, their study does raise serious questions about the viability of power-control theory.

To take into account the impact of the feminist revolution and other factors that might impact the attitudes of families in general, and women within families in particular, Hagan and associates (McCarthy, Hagan, and Woodward 1999) have incorporated a variable they call gendered schemas. Gendered-activity schemas is intended to measure the attitudes related to the role of men and women in the family unit. They use a six-item scale, including statements like, "Men should make most of the important decisions" and "Parents should encourage as much independence in their daughters as in their sons." By incorporating this measure, they shift the emphasis from an exclusive concern with the position of men and women in the work force to the actual attitudes of men and women toward gender roles. This allows them to take into account what they refer to as the mother's agency. So, even if the relative roles of the mother and father reflect a patriarchal family structure, the mother's attitudes toward gender roles may be more critical in determining the attitudes and behavior of their children.

McCarthy et al. (1999) found that males offer more support for gendered-activity schemas, especially in patriarchal families. When the intervening variables (including gendered-activity schemas) are controlled, the difference in delinquency between males and females is no longer significant in less patriarchal households. They also found that mothers in more patriarchal homes, compared to those in less patriarchal homes, more strongly discourage patriarchal schemas. Thus, living in patriarchal families appears to influence the attitudes and behavior of fathers and sons more than it does mothers and daughters. They conclude this might be due to the influence of the feminist revolution.

Other studies have extended research on power-control theory to examine some implications of the theory. One line of research has explored the implications of the theory for single-parent households. Hagan (1994) suggested that single-parent households should be balanced or egalitarian in terms of patriarchy because fathers are not an integral part of the household. In these households, then, socialization of sons and daughters should be similar and the gender gap in delinquency should not exist. Research findings have not fully supported this contention. Mack and Leiber (2005) found that there was a significant gender gap in delinquency in single-mother households, contrary to what the theory predicted. Bates, Bader, and Mencken (2003) suggest that although the theory may have correctly predicted less patriarchal attitudes in single-mother families, it has not taken into account lower levels of control in single-parent households.

Brenda Blackwell has conducted several studies in which she has explored some of the implications of power-control theory (Blackwell 2000, 2003; Blackwell and Piquero 2005; Blackwell and Reed 2003; Blackwell, Sellers, and Schlaupitz 2002; Grasmick, Hagan, Blackwell, and Arneklev 1996). The findings from a few of these are of particular interest. For instance, Blackwell (2000) suggested that power-control theory might be enhanced if it took into consideration the perceived threat of shame and embarrassment. She argued that females are more likely to be concerned about other people's impressions as well as about their parents' reactions to their misbehavior. To test this idea, she used data from a sample of adults in Oklahoma City. One drawback to the data she used is that some of the measures were collected retrospectively. Respondents, who were now adults, were asked about maternal and paternal control when they were teenagers. How reliable are such measures? Regardless, Blackwell measured embarrassment by asking respondents if individuals whose opinions they valued would lose respect for them if they committed each of a checklist of offenses. She found that females were more likely to report they would be embarrassed. Moreover, this measure accounted for a significant proportion of the gender–crime relationship. And in an earlier paper using the same data set, Grasmick et al. (1996) found that female adults who were raised in more patriarchal families had a lower taste for risk than did males. However, among adults raised in less patriarchal families, the gender differences did not exist.

Finally, Blackwell and Reed (2003) used data from the first wave of the National Youth Survey, when respondents were between the ages of 11 to 17. What is interesting about this study is the examination of both within- and between-family differences. Up to now, we have reviewed research that focused on the differences between families that were more or less patriarchal. Blackwell and Reed, however, assessed whether brothers and sisters from the same family were treated differently. Their pattern of results is complex, but the general conclusion is that they support power-control theory.

Overall Assessment of Power-Control Theory

Hagan's power-control theory has challenged the discipline in three important ways: (1) It has integrated a social structural emphasis on social class with the more process-oriented variables, such as parental control and attitudes toward risk-taking. (2) In so doing, the theory combines a framework that is derived from a more Marxian, conflict approach (see Chapter 9) with a social control approach (see Chapter 7). (3) It explicitly recognizes the importance of gender in both the role of parent and child.

The theory has certainly generated a substantial amount of research. Hagan's theoretical contribution hinges on whether the hypothesis that family control mirrors the different roles that mothers and fathers play in the work force can be supported. The results concerning this hypothesis are mixed. Even Hagan has backed off this claim somewhat, suggesting that what he refers to as mother's agency (the mother's attitude toward gender roles) can play a mitigating role in the relationship between patriarchy and delinquency. One other limitation with the theory is its attention to only common, less serious delinquent behaviors. While there may be a defensible theoretical reason to focus only on such behavior, it does limit the scope of the theory. For some scholars, power-control theory explains behaviors that are less important to account for while ignoring behaviors that have a greater impact on society.

Analytical Issues

Given what is involved, integrated theory has more than its fair share of analytical issues. Most of these do not stem from the individual integrated theories themselves, but speak to larger issues in the debate on whether or not integration is a useful tool for theory development. Given that previous chapters have spelled out the various analytical issues associated with each theory, in this section we identify some of the larger non-theory-specific analytical issues that face researchers working in this area.

Testing Complex Theory

Bernard and Snipes (1996) identify one of the most challenging of these issues. By definition, theoretical integration incorporates multiple causal factors, levels of analysis, or types of deviance into a unified framework. While this may increase the scope of the theory, it also makes it more difficult to test empirically. In other words, "[P]ractical limitations on integration arise from the complexity of the resulting theories" (p. 342). Bernard and Snipes illustrate this point using Vila's (1994) general paradigm, which is an extension of Cohen and Machalek's (1988) theory of evolutionary ecology. According to Vila, if a theory is to be sufficiently general to explain all types of criminal behavior, it must be ecological, integrative, and developmental and it must include micro- and macro-level explanations. After reviewing the basic ideas of Vila's framework, Bernard and Snipes (1996) conclude, "Vila's paradigm is frustratingly general—everything affects everything, at all levels, and these effects are continuously changing over time" (pp. 320–321). They claim, "The key question is whether social scientists are capable of testing theories that are as complex as this paradigm requires" (p. 321).

Another example of this problem is found in Pearson and Weiner (1985), who attempt to include as many prominent criminological perspectives in their dynamic integrated theory as possible. Their approach is an example of conceptual integration. They integrate concepts from various theories into a common vocabulary rather than combining different propositions into a single theory. Pearson and Weiner begin with social learning theory (more specifically, an operant conditioning framework) and build from there, mapping several major concepts from selected criminological theories (e.g., social control, deterrence, routine activities, strain, and Marxist, among others) into the integrative framework. In their original form, these concepts are relatively general and abstract, so Pearson and Weiner identify the substantive contents of these theoretical statements, which allows them to specify the kinds of criminal behaviors (e.g., general criminal behavior, violent crime, property theft, abuse of trust, vice, and threats to public order or safety) and causal factors (e.g., signs of favorable opportunities, deprivation, access to property, and technical skills) that the selected theories address. Finally, they introduce macro-level structural concepts, such as the larger distribution of opportunities or the general belief system about the probability and severity of formal and informal sanctioning of illegal behavior, that relate to the micro-level formulations.

What Pearson and Weiner end up with is an incredibly complex dynamic model of criminal behavior that is a challenge to fully comprehend. Their efforts result in converting 13 theories into 12 constructs. They do provide the reader with the following illustration to understand the occurrence of robbery (note that the concepts from various theories are italicized in their illustration):

> The *demand for utilities* such as money or property may rise due to an increase in needs or wants (e.g., for a new car) or due to a decrease in income (e.g., because of unemployment). Absent legitimate means to acquire utilities, an individual may entertain *expedient* alternatives such as robbery. The probability of a person attempting a robbery is greater if close social models are known to have engaged successfully in this behavior. Rational assessment by potential offenders may indicate that the probable gains from a robbery outweigh the probable risks.

Norms extolling smartness or toughness may bear directly on the choice because robbery can involve cleverness in selecting victims and toughness in intimidating or overcoming them. *Moral rules* also affect this choice. For example, the individual may have internalized norms supporting, permitting, or, at a minimum, tolerating illegitimate conduct, including its more serious forms, such as robbery. If *behavioral resources* like weapons are available, or if associates can be enlisted as accomplices, the chances of committing a robbery are further increased. This likelihood might rise even more if certain *behavioral skills* have been mastered that apply to the commission of robbery, such as fighting skill to overcome the victim or the skillful presentation and handling of a weapon. Even with these factors promoting the commission of the robbery, it might nevertheless not occur without *signs of favorable opportunities* such as a lone victim on an isolated and unmonitored street. (pp. 145–146)

No doubt Pearson and Weiner's integrated model addresses their major concern with existing integrated theories that "most efforts to integrate criminological theories suffer from the absence of a systematic integrative framework and from including too few of the prominent theories" (p. 148). But the results of their efforts appear to suffer from a different problem, what many refer to as "theoretical mush" (Gibbons 1994:187; Hirschi 1979). Cao (2004) notes, "integration can lead to sloppy theorizing in which scholars pick a variable they like from one theory and then a variable from another, but they do not reconcile the philosophic differences behind these variables" (p. 161).

Beyond "theoretical mush," another problem arises, similar to Vila's general paradigm: How does one empirically test this complex model? In the conclusion of their work, Pearson and Weiner (1985) call on scholars to provide "empirical substance to the theoretical concepts" (p. 149). But how would one go about testing such a theory? What types of data are available to address fully the complexities and nuances of their integrated model? In fact, the level of complexity may pose too great a challenge for researchers. Along these lines, Bernard and Snipes (1996) note, "It would seem possible to create a single theory of crime that incorporates the structural conditions that are associated with higher crime rates, the processes that explain why normal individuals who experience these structural conditions are more likely to engage in crime, and the individual characteristics that make it more or less likely that an individual will engage in crime regardless of structural conditions" (p. 342). But they also point out that this is not the same thing as arguing that we *should* construct such integrations. Can we test such a theory? Can we falsify it?

Hence, one potential problem with integration is that the resulting theory may be so complex, inclusive, and general that it is even more difficult to falsify than the component theories. Yet integration must facilitate falsification or it is not meaningful (Bernard and Snipes 1996). In this sense, theoretical integration can "muddy the empirical waters and make it more, rather than less, difficult to disentangle causal influences and to identify the differential contribution that each of them makes to the behavioral outcome"

(Gibbons 1994: 185). This moves criminological theory in precisely the wrong direction.

Integrational Chaos

Einstadter and Henry (2006) describe a related problem that may result from theoretical integration: "Since each theorist may use different criteria to construct a comprehensive approach, what emerges is 'integrational chaos'" (pp. 319–320). This became apparent in their review of Hunter and Dantzker's (2002) typology of four types of integrated theories: (1) integrated classical theories, such as routine activities, rational choice, and criminal personality; (2) integrated biological theories, such as bioconditioning and human nature; (3) integrated psychological theories, such as delinquency development, age-graded theory, and self-derogation; and (4) integrated sociological theories. As you might already guess from reading this chapter, the final category has several subcategories that can be identified, which, according to Einstadter and Henry (2006), include (a) integrated learning theories, such as network analysis and interactional theory; (b) integrated control theories, such as control balance, social developmental, and reintegrative shaming; (c) integrated strain theory, such as integrated theory and general strain; and (d) integrated conflict theory, such as power control and integrated structural Marxist theory. Einstadter and Henry also note that accompanying these integrated theories are "holistic theories" or general explanations of crime that combine multifactor perspectives. This adds another seven theories to those listed here. The end result? The number of criminological theories increases rather than decreases, which is in opposition to the overarching goals of integration. Einstadter and Henry (2006:320) question whether much is achieved in the process beyond confusion.

Where Is the Empirical Debate?

Another analytical issue has to do with the proper starting point for integrating theories, or where attention should be focused when attempting to integrate. According to some, there has been too much emphasis on the theories themselves and not enough on the observable variables and observable relations among them (Bernard and Snipes 1996:322). In other words, the thrust of the debate on integration has occurred at the conceptual, theoretical level, rather than at the empirical level, in terms of which variables are most important in predicting crime. As such, whether strain or social disorganization theory are conceptually compatible is often the focus of debate among scholars, rather than the fact that social class, an important variable for both theories, is empirically related to crime. According to Bernard and Snipes, the field would do better if we focused less on conceptual differences and got on with the task of determining which variables are related to crime and in which ways: "[T]he variables themselves and the relations among them should be the focus of attention, not the theory to which they 'belong' " (p. 341). In this sense, the competition becomes empirical rather than theoretical.

Along these lines, one useful task would be to start with the basic facts of crime that have been established in empirical research but that are not adequately explained by existing individual theories. For example, Braithwaite (1989:44–50) has suggested the following social facts of crime:

1. Crime is committed disproportionately by males.
2. Crime is committed disproportionately by 15 to 25-year-olds.
3. Crime is committed disproportionately by unmarried people.
4. Crime is committed disproportionately by people living in large cities.
5. Crime is committed disproportionately by people who have experienced high residential mobility and who live in areas characterized by high residential mobility.
6. Young people who are strongly attached to their school are less likely to engage in crime.
7. Young people who have high educational and occupational aspirations are less likely to engage in crime.
8. Young people who do poorly in school are more likely to engage in crime.
9. Young people who are strongly attached to their parents are less likely to engage in crime.
10. Young people who have friendships with criminals are more likely to engage in crime themselves.
11. People who believe strongly in the importance of complying with the law are less likely to violate the law.
12. For both women and men, being at the bottom of the class structure, whether measured by socioeconomic status, socioeconomic status of the area in which the person lives, being unemployed, or being a member of an oppressed racial minority (e.g., blacks in the United States), increases rates of offending for all types of crime apart from those for which opportunities are systematically less available to the poor (e.g., white-collar crime).
13. Crime rates have been increasing since World War II in most countries, developed and developing. The only case of a country that has been clearly shown to have had a falling crime rate in this period is Japan.

These social facts, rather than their constituent theories, should constitute the starting point for a discussion on theoretical integration. The most important question to ask is: What variables are related to crime, and in what ways? In short, according to some critics, criminologists should focus on variables and the relationships among variables, rather than on the theories themselves (Vold et al. 2002:313).

Best Method of Theoretical Development

Perhaps the greatest issue in theoretical integration is whether, at its core, this approach is the most constructive method to develop criminological theory. Theoretical integration is viewed as one means of theorizing (Liska and Messner 1999:214), but is it the preferred method? There are those who remain unconvinced (see Gibbons 1994:196–197; Short 1979), and some, in particular, who prefer theoretical competition as a way to develop better explanations. Travis Hirschi (1989) has been the most vocal proponent of theoretical competition. Again, according to this approach, theoretical development proceeds by verifying theories, which involves the evaluation of hypotheses derived from a theory. The acceptability of a theory increases as it successfully survives more and more tests. One strength of theoretical competition is its tendency to produce internal consistency and conceptual clarity (Hirschi 1989:38). Hirschi argues that a key purpose of oppositional theory is to "make the world safe for theory contrary to currently accepted views" (1989:45). His social control theory has followed the pattern of oppositional development, simultaneously attacking strain and cultural deviance theories (Hirschi 1969; see also Korn-hauser 1978), while affirming its own sharply different view of the world.

Hirschi (1989) claims that most criminological theories have incompatible essential assumptions, and, therefore, simply cannot be integrated. In fact, "theories in the oppositional tradition were constructed precisely so as to be incompatible with named enemy theories, so as to affirm what enemy theories denied and to deny what they affirmed" (p. 39). For example, social control and self-control theories assume individuals are naturally inclined to deviate but are prevented from doing so based on their bonds to society or high self-control, whereas social learning theories assume individuals are not naturally inclined to deviate but do so through a learning process that involves others. Hirschi (p. 39) questions, "If theory A asserts X and theory B asserts not-X, it would seem impossible to bring them together in a way pleasing and satisfactory to both." Accordingly, integration is considered impossible because these fundamental differences are ignored when theories are integrated (see also Akers 1989:24). To the extent that theories are incompatible with each other, they cannot be integrated.

In light of this characterization, Hirschi (1989) proposes that classical theories be developed to their full potential. He supports developing theories with a fact-based approach to theorizing, that is, one that reduces our interest in abstract, deductive theory and pays more attention to the social facts about crime, such as those listed earlier. Hirschi asserts that we currently have too much theory and too few facts to guide theory construction in criminology. Deductive theorizing, he argues, is not conducive to the discovery of ideas and is also lacking in ability to introduce empirical tension into theoretical systems. In short, "the proof is not in the argument but in the result. And the evidence, it seems to me, speaks well for an inductive or fact-oriented research strategy as opposed to the much favored deductive or theory-oriented strategy" (p. 46).

Proponents of integration disagree. Pearson and Weiner (1985:118) note, "Our conclusion . . . is that the *major concepts* of the theories can be translated into a common theoretical vocabulary, what we refer to as the integrative framework." And, in a very thorough analysis, Bernard and Snipes (1996) show that integration and falsification are not incompatible and that the purpose of integration is actually to enhance the falsification process. Bernard and Snipes additionally argue that criminological theories make different, but not contradictory, predictions, and, therefore, can in fact be integrated (whether or not this is desirable is another issue, they maintain).

Probably the most vocal opponent of theoretical competition, Delbert Elliott (Elliott 1985; Elliott et al. 1979, 1985) offers several criticisms of this approach. First, the major theories rarely permit the derivation of unambiguous, truly distinctive hypotheses. Different theories often predict similar outcomes, and a given set of empirical findings can often be reconciled with more than one theory. For example, the finding that lower social class is related to crime is consistent with both strain and social disorganization theories. Second, the results of studies are seldom definitive. Studies typically suffer from various methodological problems, including improper measurement of key concepts or a faulty analytical framework. As such, the lack of empirical support for a theory may not indicate falsification. Finally, as noted earlier, Elliott claims the explanatory power of individual theories is quite low, most likely because the causes of crime and deviance are multiple.

So the question remains: Which strategy is most promising for developing better explanations of crime and delinquency—theory competition or theory integration? Liska and Messner (1999:223) remind us that whatever strategy is adopted, the end product must be assessed with reference to the general criteria of theory evaluation. But what are these general criteria? Increasing empirical support? A reduction in the number of theories? Greater variance explained in outcomes? Liska and Messner add "logical coherence" to the list, arguing that many contemporary efforts that purport to pursue the goal of theoretical integration might be better described as attempts at prediction. They note, "[V]ariables from two or more theories are included in the same analysis, but there is little concern with relating the various concepts to one another. Instead, attention focuses on the extent to which adding variables to the analysis increases predictive power" (p. 223). The fundamental problem here is that "integration" of this nature does not address incompatibilities in basic assumptions of the constituent theories, Hirschi's (1989) precise argument. In short, theoretical growth through integration is not likely to occur unless theorists seriously attend to the logical coherence of their arguments (Liska and Messner 1999:223).

Directions for Future Research

The issues that have been raised about theoretical integration are as complex as many of the theories themselves. Should we integrate theories or not? If we do, how do we produce perspectives that have a logical coherence? Should criminological theories attempt to span the life course? If scholars develop logically coherent theories, will researchers be able to examine them as a whole, or will they continue to examine only pieces of the theory?

These are legitimate questions. Despite the difficulties in pursuing theoretical integration that these questions underscore, we contend that researchers learned much from the various attempts to generate integrated theories. For example, integrated theories have suggested how issues regarding social structure are inevitably linked to social processes. The move to integrate theoretical perspectives has served to identify the link between concepts that have previously been considered the province of a particular discipline (and not the concern of other disciplines). The developmental theories discussed here recognize the importance of considering biological and psychological variables, along with the more traditional focus on social structure and social process. Recall, too, that one of the functions of theory is to set the research agenda. Integrated theories have been an impetus to gather data sets that include measures of diverse concepts and to do so over time. While we acknowledge it is very difficult to provide an examination of all the implications of any of the theories reviewed, the research that has examined parts of those theories suggest they are on the right track. This is particularly true of the developmental theories. Results from the literature suggest the need to incorporate biological and genetic factors, to take into account developmental stages, to consider the reciprocal relationships among crime and delinquency and predictor variables, and to continue to examine changes in behavior that take place over the life course.

Over the past 30 years numerous theoretical integrations or elaborations have been proposed. Many of these have generated a vast amount of research. How can we make sense of all this complex material? David Farrington (2005) has taken a constructive first step in this process. He proposed a set of 24 key empirical and theoretical issues to the authors of eight integrated developmental theories. For example, he asked these scholars to indicate how their respective theories address issues such as why people start offending and what factors inhibit offending. Farrington hoped that the effort would highlight both the similarities and differences in key integrated theories. We have already noted that although there are important differences among the perspectives reviewed in this chapter, there is also a significant amount of overlap. One outcome of efforts such as Farrington's may be to consolidate theories or, stated alternatively, to integrate the integrated theories. This will not be an easy task but would certainly provide more logical coherence to the vast amount of material that is being generated.

Even assuming that we are successful at narrowing the field of integrated theories down to a more manageable number, we are still burdened with the arduous task of trying to empirically assess them. We have made great strides in doing so with the collection of longitudinal data and the development of highly sophisticated statistical methods to analyze the data. Even with such developments, it is very difficult to adequately assess these theories. This is not unlike what other sciences have experienced. Often methods have to catch up with scholars' theoretical ideas.

What we can say about the current efforts to integrate theories is they have instilled in researchers the motivation to consider the connections and links between disciplines and across seemingly diverse theoretical concepts. Those efforts have also generated rich data sets and advanced our analytical methods. We anticipate that the future pursuit of integrated theory will continue to make significant contributions.

Discussion Questions

1. How do theoretical falsification, theoretical competition, and theoretical integration differ from one another?
2. What is cross-level integration? Why is this type of integration valuable for criminological theory?
3. What are the differences between theoretical elaboration and theoretical integration?
4. Critics have claimed that some attempts at integration have resulted in "theoretical mush." What is the major implication of this claim for theory testing in criminology?
5. Compare and contrast the arguments of Travis Hirschi (a proponent of theoretical competition) and Delbert Elliott (a proponent of integration) in terms of theoretical development in criminology. Whose argument is more persuasive? Why?

CHAPTER 11

CONCLUSION

W hy are some individuals more or less likely to engage in crime than others? Why do some areas (e.g., neighborhoods) or groups (e.g., minorities) have higher or lower crime rates than others? These are the key questions criminologists have been struggling to answer for decades. Ever since criminology emerged as a social science, researchers have been preoccupied with determining the causes of crime and deviance. Today, as ever, the central business of criminology is causal analysis (Cao 2004:182; Gibbons 1994:200).

Yet as we discussed in Chapter 1 and as you have likely discovered in the previous chapters, identifying the causes of crime and deviance presents a formidable challenge. A major reason is that researchers examine phenomena that are not easy to study. It is very difficult, and in some cases unethical, to design a study focusing on disapproved behavior in which such behavior can be manipulated, as might be done in studying the effect of adding a chemical to a solution to determine its effect on that solution. With human behavior, many factors also operate simultaneously that are difficult to disentangle. The problem is further complicated in that individuals store numerous life experiences, and it is hard to know specifically how these experiences unconsciously influence later behavior. Add to this the fact that humans have the capacity to interpret those experiences and the task becomes even more complex. It is no wonder, then, that answering these questions is a challenging undertaking.

Of course, these challenges have not deterred researchers from searching for the causes of crime and deviance, primarily by developing and testing theories. In this book, we reviewed the major criminological theories that have resulted from these efforts. As the chapters reveal, the mysteries of crime causation have been approached from biological, psychological, and sociological perspectives. Although they offer distinctive explanations, the theories discussed generally take a scientific approach to the problem of crime. This approach focuses on relationships among observable phenomena, with the goal of identifying the causes of crime (Vold, Bernard, and Snipes 2002:319). Liska and Messner (1999:214) note, "*theorizing* constitutes an activity that organizes *empirical* findings within a general abstract framework" (emphasis added).

Criminological inquiry, therefore, is an activity in which theorizing and research are inextricably linked; theoretical considerations guide the development of research methodology to answer key questions, and theories evolve as initial formulations are modified in light of empirical evidence (or lack thereof). Cao (2004:182) claims, "Observation without a theory is chaotic ... while a theory without the support of observation is speculative." It should be apparent from the previous chapters that criminological theories differ markedly in terms of conceptual and logical rigor and empirical support. They can be arrayed along a scale with broad, sensitizing, but essentially untestable perspectives on one end and formal theories on the other (Gibbons 1994:202).

Because theory and research are interdependent, in this book we have set out to assess explicitly how criminological theories have been researched. Despite the importance of such an assessment, very few existing textbooks accomplish this task. Most textbooks are concerned with communicating the basic ideas contained within the theories. Many also include sections on the historical development of these perspectives and a critical analysis of their logic and substance. If a section on the research of theories is included, it is frequently presented in a summary fashion with little or no critical assessment of the research methods used to examine the theories. Thus, students have no way of evaluating the appropriateness of the research design and the way in which it was implemented. This can lend itself to uncritical acceptance of the research results and may lead to a naïve acceptance or rejection of the theory.

As explained in Chapter 1, in this book we have reversed the emphasis. Although we review the intellectual history and substance of criminological theories, including their concepts and hypotheses, our major focus throughout the chapters has been on critically assessing the research methods used to examine these theories. In Chapter 1, we introduced you to several standard methodological issues that are essential to understand when evaluating research on theories. In the substantive chapters that followed, we reviewed the research literature on the major theoretical perspectives, selecting studies that illustrated the theoretical, conceptual, or methodological issues in testing the particular theories. Our objective was to identify the problems and pitfalls researchers encounter in testing theories of crime and deviance. The information we have provided should enable you to become critical consumers of the research literature on criminological theories and, therefore, to be critical consumers of the theories themselves. In the remainder of the book, we consider the issues that cut across criminological theories. We discuss several methodological and analytical challenges that apply to most, if not all, of the perspectives. We also raise important questions about the future of criminological theory and theory testing.

Common Measurement and Analytical Issues

After considering the various measurement and analytical issues raised in the individual chapters, one may question whether there are common challenges to address, regardless of the theory. What has our assessment taught us about criminological theory generally? What universal concerns, if any, emerge from our analysis?

Several problems are common to nearly all of the theories reviewed in this book. These problems relate both to the theoretical concepts (e.g., their definition and operationalization) and to the research designs (e.g., selecting a sample, deciding on the unit of analysis) employed in existing studies. Next we discuss, in detail, two significant issues that have direct implications for determining causality in theories of crime and deviance.

Longitudinal Data and Analyses

One issue common to all criminological theories is the need for additional longitudinal data and analyses to properly test the theory's main hypotheses. In one way or another, the theories reviewed in this book all imply processes that occur over time, whether shorter (e.g., deterrence) or longer (e.g., labeling) time frames and whether these processes operate at the individual-level (e.g., social learning) or aggregate-level (e.g., social disorganization).

Unfortunately, as we repeatedly observed throughout the book, most studies that purport to test the main arguments of theories employ cross-sectional analyses. Cross-sectional analysis assesses the relationship between different variables at one point in time, as opposed to longitudinal studies, which analyze a series of measurements taken over a period of time. An overreliance on cross-sectional analysis in the criminological literature is problematic because, as already argued, one cannot detect causality without modeling processes over time using appropriate data.

To reiterate, several criteria must be present for inferring causality in science: correlation (the two phenomena must vary with one another), theoretical rationale (there must be good reason to believe that one phenomenon causes another), time sequence (the causal phenomenon must come first in time), and the absence of spuriousness (both phenomena must not be caused by something else) (see Vold et al. 2002:319). It is the third criterion that is critical here. To claim, for example, that weak bonds cause delinquency (social control theory), one has to determine that weak bonds precede delinquency (and not the other way around). An ideal data set to test this argument is one that contains measures of youths' bonds at an earlier time point (T1) as well as measures of their delinquency at a later time point (T2). Unfortunately, as pointed out in Chapter 7, most studies measure both—bonds and delinquency— at the same point in time. This makes it impossible to determine whether weak bonds cause delinquency (despite the fact that the two may be correlated, there is a theoretical rationale behind the proposed relationship, and both phenomena are not caused by something else). In short, two factors might be correlated and there may be a theoretical reason to believe that one causes the other, but without properly modeling processes over time, one cannot fully test the hypothesis that weak bonds cause delinquency, as the theory predicts. This is especially problematic when it is plausible to believe that the reverse may be true; it could easily be argued (and has been) that delinquency weakens bonds.

Some theories and their empirical assessments are especially vulnerable to this criticism. Labeling theory is a good example. As noted in Chapter 8, labeling theory focuses its attention on the *process* of criminalization. Recall that the theory claims that there are two types of deviance: primary and secondary. Primary deviance occurs when an individual violates norms without viewing himself or herself as being involved in a deviant social role. Primary deviance, which can arise from genetic, physiological, psychological, and sociological origins, is ignored or rationalized and transitory. As such, these acts typically do not alter an individual's self-concept. With societal reaction and labeling, however, the deviance can change in form and function. Once a label is attached to a person, sporadic deviance can stabilize into a deviant career. Secondary deviant acts, therefore, are those that result from the change in self-concept brought about by the labeling process. The sequence of interaction leading to secondary deviance is as follows: (1) primary deviation; (2) social penalties; (3) further primary deviation; (4) stronger penalties and rejection; (5) further deviation; (6) crisis reached in the tolerance quotient, expressed in formal action by the community stigmatizing the deviant; (7) strengthening of the deviant conduct as a reaction to the stigmatizing and penalties; and (8) ultimate acceptance of the deviant social status and efforts at adjustment on the basis of the associated role (Lemert 1951).

As is clear from this brief review, the theory posits that the labeling process does not occur instantaneously or even within a short period of time. The theory implies that the process can take months or even years such that the time between being labeled and engaging in secondary deviance may be quite long for some individuals. Despite these claims, most research that tests labeling theory is conducted using cross-sectional data and analyses in which labeling, self-concepts, and secondary deviance are measured at the same time point. From these studies, one can only conclude that labeling and secondary deviance are correlated. One cannot conclude that labeling causes secondary deviance.

Of course, labeling theory is not alone in this criticism. As you may have noticed, an overreliance on cross-sectional analysis plagues nearly every major criminological theory. Why is this problem so pervasive? If criminology is concerned with causal analysis, and one of the main criteria for determining causality is time sequence, why are more studies not sensitive to modeling processes over time using longitudinal data? Partly because of the expense of collecting new data, empirical examinations of criminological theories have relied on existing datasets, performing secondary data analysis. While this may be the most expedient route for theory testing, in secondary data analysis, researchers are often forced to make the existing data, typically collected for entirely different purposes, "fit" the theory they want to assess. As a result, concepts are imperfectly measured and the datasets do not include measures of the key concepts over time. Under these circumstances, causality cannot be established.

In each chapter we have concluded that there is a significant need for additional longitudinal analysis. This requires collecting data over time and carefully formulating theory-sensitive research designs, or data collection efforts that directly reflect the specific theory or theories under investigation.

In other words, data collection efforts should be informed, first and foremost, by theory. This is critical if researchers want to move beyond correlation.

Of course, devising theory-sensitive research designs and collecting longitudinal data are easier said than done. Such efforts are costly and time-consuming. It is not easy to collect survey data from thousands of individuals over several decades, years, or even months. Surveys are difficult to carry out. People are often reluctant to answer personal questions about their criminal activity or victimization experiences. And tracking individuals as they move or change jobs can be exhausting. But as we have learned from the previous chapters, such efforts are essential. And although difficult, they are not impossible. Throughout the book we have described several good examples of theory-sensitive research designs, including the Project on Human Development in Chicago Neighborhoods (PHDCN) mentioned in Chapter 4 and the Rochester Youth Development Study (RYDS) mentioned in Chapters 1, 6, 7, and 10. Developing more theory-sensitive research designs should be a top priority among scholars.

Ruling out Competing Explanations

As several others have pointed out (e.g., Cao 2004:175; Sampson 1999:447), another major challenge facing researchers testing any theory of crime and deviance is ruling out alternative or competing explanations in their empirical examinations. Existing tests of a given theory rarely, if ever, offer a critical test of competing explanations. As one example, in testing social control theory researchers typically include only measures related to youths' social bonds, as theorized by Hirschi (1969): attachment, commitment, involvement, and belief (and often these are not even measured the same way across the studies, making comparisons and the accumulation of scientific knowledge difficult). These studies, for the most part, do not incorporate measures from competing perspectives such as differential association theory. This is problematic because in cases where support for social control theory is found, by detecting a significant negative relationship between attachment and delinquency, for example, it is unclear whether incorporating measures from other perspectives would reduce or even eliminate the attachment–delinquency relationship. This makes it impossible to ascertain whether studies have documented a "true" causal relationship between, say, attachment and delinquency or whether the finding exists only because other critical variables have been excluded from the analysis. The absence of measures from competing explanations characterizes most tests of criminological theories, regardless of the perspective.

Beyond individual theories, this problem extends to groups of theories. Biological and psychological studies of crime rarely include sociological variables in their analyses and vice versa. This is problematic because the relationship between a given biological variable (e.g., arousal levels) and crime may actually be caused by a third unmeasured social variable (e.g., poor school performance). Likewise, the relationship between commitment to conventional activities and delinquency may really be caused by a biological (e.g., arousal levels) or psychological (e.g., personality) factor, yet most sociological studies do not include these measures in their analyses. Apart from the independent impact of biological and social variables, another issue has to do with the possible interaction between these factors. For example, as we discussed in Chapter 3, certain biological characteristics may have a greater impact on crime under certain social circumstances, but little or no impact under others (see Vold et al. 2002:326).

A related issue that threatens causality has to do with the fact that a given set of empirical findings can often be reconciled with various theories (Liska and Messner 1999:215). The most common example is the relationship between poverty and crime. At the individual level, several theories hypothesize that poor people will be more likely to engage in criminal behavior than wealthier people will. Anomie and strain theories claim that those living in poverty will experience greater strain pushing them into illegitimate means to obtain wealth, while rational choice and deterrence theories maintain that poor people have less to lose and more to gain from engaging in crime. Often studies report a significant relationship between poverty and crime and cite this as evidence in support of strain or rational choice perspectives. Yet which particular theory does the finding support? What is the true "cause" of the relationship between poverty and crime—arguments relating to anomie/ strain or rational choice/deterrence? In such a situation, it is impossible to answer these questions. In sum, a study attempting to test either perspective that simply reports finding a relationship between poverty and crime has not, in fact, established that the particular theory under consideration is "responsible" for the finding.

Although other examples of problems cut across the major criminological theories, we suggest that a paucity of longitudinal studies and researchers' inability to rule out competing arguments in their examinations are two of the most significant problems limiting our ability to test theoretical arguments and, ultimately, to determine the causes of crime. Unless researchers formulate more theory-sensitive research designs to carry out empirical tests and include measures of competing explanations in their assessments, these problems will continue to plague the field and undermine attempts at determining causality.

What Is the Future of Criminological Inquiry?

Throughout the book we have identified several measurement and analytical issues unique to each theory of crime and deviance. In the previous section we highlighted two issues that apply to all criminological theories. Addressing these shortcomings, no doubt, will allow researchers to reformulate theoretical arguments in light of sound empirical evidence, thereby enhancing our ability to determine the causes of crime. Apart from addressing these methodological challenges, however, what is the future of criminological inquiry? More specifically, what strategy is best employed to achieve theoretical development in the field of criminology? These questions return us to the larger debate presented in Chapter 10 on the best way to approach theoretical development. Should researchers strive to rule out competing perspectives, as theoretical competition suggests, or attempt to combine them, as theoretical integration desires?

As previously noted, some scholars claim that retaining the individual integrity of theories whose differences and applications are refined and specialized is more important than developing a grand explanatory paradigm. Along these lines, Einstadter and Henry (2006) apply the analogy of theory as a toolbox, where each perspective represents a different tool to use in best explaining and solving the problem (crime) at hand:

> Just as a construction or maintenance worker may arrive at a job with a toolbox containing several specialized tools, each designed and refined to serve a different function, so a criminologist might come analytically prepared with several different theories to explain and deal with particular kinds of crime. Just as the worker may decide that a job or a repair needs a saw to cut wood, glue or a hammer and nails to attach the wood to the existing structure, and a screwdriver and screws to secure it, so a criminologist might find that a type of crime or harm requires classical theory to analyze the offender's motives, strain theory to analyze the opportunity structure that shapes these motives, and Marxist and feminist theory to analyze the reason why there are class and gender inequalities that shape the context and relationships among people within a societal system. (p. 333)

In addition to this argument, proponents of theoretical competition claim that few criminological theories have been exploited to their full potential (consider the measurement and analytical issues presented in each chapter) and that competition between theories drives researchers toward internal consistency and conceptual clarity (Cao 2004:179). Others argue, "Theories ought to compete in the marketplace of ideas, and the winner(s) in this competition should be those that pass the test of evidence" (Gibbons 1994:200).

Yet one thing that should be apparent from all chapters is that regardless of the perspective, while some studies document empirical support for a particular theory, many do not. Theoretical competition depends on falsification, or the ability to rule out theories because of a lack of empirical support. Given this, all of the criminological theories reviewed in this book could be falsified. But where does that leave us? Obviously, rejecting all theories of crime and deviance is not useful.

Add to this the notion that inconsistent findings across studies (some suggesting support, others suggesting no support) could mean that a given theory is invalid, but it could also reflect inadequate measurement of concepts that are highly abstract and inherently difficult to measure (Liska and Messner 1999:216). Recall the opening story in Chapter 1 about the Ph.D. student who was unable to find support for a particular theory in his dissertation. Given the myriad challenges in theory testing, one is left to ponder whether a lack of empirical support is due to faulty theory, faulty theory testing, or some combination of the two. Regardless, it should be clear that many studies fail to find support or find only partial support for the major explanations of crime. According to Liska and Messner (p. 216), "Traditional theories have had only limited success in explaining crime and deviance."

Based on this, some maintain that integration may be the way to go. Given limited support, it seems only prudent to consider new points of departure such as theoretical integration. But recall how extremely complex integrated theories can be. Many cross disciplines, incorporate macro-level structural factors and micro-level processes, and predict that certain factors will affect an individual during one stage of the life course whereas other factors will affect him or her during another stage. Is it even possible to test such complex explanations?

Clearly, researchers have had more than their fair share of problems testing the *individual* perspectives that comprise integrated theory—that should be apparent from the chapters of this book. Given these challenges, it seems a near impossible feat to test integrated theory in a proper manner. Indeed, as stated in Chapter 10, most empirical tests examine just one part of the integrated theory, resulting in a body of studies that collectively addresses all aspects of the theory but do not actually test the theory as a whole. In fact, most empirical examinations of even individual criminological theories examine only one part of the theory, rather than provide a comprehensive theoretical test (see Cao 2004:174). This problem is magnified with integrated theory. One may question whether it will ever be possible to collect appropriate data, utilize sufficiently complex research designs, and employ suitably sophisticated analytical techniques to properly test integrated theory. Despite challenges to both theory competition and integration, the field must determine where its efforts are directed—at theoretical falsification, integration, or some combination of the two. The future direction of criminological inquiry depends, to a great extent, on what researchers decide in this respect.

Or does it? For the past two decades, scholars have simultaneously been pursuing both strategies. Some have chosen either to examine a single theoretical perspective or to have two discrete theories "compete" with one another so that hypotheses are either falsified or are not as meaningful as alternative hypotheses. Other scholars have proceeded to combine or integrate theoretical concepts. We are at a stage in theory building in which progress can be made pursuing either strategy. Perhaps it is premature to determine which strategy will be most efficient.

Regardless of the approach taken, theory testing will always be limited by the research methods that are currently available. We have witnessed tremendous advances in our ability to model complex processes in recent years. For example, multilevel modeling, which provides much greater capacity to model processes that inherently occur at more than one level, has recently become fairly common in criminological theory testing. Surely, then, the future of theoretical development in criminology is linked to methodological advances in theory testing. Just as Durkheim could never have imagined using a computer to support his examination of how rates of suicide covaried with other social phenomena, we cannot know what methodological advances await us to assist in theory testing and, ultimately, theory development.

Apart from testing theory for theory development's sake, there is one other critical reason why our explanations and the research methods used to verify or falsify them must be sound: criminal justice policy. Theories about crime and the evidence found to support (or refute) them affect the creation of policies aimed at crime reduction. Numerous policies have been enacted based on findings from the research literature on the causes of crime. Police crackdowns on drunk driving or drug sales (rational choice/deterrence), medication to control aggression (biosocial), therapeutic intervention (psychological), neighborhood crime watches (social disorganization), creating jobs for the poor (anomie/strain), segregating serious and nonserious youth in prison (social learning theory), programs that strengthen youths' bonds to conventional society (social control), deinstitutionalization (labeling), and decriminalization of consensual crimes and drug offenses (conflict) are just a few examples of such policies. If policies are to reduce crime successfully, they must be based on sound theory *and* empirical evidence. The link between theory and research, therefore, extends even further to include criminal justice policy as an important outcome. Thus, there is a critical link between theories of crime and the methods used to test them that we have examined throughout this book, but getting the methods right to develop sound theories of crime is no academic exercise—it is key to developing sound policies aimed at reducing crime.

REFERENCES

1: Introduction

Akers, Ronald L., James Massey, William Clarke, and Ronald M. Lauer. 1983. "Are Self-Reports of Adolescent Deviance Valid? Biochemical Measures, Randomized Response, and the Bogus Pipeline in Smoking Behavior." *Social Forces* 62 (September): 234–251.

Bachman, Ronet, and Raymond Paternoster. 2004. *Statistics for Criminology and Criminal Justice*. New York: McGraw Hill Publishers.

Champion, Dean J. 1993. *Research Methods for Criminal Justice and Criminology*. Englewood Cliffs, NJ: Regents/Prentice Hall Press.

Cuzzort, R. P. 1989. *Using Social Thought*. Mountain View, CA: Mayfield Publishing Company.

Decker, Scott H., and Barrik Van Winkle. 1996. *Life in the Gang: Family Friends, and Violence*. Cambridge, UK: Cambridge University Press.

Elliott, Delbert S., and Suzanne S. Ageton. 1980. "Reconciling Race and Class Differences in Self-Reported and Official Estimates of Delinquency." *American Sociological Review* 45(1): 95–110.

Farrington, David P., Rolf Loeber, Magda Stouthamer-Loeber, Welmoet B. Van Kammen, and Laura Schmidt. 1996. "Self-Reported Delinquency and a Combined Delinquency Seriousness Scale Based on Boys, Mothers, and Teachers: Concurrent and Predictive Validity for African Americans and Caucasians." *Criminology* 34 (November): 493–517.

Glaser, Barney G., and Anselm L. Strauss. 1967. *The Discovery of Grounded Theory: Strategies for Qualitative Research*. New York: Aldine Publishers.

Gold, Martin. 1970. *Delinquent Behavior in an American City*. Belmont, CA: Brooks/Cole Publishing Company.

Hagedorn, John M. 1988. *People and Folks: Gangs, Crime and the Underclass in a Rustbelt City*. Chicago: Lakeview Press.

Hindelang, Michael J., Travis Hirschi, and J. G. Weis. 1979. "Correlates of Delinquency: The Illusion of Discrepancy between Self-Report and Official Measures." *American Sociological Review* 44: 995–1014.

———. 1981. *Measuring Delinquency*. Beverly Hills, CA: Sage Publications.

Hirschi, Travis. 1969. *Causes of Delinquency*. Berkeley: University of California Press.

Hudson, Walter. 1982. *The Clinical Measurement Package: A Field Manual*. Homewood, IL: Dorsey Press.

———. 1996. *WALMYR Assessment Scales Scoring Manual*. Tempe, AZ: WALMYR Publishing Company.

Huizinga, David, and Delbert S. Elliott. 1986. "Reassessing the Reliability and Validity of Self-Report Delinquent Measures." *Journal of Quantitative Criminology* 2(4): 293–327.

Jankowski, Martin Sanchez. 1991. *Islands in the Street: Gangs and American Urban Society*. Berkeley: University of California Press.

Krohn, Marvin D., Susan B. Stern, Terence P. Thornberry, and Sung Joon Jang. 1992. "The Measurement of Family Process Variables: An Examination of Adolescent and Parent Perceptions of Family Life on Delinquent Behavior." *Journal of Quantitative Criminology* 8: 287–315.

Moore, Joan W. 1978. *Homeboys: Gangs, Drugs, and Prisons in the Barrios of Los Angeles.* Philadelphia: Temple University Press.

Padilla, Felix M. 1992. *The Gang as an American Enterprise.* New Brunswick, NJ: Rutgers University Press.

Porterfield, Austin L. 1943. "Delinquency and Outcome in Court and College." *American Journal of Sociology* 49: 199–208.

Runes, Dagobert D. 1962. *Dictionary of Philosophy: Ancient–Medieval–Modern.* Paterson, NJ: Littlefield, Adams, & Co.

Sellin, Thorsten. 1931. The Basis of a Crime Index." *Journal of Criminal Law and Criminology* 22: 335–356.

Thornberry, Terence P., and Marvin D. Krohn. 2000. "The Self-Report Method for Measuring Delinquency and Crime." Pp. 33–83 in *Criminal Justice 2000, Vol.4: Innovations in Measurement and Analysis*, ed. David Duffee, Robert D. Crutchfield, Steven Mastrofski, Lorraine Mazerolle, and David McDowall. Washington, DC: U.S. Department of Justice.

Thornberry, Terence, Beth Bjerregaard, and William Miles. 1993. "The Consequences of Respondent Attrition in Panel Studies: A Simulation Based on the Rochester Youth Development Study." *Journal of Quantitative Criminology* 9: 127–158.

Thornberry, Terence, Marvin D. Krohn, Alan J. Lizotte, Carolyn A. Smith, and Kimberly Tobin. 2003. *Gangs and Delinquency in Developmental Perspective.* Cambridge, UK: Cambridge University Press.

Turner, Jonathan H. 1986. *The Structure of Sociological Theory*, 4th ed. Chicago: Dorsey Press.

U.S. Department of Justice, National Institute of Justice. 1990. "Drug Use Forecasting Annual Report: Drugs and Crime in America." *Research in Action*, NCJ 122225. Washington, DC.

Vigil, James Diego. 1988. *Barrio Gangs: Street Life and Identity in Southern California.* Austin: University of Texas Press.

Wagner, David G. 1984. *The Growth of Sociological Theories.* Beverly Hills, CA: Sage Publications.

2: Rational Choice and Deterrence Theories

Akers, Ronald L. 1990. "Rational Choice, Deterrence, and Social Learning Theory: The Path Not Taken." *Journal of Criminal Law and Criminology* 81:653–676.

Akers, Ronald L., and Christine S. Sellers. 2004. *Criminological Theories: Introduction, Evaluation, and Application.* Los Angeles, CA: Roxbury Publishing.

Anderson, Linda S., Theodore G. Chiricos, and Gordon P. Waldo. 1977. "Formal and Informal Sanctions: A Comparison of Deterrent Effects." *Social Problems* 25:103–112.

Barr, Robert, and Ken Pease. 1990. "Crime Placement, Displacement, and Deflection." *Crime and Justice* 12:277–318.

Beccaria, Cesare. 1996 [1764]. *Of Crimes and Punishments.* Translated by Jane Grigson with an introduction by Marvin Wolfgang. New York: Marsilio Publishers.

Berk, Richard A., Alec Campbell, Ruth Klap, and Bruce Western. 1992. "The Deterrent Effect of Arrest in Incidents of Domestic Violence: A Bayesian Analysis of Four Field Experiments." *American Sociological Review* 57:698–708.

Bernburg, Jon Gunnar, and Thorolfur Thorlindsson. 2001. "Routine Activities in Social Context: A Closer Look at the Role of Opportunity in Deviant Behavior." *Justice Quarterly* 18:543–568.

Birkbeck, Christopher, and Gary LaFree. 1993. "The Situational Analysis of Crime and Deviance." *Annual Review of Sociology* 19:113–137.

Blumstein, Alfred, Jacqueline Cohen, and Daniel Nagin. 1978. *Deterrence and Incapacitation: Estimating the Effects of Sanctions on the Crime Rate.* Washington, DC: National Academy Press.

Braga, Anthony, David Weisburd, Elin Waring, Lorraine Green Mazerolle, William Spelman, and Francis Gajewski. 1999. "Problem-Oriented Policing in Violent Crime Places: A Randomized Controlled Experiment." *Criminology* 37:541–580.

Brantingham, Patricia L., Paul J. Brantingham, and Wendy Taylor. 2005. "Situational Crime Prevention as a Key Component in Embedded Crime Prevention." *Canadian Journal of Criminology and Criminal Justice* 47:271–292.

Briscoe, Suzanne. 2004. "Raising the Bar: Can Increased Statutory Penalties Deter Drunk-Drivers?" *Accident Analysis and Prevention* 36:919–929.

Burkett, Steven, and David Ward. 1993. "A Note on Perceptual Deterrence, Religiously Based Moral Condemnation, and Social Control." *Criminology* 31:119–134.

Chamlin, Mitchell B., Harold G. Grasmick, Robert J. Bursik Jr., and John K. Cochran. 1992. "Time Aggregation and Time Lag in Macro-Level Deterrence Research." *Criminology* 30(3):377–395.

Chiricos, Theodore G., and Gordon P. Waldo. 1970. "Punishment and Crime: An Examination of Some Empirical Evidence." *Social Problems* 18:200–217.

Clarke, Ronald. 1983. "Situational Crime Prevention: Its Theoretical Basis and Practical Scope." *Crime and Justice* 4:225–256.

———. 1992. *Situational Crime Prevention: Successful Case Studies.* Albany, NY: Harrow and Heston.

———. 1995. "Situational Crime Prevention." *Crime and Justice* 19:91–150.

———. 1997. *Situational Crime Prevention: Successful Case Studies,* 2nd ed. Albany, NY: Harrow and Heston.

Clarke, Ronald, and Derek Cornish. 1985. "Modeling Offenders Decisions: A Framework for Research and Policy." *Crime and Justice* 6:147–185.

Cochran, John K., and Mitchell B. Chamlin. 2000. "Deterrence and Brutalization: The Dual Effects of Executions." *Justice Quarterly* 17:685–706.

Cochran, John K., Mitchell B. Chamlin, and Mark Seth. 1994. "Deterrence or Brutalization? An Impact Assessment of Oklahoma's Return to Capital Punishment." *Criminology* 32:107–134.

Cohen, Jacqueline, Wilpen Gorr, and Piyusha Singh. 2003. "Estimating Intervention Effects in Varying Risk Settings: Do Police Raids Reduce Illegal Drug Dealing at Nuisance Bars?" *Criminology* 41:257–292.

Cohen, Lawrence E., and David Cantor. 1980. "Residential Burglary in the United States: Life-Style and Demographic Factors Associated with the Probability of Victimization." *Journal of Research in Crime and Delinquency* 18:588–608.

Cohen, Lawrence E., and Marcus Felson. 1979. "Social Change and Crime Rate Trends: A Routine Activities Approach." *American Sociological Review* 44:588–608.

Cohen, Lawrence E., Marcus Felson, and Kenneth C. Land. 1980. "Property Crime Rates in the United States: A Macrodynamic Analysis 1947–77 with Ex Ante Forecasts for the Mid-1980's." *American Journal of Sociology* 86:90–118.

Cohen, Lawrence E., James Kluegel, and Kenneth Land. 1981. "Social Inequality and Predatory Criminal Victimization: An Exposition and Test of a Formal Theory." *American Sociological Review* 46:505–524.

Cook, Philip J. 1980. "Research in Criminal Deterrence: Laying the Groundwork for the Second Decade." *Crime and Justice* 2:211–268.

Cornish, Derek B., and Ronald V. Clarke (Eds.). 1986. *The Reasoning Criminal: Rational Choice Perspectives on Offending*. New York: Springer.

———. 1987. "Understanding Crime Displacement: An Application of Rational Choice Theory." *Criminology* 25:933–947.

De Haan,William, and Jaco Vos. 2003. "A Crying Shame: The Over-Rationalized Conception of Man in the Rational Choice Perspective." *Theoretical Criminology* 7:29–54.

Dejong, Christina. 1997. "Survival Analysis and Specific Deterrence: Integrating Theoretical and Empirical Models of Recidivism." *Criminology* 35:561–576.

Donohue, John J., and Justin Wolfers. 2006. "The Death Penalty: No Evidence for Deterrence." *Economists' Voice*: 1–6.

Ehrlich, Isaac. 1975. "The Deterrent Effect of Capital Punishment: A Question of Life and Death." *American Economic Review* 65:397–417.

Erickson, Maynard, and Jack Gibbs. 1978. "Objective and Perceptual Properties of Legal Punishment and Deterrence Doctrine." *Social Problems* 25:253–264.

Felson, Marcus. 1998. *Crime & Everyday Life*. Thousand Oaks, CA: Pine Forge Press.

Foglia, Wanda. 1997. "Perceptual Deterrence and the Mediating Effect of Internalized Norms among Inner-City Teenagers." *Journal of Research in Crime and Delinquency* 34:414–442.

Fritsch, Eric, Tory Caeti, and Robert Taylor. 1999. "Gang Suppression Through Saturation Patrol, Aggressive Curfew, and Truancy Enforcement: A Quasi-Experimental Test of the Dallas Anti-Gang Initiative." *Crime and Delinquency* 45:122–139.

Fulkerson, Andrew. 2003. "Blow and Go: The Breath-Analyzed Ignition Interlock Device as a Technological Response to DWI." *American Journal of Drug and Alcohol Abuse* 29:219–235.

Gibbs, Jack P. 1968. "Crime, Punishment, and Deterrence." *Southwestern Social Science Quarterly* 48:515–530.

———. 1975. *Crime, Punishment, and Deterrence*. New York: Elsevier.

———. 1986. "Punishment and Deterrence: Theory, Research, and Penal Policy." Pp. 319–368 in *Law and the Social Sciences*, ed. Leon Lipson and Stanton Wheeler. New York: Russell Sage.

Gibbs, Jack P., and Glenn Firebaugh. 1990. "The Artifact Issue in Deterrence Research." *Criminology* 28:347–367.

Gottfredson, Michael R., and Travis Hirshi. 1990. *A General Theory of Crime*. Stanford, CA: Stanford University Press.

Grasmick, Harold G., and Robert J. Bursik. 1990. "Conscience, Significant Others, and Rational Choice: Extending the Deterrence Model." *Law and Society Review* 24:837–862.

Grasmick, Harold G., Robert J. Bursik, and Bruce Arneklev. 1993. "Reduction in Drunk Driving as a Response to Increased Threats of Shame, Embarrassment, and Legal Sanctions." *Criminology* 31:41–67.

Grasmick, Harold, Brenda Sims-Blackwell, and Robert Bursik. 1993. "Changes in the Sex Patterning of Perceived Threats of Sanctions." *Law and Society Review* 27:679–699.

Green, Lorraine. 1995. "Cleaning Up Drug Hot Spots in Oakland, California: The Displacement and Diffusion Effects." *Justice Quarterly* 12:737–754.

Greenberg, David. 1975. "The Incapacitative Effects of Imprisonment: Some Estimates." *Law and Society Review* 9:541–580.

Greenberg, David F., and Ronald C. Kessler. 1982. "The Effect of Arrests on Crime: A
Multivariate Panel Analysis." *Social Forces* 60:771–790.

Greenberg, David F., and Nancy Larkin. 1998. "The Incapacitation of Criminal Opiate
Users." *Crime and Delinquency* 44:205–228.

Greenberg, David F., Ronald C. Kessler, and Charles H. Logan. 1979. "A Panel Model
of Crime Rates and Arrest Rates." *American Sociological Review* 44:843–850.

Greenberg, Peter. 1982. *Selective Incapacitation*. Santa Monica: Rand Corporation.

Hawley, Amos. 1950. *Human Ecology: A Theory of Community Structure*. New York:
Ronald Press.

Huff, C. Ronald, and John M. Stahura. 1980. "Police Employment and Suburban
Crime." *Criminology* 17:461–470.

Jacob, Herbert. 1979. "Rationality and Criminality." *Social Science Quarterly* 59:584–
585.

Jacobs, Bruce. 1996. "Crack Dealers' Apprehension Avoidance Techniques: A Case of
Restrictive Deterrence." *Justice Quarterly* 13:359–381.

Jensen, Gary F., and David Brownfield. 1986. "Gender, Lifestyle, and Victimization:
Beyond Routine Activity." *Violence and Victims* 2:85–99.

Jensen, Gary F., Maynard L. Erickson, and Jack P. Gibbs. 1978. "Perceived Risk of
Punishment and Self Reported Delinquency." *Social Forces* 57:57–78.

Kelling, George, Tony Pate, Duane Dieckman, and Charles Brown. 1974. *The Kansas
City Preventative Patrol Experiment: A Summary Report*. Washington, DC: Police
Foundation.

Kennedy, David. 1998. "Pulling Levers: Getting Deterrence Right." *National Institute of
Justice Journal* (July):2–8.

Kennedy, Leslie W., and David R. Forde. 1990. "Routine Activities and Crime: An
Analysis of Victimization in Canada." *Criminology* 28:137–152.

Kleck, Gary, Brion Sever, Spencer Li, and Marc Gertz. 2005. "The Missing Link in
General Deterrence Research." *Criminology* 43:623–660.

Klepper, Steven, and Daniel Nagin. 1989. "The Deterrent Effect of Perceived Certainty
and Severity of Punishment Revisited." *Criminology* 27:721–746.

Kovandzic, Tomislav V., and John J. Sloan. 2002. "Police Levels and Crime Rates
Revisited: A County-Level Analysis from Florida." *Journal of Criminal Justice* 30:65–
76.

Kovandzic, Tomislav V., John J. Sloan III, and Lynne M. Vieraitis. 2002. "Unintended
Consequences of Politically Popular Sentencing Policy: The Homicide Promoting
Effects of 'Three Strikes' in U.S. Cities (1980–1999)." *Criminology and Public Policy*
1:399–424.

———. 2004. " 'Striking Out' as Crime Reduction Policy: The Impact of 'Three Strikes'
Laws on Crime Rates in U.S. Cities." *Justice Quarterly* 21:235–239.

Lab, Steven P. (Ed.). 1997. *Crime Prevention at a Crossroads*. Highland Heights, KY:
Academy of Criminal Justice Sciences.

Layton-MacKenzie, Doris, and Spencer De Li. 2002. "The Impact of Formal and Informal Social Controls on the Criminal Activities of Probationers." *Journal of Research in Crime and Delinquency* 39:243–276.

Levitt, Steven. 1997. "Using Electoral Cycles in Police Hiring to Estimate the Effect of
Police on Crime." *American Economic Review* 87:70–91.

———. 1998. "Why Do Increased Arrest Rates Appear to Reduce Crime: Deterrence,
Incapacitation, or Measurement Error?" *Economic Inquiry* 36:353–372.

———. 2001. "Deterrence." Pp. 435–450 in *Crime: Public Policies for Crime Control*, ed. James Q. Wilson and Joan Petersilia. Oakland, CA: ICS Press.

Loftin, Colin, and David McDowall. 1982. "The Police, Crime, and Economic Theory: An Assessment." *American Sociological Review* 47:393–401.

Lott, John, and William Landes. 1999. "Multiple Victim Public Shootings, Bombings, and Right-to-Carry Concealed Handgun Laws: Contrasting Private and Public Law Enforcement." University of Chicago Law School, John M. Olin Law and Economics working paper no. 73.

Marvell, Thomas, and Carlisle Moody. 1995. "The Impact of Enhanced Prison Terms for Felonies Committed with Guns." *Criminology* 33:247–281.

———. 1996. "Specification Problems, Police Levels, and Crime Rates." *Criminology* 34:609–646.

Massey, James, Marvin Krohn, and Lisa Bonati. 1989. "Property Crime and the Routine Activities of Individuals." *Journal of Research in Crime and Delinquency* 26:378–400.

Mendes, Silvia. 2004. "Certainty, Severity, and Their Relative Deterrent Effects: Questioning the Implications of the Role of Risk in Criminal Deterrence Policy." *Policy Studies Journal* 32:59–74.

Messner, Steven F., and Judith R. Blau. 1987. "Routine Leisure Activities and Rates of Crime: A Macro-Level Analysis." *Social Forces* 65(4):1035–1052.

Miethe, Terance D., and Robert F. Meier. 1994. *Crime and Its Social Context: Toward an Integrated Theory of Outsiders, Victims, and Situations.* New York: State University of New York.

Miethe, Terance D., Mark C. Stafford, and Scott Long. 1987. "Social Differentiation in Criminal Victimization: A Test of Routine Activities/Lifestyle Theory." *American Sociological Review* 52:184–194.

Miethe, Terance D., Michael Hughes, and David McDowall. 1991. "Social Change and Crime Rates: An Evaluation of Alternative Theoretical Approaches." *Social Forces* 70(1):165–185.

Minor, M. William, and Joseph Harry. 1982. "Deterrent and Experiential Effects in Perceptual Deterrence Research: A Replication and Extension." *Journal of Research in Crime and Delinquency* 19:190–203.

Morse, Barbara, and Delbert Elliot. 1992. "Effects of Interlock Ignition Devices on DUI Recidivism: Findings from a Longitudinal Study in Hamilton County, Ohio." *Crime and Delinquency* 38:131–157.

Nagin, Daniel S. 1978. "General Deterrence: A Review of the Empirical Evidence." Pp. 95–139 in *Deterrence and Incapacitation: Estimating the Effects of Criminal Sanctions on Crime Rates*, ed. Alfred Blumstein, Jacqueline Cohen, and Daniel S. Nagin. Washington, DC: National Academy of Sciences.

———. 1998. "Criminal Deterrence Research at the Outset of the Twenty-First Century." *Crime and Justice* 23:1–42.

Nagin, Daniel S., and Raymond Paternoster. 1994. "Personal Capital and Social Control: The Deterrence Implications of a Theory of Individual Differences in Criminal Offending." *Criminology* 32:581–606.

Nagin, Daniel S., and Greg Pogarsky. 2001. "Integrating Celerity, Impulsivity, and Extralegal Sanction Threats into a Model of General Deterrence: Theory and Evidence." *Criminology* 39:865–892.

———. 2003. "An Experimental Investigation of Deterrence: Cheating, Self-Serving Bias, and Impulsivity." *Criminology* 41:167–195.

Newman, Graeme, Ronald V. Clarke, and S. Giora Shoham (Eds.). 1997. *Rational Choice and Situational Crime Prevention: Theoretical Foundations.* Aldershot, England: Ashgate Dartmouth.

Novak, Kenneth, Jennifer Hartman, Alexander Holsinger, and Michael Turner. 1999. "The Effects of Aggressive Policing of Disorder on Serious Crime." *Policing* 22:171–190.

Osgood, D. Wayne, and Amy L. Anderson. 2004. "Unstructured Socializing and Rates of Delinquency." *Criminology* 42:519–550.

Osgood, D. Wayne, Jane K. Wilson, Patrick M. O'Malley, and Jerald G. Bachman. 1996. "Routine Activities and Individual Deviant Behavior." *American Sociological Review* 61:635–655.

Paternoster, Raymond. 1985. "Assessments of Risk and Behavioral Experience: An Explanatory Study of Change." *Criminology* 23:417–436.

———. 1988. "Examining Three-Wave Deterrence Models: A Question of Temporal Order and Specification." *Journal of Criminal Law and Criminology* 79:135–163.

Paternoster, Raymond, and Alex Piquero. 1995. "Reconceptualizing Deterrence: An Empirical Test of Personal and Vicarious Experiences." *Journal of Research in Crime and Delinquency* 32:251–258.

Paternoster, Raymond, Linda E. Saltzman, Gordon P. Waldo, and Theodore G. Chiricos. 1983a. "Perceived Risk and Social Control: Do Sanctions Really Deter?" *Law and Society Review* 17:457–480.

———. 1983b. "Estimating Perceptual Stability and Deterrent Effects: The Role of Perceived Legal Punishment in the Inhibition of Criminal Involvement." *Journal of Criminal Law and Criminology* 74:270–297.

Peete, Thomas, Trudie Milner, and Michael Welch. 1994. "Levels of Social Integration in Group Contexts and the Effects of Informal Sanction Threat on Deviance." *Criminology* 32:85–105.

Piliavin, Irving, Graig Thornton, Rosemary Gartner, and Ross L. Matsueda. 1986. "Crime, Deterrence, and Rational Choice." *American Sociological Review* 51:101–119.

Piquero, Alex, and Raymond Paternoster. 1998. "An Application of Stafford and Warr's Reconceptualization of Deterrence to Drinking and Driving." *Journal of Research in Crime and Delinquency* 35:3–39.

Piquero, Alex, and Greg Pogarsky. 2002. "Beyond Stafford and Warr's Reconceptualization of Deterrence: Personal and Vicarious Experiences, Impulsivity, and Offending Behavior." *Journal of Research in Crime and Delinquency* 39(2):153–186.

Piquero, Alex, and George F. Rengert. 1999. "Studying Deterrence with Active Residential Burglars." *Justice Quarterly* 16:451–471.

Pogarsky, Greg, and Alex Piquero. 2003. "Can Punishment Encourage Offending? Investigating the 'Resetting' Effect." *Journal of Research in Crime and Delinquency* 40:92–117.

Pudney, Stephen, Derek Deadman, and David Pyle. 2000. "The Relationship between Crime, Punishment and Economic Conditions: Is Reliable Inference Possible When Crimes Are Under-recorded?" *Journal of the Royal Statistical Society (Series A)* 163:81–97.

Roncek, Dennis W., and Pamela A. Maier. 1991. "Bars, Blocks, and Crimes Revisited: Linking the Theory of Routine Activities to the Empiricism of Hot Spots." *Criminology* 29:725–753.

Ross, H. Laurence. 1984. *Deterring the Drinking Driver: Legal Policy and Social Control.* Lexington, MA: Lexington Books.

————. 1986. "Implications of Drinking-and-Driving Law Studies for Deterrence Theory." Pp. 159–169 in *Critique and Explanation: Essays in Honor of Gwynne Nettler*, ed. Timothy F. Hartnagel and Robert A. Silverman. New Brunswick, NJ: Transaction Books.

Ross, H. Laurence, Richard McCleary, and Gary LaFree. 1990. "Can Mandatory Jail Laws Deter Drunk Driving? The Arizona Case." *Journal of Criminal Law and Criminology* 81:156–167.

Sampson, Robert, and Jacqueline Cohen. 1988. "Deterrent Effects of the Police on Crime: A Replication and Theoretical Extension." *Law and Society Review* 22:163–188.

Sampson, Robert J., and John D. Wooldredge. 1987. "Linking the Micro- and Macro-Level Dimensions of Lifestyle-Routine Activity and Opportunity Models of Predatory Victimization." *Journal of Quantitative Criminology* 3:371–393.

Shapiro, Perry, and Harold Votey. 1984. "Deterrence and Subjective Probabilities of Arrest: Modeling Individual Decisions to Drink and Drive in Sweden." *Law and Society Review* 18:111–149.

Sherman, Lawrence W. 1990. "Police Crackdowns: Initial and Residual Deterrence." *Crime and Justice* 12:1–48.

Sherman, Lawrence W., and Richard A. Berk. 1984. "The Specific Deterrent Effects of Arrest for Domestic Assault." *American Sociological Review* 49:261–272.

Sherman, Lawrence W., and Dennis P. Rogan. 1995. "Effects of Gun Seizures on Gun Violence: 'Hot Spots' Patrol in Kansas City." *Justice Quarterly* 12:673–693.

Sherman, Lawrence W., Dennis P. Rogan, Timothy Edwards, Rachel Whipple, Dennis Shreve, Daniel Witcher, William Trimble, Robert Velke, Mark Blumberg, Anne Beatty, and Carol A. Bridgeforth. 1995. "Deterrent Effects of Police Raids on Crack Houses: A Randomized, Controlled Experiment." *Justice Quarterly* 12:756–781.

Simon, Herbert. A. 1957. *Models of Man*. New York: Wiley.

Sims-Blackwell, Brenda. 2000. "Perceived Sanction Threats, Gender, and Crime: A Test and Elaboration of Power-Control Theory." *Criminology* 38:439–488.

Smith, Douglas, and Patrick Gartin. 1989. "Specifying Specific Deterrence: The Influence of Arrest on Future Criminal Activity." *American Sociological Review* 54:94–105.

Smith, Michael. 2001. "Police-Led Crackdowns and Cleanups: An Evaluation of a Crime Control Initiative in Richmond, Virginia." *Crime and Delinquency* 47:60–68.

Spohn, Cassia, and David Holleran. 2002. "The Effect of Imprisonment on Recidivism Rates of Felony Offenders: A Focus on Drug Offenders." *Criminology* 40:329–359.

Stack, Steven. 1998. "The Effect of Well-Publicized Executions on Homicide in California." *Journal of Crime and Justice* 31:1–12.

Stafford, Mark, and Mark Warr. 1993. "A Reconceptualization of General and Specific Deterrence." *Journal of Research in Crime and Delinquency* 30:123–135.

Stolzenberg, Lisa, and Stewart D'Alessio. 2004. "Capital Punishment, Execution Publicity, and Murder in Houston, Texas." *Journal of Criminal Law & Criminology* 94:351–380.

Thomas, Charles W., and Donna M. Bishop. 1984. "The Effects of Formal and Informal Sanctions on Delinquency: A Longitudinal Comparison of Labeling and Deterrence Theories." *Journal of Criminal Law and Criminology* 75:1222–1245.

Tittle, Charles. 1969. "Crime Rates and Legal Sanctions." *Social Problems* 16:409–422.

————. 1975. "Deterrents or Labeling?" *Social Forces* 53:399–410.

————. 1980. *Sanctions and Social Deviance*. New York: Praeger.

Tittle, Charles R., and Ekaterina V. Botchkovar. 2005. "Self-Control, Criminal Motivation and Deterrence: An Investigation Using Russian Respondents." *Criminology* 43:307–354.

Tunnell, Kenneth. 1992. *Choosing Crime*. Chicago: Nelson-Hall.

Uggen, Christopher, and Melissa Thompson. 2003. "The Socioeconomic Determinants of Ill-Gotten Gains: Within-Person Changes in Drug Use and Illegal Earnings." *American Journal of Sociology* 109:146–187.

Vold, George B., Thomas J. Bernard, and Jeffrey B. Snipes. 1998. *Theoretical Criminology*, 4th ed. New York: Oxford University Press.

Weisburd, David, Elin Waring, and Ellen Chayet. 1995. "Specific Deterrence in a Sample of Offenders Convicted of White-Collar Crimes." *Criminology* 33:587–607.

Weisburd, David, Laura A. Wyckof, Justin Ready, John E. Eck, Joshua C. Hinkle, and Frank Gajewski. 2006. "Does Crime Just Move around the Corner? A Controlled Study of Spatial Displacement and Diffusion of Crime Control Benefits." *Criminology* 44:549–592.

Wilcox, Pamela, Kenneth C. Land, and Scott A. Hunt. 2003. *Criminal Circumstance: A Dynamic Multicontextual Criminal Opportunity Theory*. New York: Aldine de Gruyter.

Williams, Kirk R., and Richard Hawkins. 1986. "Perceptual Research on General Deterrence: A Critical Overview." *Law and Society Review* 20:545–572.

Worrall, John L. 2004. "The Effect of Three-Strikes Legislation on Serious Crime in California." *Journal of Criminal Justice* 32:283–296.

Wright, Bradley, Avshalom Caspi, Terrie Moffitt, and Ray Paternoster. 2004. "Does the Perceived Risk of Punishments Deter Criminally Prone Individuals? Rational Choice, Self-Control, and Crime." *Journal of Research in Crime and Delinquency* 41:180–213.

Zimring, Franklin E. 1971. "Perspectives on Deterrence." *NIMH Monograph Series on Crime and Delinquency Issues*. Washington, DC: U.S. Government Printing Office.

Zimring, Franklin, and Gordon Hawkins. 1968. "Deterrence and Marginal Groups." *Journal of Research in Crime and Delinquency* 5:100–115.

———. 1973. *Deterrence*. Chicago: University of Chicago Press.

Zimring, Franklin, Gordon Hawkins, and Sam Kamin. 2001. *Punishment and Democracy: Three Strikes and You're Out in California*. New York: Oxford University Press.

3: Trait Theories

Akers, Ronald L., and Christine S. Sellers. 2004. *Criminological Theories: Introduction, Evaluation, and Application*, 4th ed. Los Angeles, CA: Roxbury.

Andrews, D. A., and James Bonta. 1998. *The Psychology of Criminal Conduct*, 2nd ed. Cincinnati, OH: Anderson.

———. 2003. *The Psychology of Criminal Conduct*, 3rd ed. Cincinnati, OH: Anderson.

Archer, John. 1991. "The Influence of Testosterone on Human Aggression." *British Journal of Psychology* 82:1–28.

Archer, John, Nicola Graham-Kevan, and Michelle Davies. 2005. "Testosterone and Aggression: A Reanalysis of Book, Starzyk, and Quinsey's (2001) Study." *Aggression and Violent Behavior* 10:241–261.

Bandura, Albert. 1973. *Aggression: A Social Learning Analysis*. Englewood Cliffs, NJ: Prentice Hall.

Berenbaum, Sheri A., and Susan M. Resnick. 1997. "Early Androgen Effects on Aggression in Children and Adults with Congential Adrenal Hyperplasia." *Psychoneuroendrocrinology* 22:501–515.

Berman, Mitchell E., Richard J. Kavoussi, and Emil F. Coccaro. 1997. "Neurotransmitter Correlates of Human Aggression." Pp. 305–313 in *Handbook of Anti-*

social Behavior, ed. David M. Stoff, James Breiling, and Jack D. Maser. New York: John Wiley and Sons.

Booth, Alan, and D. Wayne Osgood. 1993. "The Influence of Testosterone on Deviance in Adulthood: Assessing and Explaining the Relationship." *Criminology* 31:93–117.

Brain, Paul F., 1994. "Hormonal Aspects of Aggression and Violence." Pp. 173–244 in *Understanding and Preventing Violence, Vol. 2: Biobehavioral Influences*, ed. Albert Reiss Jr., Klaus A. Miczek, and Jeffrey A. Roth. Washington, DC: National Academy Press.

Brain, Paul F., and Elizabeth J. Susman. 1997. "Hormonal Aspects of Aggression and Violence." Pp. 314–323 in *Handbook of Antisocial Behavior*, ed. David M. Stoff, James Breiling, and Jack D. Maser. New York: John Wiley and Sons.

Brennan, Patricia A., Adrian Raine, Fini Schulsinger, Lis Kirkegaard-Sorenson, Joachim Knop, Barry Hutchings, Raben Rosenberg, and Sarnoff A. Mednick. 1997. "Psychophysiological Protective Factors for Male Subjects at High Risk for Criminal Behavior." *American Journal of Psychiatry* 154:853–855.

Brownlie, E. B., Joseph H. Beitchman, Michael Escobar, Arlene Young, Leslie Atkinson, Carla Johnson, Beth Wilson, and Lori Douglas. 2004. "Early Language Impairment and Young Adult Delinquent and Aggressive Behavior." *Journal of Abnormal Child Psychology* 32:453–467.

Carey, Gregory. 1994. "Genetics and Violence." Pp. 21–58 in *Understanding and Preventing Violence, Vol. 2: Biobehavioral Influences*, ed. Albert J. Reiss Jr., Klaus A. Miczek, and Jeffrey A. Roth. Washington, DC: National Academy Press.

Carey, Gregory, and David Goldman. 1997. "The Genetics of Antisocial Behavior." Pp. 243–254 in *Handbook of Antisocial Behavior*, ed. David M. Stoff, James Breiling, and Jack D. Maser. New York: John Wiley and Sons.

Caspi, Avshalom. 2000. "The Child Is Father of the Man: Personality Continuities from Childhood to Adulthood." *Journal of Personality and Social Psychology* 78: 158–172.

Caspi, Avshalom, Terrie E. Moffitt, Ohil A. Silva, Magda Stouthamer Loeber, Robert F. Krueger, and Pamela S. Schmutte. 1994. "Are Some People Crime Prone? Replications of the Personality Crime Relationship across Countries, Genders, Races, and Methods." *Criminology* 32:163–196.

Caspi, Avshalom, Joseph McClay, Terrie E. Moffitt, Jonathan Mill, Judy Martin, Ian W. Craig, Alan Taylor, and Richie Poulton. 2002. "Role of Genotype in the Cycle of Violence in Maltreated Children." *Science* 297:841–854.

Caspi, Avshalom, Brent W. Roberts, and Rebecca L. Shiner. 2005. "Personality Development: Stability and Change." *Annual Review of Psychology* 56:453–484.

Caspi, Avshalom, Karen Sugden, Terrie E. Moffitt, Alan Taylor, Ian W. Craig, HonaLee Harrington, Joseph McClay, Jonathan Mill, Judy Martin, Anthony Braithwaite, and Richie Poulton. 2003. "Influence of Life Stress on Depression: Moderation by a Polymorphism in the 5-HTT Gene." *Science* 301:386–389.

Cauffman, Elizabeth, Laurence Steinberg, and Alex R.Piquero. 2005. "Psychological, Neuropsychological and Physiological Correlates of Serious Antisocial Behavior in Adolescence: The Role of Self-Control." *Criminology* 43:133–175.

Christiansen, Karl O. 1977. "A Preliminary Study of Criminality among Twins." Pp. 89–109 in *Biosocial Bases of Criminal Behavior*, ed. Sarnoff A Mednick and Karl O. Christiansen. New York: Gardner Press, Inc.

Cloninger, C. Robert, Dragan M. Svrakic, and Thomas R. Przybeck. 1993. "A Psychobiological Model of Temperament and Character." *Archives of General Psychiatry* 50:975–990.

Cochran, John K., Peter B. Wood, and Bruce J. Arneklev. 1994. "Is the Religiosity-Delinquency Relationship Spurious? A Test of Arousal and Social Control Theories." *Journal of Research in Crime and Delinquency* 31:92–123.

Cochran, John K., Jennifer Wareham, Peter B. Wood, and Bruce J. Arneklev. 2002. "Is the School Attachment/Commitment-Delinquency Relationship Spurious? An Exploratory Test of Arousal Theory." *Journal of Crime and Justice* 25:49–71.

Cornell, Dewey G., and Wilson, Lori A. 1992. "The PIQ> VIQ Discrepancy in Violent and Nonviolent Delinquents." *Journal of Clinical Psychology* 48:256–261.

Cullen, Francis T., Paul Gendreau, G. Roger Jarjoura, and John Paul Wright. 1997. "Crime and the Bell Curve: Lessons from Intelligent Criminology." *Crime and Delinquency* 43:387–412.

Daly, Martin, and Margo Wilson. 1988. "Evolutionary Social Psychology and Family Homicide." *Science* 242:519–524.

———. 1997. "Crime and Conflict: Homicide in Evolutionary Psychological Perspective." *Crime and Justice* 22:51–100.

Dickens, William T., and James R. Flynn. 2001. "Heritability Estimates versus Large Environmental Effects: The IQ Paradox Resolved." *Psychological Review* 108:346–369.

Ellis, Lee. 1987a. "Criminal Behavior and r/K Selection: An Extension of Gene Based Evolutionary Theory." *Deviant Behavior* 8:148–176.

———. 1987b. "Religiosity and Criminality from the Perspective of Arousal Theory." *Journal of Research in Crime and Delinquency* 24:215–232.

———. 1996. "Arousal Theory and the Religiosity-Criminality Relationship." Pp. 65–84 in *Readings in Contemporary Criminological Theory*, ed. Peter Corpella and Larry Siegel. Boston, MA: Northeastern University Press.

Ellis, Lee, and Anthony Walsh. 2003. "Crime, Delinquency, and Intelligence: A Review of the Worldwide Literature." Pp. 343–365 in *The Scientific Study of General Intelligence: Tribute to Arthur R. Jensen*, ed. Robert Jensen and Helmuth Nyborg. Boston: Pergamon.

Evans, James R., and Nan-Sook Park. 1997. "Quantitative EEG Findings among Men Convicted of Murder." *Journal of Neurotherapy* 2:31–39.

Eysenck, Hans J. 1977. *Crime and Personality*. London: Routledge and Kegan Paul.

Fishbein, Diana H. 1990. "Biological Perspectives in Criminology." *Criminology* 28:27–72.

———. 1992. "The Psychobiology of Female Aggression." *Criminal Justice and Behavior* 19:99–126.

———. 2001. *Biobehavioral Perspectives on Criminology*. Belmont, CA: Wadsworth.

Fishbein, Diana H., and Susan E. Pease. 1994. "Diet, Nutrition, and Aggression." *Offender Rehabilitation* 21:117–144.

Forthun, Larry F., Nancy J. Bell, Charles W. Peek, and Sheh-Wei Sun. 1999. "Religiosity, Sensation Seeking, and Alcohol/Drug Use in Denominational and Gender Contexts." *Journal of Drug Issues* 29:75–90.

Fredl, Fritz, and Hans Toch. 1979. "The Psychoanalytic Explanation of Crime." Pp. 183–197 in *Psychology of Crime and Criminal Justice*, ed. Hans Toch. New York: Holt, Reinhart, and Winston.

Freud, Sigmund. 1953. *A General Introduction to Psychoanalysis*. New York: Permabooks.

Glueck, Sheldon, and Eleanor Glueck. 1950. *Unraveling Juvenile Delinquency*. New York: Commonwealth Fund.

Gottfredson, Michael R., and Travis Hirschi. 1990. *A General Theory of Crime*. Stanford, CA: Stanford University Press.

Grove, William M., Elke D. Eckert, Leonard Heston, Thomas J. Bouchard, Nancy Segal, and David T. Lykken. 1990. "Heritability of Substance Abuse and Antisocial Behavior: A Study of Monozygotic Twins Reared Apart." *Biological Psychiatry* 27:1293–1304.

Hart, Stephen D., and Robert D. Hare. 1997. "Psychopathy: Assessment and Association with Criminal Conduct." Pp. 22–35 in *Handbook of Antisocial Behavior*, ed. David M. Stoff, James Breiling, and Jack D. Maser. New York: John Wiley and Sons.

Hathaway, Starke, and Elio Monachesi. 1953. *Analyzing and Predicting Juvenile Delinquency with the MMPI*. Minneapolis: University of Minnesota Press.

Herrnstein, Richard J. 1995. "Criminogenic Traits." Pp. 39–64 in *Crime*, ed. James Q. Wilson and Joan Petersilia. San Francisco: ICS Press.

Herrnstein, Richard J., and Charles Murray. 1994. *The Bell Curve: Intelligence and Class Structure in American Life*. New York: Free Press.

Hirschi, Travis, and Michael J. Hindelang. 1977. "Intelligence and Delinquency: A Revisionist Review." *American Sociological Review* 42:571–587.

Horney, Julie. 2006. "An Alternative Psychology of Criminal Behavior." *Criminology* 44:1–16.

Hutchings, Barry, and Sarnoff A. Mednick. 1977. "A Review of Studies of Criminality among Twins." Pp. 45–88 in *Biosocial Bases of Criminal Behavior*, ed. Sarnoff A. Mednick and Karl O. Christensen. New York: Gardner.

Jeffery, C. Ray. 1979. *Biology and Crime*. Beverly Hills, CA: Sage.

———. 1994. "Biological and Neuropsychiatric Approaches to Criminal Behavior." Pp. 15–28 in *Varieties of Criminology: Readings from a Dynamic Discipline*, ed. Gregg Barak. Westpoint, CT: Greenwood Publishing.

Kanarek, Robin B. 1994. "Nutrition and Violent Behavior." Pp. 515–539 in *Understanding and Preventing Violence, Vol. 2: Biobehavioral Influences*, ed. Albert J. Reiss Jr., Klaus A. Miczek, and Jeffrey A. Roth. Washington, DC: National Academy Press.

Kandel, Elizabeth, and Sarnoff A. Mednick. 1991. "Perinatal Complications Predict Violent Offending." *Criminology* 29(3):519–529.

Katz, Jack. 1988. *Seductions of Crime: Moral and Sensual Attractions in Doing Evil*. New York: Basic Books.

Kohlberg, Lawrence. 1981. *Essays on Moral Development. Volume I: The Philosophy of Moral Development*. New York: Harper and Row.

Kohlberg, L., K. Kauffman, P. Scharf, and J. Hickey. 1973. *The Just Community Approach in Correction: A Manual*. Niantic: Connecticut Department of Corrections.

Krebs, Dennis L., and Kathy Denton. 2005. "Toward a More Pragmatic Approach to Morality: A Critical Evaluation of Kohlberg's Model." *Psychological Review* 112(3):629–649.

Krueger, Robert F., Pamela Schmutte, Avshalom Caspi, Terrie E. Moffit, Kathleen Campbell, and Phil A. Silva. 1994. "Personality Traits Are Linked to Crime among Men and Women: Evidence from a Birth Cohort." *Journal of Abnormal Psychology* 103(2):328–338.

Kruesi, Marcus J. P., and Teresa Jacobsen. 1997. "Serotonin and Human Violence: Do Environmental Mediators Exist?" Pp. 189–205 in *Biosocial Bases of Violence*, ed. Adrian Raine, Patricia A. Brennan, David P. Farrington, and Sarnoff A. Mednick. New York: Plenum Press.

Lave, Jean. 1988. *Cognition in Practice*. New York: Cambridge University Press.

Lipton, David N., Elizabeth C. McDonel, and Richard M. McFall. 1987. "Heterosexual Perception in Rapists." *Journal of Consulting and Clinical Psychology* 55:17–21.

Lombroso, Cesare. 1876. *The Criminal Man (L'uomo Delinquenta)*, 1st ed. Milan: Hoepli. 2nd ed. (1878) through 5th ed. (1896), Turin: Bocca.

McCrae, Robert R., and Paul T. Costa. 1990. *Personality in Adulthood*. New York: Guilford Press.

Mealey, Linda. 1995. "The Sociobiology of Sociopathy: An Integrated Evolutionary Model." *Behavioral and Brain Sciences* 18:523–599.

Mednick, Sarnoff, William Gabrielli, and Barry Hutchings. 1984. "Genetic Influences in Criminal Convictions: Evidence from an Adoption Cohort." *Science* 224:891–894.

Mednick, Sarnoff, Jan Volavka, William F. Gabrielli, and Turan M. Itil. 1981. "EEG as a Predictor of Antisocial Behavior." *Criminology* 19:219–229.

Miller, Joshua D., and Donald Lynam. 2001. "Structural Models of Personality and Their Relation to Antisocial Behavior: A Meta-Analytic Review." *Criminology* 39:765–798.

Moffitt, Terrie E. 1993. "Adolescence Limited and Life Course Persistent Antisocial Behavioral: A Developmental Taxonomy." *Psychological Review* 100:674–701.

———. 2005. "The New Look of Behavioral Genetics in Developmental Psychopathology: Gene-Environment Interplay in Antisocial Behaviors." *Psychological Bulletin* 131:533–554.

Moffitt, Terrie E., and Phil A. Silva. 1988. "IQ and Delinquency: A Direct Test of the Differential Detection Hypothesis." *Journal of Abnormal Psychology* 97:330–333.

Moffitt, Terrie E., Avshalom Caspi, and Michael Rutter. 2006. "Measured Gene-Environment Interactions in Psychopathology: Concepts, Research Strategies, and Implications for Research, Intervention, and Public Understanding of Genetics." *Perspectives on Psychological Science* 1:5–27.

Moore, Todd M., Angela Scarpa, and Adrian Raine. 2002. "A Meta-Analysis of Serotonin Metabolite 5-HIAA and Antisocial Behavior." *Aggressive Behavior* 28:299–316.

Neisser, Ulric (Ed.). 1998. *The Rising Curve: Long-Term Gains in IQ and Related Measures*. Washington, DC: American Psychological Association.

Neisser, Ulric, Gwyneth Boodoo, Thomas J. Bouchard, A. Wade Boykin, Nathan Brody, Stephen J. Ceci, Diane F. Halpern, John C. Loehlin, Robert Perloff, Robert J. Sternberg, and Susana Urbina. 1996. "Intelligence: Knowns and Unknowns." *American Psychologist* 51:77–101.

Olweus, D. 1984. "Development of Stable Aggressive Reaction Patterns in Males." Pp. 103–137 in *Advances in the Study of Aggression, Vol. 1*, ed. R. J. Blanchard and D. C. Blanchard. Orlando, FL: Academic Press.

Olweus, D., A. Mattesson, D. Schalling, and H. Low. 1988. "Circulating Testosterone Levels and Aggression in Adolescent Males: A Causal Analysis." *Psychosomatic Medicine* 50:261–272.

Ortiz, Jame B. A., and Adrian Raine. 2004. "Heart Rate Level and Antisocial Behavior in Children and Adolescents: A Meta-Analysis." *Journal of the American Academy of Child & Adolescent Psychiatry* 43(2):154–162.

Piaget, Jean. 1932. *The Moral Judgment of the Child*. London: Routledge & Kegan Paul.

Pillmann, Frank, Anke Rohde, Simone Ullrich, Steffi Draba, Ursel Sannemüller, and Andreas Marneros. 1999. "Violence, Criminal Behavior, and the EEG: Significance of Left Hemispheric Focal Abnormalities." *Journal of Neuropsychiatry and Clinical Neurosciences* 11:454–457.

Piquero, Alex. 2000. "Frequency, Specialization, and Violence in Offending Careers." *Journal of Research in Crime and Delinquency* 4:392–418.

Piquero, Alex, and Stephen G. Tibbetts. 1999. "The Impact of Pre/Perinatal Disturbances and Disadvantaged Familial Environment in Predicting Criminal Offending." *Studies on Crime and Crime Prevention* 8:52–70.

Pulkkinen, Lea, Terhi Virtanen, Britt Af Klinteberg, and David Magnusson. 2000. "Child Behavior and Adult Personality: Comparisons between Criminality Groups in Finland and Sweden." *Criminal Behavior and Mental Health* 10:155–169.

Raine, Adrian. 1993. *The Psychopathology of Crime: Criminal Behavior as a Clinical Disorder*. San Diego: Academic Press.

———. 1997. "Antisocial Behavior and Psychophysiology: A Biosocial Perspective and a Prefrontal Dysfunction Hypothesis." Pp. 289–304 in *Handbook of Antisocial Behavior*, ed. David M. Stoff, James Breiling, and Jack D. Maser. New York: John Wiley and Sons.

———. 2002a. "The Biological Basis of Crime." Pp. 43–74 in *Crime: Public Policies for Crime Control*, ed. James Q. Wilson and Joan Petersilia. Oakland, CA: ICS Press.

———. 2002b. "Biosocial Studies of Antisocial and Violent Behavior in Children and Adults: A Review." *Journal of Abnormal Child Psychology* 30:311–326.

Raine, Adrian, Patricia Brennan, and David P. Farrington. 1997. "Biosocial Bases of Violence: Conceptual and Theoretical Issues." Pp. 1–20 in *Biosocial Bases of Violence*, ed. Adrian Raine, Patricia A. Brennan, David P. Farrington, and Sarnoff A. Mednick. New York: Plenum Press.

Raine, Adrian, Patricia Brennan, David P. Farrington, and Sarnoff A. Mednick (Eds.). 1997. *Biosocial Bases of Violence*. New York: Plenum Press.

Raine, Adrian, P. Brennen, and Sarnoff A. Mednick. 1994. "Birth Complications Combined with Early Maternal Rejection at Age 1 Year Predispose to Violent Crime at Age 18 Years." *Archives of General Psychiatry* 51:984–988.

Raine, Adrian, Monte Buchsbaum, and Lori La Casse. 1997. "Brain Abnormalities in Murderers Indicated by Position Emission Tomography." *Biological Psychiatry* 42:495–508.

Raine, Adrian, Monte S. Buchsbaum, Jill Stanley, Steven Lottenberg, Leonard Abel, and Jacqueline Stoddard. 1994. "Selective Reductions in Pre-Frontal Glucose Metabolism in Murderers." *Biological Psychiatry* 36:365–373.

Raine, Adrian, Todd Lencz, Susan Bihrle, Lori La Casse, and Patrick Colletti. 2000. "Reduced Prefrontal Gray Matter Volume and Reduced Autonomic Activity in Antisocial Personality Disorder." *Archives of General Psychiatry* 57:119–127.

Raine, Adrian, Peter H. Venables, and Sarnoff A. Mednick. 1997. "Low Resting Heart Rate at Age 3 Years Predisposes to Aggression at Age 11 Years: Findings from the Mauritius Joint Child Health Project." *Journal of the American Academy of Child and Adolescent Psychiatry* 36:1457–1464.

Raine, Adrian, Peter H. Venables, and Mark Williams. 1990. "Relationships between CNS and ANS Measures of Arousal at Age 15 and Criminality at Age 24." *Archives of General Psychiatry* 47:1003–1007.

———. 1995. "High Autonomic Arousal and Electro Dermal Orienting at Age 15 Years as Protective Factors against Criminal Behavior at Age 29 Years." *American Journal of Psychiatry* 152:1595–1600.

Raine, Adrian, Terrie E. Moffitt, Avshalom Caspi, Rolf Loeber, Magda Stouthamer-Loeber, and Don Lynam. 2005. "Neurocognitive Impairments in Boys on the Life-Course Persistent Antisocial Path." *Journal of Abnormal Psychology* 114:38–49.

Reiss, Albert Jr., Klaus A. Miczek, and Jeffrey A. Roth (Eds.). 1994. *Understanding and Preventing Violence, Vol. 2: Biobehavioral Influences.* Washington, DC: National Academy Press.

Rhee, Soo Hyun, and Irwin D. Waldman. 2002. "Genetic and Environmental Influences on Antisocial Behavior: A Meta-Analysis of Twin and Adoption Studies." *Psychological Bulletin* 128:490–529.

Rosen, Gerald M., Amos S. Deinard, Samuel Schwartz, Clark Smith, Betty Stephenson, and Brenda Grabenstein. 1985. "Iron Deficiency among Incarcerated Juvenile Delinquents" *Journal of Adolescent Health Care* 6:419–423.

Rowe, David C. 1985. "Sibling Interaction and Self Reported Delinquent Behavior: A Study of 265 Twin Pairs." *Criminology* 23:223–240.

———. 1986. "Genetic and Environmental Components of Antisocial Behavior: A Study of 265 Twin Pairs." *Criminology* 24:513–532.

———. 2002. *Biology and Crime.* Los Angeles, CA: Roxbury Publishing.

Rowe, David, and David P. Farrington. 1997. "The Familial Transmission of Criminal Convictions." *Criminology* 35:177–201.

Rowe, David C., and D. Wayne Osgood. 1984. "Heredity and Sociological Theories of Delinquency: A Reconsideration." *American Sociological Review* 49:526–540.

Rushton, J. Philippe. 1990. "Race and Crime: A Reply to Roberts and Gabor." *Canadian Journal of Criminology* 32:315–334.

———. 1995. "Race and Crime: International Data for 1989–1990." *Psychological Reports* 76:307–312.

Schuessler, Karl F., and Donald R. Cressey. 1950. "Personality Characteristics of Criminals." *American Journal of Sociology* 55:476–484.

Siegel, Larry J. 2006. *Criminology*, 9th ed. Mason, OH: Thomson Wadsworth.

Simpson, M. K., and J. Hogg. 2001. "Patterns of Offending among People with Intellectual Disability: A Systematic Review. Part I: Methodology and Prevalence Data." *Journal of Intellectual Disability Research* 45:384–396.

Stattin, Hakan, and Ingrid Klackenberg-Larsson. 1993. "Early Language and Intelligence Development and Their Relationship to Future Criminal Behavior." *Journal of Abnormal Psychology* 102:369–378.

Sternberg, Robert J. 1985. *Beyond IQ: A Triarchic Theory of Human Intelligence.* New York: Cambridge University Press.

Sternberg, Robert J., and Elena L. Grigorenko (Eds.). 2002. *The General Factor of Intelligence: How General Is It?* Mahwah, NJ: Lawrence Erlbaum Associates.

Susman, E. J., and A. Ponirakis. 1997. "Hormones-Context Interactions and Antisocial Behavior in Youth." Pp. 251–270 in *Biosocial Bases of Violence*, ed. Adrian Raine, Patricia A. Brennan, David P. Farrington, and Sarnoff A. Mednick. New York: Plenum Press.

Sutherland, Edwin H. 1931. "Mental Deficiency and Crime." Pp. 357–375 in *Social Attitudes*, ed. Kimball Young. New York: Holt.

Tellegen, Auke. 1985. "Structures of Mood and Personality and Their Relevance to Assessing Anxiety, with an Emphasis on Self-report." Pp. 681–706 in *Anxiety and the Anxiety Disorders*, ed. A. Hussain Tuma and Jack D. Maser. Hillsdale, NJ: Erlbaum.

Tennenbaum, David J. 1977. "Personality and Criminality: A Summary and Implications of the Literature." *Journal of Criminal Justice* 5:225–235.

Tibbetts, Stephen G., and Alex R. Piquero. 1999. "The Influence of Gender, Low Birth Weight, and Disadvantaged Environment in Predicting Early Onset and Offending: A Test of Moffitt's Interactional Hypothesis." *Criminology* 37:843–878.

Tremblay, Richard E., Robert O. Phil, Frank Vitaro, and Patricia L. Dobkin. 1994. "Predicting Early Onset of Male Antisocial Behavior from Preschool Behavior." *Archive of General Psychiatry* 51:732–739.

Tremblay, Richard E., Benoist Schaal, Bernard Boulerice, Louise Arseneault, Robert Soussignan, and Daniel Perusse. 1997. "Male Physical Aggression, Social Dominance, and Testosterone Levels at Puberty: A Developmental Perspective." Pp. 271–291 in *Biosocial Bases of Violence*, ed. Adrian Raine, Patricia A. Brennan, David P. Farrington, and Sarnoff A. Mednick. New York: Plenum.

Turkheimer, Eric, Andreana Haley, Mary Waldron, Brian D'Onofrio, and Irving I.Gottesman. 2003. "Socioeconomic Status Modifies Heritability of IQ in Young Children." *Psychological Science* 14:623–628.

Veneziano, Carol, and Louis Veneziano. 1992. "The Relationship between Deterrence and Moral Reasoning." *Criminal Justice Review* 17:209–216.

Vold, George B., Thomas J. Bernard, and Jeffrey B. Snipes. 1998. *Theoretical Criminology*, 4th ed. New York: Oxford University Press.

Waldo, Gordon P., and Simon Dinitz. 1967. "Personality Attributes of the Criminal: An Analysis of Research Studies, 1950–1965." *Journal of Research in Crime and Delinquency* 4(2):185–202.

Walsh, Anthony. 2000. "Behavior Genetics and Anomie/Strain Theory." *Criminology* 38:1075–1108.

———. 2002. *Biosocial Criminology: Introduction and Integration*. Cincinnati, OH: Anderson Publishing

———. 2003. "Intelligence and Antisocial Behavior." Pp. 105–124 in *Biosocial Criminology: Challenging Environmentalism's Supremacy*, ed. Anthony Walsh and Lee Ellis. New York: Nova Science Publishers.

Walsh, William J., H. Ronald Isaacson, Fatima Rehman, and Anmaire Hall. 1997. "Elevated Blood Copper/Zinc Ratios in Assaultive Young Males." *Physiology and Behavior* 62:327–329.

Walters, Glenn D. 1992. "A Meta Analysis of the Gene Crime Relationship." *Criminology* 30:595–613.

Ward, David A., and Charles R. Tittle. 1994. "IQ and Delinquency: A Test of Two Competing Explanations." *Journal of Quantitative Criminology* 10:189–213.

Werbach, M. 1995. "Nutritional Influences on Aggressive Behavior." *Journal of Orthomolecular Medicine* 7:45–51.

White, Jennifer L., Terrie E. Moffitt, Avshalom Caspi, Dawn Jeglum Bartusch, Douglas J. Needles, and Magda Stouthamer-Loeber. 1994. "Measuring Impulsivity and Examining Its Relationship to Delinquency." *Journal of Abnormal Psychology* 103(2):192–205.

Wille, Reinhard, and Klaus M. Beier. 1989. "Castration in Germany." *Annals of Sex Research* 2:103–134.

Wilson, James Q., and Richard J. Herrnstein. 1985. *Crime and Human Nature*. New York: Simon and Schuster.

Wright, John Paul, and Kevin M. Beaver. 2005. "Do Parents Matter in Creating Self-Control in Their Children? A Genetically Informed Test of Gottfredson and Hirschi's Theory of Low Self-Control." *Criminology* 43:1169–1202.

Zitzmann, M., and E. Nieschlag. 2001. "Testosterone Levels in Healthy Men and the Relation to Behavioral and Physical Characteristics: Facts and Constructs." *European Journal of Endocrinology* 144:183–197.

4: Social Disorganization Theory

Akers, Ronald L., and Christine S. Sellers. 2004. *Criminological Theories: Introduction, Evaluation, and Application.* Los Angeles: Roxbury Publishing.

Anselin, Luc, Jacqueline Cohen, David Cook, Wilpen Gorr, and George Tita. 2000. "Spatial Analyses of Crime." Pp. 213–262 in *Criminal Justice, Vol. 4. Measurement and Analysis of Crime and Justice,* ed. David Duffee. Washington, DC: National Institute of Justice.

Baller, Robert D., Luc Anselin, Steven F. Messner, Glenn Deane, and Darnell F. Hawkins. 2001. "Structural Covariates of U.S. County Homicide Rates: Incorporating Spatial Effects." *Criminology* 39:561–590.

Bellair, Paul E. 1997. "Social Interaction and Community Crime: Examining the Importance of Neighbor Networks." *Criminology* 35:677–703.

———. 2000. "Informal Surveillance and Street Crime: A Complex Relationship." *Criminology* 38:137–167.

Blau, Peter M., and Joseph E. Schwartz. 1984. *Crosscutting Social Circles: Testing a Macrostructural Theory of Intergroup Relations.* Orlando, FL: Academic.

Bursik, Robert J. 1988. "Social Disorganization and Theories of Crime and Delinquency: Problems and Prospects." *Criminology* 26:519–551.

———. 1989. "Political Decisionmaking and Ecological Models of Delinquency: Conflict and Consensus." Pp. 105–117 in *Theoretical Integration in the Study of Deviance and Crime,* ed. Steven Messner, Marvin Krohn, and Allen Liska. Albany: SUNY Press.

———. 1999. "The Informal Control of Crime through Neighborhood Networks." *Sociological Focus* 32:85–97.

Bursik, Robert J., and Harold G. Grasmick. 1992. "Longitudinal Neighborhood Profiles of Delinquency: The Decomposition of Change." *Journal of Quantitative Criminology* 8:247–264.

———. 1993. *Neighborhoods and Crime: The Dimensions of Effective Community Control.* New York: Lexington.

Bursik, Robert J., and Jim Webb. 1982. "Community Change and Patterns of Delinquency." *American Journal of Sociology* 88:24–42.

Chambliss, William J. 1999. *Power, Politics, and Crime.* Boulder, CO: Westview Press.

Chamlin, Mitchell B. 1989. "A Macro Social Analysis of the Change in Robbery and Homicide Rates: Controlling for Static and Dynamic Effects." *Sociological Focus* 22:275–286.

Cohen, Albert K. 1959. "The Study of Social Disorganization and Deviant Behavior." Pp. 461–484 in *Sociology Today,* ed. Robert K. Merton, L. Broom, and L. S. Cottrell. New York: Harper & Row.

Elliott, Delbert S., William Julius Wilson, David Huizinga, Robert J. Sampson, Amanda Elliott, and Bruce Rankin. 1996. "The Effects of Neighborhood Disadvantage on Adolescent Development." *Journal of Research in Crime and Delinquency* 33:389–426.

Faris, Robert E. Lee. 1967. *Chicago Sociology, 1920–1932.* San Francisco: Chandler Publishing.

Gans, Herbert. 1968. *People and Plans: Essays on Urban Problems and Solutions.* New York: Basic Books.

Guest, Avery. 2000. "Mediate Community: The Nature of Local and Extra-Local Ties in the Metropolis." *Urban Affairs Review* 36:603–627.

Janowitz, Morris. 1975. "Sociological Theory and Social Control." *American Journal of Sociology* 81:82–108.

Kasarda, John D., and Morris Janowitz. 1974. "Community Attachment in Mass Society." *American Sociological Review* 39:328–339.

Kornhauser, Ruth. 1978. *Social Sources of Delinquency*. Chicago: University of Chicago Press.

Kubrin, Charis E. 2000. "Racial Heterogeneity and Crime: Measuring Static and Dynamic Effects." Pp. 189–218 in *Research in Community Sociology, Vol. 10*, ed. Dan A. Chekki. Stamford, CT: JAI Press.

———. 2003. "Structural Covariates of Homicide Rates: Does Type of Homicide Matter?" *Journal of Research in Crime and Delinquency* 40:1–32.

Kubrin, Charis E., and Jerald R. Herting. 2003. "Neighborhood Correlates of Homicide Trends: An Analysis Using Growth-Curve Modeling." *Sociological Quarterly* 44:329–350.

Kubrin, Charis E., and Wadsworth, Tim 2003. "Identifying the Structural Correlates of African American Killings: What Can We Learn from Data Disaggregation?" *Homicide Studies* 7:3–35.

Kubrin, Charis E., and Ronald Weitzer. 2003a. "New Directions in Social Disorganization Theory." *Journal of Research in Crime and Delinquency* 40:374–402.

———. 2003b. "Retaliatory Homicide: Concentrated Disadvantage and Neighborhood Culture." *Social Problems* 50:157–180.

Liska, Allen E. 1987. "A Critical Examination of Macro Perspectives on Crime Control." *Annual Review of Sociology* 13:67–88.

Markowitz, Fred E., Paul E. Bellair, Allen E. Liska, and Jianhong Liu. 2001. "Extending Social Disorganization Theory: Modeling the Relationships between Cohesion, Disorder, and Fear." *Criminology* 39:293–319.

Miethe, Terance D., Michael Hughes, and David McDowall. 1991. "Social Change and Crime Rates: An Evaluation of Alternative Theoretical Approaches." *Social Forces* 70:165–185.

Morenoff, Jeffrey D., and Robert J. Sampson. 1997. "Violent Crime and the Spatial Dynamics of Neighborhood Transition: Chicago, 1970–1990." *Social Forces* 76:31–64.

Morenoff, Jeffrey D., Robert J. Sampson, and Stephen W. Raudenbush. 2001. "Neighborhood Inequality, Collective Efficacy, and the Spatial Dynamics of Urban Violence." *Criminology* 39:517–559.

Park, Robert E., and Ernest W. Burgess. 1925. "The Growth of the City: An Introduction to a Research Project." Chapter 2 in *The City*, by Robert E. Park, Ernest W. Burgess and Roderick D. McKenzie. Chicago: University of Chicago Press.

Paternoster, Raymond, and Ronet Bachman (Eds.). 2001. *Explaining Criminals and Crime*. Los Angeles: Roxbury Publishing.

Plant, James S. 1937. *Personality and the Cultural Pattern*. London: Oxford University Press.

Raudenbush, Stephen W., and Robert J. Sampson. 1999. "Ecometrics: Toward a Science of Assessing Ecological Settings, with Application to the Systematic Social Observation of Neighborhoods." *Sociological Methodology* 29:1–41.

Reiss, Albert J. Jr., and Michael Tonry. 1986. *Communities and Crime, Vol. 8, Crime and Justice: An Annual Review of Research*. Chicago: University of Chicago Press.

Rosenfeld, Richard, Timothy M. Bray, and Arlen Egley. 1999. "Facilitating Violence: A Comparison of Gang-Motivated, Gang-Affiliated, and Non-Gang Youth Homicides." *Journal of Quantitative Criminology* 15:495–516.

Sampson, Robert J. 1993. "Linking Time and Place: Dynamic Contextualism and the Future of Criminological Inquiry." *Journal of Research in Crime and Delinquency* 30:426–444.

———. 1997. "Collective Regulation of Adolescent Misbehavior: Validation Results from Eighty Chicago Neighborhoods." *Journal of Adolescent Research* 12:227–244.

———. 2001. "Crime and Public Safety: Insights from Community-Level Perspectives on Social Capital." Pp. 89–114 in *Social Capital and Poor Communities*, ed. Susan Saegert, Phillips J. Thompson, and Mark R. Warren. New York: Russell Sage.

Sampson, Robert J., and W. Byron Groves. 1989. "Community Structure and Crime: Testing Social-Disorganization Theory." *American Journal of Sociology* 94:774–802.

Sampson, Robert J., and Stephen W. Raudenbush. 1999. "Systematic Social Observation of Public Spaces: A New Look at Disorder in Urban Neighborhoods." *American Journal of Sociology* 105:603–651.

Sampson, Robert J., and William Julius Wilson. 1995. "Toward a Theory of Race, Crime and Urban Inequality." Pp. 37–54 in *Crime and Inequality*, ed. John Hagan and Ruth D. Peterson. Stanford, CA: Stanford University Press.

Sampson, Robert J., Stephen W. Raudenbush, and Felton Earls. 1997. "Neighborhoods and Violent Crime: A Multilevel Study of Collective Efficacy." *Science* 277:918–924.

Schmid, Calvin. 1928. *Suicides in Seattle, 1914 to 1928*. Seattle: University of Washington Press.

Shaw, Clifford R. 1930. *The Jackroller: A Delinquent Boy's Own Story*. Chicago: University of Chicago Press.

Shaw, Clifford R., and Henry McKay. 1969 [1942]. *Juvenile Delinquency and Urban Areas*. Chicago: University of Chicago Press.

Skogan, Wesley. 1986. "Fear of Crime and Neighborhood Change. Pp. 203–229 in *Crime and Justice, Vol. 8*, ed. Albert Reiss and Michael Tonry. Chicago: University of Chicago Press.

Stark, Rodney. 1987. "Deviant Places: A Theory of the Ecology of Crime." *Criminology* 25:893–909.

Stucky, Thomas D. 2003. "Local Politics and Violent Crimes in U.S. Cities." *Criminology* 41:1101–1132.

Sutherland, Edwin H. 1947. *Principles of Criminology*, 4th ed. Philadelphia: J.B. Lippincott.

Taylor, Ralph B. 2001. *Breaking Away from Broken Windows*. Boulder, CO: Westview Press.

Velez, Maria. 2001. "The Role of Public Social Control in Urban Neighborhoods." *Criminology* 39:837–863.

Warner, Barbara D., and Glenn L. Pierce. 1993. "Reexamining Social Disorganization Theory Using Calls to the Police as a Measure of Crime." *Criminology* 31:493–517.

Warner, Barbara D., and Pamela Wilcox Rountree. 1997. "Local Social Ties in a Community and Crime Model: Questioning the Systemic Nature of Informal Social Control." *Social Problems* 44:520–536.

Whyte, William F. 1943. *Street Corner Society: The Social Structure of an Italian Slum*. Chicago: University of Chicago Press.

5: Anomie and Strain Theories

Adler, Freda. 1995. "Synnomie to Anomie: A Macrosociological Formulation." Pp. 271–283 in *The Legacy of Anomie Theory*, ed. Freda Adler and William S. Laufer. New Brunswick, NJ: Transaction.

Agnew, Robert. 1985. "A Revised Strain Theory of Delinquency." *Social Forces* 64:151–167.

———. 1987. "On Testing Structural Strain Theories." *Journal of Research in Crime and Delinquency* 24:281–286.

———. 1989. "A Longitudinal Test of the Revised Strain Theory." *Journal of Quantitative Criminology* 5:373–387.

———. 1992. "Foundation for a General Strain Theory of Crime and Delinquency." *Criminology* 30:47–88.

———. 1995a. "Testing the Leading Crime Theories: An Alternative Strategy Focusing on Motivational Processes." *Journal of Research in Crime and Delinquency* 32:363–398.

———. 1995b. "Controlling Delinquency: Recommendations from General Strain Theory." Pp. 43–70 in *Crime and Public Policy: Putting Theory to Work*, ed. Hugh Barlow. Boulder, CO: Westview Press.

———. 1995c. "The Contribution of Social Psychological Strain Theory to the Explanation of Crime and Delinquency." Pp. 3–78 and 111–122 in *Advances in Criminological Theory, Vol. 6, The Legacy of Anomie*, ed. Freda Adler and William Laufer. New Brunswick, NJ: Transaction Press.

———. 1997. "The Nature and Determinants of Strain: Another Look at Durkheim and Merton." Pp. 27–51 in *The Future of Anomie Theory*, ed. Nikos Passas and Robert Agnew. Boston: Northeastern University Press.

———. 1999. "A General Theory of Community Differences in Crime Rates." *Journal of Research in Crime and Delinquency* 36(2):125–155.

———. 2001. "Building on the Foundation of General Strain Theory: Specifying the Types of Strain Most Likely to Lead to Crime and Delinquency." *Journal of Research in Crime and Delinquency* 38:319–361.

———. 2002. "Experienced, Vicarious, and Anticipated Strain: An Exploratory Study on Physical Victimization and Delinquency." *Justice Quarterly* 19(4):603–632.

———. 2006. *Pressured into Crime: An Overview of General Strain Theory*. Los Angeles: Roxbury.

Agnew, Robert, and Timothy Brezina. 1997. "Relational Problems with Peers, Gender, and Delinquency." *Youth and Society* 29(1):1–16.

Agnew, Robert, and Nikos Passas. 1997. "Introduction." Pp. 1–26 in *The Future of Anomie Theory*, ed. Nikos Passas and Robert Agnew. Boston: Northeastern University Press.

Agnew, Robert, and Helene Raskin White. 1992. "An Empirical Test of General Strain Theory." *Criminology* 30:475–500.

Agnew, Robert, Timothy Brezina, John Paul Wright, and Francis T. Cullen. 2002. "Strain, Personality Traits, and Delinquency: Extending General Strain Theory." *Criminology* 40:43–72.

Agnew, Robert, Francis Cullen, Velmer Burton, T. David Evans, and R. Gregory Dunaway. 1996. "A New Test of Classic Strain Theory." *Justice Quarterly* 13:681–704.

Aseltine, Robert H., Susan Gore, and Jennifer Gordon. 2000. "Life Stress, Anger and Anxiety, and Delinquency: An Empirical Test of General Strain Theory." *Journal of Health and Social Behavior* 41(3):256–275.

Bao, Wan-Ning, Ain Haas, and Yiiun Pi. 2004. "Life Strain, Negative Emotions, and Delinquency: An Empirical Test of General Strain Theory in the People's Republic of China." *International Journal of Offender Therapy and Comparative Criminology* 48(3):281–297.

Baron, Stephen W. 2004. "General Strain, Street Youth and Crime: A Test of Agnew's Revised Theory." *Criminology* 42(2):457–483.

Bellair, Paul E., and Vincent J. Roscigno. 2000. "Local Labor-Market Opportunity and Adolescent Delinquency." *Social Forces* 78(4):1509–1538.

Bellair, Paul E., Vincent J. Roscigno, and Thomas L. McNulty. 2003. "Linking Local Labor Market Opportunity to Violent Adolescent Delinquency." *Journal of Research in Crime and Delinquency* 40(1):6–33.

Benda, Brent B., and Robert Flynn Corwyn. 2002. "The Effect of Abuse in Childhood and in Adolescence on Violence among Adolescents." *Youth and Society* 33(3):339–365.

Bernard, Thomas J. 1984. "Control Criticisms of Strain Theories: An Assessment of Theoretical and Empirical Adequacy." *Journal of Research in Crime and Delinquency* 21(4):353–372.

———. 1987. "Testing Structural Strain Theories." *Journal of Research in Crime and Delinquency* 24:262–290.

———. 1990. "Angry Aggression among the 'Truly Disadvantaged'." *Criminology* 28:73–96.

———. 1995. "Merton versus Hirschi: Who Is Faithful to Durkheim's Heritage?" Pp. 81–90 in *The Legacy of Anomie Theory*, ed. Freda Adler and William S. Laufer. New Brunswick, NJ: Transaction.

Blau, Judith, and Peter Blau. 1982. "The Cost of Inequality: Metropolitan Structure and Violent Crime." *American Sociological Review* 147:114–129.

Bordua, David J. 1958. "Juvenile Delinquent and 'Anomie': An Attempt at a Replication." *Social Problems* 6(3):230–238.

Braithwaite, John. 1981. "The Myth of Social Class and Criminality Reconsidered." *American Sociological Review* 46:36–57.

Brezina, Timothy. 1996. "Adapting to Strain: An Examination of Delinquent Coping Responses." *Criminology* 34:39–60.

———. 1998. "Adolescent Maltreatment and Delinquency: The Question of Intervening Processes." *Journal of Research in Crime and Delinquency* 35:71–99.

———. 1999. "Teenage Violence toward Parents as an Adaption to Family Strain: Evidence from a National Survey of Male Adolescents." *Youth and Society* 30(4):416–444.

Brezina, Timothy, Alex R. Piquero, and Paul Mazerolle. 2001. "Student Anger and Aggressive Behavior in School: An Initial Test of Agnew's Macro-Level Strain Theory." *Journal of Research in Crime and Delinquency* 38(4):362–386.

Broidy, Lisa M. 2001. "A Test of General Strain Theory." *Criminology* 39:9–36.

Broidy, Lisa, and Robert Agnew. 1997. "Gender and Crime: A General Strain Theory Perspective." *Journal of Research in Crime and Delinquency* 34:275–305.

Burton, Velmer S., and Francis T. Cullen. 1992. "The Empirical Status of Strain Theory." *Journal of Crime and Justice* 15:1–30.

Burton, Velmer, and R. Gregory Dunaway. 1994. "Strain, Relative Deprivation, and Middle-Class Delinquency." Pp. 79–96 in *Varieties of Criminology: Readings from a Dynamic Discipline*, ed. Gregg Barak. Westport, CT: Praeger.

Burton, Velmer, Frances Cullen, David Evans, and R. Gregory Dunaway. 1994. "Reconsidering Strain Theory: Operationalization, Rival Theories, and Adult Criminality." *Journal of Quantitative Criminology* 10:213–239.

Capowich, George E., Paul Mazerolle, and Alex Piquero. 2001. "General Strain Theory, Situational Anger, and Social Networks: An Assessment of Conditioning Influences." *Journal of Criminal Justice* 29:445–461.

Cernkovich, Stephen, Peggy Giordano, and Jennifer Rudolph. 2000. "Race, Crime, and the American Dream." *Journal of Research in Crime and Delinquency* 37:131–170.

Chamlin, Mitchell, and John K. Cochran. 1995. "Assessing Messner and Rosenfeld's Institutional-Anomie Theory: A Partial Test." *Criminology* 33:411.

Chilton, Roland J. 1964. "Continuity in Delinquency Area Research: A Comparison of Studies for Baltimore, Detroit, and Indianapolis." *American Sociological Review* 29(1):71–83.

Cloward, Richard. 1959. "Illegitimate Means, Anomie, and Deviant Behavior." *American Sociological Review* 24:164–177.

Cloward, Richard, and Lloyd Ohlin. 1960. *Delinquency and Opportunity.* Glencoe, IL: Free Press.

Cohen, Albert K. 1955. *Delinquent Boys: The Culture of the Gang.* New York: Free Press.

Cole, Stephen, and Harriet Zuckerman. 1964. "Inventory of Empirical and Theoretical Studies of Anomie." Pp. 243–283 in *Anomie and Deviant Behavior: A Discussion and Critique*, ed. Marshall B. Clinard. New York: Free Press.

Colvin, Mark, and Francis T. Cullen. 2002. "Coercion, Social Support, and Crime: An Emerging Theoretical Consensus." *Criminology* 40(1):19–44.

Cullen, Francis T. 1983. *Rethinking Crime and Deviance Theory: The Emergence of a Structuring Tradition.* Totowa, NJ: Rowman and Allenheld.

———. 1988. "Were Cloward and Ohlin Strain Theorists?" *Journal of Research in Crime and Delinquency* 42:80–82.

Cullen, Francis T., and John Paul Wright. 1997. "Liberating the Anomie-Strain Paradigm: Implications from Social-Support Theory." Pp. 187–206 in *The Future of Anomie Theory*, ed. Nikos Passas and Robert Agnew. Boston: Northeastern University Press.

Daly, Martin, Margo Wilson, and Shawn Vasdev. 2001. "Income Inequality and Homicide Rates in Canada and the United States." *Canadian Journal of Criminology* (April):219–236.

DeCoster, Stacy, and Karen Heimer. 2001. "The Relationship between Law Violation and Depression: An Interactionist Analysis." *Criminology* 39(4):799–836.

Dunaway, Gregory R., Francis T. Cullen, Velmer S. Burton Jr., and T. David Evans. 2000. "The Myth of Social Class and Crime Revisited: An Examination of Class and Adult Criminality." *Criminology* 38:589–632.

Durkheim, Émile. 1933. *The Division of Labor in Society.* Glencoe, IL: Free Press.

———. 1951. *Suicide: A Study in Sociology.* Glencoe, IL: Free Press.

Eitle, David, and R. Jay Turner. 2002. "Exposure to Community Violence and Young Adult Crime: The Effects of Witnessing Violence, Traumatic Victimization, and Other Stressful Life Events." *Journal of Research in Crime and Delinquency* 39(2):214–237.

Eitle, David, Steven Gunkel, and Karen Van Gundy. 2004. "Cumulative Exposure to Stressful Life Events and Male Gang Membership." *Journal of Criminal Justice* 32:95–111.

Farnworth, Margaret, and Michael J. Leiber. 1989. "Strain Theory Revisited: Economic Goals, Educational Means, and Delinquency." *American Sociological Review* 54:263–274.

Fowles, Richard, and Mary Merva. 1996. "Wage Inequality and Criminal Activity: An Extreme Bounds Analysis for the United States, 1975–1990." *Criminology* 34(2):163–182.

Hannon, Lance, and James DeFronzo. 1998. "The Truly Disadvantaged, Public Assistance, and Crime." *Social Problems* 45(3):383–392.

Hirschi, Travis. 1969. *Causes of Delinquency*. Berkeley: University of California Press.

Hoffman, John P. 2002. "A Contextual Analysis of Differential Association, Social Control, and Strain Theories of Delinquency." *Social Forces* 81(3):753–785.

Hoffman, John P., and Felicia Gray Cerbone. 1999. "Stressful Life Events and Delinquency Escalation in Early Adolescence." *Criminology* 37(2):343–373.

Hoffman, John P., and Timothy Ireland. 1995. "Cloward and Ohlin's Strain Theory Reexamined: An Elaborated Theoretical Model." Pp. 247–270 in *The Legacy of Anomie Theory*, ed. Freda Adler and William S. Laufer. New Brunswick, NJ: Transaction.

———. 2004. "Strain and Opportunity Structures." *Journal of Quantitative Criminology* 20(3):263–292.

Hoffman, John P., and Alan S. Miller. 1998. "A Latent Variable Analysis of General Strain Theory." *Journal of Quantitative Criminology* 14:83–110.

Hoffman, John P., and S. Susan Su. 1997. "The Conditional Effects of Stress on Delinquency and Drug Use: A Strain Theory Assessment of Sex Differences." *Journal of Research in Crime and Delinquency* 34:46–78.

Ireland, Timothy O., Carolyn A. Smith, and Terence P. Thornberry. 2002. "Developmental Issues in the Impact of Child Maltreatment on Later Delinquency and Drug Use." *Criminology* 40(2):359–400.

Jarjoura, G. Roger, Ruth Triplett, and Gregory P. Binker. 2002. "Growing Up Poor: Examining the Link between Persistent Childhood Poverty and Delinquency." *Journal of Quantitative Criminology* 18(2):159–187.

Jang, Sung Joon, and Byron R. Johnson. 2003. "Strain, Negative Emotions, and Deviant Coping among African Americans: A Test of General Strain Theory." *Journal of Quantitative Criminology* 19(1):79–105.

Jensen, Gary F. 1995. "Salvaging Structure through Strain: A Theoretical and Empirical Critique." Pp. 139–158 in *Advances in Criminological Theory, Vol. 6: The Legacy of Anomie*, ed. Freda Adler and William S. Laufer. New Brunswick, NJ: Transaction.

Kelly, Morgan. 2000. "Inequality and Crime." *The Review of Economics and Statistics* 82(4):530–539.

Konty, Mark. 2005. "Microanomie: The Cognitive Foundations of the Relationship between Anomie and Deviance." *Criminology* 43(1):107–131.

Kornhauser, Ruth Rosner. 1978. *Social Sources of Delinquency*. Chicago: University of Chicago Press.

Kovandzic, Tomislav, Lynne M. Vieraitis, and Mark R. Yeisley. 1998. "The Structural Covariates of Urban Homicide: Reassessing the Impact of Income Inequality and Poverty in the Post Reagan Era." *Criminology* 36(3):569–599.

Krivo, Lauren J. 1996. "Extremely Disadvantaged Neighborhoods and Urban Crime." *Social Forces* 75(2):619–650.

Krivo, Lauren J., and Ruth D. Peterson. 2000. "The Structural Context of Homicide: Accounting for Racial Differences in Process." *American Sociological Review* 65(4):547–559.

LaFree, Gary, and Kriss A. Drass. 1996. "The Effect of Changes in Intraracial Income Inequality and Educational Attainment on Changes in Arrest Rates for African Americans and Whites 1957–1990." *American Sociological Review* 61:614–634.

Landers, Bernard. 1954. *Toward an Understanding of Juvenile Delinquency*. New York: Columbia University Press.

Lee, Matthew R., and William B. Bankston. 1999. "Political Structure, Economic Inequality, and Homicide: A Cross-National Analysis." *Deviant Behavior: An Interdisciplinary Journal* 19:27–55.

Lee, Matthew, Michael O. Maume, and Graham C. Ousey. 2003. "Social Isolation and Lethal Violence across the Metro/Nonmetro Divide: The Effects of Socioeconomic Disadvantage and Poverty Concentration on Homicide." *Rural Sociology* 68(1):107–131.

Maume, Michael, and Matthew R. Lee. 2003. "Social Institutions and Violence: A Sub-National Test of Institutional Anomie Theory." *Criminology* 41(4):1137–1172.

Mazerolle, Paul. 1998. "Gender, General Strain, and Delinquency: An Empirical Examination." *Justice Quarterly* 15:65–91.

Mazerolle, Paul, and Jeff Maahs. 2000. "General Strain and Delinquency: An Alternative Examination of Conditioning Influences." *Justice Quarterly* 17:753–778.

Mazerolle, Paul, and Alex Piquero. 1997. "Violent Responses to Strain: An Examination of Conditioning Influences." *Violence and Victimization* 12:323–345.

Mazerolle, Paul, Velmer Burton, Francis Cullen, T. David Evans, and Gary Payne. 2000. "Strain, Anger, and Delinquent Adaptations: Specifying General Strain Theory." *Journal of Criminal Justice* 28:89–101.

———. 1998. "Linking Exposure to Strain with Anger: An Investigation of Deviant Adaptations." *Journal of Criminal Justice* 26:195–211.

Mazerolle, Paul, Alex R. Piquero, and George E. Capowich. 2003. "Examining the Links between Strain, Situational and Dispositional Anger, and Crime." *Youth and Society* 35(2):131–157.

Menard, Scott. 1995. "A Developmental Test of Mertonian Anomie Theory." *Journal of Research in Crime and Delinquency* 32:136–174.

———. 1997. "A Developmental Test of Cloward's Differential-Opportunity Theory." Pp. 142–186 in *The Legacy of Anomie Theory*, ed. Freda Adler and William S. Laufer. New Brunswick, NJ: Transaction.

Merton, Robert K. 1938. "Social Structure and Anomie." *American Sociological Review* 3:672–682.

———. 1968. *Social Theory and Social Structure*. New York: The Free Press, a Division of Simon and Schuster.

Messner, Steven F. 1988. "Merton's 'Social Structure and Anomie': The Road Not Taken." *Deviant Behavior* 9:33–53.

Messner, Steven F., and Richard Rosenfeld. 1994. *Crime and the American Dream*. Belmont, CA: Wadsworth.

———. 1997a. *Crime and the American Dream*, 2nd ed. Belmont, CA: Wadsworth.

———. 1997b. "Political Restraint of the Market and Levels of Criminal Homicide: A Cross-National Application of Institutional-Anomie Theory," *Social Forces* 75:1393–1416.

———. 2001a. *Crime and the American Dream*, 3rd ed. Belmont, CA: Wadsworth.

———. 2001b. "An Institutional-Anomie Theory of Crime." Pp. 151–160 in *Explaining Criminals and Crime*, ed. Raymond Paternoster and Ronet Bachman. Los Angeles: Roxbury.

Messner, Steven F., Lawrence E. Raffalovich, and Richard McMillan. 2001. "Economic Deprivation and Changes in Homicide Arrest Rates for White and Black Youths, 1967–1998: A National Time Series Analysis." *Criminology* 39(3):591–613.

Messner, Steven F., Lawrence E. Raffalovich, and Peter Shrock. 2002. "Reassessing the Cross-National Relationship between Income Inequality and Homicide Rates: Implications of Data Quality Control in the Measurement of Income Distribution." *Journal of Quantitative Criminology* 18(4):377–395.

Messner, Steven F., Richard Rosenfeld, and Eric P. Baumer. 2004. "Dimensions of Social Capital and Rates of Criminal Homicide." *American Sociological Review* 69:882–903.

Parker, Karen F., and Patricia L. McCall. 1999. "Structural Conditions and Racial Homicide Patterns: A Look at the Multiple Disadvantges in Urban Areas." *Criminology* 37(3):447–477.

Passas, Nikos. 1997. "Anomie, Reference Groups, and Relative Deprivation." Pp. 62–94 in *The Future of Anomie Theory*, ed. Nikos Passas and Robert Agnew. Boston, MA: Northeastern University Press.

Passas, Nikos, and Robert Agnew (Eds.). 1997. *The Future of Anomie Theory*. Boston: Northeastern University Press.

Paternoster, Raymond, and Paul Mazerolle. 1994. "General Strain Theory and Delinquency: A Replication and Extension." *Journal of Research in Crime and Delinquency* 32:235–263.

Piquero, Nicole Leeper, and Miriam D. Sealock. 2000. "Generalizing General Strain Theory: An Examination of an Offending Population." *Justice Quarterly* 17:449–484.

———. 2004. "Gender and General Strain Theory: A Preliminary Test of Broidy and Agnews' Gender/GST Hypotheses." *Justice Quarterly* 21(1):125–158.

Pratt, Travis C., and Timothy W. Godsey. 2002. "Social Support and Homicide: A Cross-National Test of an Emerging Criminological Theory." *Journal of Criminal Justice* 30:589–601.

———. 2003. "Social Support, Inequality, and Homicide: A Cross-National Test of an Integrated Model." *Criminology* 41(3):611–643.

Raine, Adrian. 1993. *The Psychology of Crime: Criminal Behavior as a Clinical Disorder*. San Diego, CA: Academic Press.

Rosenfeld, Richard, Steven F. Messner, and Eric P. Baumer. 2001. "Social Capital and Homicide." *Social Forces* 80(1):283–309.

Savolainen, Jukka. 2000. "Inequality, Welfare State, and Homicide: Further Support for the Institutional Anomie Theory." *Criminology* 38:983–1020.

Shihadeh, Edward S., and Graham C. Ousey. 1998. "Industrial Restructuring and Violence: The Link between Entry-Level Jobs, Economic Deprivation, and Black and White Homicide." *Social Forces* 77(1):185–206.

Simons, Ronald L., Yi-Fu Chen, Eric A. Stewart, and Gene H. Broidy. 2003. "Incidents of Discrimination and Risk for Delinquency: A Longitudinal Test of Strain Theory with an African American Sample. *Justice Quarterly* 20(4):827–854.

Slocum, Lee Ann, Sally S. Simpson, and Douglas A. Smith. 2005. "Strained Lives and Crime: Examining Intra-Individual Variation in Strain and Offending in a Sample of Incarcerated Women." *Criminology* 43:1067–1110.

Tittle, Charles R. 1983. "Social Class and Criminal Behavior: A Critique of the Theoretical Foundation." *Social Forces* 62:334–358.

Tittle, Charles R., and Robert F. Meier. 1990. "Specifying the SES/Delinquency Relationship." *Criminology* 28:271–299.

Tittle, Charles R., and Wayne J. Villemez. 1977. "Social Class and Criminality." *Social Forces* 56:474–503.

Tittle, Charles R., Wayne J. Villemez, and Douglas A. Smith. 1978. "The Myth of Social Class and Criminality: An Empirical Assessment of the Empirical Evidence." *American Sociological Review* 43:643–656.

Warner, Barbara D., and Shannon K. Fowler. 2003. "Strain and Violence: Testing a General Strain Theory Model of Community Violence." *Journal of Criminal Justice* 31:511–521.

Wright, Bradley R. Enter, Avshalom Caspi, Terrie E. Moffitt, and Phil A. Silva. 1999. "Low Self-Control, Social Bonds, and Crime: Social Causation, Social Selection, or Both?" *Criminology* 37:479–514.

6: Social Learning Theories

Agnew, Robert. 1991. "The Interactive Effects of Peer Variables on Delinquency." *Criminology* 29:47–62.

———. 1994. "The Techniques of Neutralization and Violence." *Criminology* 30:555–580.

Akers, Ronald L. 1973. *Deviant Behavior: A Social Learning Approach*. Belmont, CA: Wadsworth.

———. 1985. *Deviant Behavior: A Social Learning Approach*, 3rd ed. Belmont, CA: Wadsworth. Reprinted 1992. Fairfax, VA: Techbooks.

———. 1998. *Social Learning and Social Structure: A General Theory of Crime and Deviance*. Boston: Northeastern University Press.

Akers, Ronald L., and John K. Cochran. 1985. "Adolescent Marijuana Use: A Test of Three Theories of Deviant Behavior." *Deviant Behavior* 6:323–346.

Akers, Ronald L., and Gang Lee. 1996. "A Longitudinal Test of Social Learning Theory: Adolescent Smoking." *Journal of Drug Issues* 26:317–343.

———. 1999. "Age, Social Learning, and Social Bonding in Adolescent Substance Abuse." *Deviant Behavior: An Interdisciplinary Journal* 19:1–25.

Akers, Ronald L., and Christine Sellers. 2004. *Criminological Theories: Introduction, Evaluation, and Application*. Los Angeles, CA: Roxbury Publishing.

Akers, Ronald L., Marvin D. Krohn, Lonn Lanza-Kaduce, and Marcia Radosevich. 1979. "Social Learning and Deviant Behavior: A Specific Test of a General Theory." *American Sociological Review* 44:635–655.

Akers, Ronald L., Anthony J. La Greca, John Cochran, and Christine Sellers. 1989. "Social Learning Theory and Alcohol Behavior among the Elderly." *Sociological Quarterly* 30:625–638.

Alarid, Leanne Fiftal, Velmer S. Burton Jr., and Francis T. Cullen. 2000. "Gender and Crime among Felony Offenders: Assessing the Control and Differential Association Theories." *Journal of Research in Crime and Delinquency* 37:171–199.

Anderson, Elijah. 1999. *Code of the Street: Decency, Violence, and the Moral Life of the Inner City*. New York: W.W. Norton

Andrews, D. A. 1980. "Some Experimental Investigations of the Principals of Differential Association through Deliberate Manipulations of the Structure of Service Systems." *American Sociological Review* 45:448–462.

Ardelt, Monika, and Laurie Day. 2002. "Parents, Siblings, and Peers: Close Social Relationships and Adolescent Deviance." *Journal of Early Adolescence* 22:310–349.

Aseltine, Robert H. Jr. 1995. "A Reconsideration of Parental and Peer Influences on Adolescent Behavior." *Journal of Health and Social Behavior* 36:103–121.

Ball, Richard A. 1968. "An Empirical Exploration of Neutralization Theory." Pp. 255–265 in *Approaches to Deviance*, ed. Mark Lefton, James E. Skipper, and Charles H. McCaghy. New York: Appleton-Century-Crofts.

Becker, Howard S. 1953. "On Becoming a Marijuana User." *American Journal of Sociology* 59:235–242.

Benda, Brent B. 1994. "Testing Competing Theoretical Concepts: Adolescent Alcohol Consumption." *Deviant Behavior* 15:375–396.

Brezina, Timothy, and Alex R. Piquero. 2003. "Exploring the Relationship between Social and Non-Social Reinforcement in the Context of Social Learning Theory." Pp. 265–288 in *Social Learning Theory and the Explanation of Crime*, ed. Ronald L. Akers and Gary F. Jensen. New Brunswick, NJ: Transaction Publishers.

Briar, Scott, and Irving Piliavin. 1965. "Delinquency, Situational Inducements, and Commitment to Conformity." *Social Problems* 13:35–45.

Brownfield, David. 2003. "Differential Association and Gang Membership." *Journal of Gang Research* 11:1–12.

Bruinsma, Gerben J. N. 1992. "Differential Association Theory Reconsidered: An Extension and Its Empirical Test." *Journal of Quantitative Criminology* 8:175–187.

Burgess, Robert, and Ronald Akers. 1966. "A Differential Association Reinforcement Theory of Criminal Behavior." *Social Problems* 14:128–147.

Cernkovich, Stephan A., and Peggy C. Giordano. 1987. "Family Relationships and Delinquency." *Criminology* 25:295–321.

Chappell, Allison T., and Alex R. Piquero. 2004. "Applying Social Learning Theory to Police Misconduct." *Deviant Behavior* 25:89–108.

Cloward, Richard, and Lloyd Ohlin. 1960. *Delinquency and Opportunity: A Theory of Delinquent Gangs*. New York: Free Press.

Cohen, Albert K. 1955. *Delinquent Boys: The Culture of the Gang*. New York: Free Press.

Cohen, Albert, Alfred Lindesmith, and Carl Schuessler. 1956. *The Sutherland Papers*. Bloomington: Indiana University Press.

Conger, Rand. 1976. "Social Control and Social Learning Models of Delinquency: A Synthesis." *Criminology* 14:17–40.

Costello, Barbara J., and Paul R. Vowell. 1999. "Testing Control Theory and Differential Association: A Reanalysis of the Richmond Youth Project Data." *Criminology* 37:815–843.

Cressey, Donald. 1952. "Application and Verification of the Differential Association Theory." *Journal of Criminal Law, Criminology, and Police Science* 43:43–52.

Dabney, Dean. 1995. "Neutralization and Deviance in the Workplace: Theft of Supplies and Medicines by Hospital Nurses." *Deviant Behavior* 16:313–331.

DeCoster, Stacey. 2003. "Delinquency and Depression: A Gendered Role-Taking and Social Learning Perspective." Pp. 129–150 in *Social Learning Theory and the Explanation of Crime*, ed. Ronald L. Akers and Gary F. Jensen. New Brunswick, NJ: Transaction Publishers.

Dull, R. Thomas. 1983. "Friends' Use and Adult Drug and Drinking Behavior: A Further Test of Differential Association Theory." *Journal of Criminal Law and Criminology* 74:1608–1619.

Elliott, Delbert, and Susan S. Ageton. 1980. "Reconciling Race and Class Differences in Self Reported and Official Estimates of Delinquency." *American Sociological Review* 45:95–110.

Erickson, Kristan G., Robert Crosnoe, and Sanford M. Dornbusch. 2000. "A Social Process Model of Adolescent Deviance: Combining Social Control and Differential Association Perspectives." *Journal of Youth and Adolescence* 29:395–425.

Glaser, Daniel. 1960. "Differential Association and Criminological Prediction." *Social Problems* 8:6–14.

Glueck, Sheldon, and Eleanor Glueck. 1950. *Unraveling Juvenile Delinquency*. Cambridge, MA: Harvard University Press.

Gottfredson, Michael, and Travis Hirschi. 1990. *A General Theory of Crime*. Stanford, CA: Stanford University Press.

Griffin, Brenda S., and Charles T. Griffin. 1978. "Drug Use and Differential Association." *Drug Forum* 7:1–8.

Hayes, Hennessey D. 1997. "Using Integrated Theory to Explain the Movement into Juvenile Delinquency." *Deviant Behavior* 18:161–184.

Haynie, Dana L. 2001. "Delinquent Peers Revisited: Does Network Structure Matter?" *American Journal of Sociology* 106:1013–1057.

———. 2002. "Friendship Networks and Delinquency: The Relative Nature of Peer Delinquency." *Journal of Quantitative Criminology* 18:99–134.

Haynie, Dana L., and Danielle C. Payne. 2006. "Race, Friendship Networks, and Violent Delinquency." *Criminology* 44:775–805.

Heider, Fritz. 1958. *The Psychology of Interpersonal Relations*. New York: Wiley.

Heimer, Karen. 1997. "Socio-Economic Status, Subcultural Definitions, and Violent Delinquency." *Social Forces* 75:799–833.

Heimer, Karen, and Ross Matsueda. 1994. "Role-Taking, Role-Commitment, and Delinquency: A Theory of Differential Social Control." *American Sociological Review* 59:365–390.

Heimer, Karen, and Stacey DeCoster. 1999. "The Gendering of Violent Delinquency." *Criminology* 37:277–317.

Hirschi, Travis, and Michael Gottfredson. 1983. "Age and the Explanation of Crime." *Journal of Research in Crime and Delinquency* 30:47–54.

Hochstetler, Andy, Heith Copes, and Matt DeLisi. 2002. "Differential Association in Group and Solo Offending." *Journal of Criminal Justice* 30:559–566.

Hollinger, Richard C. 1991. "Neutralizing in the Workplace: An Empirical Analysis of Property Theft and Production Deviance." *Deviant Behavior* 12:169–202.

Huizinga, David, Ann Weiher, and Finn-Aage Esbensen. 1992. "Intergenerational Transmission of Delinquency and Drug Use." Prepared for the meeting of the Society for Research on Adolescence, Washington, DC.

Jackson, Elton F., Charles R. Tittle, and Mary Jean Burke. 1986. "Offense-Specific Models of the Differential Association Process." *Social Problems* 33:335–356.

Jeffery, C. Ray. 1965. "Criminal Behavior and Learning Theory." *Journal of Criminal Law, Criminology, and Police Science* 56:294–300.

Jensen, Gary F. 1972. "Parents, Peers, and Delinquent Action: A Test of the Differential Association Perspective." *American Journal of Sociology* 78:562–575.

Johnson, Richard E., Anastasios C. Marcos, and Stephen J. Bahr. 1987. "The Role of Peers in the Complex Etiology of Adolescent Drug Use." *Criminology* 25:323–340.

Jussim, Lee, and D. Wayne Osgood. 1989. "Influence and Similarity among Friends: An Integrative Model Applied to Incarcerated Adolescents." *Social Psychology Quarterly* 52:98–112.

Kandel, Denise B. 1978. "Homophily, Selection, and Socialization in Adolescent Friendships." *American Journal of Sociology* 84:427–436.

Krohn, Marvin D. 1999. "Social Learning Theory: The Continuing Development of a Perspective." *Theoretical Criminology* 3:462–476.

Krohn, Marvin D., Alan J. Lizotte, Terence P. Thornberry, Carolyn Smith, and David McDowall. 1996. "Reciprocal Causal Relationships among Drug Use, Peers, and Beliefs: A Five-Wave Panel Model." *Journal of Drug Issues* 26:405–428.

Krohn, Marvin D., William Skinner, James L. Massey, and Ronald Akers. 1985. "Social Learning Theory and Adolescent Cigarette Smoking: A Longitudinal Study." *Social Problems* 32:455–473.

Lanza-Kaduce, Lonn, and Michael Capece. 2003. "Social Structure-Social Learning (SSSL) and Binge Drinking: A Specific Test of an Integrated General Theory." Pp. 179–196 in *Social Learning Theory and the Explanation of Crime: A Guide for the New Century. Advances in Criminological Theory, Vol. 11*, ed. Ronald Akers and Gary F. Jensen. New Brunswick, NJ: Transaction Publishers.

Laub, John H., and Robert J. Sampson. 2003. *Shared Beginnings, Divergent Lives: Delinquent Boys to Age 70.* Cambridge, MA: Harvard University Press.

Lo, Celia C. 2000. "The Impact of First Drinking and Differential Association on Collegiate Drinking." *Sociological Focus* 33:265–280.

Marcos, Anastasios C., Stephen J. Bahr, and Richard E. Johnson. 1986. "Test of a Bonding/Association Theory of Adolescent Drug Use." *Social Forces* 65:135–161.

Massey, James L., and Marvin D. Krohn. 1986. "A Longitudinal Examination of an Integrated Social Process Model of Deviant Behavior." *Social Forces* 65:106–134.

Matsueda, Ross L. 1982. "Testing Control Theory and Differential Association." *American Sociological Review* 47:489–504.

———. 1988. "The Current State of Differential Association." *Crime and Delinquency* 34:277–306.

Matsueda, Ross L., and Kathleen Anderson. 1998. "The Dynamics of Delinquent Peers and Delinquent Behavior." *Criminology* 36:269–309.

Matsueda, Ross L., and Karen Heimer. 1987. "Race, Family Structure, and Delinquency: A Test of Differential Association and Social Control Theories." *American Sociological Review* 52:826–840.

Mazerolle, Paul. 1998. "Gender, General Strain, and Delinquency: An Empirical Examination." *Justice Quarterly* 15:65–91.

McCarthy, Bill. 1996. "The Attitudes and Actions of Others: Tutelage and Sutherland's Theory of Differential Association." *The British Journal of Criminology* 36:135–147.

McCord, Joan. 1991. "Family Relationships, Juvenile Delinquency, and Adult Criminality." *Criminology* 29:397–418.

Mears, Daniel, Matthew Ploeger, and Mark Warr. 1998. "Explaining the Gender Gap in Delinquency: Peer Influence and Moral Evaluations of Behavior." *Journal of Research in Crime and Delinquency* 35:251–266.

Miller, Walter B. 1958. "Lower Class Culture as a Generating Milieu of Gang Delinquency." *Journal of Social Issues* 14:5–19.

Miller, William J., and Rick A. Matthews. 2001. "Youth Employment, Differential Association, and Juvenile Delinquency." *Sociological Focus* 34:251–268.

Minor, W. William. 1980. "The Neutralization of Criminal Offense." *Criminology* 18:103–120.

———. 1981. "Techniques of Neutralization: A Reconceptualization and Empirical Examination." *Journal of Research in Crime and Delinquency* 18:295–318.

———. 1984. "Neutralization as a Hardening Process: Consideration in the Modeling of Change." *Social Forces* 62:995–1019.

Morash, Merry. 1999. "A Consideration of Gender in Relation to Social Learning and Social Structure: A General Theory of Crime and Deviance." *Theoretical Criminology* 3(4):451–462.

Orcutt, James D. 1983. *Analyzing Deviance*. Homewood, IL: Dorsey.

———. 1987. "Differential Association and Marijuana Use: A Closer Look at Sutherland (with a Little Help from Becker)." *Criminology* 25:341–358.

Poole, Eric D., and Robert Regoli. 1979. "Parental Support, Delinquent Friends, and Delinquency: A Test of Interaction Effects." *Journal of Criminal Law and Criminology* 70:188–193.

Reed, Mark D., and Pamela Wilcox Rountree. 1997. "Peer Pressure and Adolescent Substance Use." *Journal of Quantitative Criminology* 13:143–181.

Sampson, Robert J. 1999. "Techniques of Research Neutralization." *Theoretical Criminology* 3(4):438–451.

Sampson, Robert J., and John H. Laub. 1993. *Crime in the Making: Pathways and Turning Points through Life*. Cambridge, MA: Harvard University Press.

Scully, Diana, and Joseph Moralla. 1984. "Convicted Rapists' Vocabulary of Motives: Excuses and Justifications." *Social Problems* 31:530–544.

Sellers, Christine S., and Thomas L. Winfree. 1990. "Differential Associations and Definitions: A Panel Study of Youthful Drinking Behavior." *International Journal of the Addictions* 25:755–771.

Sherif, Muzafer, and Carl Iver Hovland. 1961. *Social Judgment: Assimilation and Contrast Effects in Communication and Attitude Change*. New Haven, CT: Yale University Press.

Short, James F. 1957. "Differential Association and Delinquency." *Social Problems* 4:233–239.

———. 1958. "Differential Association with Delinquent Friends and Delinquent Behavior." *Pacific Sociological Review* 1:20–25.

Skinner, William F., and Anne M. Fream. 1997. "A Social Learning Theory Analysis of Computer Crime among College Students." *Journal of Research in Crime and Delinquency* 34:495–518.

Stafford, Mark C., and Sheldon Ekland-Olson. 1982. "On Social Control and Deviant Behavior: A Reappraisal of the Findings." *American Sociological Review* 47:167–169.

Strickland, Donald E. 1982. "Social Learning and Deviant Behavior: A Specific Test of a General Theory: A Comment and Critique." *American Sociological Review* 47:162–167.

Sutherland, Edwin H. 1937. *The Professional Thief*. Chicago: University of Chicago Press.

———. 1940. "White Collar Criminality." *American Sociological Review* 5:1–12.

———. 1947. *Principles of Criminology*, 4th ed. Philadelphia: J.B. Lippincott.

———. 1949. *White-Collar Crime*. New York: Holt, Rinehart, and Winston.

Sutherland, Edwin H., and Donald R. Cressey. 1955. *Principles of Criminology*, 5th ed. Philadelphia: J.B. Lippincott.

Sutherland, Edwin H., Donald R. Cressey, and David F. Luckenbill. 1992. *Principles of Criminology*, 11th ed. Philadelphia: J.B. Lippincott.

Sykes, Gresham, and David Matza. 1957. "Techniques of Neutralization: A Theory of Delinquency." *American Sociological Review* 22:664–670.

Thornberry, Terence P. 1987. "Toward an Interactional Theory of Delinquency." *Criminology* 25:863–891.

Thornberry, Terence P., and Marvin D. Krohn. 1997. "Peers, Drug Use, and Delinquency." Pp. 218–233 in *Handbook of Antisocial Behavior*, ed. David M. Stoff, James Breilig, and Jack D. Maser. New York: John Wiley and Sons.

Thornberry, Terence P., Marvin D. Krohn, Alan J. Lizotte, Carolyn A. Smith, and Kimberly Tobin. 2003. *Gangs and Delinquency in Developmental Perspective*. New York: Cambridge University Press.

Thornberry, Terence P., Alan J. Lizotte, Marvin D. Krohn, Margaret Farnworth, and Sung Joon Jang. 1994. "Delinquent Peers, Beliefs, and Delinquent Behavior: A Longitudinal Test of Interactional Theory." *Criminology* 32:47–83.

Tittle, Charles R., Mary Jean Burke, and Elton F. Jackson. 1986. "Modeling Sutherland's Theory of Differential Association: Toward an Empirical Clarification." *Social Forces* 65:405–432.

Vold, George B., Thomas J. Bernard, and Jeffrey B. Snipes. 1998. *Theoretical Criminology*. New York: Oxford University Press.

Vowell, Paul R., and Jieming Chen. 2004. "Predicting Academic Misconduct: A Comparative Test of Four Sociological Explanations." *Sociological Inquiry*. 74:226–249.

Warr, Mark. 1993a. "Parents, Peers, and Delinquency." *Social Forces* 72:247–264.

———. 1993b. "Age, Peers, and Delinquency." *Criminology* 31:17–40.

Warr, Mark. 2002. *Companions in Crime: The Social Aspects of Criminal Conduct*. Cambridge: Cambridge University Press.

Warr, Mark, and Mark Stafford. 1991. "The Influence of Delinquent Peers: What They Think or What They Do?" *Criminology* 4:851–866.

Winfree, L. Thomas Jr., G. Larry Mays, and Teresa Vigil-Backstrom. 1994. "Youth Gangs and Incarcerated Delinquents: Exploring the Ties between Gang Membership, Delinquency and Social Learning Theory." *Justice Quarterly* 11:229–256.

Winfree, L. Thomas Jr., Teresa Vigil-Backstrom, and G. Larry Mays. 1994. "Social Learning Theory, Self-Reported Delinquency, and Youth Gangs: A New Twist on a General Theory of Crime and Delinquency." *Youth & Society* 26:147–177.

Wood, Peter B., John K. Cochran, Betty Pfefferbaum, and Bruce J. Arneklev. 1995. "Sensation-Seeking and Delinquent Substance Use: An Extension of Learning Theory." *Journal of Drug Issues* 25:173–193.

Wood, Peter, Walter Grove, James A. Wilson, and John Cochran. 1997. "Nonsocial Reinforcement and Habitual Criminal Conduct: An Extension of Learning Theory." *Criminology* 35:335–366.

Zhang, Lening, and Steven F. Messner. 1995. "Family Deviance and Delinquency in China." *Criminology* 33:359–388.

———. 2000. "The Effects of Alternative Measures of Delinquent Peers on Self-Reported Delinquency." *Journal of Research in Crime and Delinquency* 37:323–337.

7: Control Theories

Achenbach, T. M. 1991. *Manual for the Child Behavior Checklist/4-18 and 1991 Profile*. Burlington: University of Vermont.

———. 1992. *Manual for the Child Behavior Checklist/2-3 and 1992 Profile*. Burlington: University of Vermont.

Agnew, Robert. 1985. "Social Control and Delinquency: A Longitudinal Test." *Criminology* 23:47–61.

———. 1991. "A Longitudinal Test of Social Control Theory and Delinquency." *Journal of Research in Crime and Delinquency* 28:126–156.

Benda, Brent B. 2005. "The Robustness of Self-Control in Relation to Form of Delinquency." *Youth & Society* 36(4):418–444.

Burkett, Steven R., and Bruce O. Warren. 1987. "Religiosity, Peer Association, and Adolescent Marijuana Use: A Panel Study of Underlying Causal Structures." *Criminology* 25(1):109–132.

Cernkovich, Stephen A., and Peggy C. Giordano. 1992. "School Bonding, Race, and Delinquency." *Criminology* 30:261–291.

Chapple, Constance L. 2005. "Self-Control, Peer Relations, and Delinquency." *Justice Quarterly* 22(1):89–106.

Chard-Wierschem, Deborah J. 1998. *In Pursuit of the "True" Relationship: A Longitudinal Study of the Effects of Religiosity on Delinquency and Substance Use.* Unpublished doctoral dissertation, Albany, State University of New York.

Conger, Rand D., Lora E. Wallace, Yumei Sun, Ronald L. Simons, Vonnie C. McLoyd, and Gene H. Brody. 2002. "Economic Pressure in African American Families: A Replication and Extension of the Family Stress Model. *Developmental Psychology* 38(2):179–193.

Durkheim, Emile. 1951. "Anomic Suicide." Pp. 241–276 in *Suicide.* New York: The Free Press.

Elliott, Delbert S., David Huizinga, and Susan Ageton. 1985. *Explaining Delinquency and Drug Use.* Beverly Hills, CA: Sage Publications.

Gibson, Chris, Christopher J. Schreck, and J. Mitchell Miller. 2004. "Binge Drinking and Negative Alcohol-Related Behaviors: A Test of Self-Control Theory." *Journal of Criminal Justice* 32(5):411–420.

Glueck S., and Glueck, E. 1950. *Unraveling Juvenile Delinquency.* New York: The Commonwealth Fund.

Gottfredson, Michael R., and Travis Hirschi. 1990. *A General Theory of Crime.* Stanford, CA: Stanford University Press.

Grasmick, Harold G., Charles R. Tittle, Robert J. Bursik Jr., and Bruce J. Arneklev. 1993. "Testing the Core Empirical Implications of Gottfredson and Hirschi's General Theory of Crime." *Journal of Research in Crime and Delinquency* 30(1):5–29.

Hirschi, Travis. 1969. *Causes of Delinquency.* Berkeley: University of California Press.

Hirschi, Travis, and Michael Gottfredson. 1993. "Commentary: Testing the General Theory of Crime." *Journal of Research in Crime and Delinquency* 30(1):47–54.

Hudson, Walter. 1982. *The Clinical Measurement Package: A Field Manual.* Homewood, IL: Dorsey Press.

Jones, Shayne, and Neil Quisenberry. 2004. "The General Theory of Crime: How General Is It?" *Deviant Behavior* 25:401–426.

Kandel, D. B., and K. Yamaguchi. 1987. "Job Mobility and Drug Use: An Event History Analysis." *American Journal of Sociology* 92:836–878.

Keane, Carl, Paul S. Maxim, and James J. Teevan. 1993. "Drinking and Driving, Self-Control and Gender: Testing a General Theory of Crime." *Journal of Research in Crime and Delinquency* 30:30–46.

Kempf, Kimberly L. 1993. "The Empirical Status of Social Control Theory." Pp. 143–185 in ed. Freda Adler and William S. Laufer. *New Directions in Criminological Theory, Vol. 4,* New Brunswick, NJ: Transaction.

Kornhauser, Ruth R. 1978. *Social Sources of Delinquency: An Appraisal of Analytic Models.* Chicago: University of Chicago Press.

Krohn, Marvin D., and James L. Massey. 1980. "Social Control and Delinquent Behavior: An Examination of the Elements of the Social Bond." *Sociological Quarterly* 21:529–543.

Krohn, Marvin D., Terence P. Thornberry, Lori Collins-Hall, and Alan J. Lizotte. 1995. "School Dropout, Delinquent Behavior, and Drug Use: An Examination of the

Causes and Consequences of Dropping Out of School. Pp. 163–183 in *Drugs, Crime, and Other Deviant Adaptations: Longitudinal Studies*, ed. Howard B. Kaplan. New York: Plenum Press.

Krohn, Marvin D., Terence P. Thornberry, Craig Rivera, and Marc LeBlanc. 2001. "Later Delinquency Careers. Pp. 67–93 in *Child Delinquents: Development, Intervention, and Service Needs*, ed. Rolf Loeber and David P. Farrington. Thousand Oaks, CA: Sage.

LaGrange, Randy L., and Helene R. White. 1985. "Age Difference in Delinquency: A Test of Theory." *Criminology* 23(1):19–46.

Laub, John H, and Robert J. Sampson. 2003. *Shared Beginnings, Divergent Lives: Delinquent Boys to Age 70*. Cambridge: Harvard University Press.

Longshore, Douglas, Eunice Chang, and Nena Messina. 2005. "Self-Control and Social Bonds: A Combined Control Perspective on Juvenile Offending." *Journal of Quantitative Criminology* 21(4):419–437.

Maddox, Samuel J., and Ronald J. Prinz. 2003. "School Bonding in Children and Adolescents: Conceptualization, Assessment, and Associated Variables." *Clinical Child and Family Psychology Review* 6:31–49.

Marcos, Anastasios C., Stephen J. Bahr, and Richard E. Johnson. 1986. "Test of a Bonding/Association Theory of Adolescent Drug Use." *Social Forces* 65(1):135–161.

Massey, James L., and Marvin D. Krohn. 1986. "A Longitudinal Examination of an Integrated Social Process Model of Deviant Behavior." *Social Forces* 65:106–134.

McCarthy, John D., and Dean R. Hoge. 1984. "The Dynamics of Self-Esteem and Delinquency." *American Journal of Sociology* 90(2):396–410.

Nye, F. Ivan. 1958. *Family Relationships and Delinquent Behavior*. New York: John Wiley.

Paternoster, Raymond. 1988. "Criminology: Examining Three-Wave Deterrence Models: A Question of Temporal Order and Specification." *The Journal of Criminal Law & Criminology* 79(1):135–179.

Paternoster, Raymond, and Leeann Iovanni. 1986. "The Deterrent Effect of Perceived Severity: A Reexamination." *Social Forces* 64(3):751–777.

Pratt, T. C., and F. T. Cullen. 2000. "The Empirical Status of Gottfredson and Hirschi's General Theory of Crime: A Meta-Analysis." *Criminology* 38:931–964.

Province of Ontario, Interministerial Committee on Drinking Driving. 1988. *The 1986 Ontario Survey of Night-Time Drivers—Summary Report*. Downsview, Canada: Ministry of Transportation.

Reckless, Walter C. 1961. *The Crime Problem*, 3rd ed. New York: Appleton-Century-Crofts.

Reiss, Albert J. 1951. "Delinquency as the Failure of Personal and Social Control." *American Sociological Review* 16:196–207.

Sampson, Robert J., and John H. Laub. 1993. *Crime in the Making: Pathways and Turning Points Through Life*. Cambridge, MA: Harvard University Press.

Simons, Ronald L., Eric A. Stewart, Leslie Gordon, Rand D. Conger, and Glen H. Elder. 2002. "Explaining Stability and Change in Antisocial Behavior from Adolescence to Young Adulthood." *Criminology* 40:401–434.

Smith, C. A., and M. D. Krohn. 1995. "Delinquency and Family Life among Male Adolescents: The Role of Ethnicity." *Journal of Youth and Adolescence* 24:69–93.

Smith, Carolyn, Anne W. Weiher, and Welmoet B. Van Kammen. 1991. "Family Attachment and Delinquency." Pp. 8.1–8.28 in *Urban Delinquency and Substance Abuse: Technical Report*, Vol. 1, ed. David Huizinga, Rolf Loeber, and Terence P. Thornberry. Washington, DC: Program of Research on the Causes and Correlates of Delinquency, The Office of Juvenile Justice and Delinquency Prevention, U.S. Department of Justice.

Stewart, Eric A., and Ronald L. Simons. 2006. "Structure and Culture in African-American Adolescent Violence: A Partial Test of the Code of the Street Thesis." *Justice Quarterly* 23:1–33.

Stewart, Eric A., Ronald L. Simons, and Rand D. Conger. 2002. "Assessing Neighborhood and Social Psychological Influences on Childhood Violence in an African American Sample." *Criminology* 40:801–830.

Stewart, Eric A., Ronald L. Simons, Rand D. Conger, and Laura V. Scaramella. 2002. "Beyond the Interactional Relationship between Delinquency and Parenting Practices: The Contribution of Legal Sanctions." *Journal of Research in Crime and Delinquency* 39:36–59.

Sykes, Gresham M., and David Matza. 1957. "Techniques of Neutralization: A Theory of Delinquency." *American Sociological Review* 22(6):664–670.

Thornberry, Terence P., Alan J. Lizotte, Marvin D. Krohn, Margaret Farnworth, and Sung Joon Jang. 1991. "Testing Interactional Theory: An Examination of Reciprocal Causal Relationships among Family, School, and Delinquency." *The Journal of Criminal Law and Criminology* 82:3–35.

Tittle, Charles R., David A. Ward, and Harold G. Grasmick. 2003. "Gender, Age, and Crime/Deviance: A Challenge to Self-Control Theory." *Journal of Research in Crime & Delinquency* 40(4):426–453.

Warr, Mark. 2002. *Companions in Crime: The Social Aspects of Criminal Conduct.* New York: Cambridge University Press.

Wiatrowski, Michael D., David B. Griswold, and Mary K. Roberts. 1981. "Social Control Theory and Delinquency." *American Sociological Review*, 46(5):525–541.

Winfree, L. Thomas, and Francis P. Bernat. 1998. Social Learning, Self-Control, and Substance Abuse by Eighth Grade Students: A Tale of Two Cities." *Journal of Drug Issues* 28(2):539–558.

Wright, Bradley R. E., Avshalom Caspi, Terry E. Moffitt, and Phil A. Silva. 1999. "Low Self-Control, Social Bonds, and Crime: Social Causation, Social Selection, or Both?" *Criminology* 37(3):479–514.

Yamaguchi, Kazuo, and Denise B. Kandel. 1985. "On the Resolution of Role Incompatibility: A Life Event History Analysis of Family Roles and Marijuana Use." *American Journal of Sociology* 90:1284–1325.

8: Labeling Theory

Adams, Mike S., Craig T. Robertson, Phyllis Gray-Ray, and Melvin C. Ray. 2003. "Labeling and Delinquency." *Adolescence* 38:171–186.

Adler, Freda, Gerhard O. W. Mueller, and William S. Laufer. 1991. *Criminology.* New York: McGraw-Hill.

Ageton, Suzanne, and Delbert S. Elliott. 1974. "The Effects of Legal Processing on Delinquent Orientation." *Social Problems* 22:87–100.

Akers, Ronald L. 1968. "Problems in the Sociology of Deviance." *Social Forces* 46:455–465.

Akers, Ronald L. 1994. *Criminological Theories: Introduction and Evaluation.* Los Angeles, CA: Roxbury.

Akers, Ronald L., and Christine S. Sellers. 2004. *Criminological Theories: Introduction, Evaluation, and Application,* 4th ed. Los Angeles, CA: Roxbury.

Aultman, Madeline, and Charles F. Wellford. 1979. "Towards an Integrated Model of Delinquency Causation: An Empirical Analysis." *Sociology and Social Research* 63:316–327.

Barkan, Steven E. 1997. *Criminology: A Sociological Understanding.* New Jersey: Prentice Hall.

Becker, Howard S. 1963. *Outsiders: Studies in the Sociology of Deviance.* New York: Macmillan.

———. 1967. "History, Culture and Subjective Experience: An Exploration of the Social Bases of Drug-Induced Experiences." *Journal of Health and Social Behavior* 3:163–176.

Bernburg, Jon Gunnar, Marvin D. Krohn, and Craig J. Rivera. 2006. "Official Labeling, Criminal Embeddedness, and Subsequent Delinquency: A Longitudinal Test of Labeling Theory." *Journal of Research in Crime and Delinquency* 43:67–88.

Bliss, D. C. 1977. "The Effects of the Juvenile Justice System on Self-Concept." San Francisco: R&E Associates. As cited in *Criminal Justice Abstracts* 10:297–298.

Blumer, Herbert. 1969. "Sociological Implications of the Thought of George Herbert Mead." Pp. 61–77 in *Symbolic Interactionism*, ed. Herbert Blumer. Englewood Cliffs, NJ: Prentice Hall.

Braithwaite, John. 1989. *Crime, Shame, and Reintegration.* Cambridge, UK: Cambridge University Press.

Chassin, Laurie, and Richard D. Young. 1981. "Salient Self-Conceptions in Normal and Deviant Adolescents." *Adolescence.* 16:613–620.

Conklin, John E. 1992. *Criminology*, 4th ed. New York: Macmillan.

Cooley, Charles Horton. 1902. *Human Nature and the Social Order.* New York: Scribner.

Curra, John. 2000. "The Dynamic Nature of Deviance." Pp. 1–19 in *The Relativity of Deviance*, by J. Curra. Thousand Oaks, CA: Sage.

Davies, Scott, and Julian Tanner. 2003. "The Long Arm of the Law: Effects of Labeling on Employment." *Sociological Quarterly* 44:385–404.

Davis, F. 1961. "Deviance Disavowal: The Management of Strained Interaction by the Visibly Handicapped." *Social Problems* 9:120–132.

Davis, N. 1972. "Labelling Theory in Deviance Research: A Critique and Reconsideration." *Sociological Quarterly* 13:447–474.

Downs, William R., and Joan F. Robertson. 1990. "Referral for Treatment among Adolescent Alcohol and Drug Abusers." *Journal of Research in Crime and Delinquency* 27:190–209.

Erickson, Patricia G., and Michael S. Goodstadt. 1979. "Legal Stigma for Marijuana Possession." *Criminology* 17:208–216.

Felson, Richard B. 2000. "Self-Concept." Pp. 2505–2510 in *Encyclopedia of Sociology*, ed. Edgar Borgatta and Rhonda J. V. Montgomery. New York: Macmillan.

Garfinkel, Harold. 1956. "Conditions of Successful Degradation Ceremonies." *American Journal of Sociology* 61:420–424.

Gibbons, Don C. 1994. *Talking about Crime and Criminals: Problems and Issues in Theory Development in Criminology.* Englewood Cliffs, NJ: Prentice Hall.

Gibbs, Jack P. 1966. "Conceptions of Deviant Behavior: The Old and the New." *Pacific Sociological Review* 9:9–14.

Gove, Walter. 1980. "The Labelling Perspective: An Overview." Pp. 9–33 in *The Labeling of Deviance*, 2nd ed., ed. Walter R. Gove. Beverly Hills, CA: Sage.

Hagan, John. 1974. "Extra-Legal Attributes and Criminal Sentencing: An Assessment of a Sociological Viewpoint." *Law and Society Review* 8:357–383.

Hagan, John, and Alberto Palloni. 1990. "The Social Reproduction of a Criminal Class in Working-Class London, Circa 1950–1980." *American Journal of Sociology* 96:265–299.

Hirschi, Travis. 1975. "Labelling Theory and Juvenile Delinquency: An Assessment of the Evidence." Pp. 181–203 in *The Labeling of Deviance: Evaluating a Perspective*, ed. Walter Gove. Beverly Hills, CA: Sage.

Johnson, Lee Michael, Ronald L. Simons, and Rand D. Conger. 2004. "Criminal Justice System Involvement and Continuity of Youth Crime." *Youth and Society* 36:3–29.

Kronick, Robert F., Dorothy E. Lambert, and W. Warren Lambert. 1998. "Recidivism among Adult Parolees: What Makes the Difference?" *Journal of Offender Rehabilitation* 28:61–69.

Lemert, Edwin M. 1951. *Social Pathology*. New York: McGraw-Hill.

———. 1967. *Human Deviance, Social Problems, and Social Control*. Englewood Cliffs, NJ: Prentice Hall.

———. 1981. "Issues in the Study of Deviance." *Sociological Quarterly* 22:285–305.

Liazos, Alexander. 1972. "The Poverty of the Sociology of Deviance: Nuts, Sluts and Perverts." *Social Problems* 20:103–120.

Link, Bruce G., and Francis T. Cullen. 1983. "Reconsidering the Social Rejection of Ex-Mental Patients: Levels of Attitudinal Response." *American Journal of Community Psychology* 11:261–273.

Link, Bruce G., John Monahan, Ann Stueve, and Francis T. Cullen. 1999. "Real in Their Consequences: A Sociological Approach to Understanding the Association between Psychotic Symptoms and Violence." *American Sociological Review* 64:316–332.

Liska, Allen. 1987. *Perspectives on Deviance*. Englewood Cliffs, NJ: Prentice Hall.

Lotz, Roy, and Leona Lee. 1999. "Sociability, School Experience, and Delinquency." *Youth and Society* 31:199–223.

Mankoff, M. 1971. "Societal Reaction and Career Deviance: A Critical Analysis." *Sociological Quarterly* 12:204–218.

Margolin, Leslie. 1992. "Deviance on the Record: Techniques for Labeling Child Abusers in Official Documents." *Social Problems* 39:58–70.

Matsueda, Ross. 1992. "Reflected Appraisals, Parental Labeling, and Delinquency: Specifying a Symbolic Interactionist Theory." *American Journal of Sociology* 97:1577–1611.

———. 2001. "Labeling Theory: Historical Roots, Implications, and Recent Developments." Pp. 223–241 in *Explaining Criminals and Crime: Essays in Contemporary Criminological Theory*, ed. Raymond Paternoster and Ronet Bachman. Los Angeles, CA: Roxbury.

Mead, George Herbert. 1934. *Mind, Self, and Society*. Chicago: University of Chicago Press.

Meade, A. C. 1974. "The Labeling Approach to Delinquency: State of the Theory as a Function of Method." *Social Forces* 53:83–91.

Pager, Devah. 2003. "The Mark of a Criminal Record." *American Journal of Sociology* 108:937–975.

Palamara, Frances, Francis T. Cullen, and Joanne C. Gersten. 1986. "The Effect of Police and Mental Health Intervention on Juvenile Deviance: Specifying Contingencies in the Impact of Formal Reaction." *Journal of Health and Social Behavior* 27:90–105.

Paternoster, Raymond, and Ronet Bachman. 2001. *Explaining Criminals and Crime: Essays in Contemporary Criminological Theory*. Los Angeles, CA: Roxbury.

Paternoster, Raymond, and LeeAnn Iovanni. 1989. "The Labeling Perspective and Delinquency: An Elaboration of the Theory and Assessment of the Evidence." *Justice Quarterly* 6:359–394.

Ray, M. C., and W. R. Downs. 1986. "An Empirical Test of Labeling Theory Using Longitudinal Data." *Journal of Research in Crime and Delinquency* 23:169–194.

Rosenhan, David L. 1973. "On Being Sane in Insane Places." *Science* 179:205–258.

Scheff, Thomas. 1963. "The Role of the Mentally Ill and the Dynamics of Mental Disorder." *Sociometry* 26:436–453.

———. 1974. "The Labelling Theory of Mental Illness." *American Sociological Review* 39:444–452.

Schneider, Andreas, and Wayne McKim. 2003. "Stigmatization among Probationers." *Journal of Offender Rehabilitation* 38:19–31.

Schur, Edwin. 1965. *Crimes without Victims*. Englewood Cliffs, NJ: Prentice Hall.

———. 1969. "Reactions to Deviance: A Critical Assessment." *American Journal of Sociology* 75:309–322.

———. 1971. *Labeling Deviant Behavior: Its Sociological Implications*. New York: Harper & Row.

———. 1973. *Radical Non-Intervention: Rethinking the Delinquency Problem*. Englewood Cliffs, NJ: Prentice-Hall.

Schwartz, Richard D., and Jerome H. Skolnick. 1962. "Two Studies of Legal Stigma." *Social Problems* 10:133–138.

Scimecca, Joseph A. 1977. "Labeling Theory and Personal Construct Theory: Toward the Measurement of Individual Variation." *Journal of Criminal Law and Criminology* 68:652–659.

Sheley, Joseph F. 1991. *Criminology: A Contemporary Handbook*. Belmont, CA: Wadsworth.

Shoemaker, Donald J. 1996. *Theories of Delinquency: An Examination of Explanations of Deviant Behavior*, 3rd ed. New York: Oxford University Press.

Tannenbaum, Frank. 1938. *Crime and the Community*. Boston: Ginn.

Tittle, Charles. 1975. "Labelling and Crime: An Empirical Evaluation." Pp. 157–179 in *The Labelling of Deviance: Evaluating a Perspective*, ed. Walter Gove. Beverly Hills, CA: Sage.

———. 1980. "Labelling and Crime: An Empirical Evaluation." Pp. 241–263 in *The Labelling of Deviance*, 2nd ed., ed. Walter Gove. Beverly Hills: Sage.

Triplett, Ruth. 2000. "The Dramatization of Evil: Reacting to Juvenile Delinquency during the 1990s." Pp. 121–138 in *Of Crime and Criminality*, ed. Sally S. Simpson. Thousand Oaks, CA: Pine Forge Press.

Warren, C., and J. Johnson. 1972. "A Critique of Labelling Theory from the Phenomenological Perspective." Pp. 69–92 in *Theoretical Perspective on Deviance*, ed. R. Scott and J. Douglas. New York: Basic Books.

Wellford, Charles F. 1975. "Labeling Theory and Criminology: As Assessment." *Social Problems* 22:313–332.

Wellford, Charles F., and Ruth A. Triplett. 1993. "The Future of Labeling Theory: Foundations and Promises." Pp. 1–22 in *New Directions in Criminological Theory: Advances in Criminological Theory*, ed. F. Adler and W. Laufer. Rutgers, NJ: Transaction Press.

Wenz, F. V. 1978. "Multiple Suicide Attempts and Informal Labeling: An Exploratory Study." *Suicide and Life-Threatening Behavior* 8:3–13.

Western, Bruce. 2002. "The Impact of Incarceration on Wage Mobility and Inequality." *American Sociological Review* 67:526–546.

9: Conflict Theory

Adler, Freda, Gerhard O. W. Mueller, and William S. Laufer. 1991. *Criminology*. New York: McGraw-Hill.

Akers, Ronald L., and Christine S. Sellers. 2004. *Criminological Theories: Introduction, Evaluation, and Application*, 4th ed. Los Angeles, CA: Roxbury.

Albonetti, Celesta A., and John R. Hepburn. 1996. "Prosecutorial Discretion to Defer Criminalization: The Effects of Defendant's Ascribed and Achieved Status Characteristics." *Journal of Quantitative Criminology* 12:63–81.

Alix, E. K. 1978. *Ransom Kidnapping in America 1874–1974*. Carbondale, IL: Southern Illinois University Press.

Arvanites, Thomas M. 1993. "Increasing Imprisonment: A Function of Crime or Socio-Economic Factors?" *American Journal of Criminal Justice* 17:19–38.

Barkan, Steven E. 1997. *Criminology: A Sociological Understanding*. Upper Saddle River, NJ: Prentice Hall.

Beckett, Katherine, and Theodore Sasson. 2000. "The War on Crime as Hegemonic Strategy." Pp. 61–84 in *Of Crime and Criminality*, ed. Sally S. Simpson. Thousand Oaks, CA: Pine Forge Press.

Behrens, A., Christopher Uggen, and Jeff Manza. 2003. "Ballot Manipulation and the Menace of Negro Domination: Racial Threat and Felon Disenfranchisement in the United States, 1850–2002." *American Journal of Sociology* 10:559–605.

Beirne, Piers. 1979. "Empiricism and the Critique of Marxism on Law and Crime." *Social Problems* 26:373–385.

Bernstein, Ilene Nagel, William R. Kelly, and Patricia A. Doyle. 1977. "Societal Reaction to Deviants: The Case of Criminal Defendants." *American Sociological Review* 42:743–755.

Bertrand, Marie Andree. 1969. "Self-Image and Delinquency: A Contribution to the Study of Female Criminality and Women's Image." *Acta Criminologia: Etudes sur la Conduite Antisociale* 2(January):71–144.

Bishop, Donna M., and Charles S. Frazier. 1996. "Race Effects in Juvenile Justice Decision-Making." *Journal of Criminal Law and Criminology* 86:392–413.

———. 1988. "The Influence of Race in Juvenile Justice Processing." *Journal of Research in Crime and Delinquency* 25:242–263.

Blumberg, P. 1989. *The Predatory Society: Deception in the American Marketplace*. New York: Oxford University Press.

Blumstein, Alfred. 1982. "On the Racial Disproportionality of the United States Prison Population." *Journal of Criminal Law and Criminology* 73:1259–1281.

Blumstein, Alfred, and Jacqueline Cohen. 1980. "Sentencing of Convicted Offenders: An Analysis of the Public's View." *Law and Society Review* 14:223–262.

Bonacich, Edna. 2000. "Class and Race." Pp. 319–323 in *Encyclopedia of Sociology*, 2nd ed., ed. Edgar F. Borgatta and Rhonda J. V. Montgomery. New York: Macmillan.

Bontrager, Stephanie, William Bales, and Ted Chiricos. 2005. "Race, Ethnicity, Threat and the Labeling of Convicted Felons." *Criminology* 43:589–622.

Box, S., and C. Hale. 1985. "Unemployment, Imprisonment and Prison Overcrowding." *Contemporary Crises* 9:209–228.

Brenner, H. M. 1976. "Estimating the Social Costs of National Economic Policy." Washington, DC: U.S. Government Printing Office.

Bridges, George S., and Robert D. Crutchfield. 1988. "Law, Social Standing and Racial Disparities in Imprisonment." *Social Forces* 66:699-724.

Bridges, George S., and Sara Steen. 1998. "Racial Disparities in Official Assessments of Juvenile Offenders over.

Britt, Chester. 2000. "Social Context and Racial Disparities in Punishment Decisions." *Justice Quarterly* 17:707-732.

Bush-Baskette, Stephanie. 2004. "The War on Drugs and the Incarceration of Mothers." Pp. 236-244 in *Gendered (In)justice: Theory and Practice in Feminist Criminology*, ed. Pamela J. Schram and Barbara Koons-Witt. Long Grove, IL: Waveland Press.

Chambliss, William J. 1964. "A Sociological Analysis of the Law of Vagrancy." *Social Problems* 12:67-77.

———. (Ed.). 1969. *Crime and the Legal Process*. New York: McGraw Hill.

———. (Ed.). 1975a. *Criminal Law in Action*. Santa Barbara, CA: Hamilton.

———. 1975b. "Toward a Political Economy of Crime." *Theory and Society* 2:149-170.

———. 1988. *On the Take*. Bloomington: Indiana University Press.

———. 1999. "The State, the Law, and the Definition of Behavior as Criminal or Delinquent." Pp. 18-24 in *Crime and Criminals: Contemporary and Classic Readings in Criminology*, ed. Frank R. Scarpitti and Amie L. Nielsen. Los Angeles, CA: Roxbury.

Chambliss, William J., and Robert Seidman. 1971. *Law, Order and Power*. Reading, MA: Addison-Wesley.

Chambliss, William J., and Marjorie S. Zatz. 1993. Making Law: *The State, The Law, and Structural Contradictions*. Bloomington: Indiana University Press.

Chamlin, Mitchell B. 1989a. "A Macro Social Analysis of Change in Police Force Size, 1972-1982." *Sociological Quarterly* 30:615-624.

———. 1989b. "Conflict Theory and Police Killings." *Deviant Behavior* 10:353-368.

Chiricos, Theodore G., and Charles Crawford. 1995. "Race and Imprisonment: A Contextual Assessment of the Evidence." Pp. 281-309 in *Ethnicity, Race and Crime*, ed. Darnell F. Hawkins. Albany: SUNY Press.

Chiricos, Theodore G., and Miriam A. DeLone. 1992. "Labor Surplus and Punishment: A Review and Assessment of Theory and Evidence." *Social Problems* 39:421-446.

Chiricos, Theodore G., and Gordon P. Waldo. 1975. "Socioeconomic Status and Criminal Sentencing." *American Sociological Review* 40:753-772.

Conklin, John E. 1996. *Criminology*, 9th ed. Boston: Pearson.

Crawford, Charles, Ted Chiricos, and Gary Kleck. 1998. "Race, Racial Threat, and Sentencing of Habitual Offenders." *Criminology* 36:481-512.

Dahrendorf, Ralf. 1959. *Class and Class Conflict in Industrial Society*. Stanford, CA: Stanford University Press.

Daly, Kathleen, and Lisa Maher. 1998. "Crossroads and Intersections: Building from Feminist Critique." Pp. 1-17 in *Criminology at the Crossroads: Feminist Readings in Crime and Justice*, ed. Kathleen Daly and Lisa Maher. Oxford: Oxford University Press.

Demuth, Stephen. 2003. "Racial and Ethnic Differences in Pretrial Release Decisions and Outcomes: A Comparison of Hispanic, Black, and White Felony Arrestees." *Criminology* 41:873-908.

Duster, Troy. 1970. *The Legislation of Morality: Law, Drugs and Moral Judgment*. New York: Free Press.

Engel, Robin S., J. M. Calnon, and T. J. Bernard. 2002. "Theory and Racial Profiling: Shortcomings and Future Directions in Research," *Justice Quarterly* 19:249–273.

Engels, F. 1958 [1895]. *The Condition of the Working Class in England.* Translated by W. O. Henderson and W. H. Chaldner. Stanford, CA: Stanford University Press.

Galliher, John F. and Allynn Walker. 1977. "The Puzzle of the Social Origins of the Marihuana Tax Act of 1937." *Social Problems* 24:367–376.

Garofalo, J. 1980. "Social Structure and Rates of Imprisonment: A Research Note." *Justice System Journal* 5:299–305.

Gartner, Rosemary and Bill McCarthy. 2005. "Killing One's Children: Maternal Infanticide and the Dark Figure of Homicide." Pp. 185–233 in Gender and Crime: Patterns of Victimization and Offending, edited by Karen Hermes and Candace Kruttschnitt.

Gibbons, Don C. 2000. "Criminology, Criminologists, and Criminological Theory." Pp. vxii–xxxiii in *Of Crime and Criminality*, ed. Sally Simpson. Thousand Oaks, CA: Pine Forge Press.

Giordano, Peggy G., Jill A. Deines, and Stephen A. Cernkovich. 2006. "In and Out of Crime: A Life Course Perspective on Girls' Delinquency." Pp. 17-40 in *Gender and Crime*, ed. Karen Heimer and Candace Kruttschnitt. New York: New York University Press.

Gordon, D. M. 1976. "Class and the Economics of Crime." Pp. in *Whose Law What Order?*, ed. William J. Chambliss and M. Mankoff. New York: Wiley.

Greenberg, David F. 1977. "The Dynamics of Oscillatory Punishment Processes." *Journal of Criminal Law and Criminology* 68:643–651.

———. 1993. *Crime and Capitalism: Essays in Marxist Criminology,* 2nd ed. Philadelphia: Temple University Press.

Greider, W. 2002. "William Lerachis' Legal Crusade against Enron and Infectious Greed." *The Nation* (August 5/12):11–15.

Gusfield, Joseph R. 1963. *Symbolic Crusade.* Urbana, IL: University of Illinois Press.

Gusfield, Joseph R. 1986. *Symbolic Crusade: Status Politics and the American Temperance Movement,* 2nd ed. Urbana, IL: University of Illinois Press.

Hagan, John. 1974. "Extra-legal Attributes and Criminal Sentencing: An Assessment of a Sociological Viewpoint." *Law and Society Review* 8:357–383.

Hagan, John, and Celesta Albonetti. 1982. "Race, Class and the Perception of Criminal Injustice in America." *American Journal of Sociology* 88:329–355.

Hagan, John and Jeffrey Leon. 1977. "Rediscovering Delinquency: Social History, Political Ideology, and the Sociology of Law." *American Sociological Review* 42:587–598.

Hagan, John, Llene Bernstein Nagel, and Celesta Albonetti. 1980. "The Differential Sentencing of White-Collar Offenders in Ten Federal District Courts." *American Sociological Review* 45:802–820.

Hagan, John, A. R. Gillis, and John Simpson. 1985. "The Class Structure of Gender and Delinquency: Toward a Power-Control Theory of Common Delinquent Behavior." *American Journal of Sociology* 90:1151–1178.

———. 1990. "Clarifying and Extending Power-Control Theory." *American Journal of Sociology* 95:1024–1037.

Hagan, John, Monique Payne, and Carla Shedd. 2005. "Race, Ethnicity, and Youth Perceptions of Criminal Justice." *American Sociological Review* 70:381–407.

Hall, Jerome. 1952. *Theft, Law and Society.* Indianapolis: Bobbs-Merrill.

Hawkins, Darnell F. 1987. "Beyond Anomalies: Rethinking the Conflict Perspective on Race and Criminal Punishment." *Social Forces* 65:719–745.

Heidensohn, Frances M. 1968. "The Deviance of Women: A Critique and an Enquiry." *British Journal of Sociology* 19:160–176.

Heimer, Karen. 2000. "Changes in the Gender Gap in Crime and Women's Economic Marginalization." *Criminal Justice* 1:427–483.

Helmkamp, J., R. Ball, and K. Townsend (Eds.). 1996. *Definitional Dilemma: Can and Should There Be a Universal Definition of White Collar Crime?* Morgantown, WV: National White Collar Crime Center.

Hochstetler, Andrew L., and Neal Shover. 1997. "Street Crime, Labor Surplus, and Criminal Punishment, 1980–1990." *Social Problems* 44:358–368.

Hollinger, Richard C., and Lonn Lanza-Kaduce. 1988. "The Process of Criminalization: The Case of Computer Crime Laws." *Criminology* 26:101–126.

Holmes, Malcolm D. 2000. "Minority Threat and Police Brutality: Determinants of Civil Rights Complaints in U.S. Municipalities." *Criminology* 38:343–365.

Inverarity, Jim, and R. Grattet. 1989. "Institutional Reponses to Unemployment: A Comparison of U.S. Trends, 1948–1985." *Contemporary Crises* 13:351–370.

Inverarity, Jim, and D. McCarthy. 1988. "Punishment and Social Structure Revisited: Unemployment and Imprisonment in the U.S.: 1948–1984." *Sociological Quarterly* 29:263–279.

Jackson, P., and L. Carroll. 1981. "Race and the War on Crime: The Sociopolitical Determinants of Municipal Police Expenditures in 90 Non-Southern Cities." *American Sociological Review* 46:390–405.

Jacobs, David. 1978. "Inequality and the Legal Order: An Ecological Test of the Conflict Model." Social Problems 25:515–525.

Jacobs, David. 1979. "Inequality and Police Strength: Conflict Theory and Coercive Control in Metropolitan Areas." *American Sociological Review* 44:913–925.

Jacobs, David, and D. Britt. 1979. "Inequality and Police Use of Deadly Force: An Empirical Assessment of a Conflict Hypothesis." *Social Problems* 26:403–412.

Jacobs, David, and Robert O'Brien. 1998. "The Determinants of Deadly Force: A Structural Analysis of Police Violence." *American Journal of Sociology* 103:837–862.

Jacobs, David, Jason T. Carmichael, and Stephanie L. Kent. 2005. "Vigilantism, Current Racial Threat, and Death Sentences." *American Sociological Review* 70:656–677.

Jacoby, Joseph E., and Francis T. Cullen. 1998. "The Structure of Punishment Norms: Applying the Rossi-Berk Model." *Journal of Criminal Law and Criminology* 89:245–312.

Jankovic, I. 1977. "Labor Market and Imprisonment." *Crime and Social Justice* 8:17–31.

Johnson, Brian D. 2005. "Contextual Disparities in Guidelines Departures: Courtroom Social Contexts, Guidelines Compliance, and Extralegal Disparities in Criminal Sentencing." *Criminology* 43:761–796.

Kappeler, V., M. Blumberg, and G. Potter. 2000. *The Mythology of Crime and Criminal Justice*. Prospect Heights, IL: Waveland Press.

Kautt, Paula M. 2002. "Interdistrict and Intercircuit Variation in Sentencing Outcomes for Federal Drug-Trafficking Offenses." *Justice Quarterly* 19:633–671.

Kent, Stephanie, and David Jacobs. 2004. "Social Divisions and Coercive Control in Advanced Societies: Law Enforcement Strength in Eleven Nations from 1975 to 1994." *Social Problems* 51:343–361.

Kleck, Gary. 1981. "Racial Discrimination in Sentencing: A Critical Evaluation of the Evidence with Additional Evidence on the Death Penalty." *American Sociological Review* 43:783–805.

Koons-Witt, Barbara A., and Pamela J. Schram. 2004. "The Prevalence and Nature of Violent Offending by Females." Pp. 176–194 in *Gendered (In)justice: Theory and Practice in Feminist Criminology*, ed. Pamela J. Schram and Barbara Koons-Witt. Long Grove, IL: Waveland Press.

Krisberg, Barry, I. Schwartz, G. Fishman, E. Eisikovits, E. Guttman, and K. Joe. 1987. "The Incarceration of Minority Youth." *Crime and Delinquency* 33:173–205.

Lamberth, J. D. 1997. Report of John Lamberth, Ph.D. American Civil Liberties Union.

Lea, John. 1987. "Left Realism: A Defence." *Contemporary Crises* 11:357–370.

Lessan, Gloria. 1991. "Macro-Economic Determinants of Penal Policy: Estimating the Unemployment and Inflation Influences on Imprisonment Rate Changes in the United States, 1948–1985." *Crime, Law and Social Change* 16:177–198.

Liazos, Alexander. 1972. "The Poverty of the Sociology of Deviance: Nuts, Sluts and Perverts." *Social Problems* 20:103–120.

Liska, Allan E. 1987. "A Critical Examination of Macro Perspectives on Crime Control." *Annual Review of Sociology* 13:67–88.

Liska, Allan E., and Mitchell Chamlin. 1984. "Social Structure and Crime Control among Macrosocial Units." *American Journal of Sociology* 90:383–395.

Liska, Allan E., and Steven F. Messner. 1999. *Perspectives on Crime and Deviance*, 3rd ed. Upper Saddle River, NJ: Prentice Hall.

Liska, Allan E., and Mark Tausig. 1979. "Theoretical Interpretations of Social Class and Racial Differentials in Legal Decision-Making for Juveniles." *Sociological Quarterly* 20:197–207.

Liska, Allan E., Mitchell Chamlin, and Mark Reed. 1985. "Testing the Economic Production and Conflict Models of Crime Control." *Social Forces* 64:119–138.

Liska, Allan E., J. Lawrence, and M. Benson. 1981. "Perspectives on the Legal Order: The Capacity for Social Control." *American Journal of Sociology* 87:413–426.

Lizotte, Alan J. 1978. "Extra-Legal Factors in Chicago's Criminal Courts: Testing the Conflict Model of Criminal Justice." *Social Problems* 25:564–580.

Lynch, Michael J., and Paul B. Stretesky. 2001. "Radical Criminology." Pp. 267–286 in *Explaining Criminals and Crime*, ed. Raymond Paternoster and Ronet Bachman. Los Angeles, CA: Roxbury.

Mankoff, Milton. 1978. "On the Responsibility of Marxist Criminology: A Reply to Quinney." *Contemporary Crisis* 2:293–301.

Marx, Karl and Friedrich Engels. 1848/1978. "The Communist Manifesto." Pp. 469–500 in *The Marx-Engels Reader*, edited by Robert C. Tucker. New York: W.W. Norton.

McCarthy, Belinda, and Brent L. Smith. 1986. "The Conceptualization of Discrimination in the Juvenile Justice Process." *Criminology* 24:41–64.

McGarrell, Edmund F. 1993. "Institutional Theory and the Stability of a Conflict Model of the Incarceration Rate." *Justice Quarterly* 10:7–27.

Miethe, Terance D. 1982. "Public Consensus on Crime Seriousness: Normative Structure or Methodological Artifact?" *Criminology* 20:515–526.

Miller, Jody and Clintopher W. Mullins. 2005. "Tough Girls: Dating and Young Women's Violence." Pp. 82–135 in Gender and Crime: Patterns of Victimization and Offending, edited by Karen Heimer and Candace Kruttschnitt. New York: New York University Press.

Millett, Kate. 1970. *Sexual Politics*. New York: Doubleday.

Mosher, Clayton. 2001. "Predicting Drug Arrest Rates: Conflict and Social Disorganization Perspectives." *Crime and Delinquency* 47:84–104.

Myers, Martha A., and Susette M. Talarico. 1987. *The Social Contexts of Criminal Sentencing*. New York: Springer Verlag.

Paternoster, Raymond. 1991. *Capital Punishment in America*. New York: Lexington Books.

Paternoster, Raymond, and Ronet Bachman. 2001. *Explaining Criminals and Crime*. Los Angeles, CA: Roxbury.

Pearce, F. 1976. *Crimes of the Powerful*. London: Pluto Press.

Pease, Kenneth, Judith Ireson, and Jennifer Thorpe. 1975. "Modified Crime Indices for Eight Countries." *Journal of Criminal Law and Criminology* 66:209–214.

Pepinsky, Harold, and Richard Quinney (Eds.). 1991. *Criminology as Peacemaking*. Bloomington: Indiana University Press.

Petrocelli, Matthew, Alex R. Piquero, and Michael R. Smith. 2002. "Conflict Theory and Racial Profiling: An Empirical Analysis of Police Traffic Stop Data." *Journal of Criminal Justice* 31:1–11.

Platt, Anthony M. 1969. *The Child Savers: The Invention of Delinquency*. Chicago: University of Chicago Press.

Polk, Kenneth. 1998. "Masculinity, Honour, and Confrontational Homicide." Pp. 188–205 in *Criminology at the Crossroads: Feminist Readings in Crime and Justice*, ed. Kathleen Daly and Lisa Maher. Oxford: Oxford University Press.

Pope, Carl E., and William H. Feyerherm. 1990. "Minority Status and Juvenile Justice Processing: An Assessment of the Research Literature." *Criminal Justice Abstracts* 22:327–335, 527–542.

Quinney, Richard. 1970. *The Social Reality of Crime*. New York: Little, Brown.

———. 1974. *Critique of the Legal Order: Crime Control in Capitalist Society*. Boston: Little, Brown.

———. 1977. *Class, State and Crime*. New York: David McKay.

———. 1980. *Class, State and Crime*. New York: Longman.

Ramirez, Deborah, Jack McDevitt, and Amy Farrell. 2000. A Resource Guide on Racial Profiling Data Collection Systems: Promising Practices and Lessons Learned. Washington, DC: U.S. Department of Justice.

Reiman, Jeffrey H. 2007. The Rich Get Richer and The Poor Get Prison, 8th Edition. Boston: Allyn on Bascon.

———. 1999. "A Crime by Any Other Name..." Pp. 25–33 in *Crime and Criminals: Contemporary and Classic Readings in Criminology*, ed. Frank R. Scarpitti and Amie L. Nielsen. Los Angeles, CA: Roxbury.

———. 2004. *And the Poor Get Prison: Economic Bias in American Criminal Justice*. Boston: Allyn and Bacon.

Rossi, Pater H., Emily Waite, Christine E. Bose, and Richard E. Berk. 1974. "The Seriousness of Crimes: Normative Structure and Individual Differences." *American Sociological Review* 39:224–237.

Rubenstein, Jonathan. 1973. *City Police*. New York: Farrar, Straus, and Giroux.

Russell, Kathryn. 1998. *The Color of Crime: Racial Hoaxes, White Fear, Black Protectionism, Police Harassment, and Other Macroagressions*. New York: NYU Press.

Sampson, Robert J., and John H. Laub. 1993. "Structural Variations in Juvenile Court Processing: Inequality, the Underclass, and Social Control." *Law & Society Review* 27:285–311.

Schlegel, K. 2000. "Transnational Crime." *Journal of Contemporary Criminal Justice* 16:365–385.

Sellin, Thorsten. 1938. *Culture Conflict and Crime*. New York: Social Science Research Council.

Schwartz, Martin D. and David O. Friedrichs. 1994. "Postmodern Thought and Criminological Discontent: New Metaphors for Understanding Violence." *Criminology* 32:221–246.

Sharp, Susan F., and Kristen Hefley. 2007. "This Is a Man's World: Or Least That's How It Looks in the Journals." *Critical Criminology* 15:3–18.

Sorenson, J., J. Marquart, and D. Brock. 1993. "Factors Related to Killings of Felons by Police Officers: A Test of the Community Violence and Conflict Hypotheses." *Justice Quarterly* 10:417–440.

Steffensmeier, Darrell, and Stephen Demuth. 2001. "Ethnicity and Judges' Sentencing Decisions. Hispanic-Black-White Comparisons." Criminology 39:145–178.

Steffensmeier, Darrell and Stephen Demuth. 2000. "Ethnicity and Sentencing Outcomes in U.S. Federal Courts: Who Is Punished More Harshly? American Sociological Review 65:705–729.

Spitzer, Steven. 1975. "Toward a Marxian Theory of Deviance." *Social Problems* 22:638–651.

Stolzenberg, Lisa, Stewart J. D'Alessio, and David Eitle. 2004. "A Multilevel Test of Racial Threat Theory." *Criminology* 42:673–698.

Swigert, Victoria, and Ronald A. Farrell. 1977. "Normal Homicides and the Law." *American Sociological Review* 42:16–32.

Thornberry, Terence P. 1973. "Race, Socioeconomic Status and Sentencing in the Juvenile Justice System." *The Journal of Criminal Law and Criminology* 64:90–98.

Tonry, Michael. 1995. *Malign Neglect: Race, Crime and Punishment in America*. Oxford: Oxford University Press.

Troyer, Ronald J. and Gerald E. Markle. 1983. *Cigarettes: The Battle over Smoking*. New Brunswick: Rutgers University.

Turk, Austin T. 1969. *Criminality and Legal Order*. Chicago: Rand McNally.

———. 1976. "Law as a Weapon in Social Conflict." *Social Problems* 23:276–291.

Ulmer, Jeffery T. 1997. *Social Worlds of Sentencing: Court Communities under Sentencing Guidelines*. Albany: SUNY Press.

Ulmer, Jeffery T., and Brian D. Johnson. 2004. "Sentencing in Context: A Multilevel Analysis." *Criminology* 42:137–177.

Vold, George. 1958. *Theoretical Criminology*. New York: Oxford University Press.

Vold, George B., Thomas J. Bernard, and Jeffrey B. Snipes. 2002. *Theoretical Criminology*. Oxford: Oxford University Press.

Walker, Samuel, Cassia Spohn, and Miriam DeLone. 2000. *The Color of Justice: Race, Ethnicity, and Crime in America*, 2nd ed. Belmont, CA: Wadsworth.

Warr, Mark, Jack P. Gibbs, and Maynard L. Erickson. 1982. "Contending Theories of Criminal Law: Statutory Penalties versus Public Preferences." *Journal of Research in Crime and Delinquency* 19:25–46.

Wellford, Charles. 1975. "Labeling Theory and Criminology: An Assessment." *Social Problems* 22:332–345.

Westley, William A. 1972. *Violence and the Police: A Sociological Study of Law, Custom, and Morality*. Cambridge, MA: MIT Press.

Wheeler, Stanton. 1976. "Trends and Problems in the Sociological Study of Crime." *Social Problems* 23:525–534.

Wolfgang, Marvin E., Robert E. Figlio, Paul E. Tracey, and Simon I. Singer. 1985. *The National Survey of Crime Severity*. Bureau of Justice Statistics: U.S. Department of Justice. Washington, D.C.

Wooldredge, John, and Amy Thistlethwaite. 2004. "Bilevel Disparities in Court Dispositions for Intimate Assault." *Criminology* 42:417–456.

Young, Jock. 1997. "Left Realism: The Basics." Pp. 28–36 in *Thinking Critically about Crime*, ed. Brian D. MacLean and Dragan Milovanovic Richmond, British Columbia: Collective Press.

Zingraff, M. T., M. Mason, W. Smith, D. Tomaskovic-Devey, P. Warent, H. L. McMurray, and R. C. Fenlon. 2000. "Evaluating North Carolina State Highway Patrol Data: Citation, Warnings, and Searches in 1998." Report submitted to North Carolina Department of Crime Control and Public Safety and North Carolina State Highway Patrol.

10: Integrated Theory

Akers, Ronald L. 1989. "A Social Behaviorist's Perspective on Integration of Theories of Crime and Deviance." Pp. 23–36 in *Theoretical Integration in the Study of Deviance and Crime*, ed. Steven F. Messner, Marvin D. Krohn, and Allen E. Liska. Albany: SUNY Press.

———. 1999. *Criminological Theories*, 2nd ed. Chicago: Fitzroy Dearborn Publishers.

Akers, Ronald L., and Christine S. Sellers. 2004. *Criminological Theories: Introduction, Evaluation, and Application*, 4th ed. Los Angeles: Roxbury.

Barak, Gregg. 1998. *Integrating Criminologies*. Boston: Allyn and Bacon.

Bates, Kristin A., Christopher D. Bader, and F. Carson Mencken. 2003. "Family Structure, Power-Control Theory, and Deviance: Extending Power-Control Theory to Include Alternate Family Forms." *Western Criminology Review* 4:170–190.

Benson, Michael L. 2002. *Crime and the Life Course: An Introduction*. Los Angeles, CA: Roxbury.

Bernard, Thomas J. 1991. "Twenty Years of Testing Theories." *Journal of Research in Crime and Delinquency* 27:325–347.

Bernard, Thomas J., and Jeffrey B. Snipes. 1996. "Theoretical Integration in Criminology." *Crime and Justice* 20:301–348.

Blackwell, Brenda S. 2000. "Perceived Sanction Threats, Gender, and Crime: A Test and Elaboration of Power-Control Theory." *Criminology* 38:439–488.

———. 2003. "Power-Control and Social Bonds: Exploring the Effect of Patriarchy." *Criminal Justice Studies* 16:131–152.

Blackwell, Brenda Sims, and Alex R. Piquero. 2005. "On the Relationships between Gender, Power Control, Self-Control, and Crime." *Journal of Criminal Justice* 33:1–17.

Blackwell, Brenda S., and Mark D. Reed. 2003. "Power-Control as a Between- and Within-Family Model: Reconsidering the Unit of Analysis." *Journal of Youth and Adolescence* 32:385–399.

Blackwell, Brenda S., Christine S. Sellers, and Sheila M. Schlaupitz. 2002. "A Power-Control Theory of Vulnerability to Crime and Adolescent Role Exits—revisited." *The Canadian Review of Sociology and Anthropology* 39:199–218.

Braithwaite, John. 1989. *Crime, Shame and Reintegration*. Cambridge: Cambridge University Press.

Burgess, Robert L., and Ronald L. Akers. 1966. "A Differential Association-Reinforcement Theory of Criminal Behavior." *Social Problems* 14:128–147.

Bursik, Robert J. 1989. "Political Decisionmaking and Ecological Models of Delinquency: Conflict and Consensus." Pp. 105–117 in *Theoretical Integration in the Study of Deviance and Crime*, ed. Steven F. Messner, Marvin D. Krohn, and Allen E. Liska. Albany: SUNY Press.

Cao, Liqun. 2004. *Major Criminological Theories: Concepts and Measurement*. Belmont, CA: Wadsworth/Thomson.

Cloward, Richard, and Lloyd Ohlin. 1960. *Delinquency and Opportunity: A Theory of Delinquent Gangs*. Glencoe, IL: Free Press.

Cohen, Lawrence E., and Richard Machalek. 1988. "A General Theory of Expropriative Crime: An Evolutionary Ecological Approach." *American Journal of Sociology* 94:465–501.

Colvin, Mark, and John Pauly. 1983. "A Critique of Criminology: Toward an Integrated Structural-Marxist Theory of Delinquency Production." *American Journal of Sociology* 89:513–551.

Denno, Deborah W. 1990. *Biology and Violence: From Birth to Adulthood*. Cambridge: Cambridge University Press.

Einstadter, Werner J., and Stuart Henry. 2006. *Criminological Theory*, 2nd ed. Lanham, MD: Rowman and Littlefield.

Elliott, Delbert H. 1985. "The Assumption That Theories Can Be Combined with Increased Explanatory Power: Theoretical Integration." Pp. 123–149 in *Theoretical Methods in Criminology*, ed. Robert M. Meier. Beverly Hills, CA: Sage Publication.

Elliott, Delbert H., Suzanne S. Ageton, and Rachelle J. Cantor. 1979. "An Integrated Theoretical Perspective on Delinquent Behavior." *Journal of Research in Crime and Delinquency* 16:3–27.

Elliott, Delbert H., David Huizinga, and Suzanne S. Ageton. 1985. *Explaining Delinquency and Drug Use*. Beverly Hills, CA: Sage.

Farnworth, Margaret. 1989. "Theory Integration versus Model Building. Pp. 93–103 in *Theoretical Integration in the Study of Deviance and Crime*, ed. Steven F. Messner, Marvin D. Krohn, and Allen E. Liska. Albany, NY: SUNY Press.

Farrington, David P. (Ed.). 2005. *Integrated Developmental and Life-Course Theories of Offending*. New Brunswick, NJ: Transaction Publishers.

Gibbons, Don C. 1994. *Talking about Crime and Criminals: Problems and Issues in Theory Development in Criminology*. Englewood Cliffs, NJ: Prentice Hall.

Gibbons, Don C., and Kathryn A. Farr. 2001. Defining Patterns of Crime and Types of Offenders." Pp. 37–64 in *What Is Crime? Controversies over the Nature of Crime and What to Do about It*, ed. Stuart Henry and Mark M. Lanier. Latham, MD: Rowman and Littlefield.

Glueck, Sheldon, and Eleanor Glueck. 1950. *Unraveling Juvenile Delinquency*. New York: The Commonwealth Fund.

Grasmick, Harold G., John Hagan, Brenda S. Blackwell, and Bruce J. Arneklev. 1996. "Risk Preferences and Patriarchy: Extending Power-Control Theory." *Social Forces* 75:177–199.

Hagan, John. 1989. *Structural Criminology*. New Brunswick, NJ: Rutgers University Press.
———. 1994. *Crime and Disrepute*. Thousand Oaks, CA: Pine Forge Press.

Hagan, John, and Alberto Palloni. 1986. "Toward a Structural Criminology." *Annual Review of Sociology* 12:431–449.

Hagan, John, A. R. Gillis, and John Simpson. 1985. "The Class Structure of Gender and Delinquency: Toward a Power-Control Theory of Common Delinquent Behavior." *American Journal of Sociology* 90:1151–1178.

Hempel, Carl G. 1966. *Philosophy of Natural Science*. Princeton, NJ: Princeton University Press.

Hirschi, Travis. 1969. *Causes of Delinquency*. Berkeley: University of California Press.
———. 1979. "Separate and Unequal Is Better." *Journal of Research in Crime and Delinquency* 16:34–38.

————. 1989. "Exploring Alternatives to Integrated Theory." Pp. 37–49 in *Theoretical Integration in the Study of Deviance and Crime,* ed. Steven F. Messner, Marvin D. Krohn, and Allen E. Liska. Albany, NY: SUNY Press.

Hudson, W. H. 1996. *WALMYR Assessment Scales Scoring Manual.* Tempe, AZ: WALMYR Publishing Company.

Hunter, Ronald D., and Mark L. Dantzker. 2002. *Crime and Criminality: Causes and Consequences.* Upper Saddle River, NJ: Prentice Hall

Kornhauser, Ruth Rosner. 1978. *Social Sources of Delinquency: An Appraisal of Analytic Models.* Chicago: University of Chicago Press.

Krohn, Marvin D., Alan J. Lizotte, and Cynthia M. Perez. 1997. "The Interrelationship between Substance Use and Precocious Transitions to Adult Statuses." *Journal of Health and Social Behavior* 38:87–103.

Krohn, Marvin D., Alan J. Lizotte, Terence P. Thornberry, Carolyn Smith, and David McDowall. 1996. "Reciprocal Causal Relationships among Drug Use, Peers, and Beliefs: A Five-Wave Panel Model." *Journal of Drug Issues* 26:405–428.

Lanier, Mark, and Stuart Henry. 2004. *Essential Criminology,* 2nd ed. Boulder, CO: Westview Press.

Laub, John H., and Robert J. Sampson. 2003. *Shared Beginnings, Divergent Lives: Delinquent Boys to Age 70.* Cambridge, MA: Harvard University Press.

Liska, Allan E., and Steven F. Messner. 1999. *Perspectives on Crime and Deviance,* 3rd ed. Upper Saddle River, NJ: Prentice Hall.

Liska, Allan E., Marvin D. Krohn, and Steven F. Messner. 1989. "Strategies and Requisites for Theoretical Integration in the Study of Crime and Deviance." Pp. 1–19 in *Theoretical Integration in the Study of Deviance and Crime,* ed. Steven F. Messner, Marvin D. Krohn, and Allen E. Liska. Albany: SUNY Press.

Lynam, Donald R., Terrie E. Moffitt, and Magda Stouthamer-Loeber. 1993. "Explaining the Relation between IQ and Delinquency: Class, Race, Test Motivation, School Failure or Self-Control." *Journal of Abnormal Psychology* 102:187–196.

Mack, Kristin Y., and Michael J. Leiber. 2005. "Race, Gender, Single-Mother Households, and Delinquency: A Further Test of Power-Control Theory." *Youth and Society* 37:115–144.

McCarthy, Bill, John Hagan, and Todd S. Woodward. 1999. "In the Company of Women: Structure and Agency in a Revised Power-Control Theory of Gender and Delinquency." *Criminology* 37:761–788.

Menard, Scott, and Delbert S. Elliott. 1994. Delinquent Bonding, Moral Beliefs, and Illegal Behavior: A Three-Wave Panel Model." *Justice Quarterly* 11:173–188.

Messner, Steven F., Marvin D. Krohn, and Allen E. Liska (Eds.). 1989. *Theoretical Integration in the Study of Deviance and Crime: Problems and Prospects.* Albany: SUNY Press.

Moffitt, Terrie. 1990a. "Juvenile Delinquency and Attention Deficit Disorder: Boys' Developmental Trajectories from Age 3 to Age 15." *Child Development* 61:893–910.

————. 1990b. "The Neuropsychology of Juvenile Delinquency: A Critical Review." Pp. 99–169 in *Crime and Justice: An Annual Review of Research,* Vol. 12, ed. M. Tonry and N. Morris. Chicago: University of Chicago Press.

————. 1993. " 'Life-Course-Persistent' and 'Adolescence-Limited' Antisocial Behavior: A Developmental Taxonomy." *Psychological Review* 100:674–701.

————. 1997. "Adolescence-Limited and Life-Course-Persistent Offending: A Complementary Pair of Developmental Theories." Pp. 11–54 in *Developmental Theories of*

Crime and Delinquency, ed. Terence P. Thornberry. New Brunswick, NJ: Transaction Publishers.

———. 2003. "Life-Course-Persistent and Adolescence-Limited Antisocial Behavior: A 10-Year Research Review and a Research Agenda." Pp. 49–75 in *Causes of Conduct Disorder and Juvenile Delinquency*, ed. B. Lahey, T. Moffitt, and A. Caspi. New York: The Guilford Press.

Moffitt, Terrie E., William F. Gabrielli, Sarnoff A. Mednick, and Fini Schulsinger. 1981. "Socioeconomic Status, IQ, and Delinquency." *Journal of Abnormal Psychology* 90:152–156.

Moffitt, Terrie E., Donald R. Lyman, and Phil A. Silva. 1994. "Neuropsychological Tests Predicting Persistent Male Delinquency." *Criminology* 32:277–300.

Moffitt, Terrie E., Aushalom Caspi, M. Rutter, and Phil A. Silva. 2001. Sex Differences in Antisocial Behaviour: Conduct Disorder, Delinquency, and Violence in the Dunedin Longitudinal Study. Cambridge: Cambridge University Press.

Paternoster, Raymond, and Ronet Bachman (Eds.). 2001. *Explaining Criminals and Crime: Essays in Contemporary Criminological Theory*. Los Angeles, CA: Roxbury.

Pearson, Frank S., and Neil A. Weiner. 1985. "Toward an Integration of Criminological Theories." *Journal of Criminal Law and Criminology* 76:116–150.

Piquero, Alex R., and Terrie E. Moffitt. 2005. "Explaining the Facts of Crime: How the Developmental Taxonomy Replies to Farrington's Invitation." Pp. 51–72 in *Integrated Developmental and Life-Course Theories of Offending*, ed. David P. Farrington. New Brunswick, NJ: Transaction Publishers.

Rutter, Michael, Jack Tizard, and Kingsley Whitmore. 1970. *Education, Health, and Behaviour*. New York: John Wiley and Sons.

Sampson, Robert J., and John H. Laub. 1993. *Crime in the Making*. Cambridge, MA: Harvard University Press.

———. 2005. "A General Age-Graded Theory of Crime: Lessons Learned and the Future of Life-Course Criminology. Pp. 165–182 in *Integrated Developmental and Life-Course Theories of Offending*, ed. David P. Farrington. New Brunswick, NJ: Transaction Publishers.

Short, James F. 1979. "On the Etiology of Delinquent Behavior." *Journal of Research in Crime and Delinquency* 16:28–33.

Singer, Simon I., and Murray Levine. 1988. "Power Control Theory, Gender, and Delinquency: A Partial Replication with Additional Evidence on the Effects of Peers." *Criminology* 26:627–648.

Stinchcombe, Arthur L. 1968. *Constructing Social Theories*. New York: Harcourt, Brace and World.

Thornberry, Terence P. 1987. "Toward an Interactional Theory of Delinquency." *Criminology* 25:863–891.

———. 1989. "Reflections on the Advantages and Disadvantages of Theoretical integration." Pp. 51–60 in *Theoretical Integration in the Study of Deviance and Crime*, ed. Steven F. Messner, Marvin D. Krohn, and Allen E. Liska. Albany: SUNY Press.

Thornberry, Terence P., and Marvin D. Krohn (Eds.). 2003. *Taking Stock of Delinquency: An Overview of Findings from Contemporary Longitudinal Studies*. New York: Kluwer Academic/Plenum Publishers.

Thornberry, Terence P., Marvin D. Krohn, Alan J. Lizotte, Carolyn A. Smith, and Kimberly Tobin. 2003. *Gangs and Delinquency in Developmental Perspective*. New York: Cambridge University Press.

Thornberry, Terence P., Alan J. Lizotte, Marvin D. Krohn, M. Farnworth, and S. J. Jang. 1991. "Testing Interactional Theory: An Examination of Reciprocal Causal

Relationships among Family, School and Delinquency." *Journal of Criminal Law and Criminology* 82:3–35.

———. 1994. "Delinquent Peers, Beliefs, and Delinquent Behavior: A Longitudinal Test of Interactional Theory." *Criminology* 32:47–83.

Tittle, Charles R. 1995. *Control Balance: Toward a General Theory of Deviance.* Boulder, CO: Westview Press.

———. 1997. "Thoughts Stimulated by Braithwaite's Analysis of Control Balance Theory." *Theoretical Criminology* 3:344–352.

———. 1999. "Continuing the Discussion of Control Balance." *Theoretical Criminology* 3:344–352.

Vila, Bryan. 1994. "A General Paradigm for Understanding Criminal Behavior: Extending Evolutionary Ecological Theory." *Criminology* 32:311–360.

Vold, George B., Thomas J. Bernard, and Jeffrey B. Snipes. 2002. *Theoretical Criminology*, 5th ed. Oxford: Oxford University Press.

White, J., Terrie E. Moffitt, Felton Earls, Lee N. Robins, and Phil A. Silva. 1990. "How Early Can We Tell? Preschool Predictors of Boys' Conduct Disorders and Delinquency." *Criminology* 28:507–533.

Wilson, James Q., and Richard J. Herrnstein. 1985. *Crime and Human Nature.* New York: Simon and Schuster.

Wolfgang, Marvin E., Robert M. Figlio, and Terence P. Thornberry. 1978. *Evaluating Criminology.* New York: Elsevier.

11: Conclusion

Cao, Liqun. 2004. *Major Criminological Theories: Concepts and Measurement.* Belmont, CA: Wadsworth/Thompson Publishing.

Einstadter, Werner J., and Stuart Henry. 2006. *Criminological Theory: An Analysis of Its Underlying Assumptions*, 2nd ed. Lanham, MD: Rowman & Littlefield.

Gibbons, Don C. 1994. *Talking about Crime and Criminals: Problems and Issues in Theory Development in Criminology.* Upper Saddle River, NJ: Prentice Hall.

Hirschi, Travis. 1969. *Causes of Delinquency.* Berkeley: University of California Press.

Lemert, Edwin M. 1951. *Social Pathology.* New York: McGraw-Hill.

Liska, Allen E., and Steven F. Messner. 1999. *Perspectives on Crime and Deviance*, 3rd ed. Upper Saddle River, NJ: Prentice Hall.

Sampson, Robert J. 1999. "Techniques of Research Neutralization." *Theoretical Criminology* 3:438–450.

Vold, George B., Thomas J. Bernard, and Jeffrey B. Snipes. 2002. *Theoretical Criminology*, 5th ed. New York: Oxford University Press.

INDEX

A

absolutist approach to deviance, 199
abstract concepts, 4
"adaptive," criminal behavior as, 53
adolescence-limited (AL) offenders,
    70, 255, 257
adoption studies, 57, 62–63
adult status, passage to, 171
affection, parental, 174
age-graded theory of informal social
    control, 261–67
agency, 207. *See also* free will
aggression, 59
    types of, 59
Agnew, Robert, 114, 128, 131, 134
    on anger, 128–29, 131–32
    general strain theory, 110–11, 120–23,
        128, 131, 136. *See also* anomie
        and strain theories
    Hirschi's social control theory and,
        181–82, 184
    macro-level strain theory, 116–17,
        129, 136
    peer influence and, 149
    on satisfaction with monetary
        status, 119
Akers, Ronald L., 156
    concept of imitation, 155, 158
    concepts of reinforcement, 154, 158
    social learning theories and, 137,
        140–41, 156, 158, 252
    social structure and social learning
        (SSSL) theory, 141–42, 159, 166
    on structural theories, 252
alcohol use, 161
androgens, 65
anger, 122–24, 128–29, 131–32. *See also*
    negative affective states
    trait/dispositional *vs.* situational,
        125, 129, 135

"anger people," 73, 135
anomie, 111, 114–17
    institutional, 109–10, 112, 114–16,
        125–26
anomie and strain theories, 107
    analytical issues, 129
        causal order issues, 134
        model specification and causal
            ordering, 132–34
        potential alternative explanations,
            134–35
        study design, 129–32
    concepts and measurement issues,
        111–29
    directions for future research,
        135–36
    hypotheses based on, 111–14
    intellectual history of, 107
    limitations of classic strain
        research, 127
    macro-level implications, 114–17
    modern, 107–11
antisocial behavior, 60–61
antisocial personality disorder
    (APD), 60
arousal theory, 52, 58, 66–68
aspirations, 117–19
atavistic anomolies, 49
attachment. *See also* neighborhood
    bonding; social bond
    to child, parental, 10, 11
    to others, 170
    to parents, 174–75
attention deficit/hyperactivity
    disorder (ADHD), 52

B

Beccaria, Cesare, 22
Becker, Howard S., 201

CPSIA information can be obtained at www.ICGtesting.com
Printed in the USA
BVOW041143091212

307580BV00005B/13/P

9 780195 340860